DATE DUE

MAR 2 2	

Labour and Russia

To Jane

LABOUR AND RUSSIA

The attitude of the Labour Party to the USSR, 1924–34

Andrew J. Williams

Manchester University Press

Manchester and New York

Distributed exclusively in the USA and Canada by St Martin's Press

Published by Manchester University Press
Oxford Road, Manchester M13 9PL, UK
and Room 400, 175 Fifth Avenue,
New York, NY 10010, USA

Distributed exclusively in the USA and Canada
by St. Martin's Press, Inc.,
175 Fifth Avenue, New York, NY 10010, USA

British Library cataloguing in publicaion data
Wiliams, Andrew J.
Labour and Russia: the attitude of the Labour
Party to the USSR, 1924–1934.
1. Soviet Union. Attitudes of Labour Party
(Great Britain)
1924–1953
I. Title
947.084'2

Library of Congress cataloguing in publication data
Wiliams, Andrew J.
Labour and Russia: the attitude of the Labour Party to the USSR,
1924–1934/Andrew J. Williams.
p.cm.
Bibliography: p.
Includes index.
ISBN 0-7190-2624-5
1. Great Britain—Foreign relations—Soviet Union.
2. Great Britain—Foreign relations—1910-1936.
3. Soviet Union—Foreign relations—Great Britain.
4. Soviet Union—Foreign relations—1917-1945.
5. Labour Party (Great Britain)
I. Title
DA47.65.W55 1989
327.41047—dc19 88-38146

ISBN 0-7190-2624-5 *hardback*

Printed in Great Britain
by Billings and Son, Worcester.

Contents

Introduction 1

1 Anglo-Soviet relations before and during the 1924 Labour Government 6

2 Labour Party, TUC and the USSR, 1925–7 22

3 Russia as an element in the power struggles within the Labour Party, 1927–9 41

4 Russia, peace and the elaboration of Labour Party foreign policy aims, 1927–8 53

5 'Russia the enigma': Labour party opinion leaders' analyses of the USSR, 1927–end 1928 65

6 Russia and the Labour Party during the 1929 election 77

7 The Russian element in the Labour Government's politics, June-December 1929 88

8 The Russian element in the Labour Government's domestic politics, January 1930–August 1931 102

9 The Labour Party's foreign policy and Russia, 1927–31 119

10 Looking at the Soviet Union through Labour Party eyes during 1929–31 134

11 The Labour Party in crisis and reconstruction, 1931–34: Russia the 'exemplar'? 150

12 Gathering evidence for the blueprint: Labour Party visitors to the USSR, 1932–3 164

13 The Webbs' visits to the USSR in 1932 and 1934 and their impact on Labour Party thinking about it 181

14 The Russian impact on the Labour Party's domestic economic policies, 1932–34 197

15 Russia as an element in the Labour Party's foreign policy, October 1931–end 1932 211

16 Russia as an element in the elaboration of the Labour Party's foreign policy, 1933–4 224

Conclusions 239

Bibliography 244

Index 257

Introduction

A great deal has been written about both the Labour Party and the USSR, enough to be the subject of magisterial bibliographical tomes in the case of the USSR, and even of modest volumes in the case of the Labour Party.[1] However, a close look at the literature on the links between the two, or even of the links between the USSR and Great Britain, reveals a very meagre harvest.

The most recent and the only comprehensive survey of Anglo-Soviet relations of the period 1917-80, by Northedge and Wells, pointed out that:

> few subjects which deeply affect our lives have had so little written about them as relations between Britain and the Soviet Union ... Since the revolution in 1917, the issues raised by Soviet communism have provoked as intense a debate in Britain as any in our history. It is all too obvious today that our relations with the Soviet state, along with those of our allies, could go far to determine, not only the future of the human race, but whether there will be any future at all. And yet serious studies of Anglo-Soviet affairs are few.[2]

This book hopes to clarify a particularly important, but relatively neglected, period of Anglo-Soviet relations, between 1924 and 1934,[3] and particularly the section of this period after the breach of diplomatic relations in 1927. This era spanned the transition in the USSR from Lenin's 'New Economic Policy' (NEP) through collectivisation and industrialisation to the first great purge trials, which really got under way after 1934. In Britain the period was marked by the first two Labour Governments (of 1924 and 1929-31) in coalition with an enfeebled Liberal Party, and the most difficult period of the Depression. For both the USSR and Britain, indeed for Europe as a whole, the period saw the defeat of the forces of international reason and the gathering clouds of war. This book therefore ends on a sombre note, with the Spanish Civil War in the near future, the tragedy of the purges yet to get fully under way, and the full implications of British 'appeasement' of Hitler still to be seen.

The Labour Party has been chosen as the main vehicle of this story mainly because the party has, by its ideological leanings and internationalist aspirations, had to face up to the challenge of the USSR more than any other British political entity with the obvious exception of the Communist Party of Great Britain (CPGB).

Only one book solely dedicated to the Labour Party's attitude to the USSR is extant, by Bill Jones.[4] Jones generally accepts the extreme view that the Labour Party had a 'love affair' with the Soviet Union in the inter-war period. However vague a concept this might appear to be, and the following pages hope to show just how vague, Jones provided the literature with an initial and long-due overview. But there are none the less huge gaps. John Naylor's book on *Labour's International Policy* in the 1930s deals mainly with the period after 1935 and has little to say on the USSR.[5] As we shall see, there are two good reviews of Labour's internal disputes in the 1930s.[6] The main gaps are in discussion of Labour's internal disputes about foreign policy, especially in our area of interest. The explanation of this may lie in the relatively recent opening of the National Executive Committee (NEC) files for the period, Naylor for example complaining that he did not get access. The Independent Labour Party's files are also now fully available, as are the papers of Hugh Dalton, the Webbs, James Ramsay MacDonald, and Philip Noel-Baker, to name but some of the more illustrious.

It must also be said that a great deal had, and has, still to be unearthed from both local and national Labour Party press organs. One weakness of this book is the difficulty I have found in doing full justice to the relations of party leadership and rank and file. Given the plethora of possible sources this was perhaps an impossible task, and of course it could still be attempted by future scholars. What has been concentrated on here is the developing feelings of the leadership of the party to the USSR, be they in parliament, at party headquarters or on the General Council of the Trades Union Congress (TUC); for let it not be forgotten, this was a Labour *movement*, not just a party. That movement has defied categorisation many times. It is a 'broad church', pluralist, sectarian, dubiously 'socialist', pace Clause IV of its Constitution.[7] Certainly it has never been revolutionary.[8] It has usually disliked 'intellectuals', even though increasingly its parliamentary ranks came to be filled with middle-class members of the genre.

Various themes will therefore be developed throughout in the hope of showing the evolution of attitudes among different sections of the party and within the psyches of individuals of importance. This aim will be developed within an overall analysis of the changing structure and membership of the Labour Party itself. This is, of course, a difficult task but by no means an impossible one, as the following pages hope to prove. The success of the enterprise hinges around asking the right questions. The initial questions must be the following:

1 What was the Labour Party that confronted the problem of the USSR throughout the period in question? Did it change, and if so, how? What were its perceived policy options and limitations, be they electoral, internal or external? What, in short, was its place within British politics?
2 What complexion did the USSR assume within this domestic constellation? Was it viewed as a promising model or as a damning contradiction of Labour Party principles? Once in power, what was the foreign policy on the USSR to be for a Labour Party that had no particular tradition of foreign policy making? It was after all a *new* party.
3 What was known about the USSR? On what basis could such a policy be developed? The USSR was after all even younger than the Labour Party, the subject of much passion and much ignorance.

Moreover, a great deal of ink has flowed in recent years denouncing those who saw anything whatsoever to admire in the inter-war USSR, and many of these people had formal or informal links with the Labour Party.

This literature varies from the thoughful to the lurid. In the last category can be mentioned the work of Chapman Pincher and Andrew Boyle,[9] in a more analytical framework David Caute's *Fellow Travellers* and Sylvia Margulies' *The Pilgrimage to Russia*.[10] Both genres have a tendency towards a constant implication that those who found something of value in the USSR inevitably, or at least usually, lacked both judgement and, in some cases, loyalty to their country and its values.

This is not to let those that did adulate the USSR completely off the hook. Intellectuals of the stature of Beatrice Webb would not have welcomed a condescending forgiveness for what were great errors of judgement. But they should at least be errors put into context. And it must be admitted that many others have been utterly and criminally wrong about Adolf Hitler, Benito Mussolini, Mao-Tse Tung, the Ayatollah Khomeini and other revolutionary leaders. The explanation for the refusal to forgive or forget in the case of the Webbs and the 'Fellow Travellers' has many facets and is one that we must also try to explore. A major task in the following pages is therefore to shed some light on the visitors to Russia, their motives, hopes, fears and discoveries. It is perhaps time to introduce some new ideas into this debate.

In a broader context it is hoped to shed some light on some of the enduring debates of twentieth-century politics. The dangers of drawing from exterior 'exemplars' in the pursuit of domestic inspiration has been a constant since at least the First World War. The world has made a fetish of 'experiments' of all kinds, adopting economic and political fashions with great alacrity and regularity. This book is the description of how one experiment was viewed, used and arbitrarily discarded. I hope that it will both demonstrate the intrinsically difficult nature of borrowing from one system for use in another, but also explain the enormous temptation to do so. It does not attempt to condemn or justify, but in explaining the process will inevitably do both.

I would like to express my thanks and appreciation for all those who have contributed to the writing of this work.

Among the many librarians and archivists I should particularly like to thank are Mrs Irene Wagner, Ms Pat Francis and Mr Stephen Bird of the Labour Party. Ms Angela Raspin of the British Library of Political and Economic Science (BLPES) at the London School of Economics not only inspired me with her immense knowledge of the Webbs and Hugh Dalton, but also with all the copious material in her charge. Thanks must be extended to the various other libraries whose librarians remained extremely helpful but anonymous, and in particular the staff of the Birmingham Public Library, of Churchill College, Cambridge, the Cooperative Union, Manchester and Nuffield College, Oxford. As any historian who has studied British history, I must include in my thanks the British Library, and especially its Manuscripts Room and Newspaper Library at Colindale, London, and the Public Record Office at Kew where I spent weeks, if not months.

I should also like to thank those who guided this manuscript throughout its life. Naturally my thesis adviser, Professor Miklos Molnar, has taken the brunt of this task, but I also owe a great debt to Professors Jacques Freymond and Asa Briggs.

This book is dedicated to Jane Williams for her perseverance and friendship, without which none of this would have been possible.

A. J. Williams
Canterbury, February 1989

Notes

1 Perhaps the best example on the USSR is HAMMOND, Thomas T., *Soviet Foreign Relations and World Communism, A Selected Bibliography*, Princeton, New Jersey, Princeton University Press, 1965 (with subsequent reprints). On the Labour Party see Victor F. Gilbert (compiled), *Labour and Social History Theses, 1900-1978*, London, Mansell Publishing, 1982, for the latest research. Updates are published periodically in the *Bulletin* of the Society for the Study of Labour History.

2 NORTHEDGE, F.S., and WELLS, Audrey, *Britain and Soviet Communism: The Impact of a Revolution*, London, Macmillan, 1982.

3 The most comprehensive survey of Anglo-Soviet relations between 1917 and 1921 is ULLMAN, Richard Henry, *Anglo-Soviet Relations, 1917-1921*, vol. 1: *Intervention and the War*; vol. 2: *Britain and the Russian Civil War*; vol. 3: *The Anglo-Soviet Accord.* All published by Princeton University Press, respectively 1961, 1968 and 1972. The best survey of the period between 1920 and 1924 is WHITE, Stephen, *Britain and the Bolshevik Revolution*, London, Macmillan, 1979. For the period 1924-7 Gabriel GORODETSKY's *The Precarious Truce: Anglo-Soviet Relations 1924-1927*, Cambridge University Press, 1977, covers the diplomatic relations of that period well. But the best book for conveying the atmosphere of Anglo-Soviet relations, and especially the Labour movement's feeling about them is Daniel CALHOUN's *The United Front: The TUC and the Russians*, Cambridge University Press, 1976. Extensive use of this book will be made in early chapters. For the period after 1927 there is little of use, with the exception of Jonathan HASLAM's *Soviet Foreign Policy, 1930-33*, London, Macmillan, 1983.

4 JONES, William, *The Russia Complex: The British Labour Party and the Soviet Union*, Manchester University Press, 1971.

5 NAYLOR, John F., *Labour's International Policy, The Labour Party in the 1930s*, London, Weidenfeld and Nicolson, 1969.

6 PIMLOTT, Ben, *Labour and the Left in the 1930s*, Cambridge University Press, 1977 and JUPP, James, *The Radical Left in Britain, 1931-41*, London, Frank Cass, 1982.

7 On this the literature is naturally vast. There are many who bewail the Labour Party's lack of 'socialism', Ralph Miliband being a good example. Perhaps the best comment on this debate has been that 'it has been a significant fact of the party's history that its identity has regularly drawn conflicting perceptions and prescriptions from the various members of the 'Great Alliance'; MINKIN, Lewis and SEYD, Patrick in PATERSON, William and THOMAS, Alistair, *Social Democratic Parties in Western Europe*, London, Croom Helm, 1977, p. 101.

8 Strong evidence to support this view can be found in McKIBBIN, Ross, *The Evolution of the Labour Party, 1910-1924*, Oxford, Clarendon Press, 1974.

9 BOYLE, Andrew, *The Climate of Treason*, London, Hutchinson, 1979 and PINCHER, Chapman, *Their Trade is Treachery*, London, Sidgewick, 1981, are good examples of the genre. The accused persons vary from the obvious members of the Communist Party right up to the top of the British establishment.

10 CAUTE, David, *The Fellow Travellers: A Postscript to the Enlightenment*, London, Quartet, 1977. MARGULIES, Sylvia, *The Pilgrimage to Russia; The Soviet Union and the Treatment of Foreigners, 1924-1937*, Madison, University of Wisconsin Press, 1968.

chapter one

Anglo-Soviet relations before and during the 1924 Labour Government

The basis for an Anglo-Soviet rapprochement

Before the First World War the Labour Party, young as it then was, could condemn Czarist Russia wholeheartedly and still appear both moderate and conciliatory. Few within British society, of whatever political colour, liked this old Russia. It was necessary to do business with it on occasion, but no affection was possible or necessary. Excessive hysteria was kept to a minimum out of respect for the English monarchy, which was unfortunately related to the Czars, but it did not take much to inspire righteous indignation. The visit of the Czar to London in 1909 to the King at Cowes led the Labour Party to issue a pamphlet roundly condemning such contacts. The presence of such a representative of a 'system of murder ... is an insult to our national good name and to our self-respect'. The Czar and his monarchy were 'tainting the world'. Moreover, he was in no way representative of his people, 'who are no more represented by the Czar than victims can be represented by their oppressors'.[1]

This condemnation was shaken, as was virtually everything else, by the shock of 1914-18. The very raison d'etre of the organised opposition to the war lay at least partly in a desire to have nothing whatsoever to do with the 'asiatic' Czarist regime. The assault on 'secret diplomacy' was directed mainly against this Russian regime and became inextricably linked with an assault on Russian anti-democratic methods in the main anti-war organisation, the Union of Democratic Control. The Labour Party was split down the middle by its attitude to the war, Ramsay MacDonald and Philip Snowden being sent into a temporary political wilderness, while Arthur Henderson, with whom they had built up the party, went into the Cabinet. The generally recognised incompetence with which the war was being waged and weariness with the slaughter slowly brought these two factions back onto speaking terms. But it needed the political equivalent of the tank to break the deadlock and bring the party to unity on a major issue. This was at least partly provided by the February Revolution of 1917.

A spontaneous reaction of joy greeted this event. A huge crowd gathered in the Albert Hall on 18 March and support for the Kerensky Government because synonymous with a desire for a just and swift peace. The Cabinet, alarmed as to what this could mean, sent its most conciliatory representative to St Petersburg in June to find out what might be the result of the changes. This was Arthur Henderson. He found himself in the midst of a 'situation most perplexing owing to its uncertainty'. He could not choose between those who claimed that the revolution would lead to better things and those who saw inevitable chaos. Henderson urged moderation and no precipitate plunge into socialism. He also introduced a notion that was to dominate one area of the Labour Party's thinking about the USSR, by saying: 'I think the risks of the experiment ... are so great that not only might it prove a disaster to Russia but to the Allied cause'. He was particularly alarmed at the lack of 'steadying influences akin to our trade unions' and the consequent risks of economic collapse.

But at the same time as he was alarmed, he was fascinated. He quite openly suggested himself as ambassador to the new regime. A subsequent letter to his Labour Cabinet colleague, G. H. Roberts, urged the organisation of a conference to discuss this new phenomenon. He saw a crisis occurring in the near future between the existing and, in his eyes, admirable 'moderate socialists' and the 'extremists' who would hang them all from lamp-posts, Lenin's group representing the latter tendency.[2] The duly convened conference thus hailed the installation of a moderate Russian democracy, not the Bolsheviks, a point deliberately misunderstood by certain Conservatives at several inter-war general elections.[3]

Although this convention did much to bring about the reunification of the Labour Party in a refound common desire to extend the principles of civil liberty in Britain in the image of their Russian comrades, the provisional government did not last. Could the new October regime be counted on to continue 'the intellectual and social development of Russia', in the words of the Leeds Manifesto? Henderson feared that 'extremists' would win the day.[4]

In the immediate post-war period a major test of the reaction of the Labour Party to the new Russia was the Allied intervention of 1919-21.[5] One element of the Labour Party left's mythology is still that 'Councils of Action' set up by various local labour and union branches forced Lloyd George to withdraw Allied, or at least British, help from the Whites in Russia. Stephen White has attacked this view by showing that it was war weariness that really prompted what Labour Party opposition existed to intervention, not support for the Bolsheviks.[6]

The main conclusions of one major fact-finding mission sent by the TUC and Labour Party, in 1920, were not ones of overwhelming enthusiasm, but rather a very British appeal to 'fair play'.[7]

This is why the analysis of the Labour Party's relationship with the USSR really has to start in 1924. Until the end of warfare and a kind of normalcy on Russian territory the Labour Party leadership could not make up its mind about even the bare essentials of the phenomenon with which it would have to deal. All that existed before was genuine sorrow at the plight of the ordinary Russian and a mixture of suspicion and hope for what the new Russia might produce.

Three major points must be made to conclude this brief examination of the Labour Party and its relations with Russia before and after 1917 until about 1923. Firstly, the Labour Party and the Soviet Union were born (to a large extent) together and the USSR's birth greatly influenced the post-1918 Labour Party. Secondly, it demonstrates that from 1917 onwards happenings in the USSR had some direct effect, which varied from period to period in intensity, on domestic Labour Party concerns. Much of the material in the following pages is intended to explore these links. Lastly, the initial analysis has tried to show that the new Russia had by no means an automatic friend in the Labour Party. The relationship was from the beginning ambiguous and difficult.

Until 1924 the Labour Party had no experience of government, except for those few such as Henderson and some of the incoming Liberals who had served under war-time coalition or Liberal administrations. Dealing with any problem of domestic or foreign policy with such an inexperienced cabinet was a source of some worry to James Ramsay MacDonald, the new Prime Minister. Given his election pledge to re-establish contacts with the USSR he was particularly aware of the need not to make mistakes in dealing with a country that could prove to be a poisonous ally.[8] This was especially so given the ostentatious antagonism to the USSR displayed by the outgoing Conservative Foreign Secretary, Lord Curzon, and other 'diehards', as the Conservative lobby for isolating Russia became known.

The principle themes that emerged from the Labour Party critique of Conservative intransigence over the USSR come out strongly in the 1923 debate over the practical consequences of Curzon's famous 'note'.[9]

The Labour Party leadership had become aware in April 1923 that Curzon and the Cabinet were building up to some kind of showdown with the USSR, enraged about propaganda in the Empire and the persecution of religion in the USSR. The Labour Party in turn had some reason to feel annoyed about propaganda in its 'empire' from the Communist Party of Great Britain (CPGB), although relations in 1923 were not nearly so bad between the CPGB and the Labour Party as they later became, especially after 1924. Religion was also a subject upon which many Labour Party members were somewhat touchy, as will be seen later, and the USSR was vociferously 'anti-God'.

Henderson, as Secretary of the Labour Party, therefore wrote in April 1923 to the Prime Minister, Bonar Law, appealing for a change in the debate about Russia. His letter was mainly directed at 'the campaign which is being conducted against the Russian trade delegation', although expressing shock over the 'recent trials and the subsequent execution of a bishop ... [which] I need hardly say the Parliamentary Labour Party deeply deplores'. However 'this unfortunate incident' in no way excused the 'breaking off of official trade relationships ... thereby inflicting economic injury on the people of this country'. Moreover, 'the results upon this country would far outweigh any possible injury which might be inflicted upon the Russian Republic'. Trade was likely to increase, he added, since 'Russia's industrial prospects are certain to improve with the anticipated agricultural revival'.[10]

Bonar Law's reply showed that the government gave other matters more weight:

> The proceedings of the Soviet Government ... towards the ministers of religion, the nature and terms of their official communications to the British Government, their seizure of British trawlers, and their violation of the preliminary conditions of the trade agreement [on propaganda] are serious matters.[11]

To some extent the Labour Party leadership shared Curzon's fears about the intentions of the Soviet Government, including those of propaganda (point 4 of Curzon's 'ultimatum' of May 1923). However, it still shared Lloyd George's hopes of 1919 and 1920, those of helping the cause of peace by bringing the Russians into the 'comity of nations' and taming the bear through commerce, helping British unemployment figures as a useful side-benefit. The Anglo-Soviet Trade Agreement of 1921 was the fruit of this reasoning – one not shared by most Conservatives. The party's subsequent National Joint Council (NJC) statement, published in the *Daily Herald*, protested 'against any rupture of trade relations with Russia, which will result not only in increased unemployment here, but also in political unsettlement, which will add to the danger of war'.[12]

The Soviet reply to the Curzon note was fairly conciliatory, and both Labour Party and Trades Union Congress (TUC) chose to accept it in a similar spirit. The *Daily Herald* diplomatic correspondent pointed out that the propaganda charges may well have been true but that the capitals (Kabul and Teheran), from where Russian diplomats were supposed to fund newspapers hostile to British interests were also the scene of a massive British subsidy of papers hostile to the Soviet Union.[13]

The episode was closed when the British Conservative Government accepted Soviet assurances, with bad grace, on 18 June 1923. White assures us that the various elements of Labour's response were not 'derived from a feeling of political community with the Soviet Government', but from the fact that the Labour Party was struggling with the Communist Party. In fact, 'British Labour, far from manifesting any sympathy for Bolshevism, was among its most determined and vigorous opponents on both the national and international arenas', and even the Comintern realised this.[14] Among the leadership this was undoubtedly the prevalent opinion, even though a distinct difference must be made between the views of the CPGB and the Comintern on the one hand and of the 'official' USSR on the other. This is a distinction that will be developed throughout the following pages.

This, it must be repeated, was to be the first ever Labour Government. It was also an unexpected victory for the Labour Party.[15] The new administration was inevitably in a bewildering position, with huge organisational problems and an insecure position of keeping power only on Liberal sufference. On foreign policy questions the approach to take was even more complicated, with a Foreign Office state and representation abroad that was almost, if not totally, made up of members of the upper classes who had little sympathy for the men now in office. Duff Cooper was a good example of this attitude and was very frank in admitting that the reason he got on well with Arthur Ponsonby, the new Under-Secretary of State for Foreign Affairs, was because of Ponsonby's (upper-) class origins. The Labour Party as a whole struck Cooper as 'very dull', but Ponsonby, who Cooper characterises as 'far left' was 'considering his detestable principles ... a decent enough fellow'.[16] MacDonald, as Foreign Secretary, as well as Prime Minister, gave most of the responsibility for foreign affairs to Ponsonby.[17]

Nineteen twenty-three had been a year of no small impact on foreign affairs in Britain. Apart from the Curzon ultimatum, reparations had been a major issue and MacDonald devoted much of his time to this question in 1924. As Marquand says: 'it was clear that foreign policy would be just as important politically as it had been in 1923'.[18] It was at the 8 January 1924 post-election rally at the Albert Hall (where Cooper had seen the party as 'very dull') that MacDonald said that 'the pompous folly of standing aloof from the Russian Government' would be ended.[19] But MacDonald and Ponsonby were presented with the same advice by the same officials who had advised Curzon, the only difference being pressure from their own backbenches, 'who are impatient for the recognition of Russia and cannot understand why there should be an hour's delay'.[20] Given that Parliament had met for the first time on 15 January and that MacDonald was not made Prime Minister until 23 January, the new administration was already under considerable pressure with an enormous number of decisions to take, most of which were delicate.

The first most important point – that of recognition – had already been conceded by MacDonald. What concrete information could have been used by MacDonald to know to what point he could trust the Russians not to exploit an opening up on his side, particularly on the questions of bond-holders and propaganda? Talks on these subjects took place within the Anglo-Soviet Conference that started in April 1924. But before that MacDonald was presented with a despatch from R. M. Hodgson (British Chargé d'Affaires in Moscow) addressed to the previous Foreign Secretary, Curzon.[21] It was dated 18 January but was received, significantly, on 28 January, that is to say only five days after MacDonald became Prime Minister and only three days before Hodgson was instructed to make the initial declaration of an official wish for recognition (the official despatch left London on 1 February). It has been noted that the Italians nearly beat the British to the post of recognition and, Gorodetsky feels, these were the circumstances that 'dictated swift action'.[22] This may be partly true, but Hodgson's despatch of 18 January was possibly more crucial.[23]

Hodgson felt that the Communist Party of the Soviet Union (CPSU) was 'sick physically and morally. Lenin is gone ... Trotsky is an invalid; and a whole group of the more prominent figures in the Bolshevik world are either prostrated by illness or are incapacitated to a greater or lesser degree. Morally, the party is more gravely affected than physically'. Moreover:

> Zinoviev, a poor creature at best, finds his influence rapidly waning since the Communist debacle in Germany; Kamenev is a depressing personality incapable of giving inspiration to the mass; Stalin, 'the man of steel', a narrow-minded,

> obstinate Georgian, entangled in the intricacies of party doctrine; Bukharin, a fanatic, popular with the working man, but without the makings of a leader. Of the others among the old Communists none is of eminence while the 'Young Guard' of Communism is barren.

The CPSU was also portrayed as untrustworthy. It had reneged on clauses stopping propaganda (including under the terms of the 1921 Anglo-Soviet Trade Agreement), but Hodgson was convinced that although still 'the victim of a revolutionary mentality' Russia could not stay this way. This was because:

> closer relations with the outside world and, above all, the necessities imposed by economic laws ... will bring this country, in spite of the intractability of its rulers, who are personally refractory to evolution, back into the normal current of international relations. The Communist Party has, I believe, had its day, and the play of elemental forces within it is leading to its disruption, but there are signs that out of it is gradually emerging a national Russian Government whose policy will be less and less dictated by political charlatans like Zinoviev, or gutter journalists like Radek.

Although acknowledging that the CPSU was by no means yet finished the tone of the whole despatch led the reader to believe that its necessity to 'compromise with bourgeois states' would bring the party to an eventual nemesis, and has a 'hopeful augury for the future'.[24]

How seriously this despatch was taken by MacDonald is difficult to relate, but it does perhaps throw light on a question that had been a major problem for the Labour Party, and continued to be – that of the CPGB being under orders from Moscow. A weak CPSU, or one that could be weakened by 'compromise' would inevitably mean confused orders for its British satellite, which would in turn perish. In these circumstances the best way to encourage still further a decline in Moscow-based propaganda would be to pursue trade links with the USSR. Confirmation that this line was accepted by the Labour Cabinet of 1924 lies in Ponsonby's preface to an explanatory booklet on the Anglo-Soviet treaties (on trade) signed in the last weeks of the Labour Government. As well as the obvious benefits for the czarist bondholders, Ponsonby suggested that a Labour Government must right the wrongs done by seven years of isolation and decay: 'Russia must first of all be set on its legs in order that by the restoration of its economic life it can be in a position to meet the claims made against it'. Hence the 'recognition of the Soviet Government thereby creating the friendly atmosphere which is the essential preliminary to successful negotiations. The present treaties are the next step' (the third would be that of an export-oriented loan to enable the Soviet Government to 'buy British' and the settling of czarist debts). Without the treaties the Russians would stay out in the cold and hence not pay their debts, the chance to reduce unemployment would be missed but, most importantly from the political point of view, '*the extremist elements in Russia will be strengthened*; and, worst of all, a disappointed and offended Russia once more treated as a pariah and an outcast will become a standing menace to European peace'.[25]

Hence, although MacDonald told Rakovsky at their first meeting that it would be a 'great mistake' to mix diplomatic recognition with economic discussions', (the Foreign Office's view, according to Gorodetsky), MacDonald none the less wanted all issues to be discussed together, which did not please the Russians, but which they accepted. MacDonald seems to have been attempting a rather subtle game that does not make sense unless he took at least some of the Hodgson memorandum to heart. Indeed, he seems to have made the final decision to extend recognition alone, even over the King's entreaties, and without consulting his Cabinet.[26]

The Anglo-Soviet Conference of 1924

Perhaps one should also see the opening of the famous Anglo-Soviet Conference in a different light from that given it by many writers. MacDonald did give over power to Ponsonby in the negotiations after only one meeting but his excuse – that of his 'other' duties[27] – for not taking the leading role as British negotiator was perhaps a real one. The quality-bereft nature of MacDonald's 1924 administration meant he had to delegate even decisions of a primordial nature where he could, and Ponsonby was universally held to be among the best of a rather administratively weak cuvee. MacDonald, then, probably meant it when he said at this opening meeting: 'It is my intention to give close and constant attention to all the questions with which both the political and economic committees will deal ... I hope to preside over the joint sittings as regularly as possible, and especially when the work is of definite importance'. If we take an even slightly less-jaundiced view of MacDonald's sincerity than has become fashionable since 1931, then his giving the main task to Ponsonby may be a sign of the importance he attached to the proceedings, not the other way round. It should also be noted that the King had made a particular point of showing his disapproval of any contact with the 'murderers of his relatives'.[28] This may have been part of the sensitivity to which he referred in a letter to Soviet Commissar for Foreign Affairs, Chicherin, the very day that the intention of a resumption of diplomatic relations was sent to Moscow.

This warm letter ('official communications are apt to appear cold and lifeless, and necessarily leave unexpressed the sentiments which underly them') hoped for both 'a friendship between our two peoples which will lead to their understanding each other to a degree hitherto impossible and to a settlement of their differences'. MacDonald felt the choice of Soviet ambassador would be a crucial first step: 'for instance ... [someone who has had] personal ties with this country, or have known it for other than political interests'.[29]

Chicherin's reply, ominously linked his best greetings with a wish for 'success in your really difficult task'. But he gave MacDonald cause for feeling that even the existing contact was helping the cause of the Russian moderates. 'Peace is our watchword', wrote Chicherin, 'if only we could work together with the British Labour Party for the sake of universal settlement ... [the] need is now for "civilisation" as a motto'. Given Chicherin's dislike of the Comintern, they probably were on the same wavelength.[30] But it was not to be until 1930 that a Soviet ambassador actually arrived in London, as will be seen later.

When the Anglo-Soviet Conference finally opened, MacDonald gave an impressive inaugural speech covering all the issues before leaving the technical questions to Ponsonby. Good trade, said MacDonald, was dependent on 'mutual confidences' and (1) a 'liquidation of the past'; (2) a definition of 'rights and obligations actually existing as between the two countries' in order to (3) 'provide as far as possible for peaceful and profitable relations in the future'. The question of the bond-holders and personal (economic grievances) came under the first category; under the second came a discussion of the existing treaties 'concluded with your predecessors', while under the third came an upgrading of the 1921 Trade Agreement into a proper commercial treaty. Propaganda made up another category: 'we shall desire to have a very frank discussion on what has been alluded to in previous correspondence between the two governments as "propaganda" or "hostile activities" ... [so] as to see whether difficulties of this kind cannot be effectively prevented from recurring under our new relations'.[31]

In the ensuing conference there was clearly ground for cooperation on the trade issues; the financial aspects gave more problems. The key one was that of a loan to the Soviet Government which the Foreign Office, in a long memo of 28 July, felt was the only solution, with a refusal having 'serious political consequences', both 'negatively' where 'a great chance of conciliation tending towards general recovery in Europe could have been lost' and 'positively ... Soviet Russia ... cut off from Western Europe, might become the focus of dangerous activities in

Eastern Europe'. Lastly, it would be 'very bitterly resented by the party, not only in the House of Commons but also in the country. A chance of getting work for the unemployed would again have been missed'.[32] The same memo did not anticipate opposition from the other parties. This was clearly optimistic, for even within his own party MacDonald met opposition notably to the offering of a loan to the USSR from the Chancellor of the Exchequer, Philip Snowden, who was certain the City would not approve.[33] Ponsonby agreed with the Foreign Office belief in the necessity of a loan as did MacDonald himself, so it seems, for his only comments were on shipping problems.[34] This Foreign Office/ Treasury difference over the desirability or indeed feasibility of a British loan to the USSR was the harbinger of a quarrel that was to haunt all British relations with the USSR during the 1920s and 1930s.[35]

Sources of pressure on the Government's Russian policy

We must ask what other pressures MacDonald came under from elsewhere. They were of three major kinds. Firstly from the rank and file of the Labour Party, and from the international allies of the Labour Party, secondly from the Foreign Office, and lastly from elements essentially hostile to the Soviet Union, in particular the City of London where many remembered the Czarist loans that had never been repaid.

The main pressure from the rank and file was on the subject of pushing through a trade agreement as fast as possible. The commercial element was separated from that of the bond-holders, the negotiations on the latter having proved so thorny that they were relegated to a 'general' treaty that allowed for further discussion.[36] The bond-holders claims were probably of little interest to Labour supporters (the large majority of whom cannot have been claimants), but Snowden in particular felt it essential to minimise City opposition to the treaty, which meant treating the debt problem seriously. Hence Ponsonby was forced to treat trade and financial questions together, thus reducing the chances of an improvement of either.

At times the relatively slow pace of the conference (also due, it must be said, to the Russians' hard negotiating), often put MacDonald under a great deal of pressure from his own supporters in Parliament and led to some confusion in Labour ranks. MacDonald had to reproach Sidney Webb (President of the Board of Trade, and thus particularly open to pressure) for giving the impression to a rank-and-file delegation that 'we are not acting in full agreement'.[37]

The treaties were signed on 8 August. MacDonald was probably sincere when he declared at a meeting in late September 1924: 'An agreement with Russia on these lines [i.e. the two treaties] is now an essential part of the Labour Party's policy, and if the House of Commons will not allow it, the House of Commons had better censure us (loud cheers)'.[38]

What also separated the rank and file of the party from the leadership was their access to information. Clearly some of the rank and file were aware of the horrors perpetrated in the name of progress in the USSR but these stories were often discounted as diehard rubbish. After 1924 an 'Anglo-Russian Parliamentary Committee' run by William and Zelda Coates made a full-time career of exposing 'Tory lies' about Russia, to which prominent and respected members of the British labour movement gave their support on occasion.

It was more difficult to refute the charges of fellow socialists in the Labour and Socialist International (LSI) although here again, during 1924 at least, the main criticisms came from a source that it was relatively easy to ignore, the Socialist Revolutionary Party of Russia. The Socialist Revolutionaries (SRs) were members of the LSI (as were the Mensheviks under Abramovitch). In mid-June 1924 Vandervelde had written to MacDonald asking him to intercede with the Russians for SRs imprisoned in the USSR.[39]

He also received a memo from Socialist Revolutionary, Soukhoumlin, which dwelt principally and at great length on the persecution of Socialists, and especially SRs in the USSR, information later published in full by the LSI.[40] The Northern Department of the Foreign Office wrote full comments. This, they said, was a Labour Party affair but they 'felt it inadvisable to have any direct dealings with the representative of the Socialist Revolutionaries'. They none the less said they liked point 4 (on propaganda). On the details of persecution and the internal crisis (also discussed), 'this is more or less fully borne out by our reports from Moscow ... and adds little to our knowledge' and advised no action that would 'savour too much of interference in the internal party politics of Russia' except, perhaps, to reply to Trotsky's allegations about the Labour Party being the 'screen of British Imperialists'. Poor MacDonald could only minute it: 'I can take no part in this. If there are to be any approaches made, they must not be with my knowledge or consent'. To have done otherwise would have seriously compromised the treaty discussions.

As to the matters that the Foreign Office were aware of, MacDonald was, as Foreign Secretary, given all the confidential embassy reports even before Ponsonby. He alone had the possibility of a clear view of persecution and the power struggle in the USSR. Even if he had reason to doubt the motives of some Foreign Office officials he never seems to have questioned too much the integrity of their information or actions. They seem to have continued to play the traditional role of protecting their Foreign Minister from too many unpleasant surprises. Their action in the Soukhoumlin affair is typical of this. Equally so was that of the King, outraged at insults being heaped upon MacDonald by Zinoviev and well reported in the British press,[41] Selby (his Foreign Office Private Secretary) replied to the King that MacDonald 'fully adheres to his Majesty's view' and was writing to Rakovsky 'to stem the tide of abuse'.[42]

On the information side, the Foreign Office was even more helpful. Hodgson continued to send detailed reports on the political situation in Leningrad. In an April despatch he said changes since Lenin's death 'can only be described as a tidal wave',[43] the destruction being among Trotsky's followers and the left oppositionists as well as among 'bourgeois elements'.[44] Generally speaking the Foreign Office despatches told MacDonald what he wanted to hear, i.e. that the treaties would bolster 'moderation'. It will never be elucidated whether the Foreign Office did sincerely stay neutral or whether class predilections spoken of by Duff Cooper won through in the end. Such would have been a departure from tradition, but then many Foreign Office officials considered both the advent of the Labour Party and relations with Soviet Russia as equal departures from sane and normal practice.

Russia and the general election of 1924

The election was forced on MacDonald by the Liberal defection over the signing of the Russian treaties, a defection that clearly surprised him.[45] The most damaging event of the whole election campaign was the publishing of a letter, probably forged, purporting to have been written by Comintern supremo Zinoviev, in the *Daily Mail* and simultaneously by the Foreign Office. The truth or non-truth of this letter has been debated at great length elsewhere, as has another issue, carrying the Russian link further. This was the 'Campbell case' where a prominent communist was prosecuted for 'incitement to mutiny' which turned into an outcry about communist propaganda in Britain.[46] It was over the Campbell case that the Labour Party was censured in the House of Commons on 8 October; the Zinoviev letter exploded (no other word is possible) on 29 October during the campaign in an atmosphere of anti-Soviet hysteria.

The overall Labour vote on polling day, 1 November, was actually increased by 1 million, but the forward march of Labour was slowed down due to a collapse of the Liberal vote. It is doubtful that many believed the veracity of the Zinoviev letter (it has never been proved one way or the other), and the Campbell case was seen widely as a blunder rather than a deliberate pro-communist act by MacDonald. But it was the party leader himself who suffered most from the two scandals. All his hopes were dashed on a recognisably Russian rock, to which he had devoted his reputation and care. He had all his belief in the still extremist nature of the USSR's leadership confirmed by the Zinoviev letter. Gorodetsky's comments sum up the probable truth of the matter:

> The immediate reaction of Labour Ministers after the elections was to blame their defeat on the 'Zinoviev letter' affair. A careful study of the election results, however, suggests that the Liberal decline rather than the 'Zinoviev letter' was responsible for the Conservative victory, though the affair probably made the majority an overwhelming one.[47]

But when he saw the King for the last time on 4 November MacDonald told him that 'my successors would have to carry out the same policy'.[48] Baldwin clearly seemed to disagree with this opinon, and most of MacDonald's opening up to Russia was undone by 1927.

The lessons of 1924

As to the Labour Party leadership, and particularly MacDonald, its feeling was clearly one of having burnt its fingers. The difficult balance of pragmatic needs and humanitarian and ideological misgivings was a difficult one to maintain and it got no easier. The next time he was in office MacDonald was going to treat the Russian question with a great deal more distance. There would be no more friendly letters to Chicherin.

On a more general level the 1924 Labour Government's experience of relations with the USSR seems to confirm the theory that the making of any foreign policy can never be unfettered. The government was by no means monolithic in its power, even when the pressure groups that pushed it on generally agreed with its aims. The Labour Party's whole previous belief in open diplomacy made it prey to the kinds of problem that any traditionalist would have foreseen. But whereas the traditionalists of the Curzon period had chosen to try and ignore Russia as much as possible in public and attack it when this proved impossible, a Labour Government could not do this, especially with Russia as the self-proclaimed 'homeland of the working class'. Nineteen twenty-four was only a preliminary skirmish in what became and remained a very complex love-hate relationship between the British Labour movement and the Soviet Union.

Ponsonby summed up the party organs' and leadership's attitude very well in a debate a month before the signing of the treaties when he said:

> The middle course is a difficult one. I believe the policy which the Labour Party has always advocated, the policy of conciliation, ought to guide us for the sake of British trade and for the sake of the revival of Russia itself. I have a great belief in the future of Russia, and it is with this consideration in view, and for the sake of healing the wounds of Europe, that we are desirous of bringing Russia into the comity of nations'.[49]

Notes

1 Labour Party, *The Visit of the Czar of Russia* ('issued by instructions of the Executive Committee of the Labour Party'), 26 June 1909, 2 pp.

2 Henderson to G. H. Roberts, 21 June 1917, Labour Party Archives, HEN/1/31. For further discussions of Hendersons's feelings, see WINTER, J. M. 'Arthur Henderson, the Russian Revolution and the Reconstruction of the Labour Party', *Historical Journal*, 15, 4 (1972), pp. 733-73.

3 Labour Party, 'Great Labour, Socialist and Democratic Convention to Hail the Russian Revolution and to Organise the British Democracy: to Follow Russia', Manchester, Labour Party Press, 23 May 1917, 3 pp. The conference was held on 3 June 1917.

4 Henderson's letters and a poem ('Skin a Russian and Discover a Tartar') can be found in the Labour Party Archives, under HEN/14/3.

5 Cf. ULLMAN, op. cit, vol. 3 and White, op. cit, Ch. 1.

6 WHITE, *Britain and the Bolshevik Revolution*, op. cit, Ch. 2.

7 *British Labour Delegation to Russia, 1920 – Report*, London, TUC and Labour Party, 1920.

8 The details of the negotiation are covered in extensive detail elsewhere. Gorodetsky is one good source, op. cit.

9 For full details of the circumstances around this 'Note' see correspondence between His Majesty's Government and the Soviet Government with respect to the relations between the two Governments: Cmd 1869, 1923, (xxv) 497 pp. and reply of the Soviet Government, Cmd 1894, 1923, (xxv) 511 pp.

10 Henderson to Bonar Law, 17 April 1923, FO 800/219.

11 Bonar Law to Henderson, 18 April 1923, FO 800/219. An Anglo-Soviet agreement on trade had been signed in 1921, which had contained clauses limiting Soviet propaganda. The Soviet Government always claimed after this date that propaganda emanated not from official sources but from the Communist International, over which it had no control. Cf. EUDIN, J. and FISHER, H., *Soviet Russia and the West, 1920-1927*, Stanford, California, 1957, pp. 20-23.

12 *Daily Herald*, 12 May 1923.

13 *Daily Herald*, 5 June 1923.

14 WHITE, pp. 217-18.

15 According to Morrison in MORRISON, Herbert, *An Autobiography of Lord Morrison of Lambeth*, London, Odhams, 1960, p. 90. Attlee supports the view in *As It Happened*, London, Heinemann, 1954, pp. 60-61.

16 COOPER, Duff, *Old Men Forget*, London, Rupert Hart-Davies, 1953, p. 123. Duff Cooper was Ponsonby's Private Secretary until 13 February 1924, as he had been to Curzon's

Under-Secretary of State, Cecil Harmsworth. He became a Conservative MP in October 1924, and pursued an illustrious career in politics.

17 Ponsonby was also suggested by Christopher Addison to MacDonald as a good choice, cf. Addison to MacDonald, 19 December 1923 PRO 30/69/685.

18 MARQUAND, David, *Ramsay MacDonald*, London, Jonathan Cape, 1977, p. 299.

19 *Daily Herald*, 9 January 1924.

20 COOPER, *Old Men Forget*, p. 123.

21 Hodgson to Curzon, 18 January 1924, PRO 30/69/104.

22 GORODETSKY, *The Precarious Truce*, p 10.

23 Neither Calhoun, Gorodetsky or White consider this despatch. It was probably not considered (1) because it referred to Curzon not MacDonald, although MacDonald actually received it, and (2) because the MacDonald papers were by no means fully available to the three researchers when they wrote their books.

24 Hodgson to Curzon, 18 January 1924, PRO 30/69/104.

25 *The Anglo-Soviet Treaties*, introduction by Arthur Ponsonby, MP. Published Labour Party Publications Department, September 1924, pp. 1-2 (my emphasis).

26 Gorodetsky once again puts this down to the 'Mussolini factor' and notes: 'In view of the short time remaining [before Italian recognition], MacDonald acted in great haste and without consulting other members of the Cabinet'. He supports my view in his footnote to p. 11 (no.15) when he says: 'There is no evidence to suggest whether the imminent Soviet – Italian agreement or the wish to allow the announcement to be made to the Congress [of Soviets] was the decisive factor'.

27 Anglo-Soviet Conference. First meeting 14 April 1924, PRO 30/69/105.

28 Diary entry for 22 January 1924, PRO 30/69/1753.

29 MacDonald to Chicherin, 1 February 1924, FO 800/219. Other evidence of sensitivity is to be found in the opening remarks to the Anglo-Soviet Conference: 'It would be most inconvenient if reports of our proceedings went to the press piecemeal and in perhaps a distorted way from either one source or the other' (Anglo-Soviet Conference opening speech by MacDonald, 14 April 1924, PRO 30/69/105, N3386/3377/85.

30 Chicherin to MacDonald. No date (probably mid-February 1924), PRO FO 800/219. ULDRICKS, Teddy, J., *Diplomacy and Ideology. The Origins of Soviet Foreign Relations, 1917-1930*, London and Beverley Hills, Sage Publications, 1979 (especially Ch. 6).

31 Opening speech to Anglo-Soviet Conference, PRO 30/69/105, op. cit., pp. 2–3.

32 Foreign Office memo in MacDonald papers, PRO 30/69/106 of 28 July 1924.

33 Cf. Marquand, p. 362, who said the debate in Cabinet was fierce.

34 MacDonald papers, PRO 30/69/106 (written on the document).

35 Cf. especially Ch. 8.

36 This was discussed throughout, with a particularly tough seventh meeting on 27 May 1924 (PRO 30/69/105).

37 MacDonald to Webb, 19 March 1924, FO 800/219.

38 *The Times*, 29 September 1924. Quoted by Marquand, p. 364.

39 Vandervelde to MacDonald, 19 June 1924, FO 800/219. I have found no trace of a reply by MacDonald.

40 'Bolshevik Terror Against Socialists' published by the Committee for Political Prisoners in Russia, documents collected on the authority of the LSI, New York, 1925, 60 pp.

41 Stamfordham (George V's private secretary) to Sir R. Waterhouse (Downing Street), 22 July 1924, FO 800/219.

42 Selby to Stamfordham, 26 July 1924, FO 800/219.

43 Hodgson to MacDonald, 28 April 1924, PRO 30/69/104.

44 Hodgson to MacDonald, 12 May 1924, PRO 30/69/104.

45 MacDonald private diary entries of 27 September 1924 and 31 October 1924, PRO 30/69/1753.

46 For details of the Zinoviev and Campbell cases, see GORODETSKY, *The Precarious Truce*, pp. 35-52, and the *Survey of International Affairs*, 1924, RIIA, London, 1926, pp. 244-251.

47 GORODETSKY, *The Precarious Truce*, p. 48.

48 Diary entry, 4 November 1924: the 'King had chaffed me about the Russian Treaty', he wrote.

49 House of Commons *Debates*, vol. 175, 7 July 1924, col. 1924.

chapter two

Labour Party, TUC and the USSR 1925-7

The Anglo-Russian Joint Advisory Committee (ARJAC)

The TUC rapprochement with Moscow: the background to ARJAC

The contacts that had been created, albeit tentatively, during the period of the 1924 government between the Labour movement and the Russians were not broken by the electoral defeat. The defeat did, however, change their focus. Certain reservations had been created in the Labour Party leadership about contacts with Russia for purely political reasons. The pragmatic rapprochement on the political level in the trade and diplomatic talks was echoed by the TUC's awareness that Bolshevik Russia would not only not go away, but that it was a force to be reckoned with in world affairs.

In the mid-1920s the Soviet Union's problem was to find a foreign policy that would reconcile its different ideological, material and military needs. It is clear that the first of these categories often clashed with the latter two, and indeed it could be argued that they still do. 'Detente' may have been invented as a word applied to East–West relations in the early 1970s, but its essence was clearly there in the 1920s and 1930s. The Soviet Union could not exist in a vacuum if it wished to develop and this is in many ways the key to the internecine struggles within the Bolshevik ranks until the definitive victory of Stalin in the 1930s. Only then was ideology, as incarnated by the Comintern, subordinated to 'peaceful co-existence', as incarnated in foreign policy by the Narkomindel, the Commissariat for Foreign Affairs. In his work on the Narkomindel,[1] Uldricks shows clearly that the formative hand that shaped this body was not that of Zinoviev or Trotsky, but rather that of Chicherin (Commissar until 1930) and Litvinov after him, who viewed 'the very existence of the Communist International, openly dedicated to the overthrow of the capitalist order ... as a great source of embarrassment for the Soviet diplomats'.[2] The contact between the Russian trade unions, led by Tomsky, and the British TUC General Council must therefore be seen in a wider context of a power struggle within the USSR.

The ARJAC period 1924–7

A joint committee, the Anglo-Russian Joint Advisory Committee, was established in late 1924 after a visit of the members of the TUC General Council to Russia. This committee has been well described by American writer Daniel Calhoun, and all writings on the episode must acknowledge a great debt to his work.

In instigating this discussion with the Russians, the TUC had pushed itself out on a precarious limb in its relations with its own natural allies, the International Federation of Free Trade Unions (IFTU), who had been at daggers drawn with the Red International of Labour Unions (RILU) linked to the Comintern, since the historic breaches of the immediate post-war period. The 1924 Comintern proposals for a 'united front' did little to impress the IFTU Executive which felt that the proposed 'unity' was 'a kind of cheap rubbish novel in letter form'.[3] As Calhoun points out: 'It was at this low point in negotiations for unity that help arrived from an unexpected source – the most ancient and tradition-bound trade union movement in the world – the British'.[4]

What provoked the TUC into such an attempted alliance? Calhoun cites the largely trades-union element of the 1919 'Hands Off Russia' movement, in contrast to what he categorises as the cool approach of the 'official Labour Party'.[5] TUC members had been impressed, in spite of themselves in some cases, by the spirit they had experienced during the May 1920 joint TUC–Labour Party visit to the USSR.[6] Some of the TUC members of this expedition were later, during ARJAC, the most prominent supporters of cooperation with the Russians – A. A. Purcell and George Hicks, both future chairmen of the TUC General Council, being perhaps the most notable examples. These men were on the left of the TUC, and many of the international questions dealt with by the General Council tended to fall into their hands. The right, represented by J. H. Thomas of the railwaymen, a future 'traitor' of 1931, preferred the practical questions of wage bargaining and therefore tended to 'abdicate leadership claims to such trustworthy Labour Party politicians as MacDonald and Philip Snowden' at the party level.[7] This left Purcell, Hicks and others the task of reacting to the Soviet proposals for unity within the TUC itself, helped by their feelings of benign interest towards the Soviet experiment. These feelings were particularly nurtured by a violent dislike of Tory foreign policy.

With a move to the left in 1924 of the TUC General Council, Purcell gained the post of chairman and that of president of the IFTU, while Hicks replaced Thomas on the key International Committee.[8] The Russians intended to exploit this leftwards surge. They had also been encouraged by the Labour Government's evident interest in better Anglo-Soviet relations during the Labour Government of 1924. However, at the beginning of ARJAC, in early 1925, it is not at all clear what exactly the Russians expected from these talks. The TUC General Council was clearly split, the left hoping for a strengthening of the international labour movement, the right thinking it would probably do no harm to talk to the Russians.

Thus there was a situation of a left of the TUC more or less in control of international contacts and a right largely indifferent to international questions. The indifference of the right at this initial stage can perhaps be best explained by saying that the TUC had that precious commodity in 1924 - unity at home. It was untroubled by communist-led breakaway unions such as plagued its counterpart organisations on the continent. There seemed no bar to good relations with Moscow on the trade-union level, save from the IFTU, whose other members had active reason to dislike communist infiltration of their ranks. However, it appeared to the TUC that not to have close relations with the Russians was an absurdity. Why, even confirmed pragmatists like MacDonald and Snowden had reopened trade and diplomatic relations. With this the right was lulled and the left went ahead, open-armed to its blind date with destiny. As Calhoun says, it indeed had all the impression of a 'courtship', leading to 'engagement' and 'marriage'.[9] Whatever the intentions of the machiavellian Russian 'groom', the TUC 'bride' went to her tryst with a dowry of goodwill that was later to seem preposterous. The IFTU, and especially Oudegeest, was understandably suspicious from the beginning and the Soviet approaches to Amsterdam, parallel to those to London, were met with the coldest possible cooperation.[10] But 'so long as the TUC insisted on supporting the unity campaign, Amsterdam had to take it seriously'.[11]

However, clouds were beginning to accumulate even before the first major meeting. The national Minority Movement of largely communist trade unionists met on 24-5 August 1924 for the first time. The TUC could no longer count entirely on unity at home, any more than could the Labour Party, burdened by communists in its ranks. As yet no serious moves were made to exclude either minorities from membership of the TUC or the Labour Party, but the new clamour of a vocal communist minority for 'class struggle' could not help but embarrass the right-wing leadership and, indeed, most of the membership. So even at the Hull Congress of the TUC in September 1924, 'not all delegates were so sure the Russians could be dealt with at all'.[12] However, a conciliatory speech by Tomsky himself seems to have dispelled whatever major doubts existed about the impossible nature of dealing with the 'abuse' of the Comintern and Profintern. Here was a Russian trade unionist with whom debate was possible, and such was the impact of his 'effective speech' that his proposal for talks was 'agreed, without debate, by acclamation and enthusiastically'.[13] This Congress also authorised contacts, with a view to bringing about a reconciliation between Amsterdam and Moscow, and between the TUC and its Russian counterpart. On the face of it, the TUC showed a remarkable sensitivity to personal charm, surprising given the issues at stake. It also obviously believed that the best way to deal with such execrations as the Minority Movement was to outflank it by dealing directly with the Russians.

Thus, however alienated the leadership of the official Labour Party was by the appalling mixture of insensitivity and circumstance represented by the Campbell case and the Zinoviev letter, the TUC General Council still wished to enter into discussions with Tomsky in the aftermath of the election defeat of 1924.

The struggle for power in the USSR and the ARJAC period

It is necessary to consider briefly why the Russians felt the negotiations with the TUC were worthwhile. A recent writer has stated that the whole ARJAC period and in particular the question of how to react to the 1926 General Strike in Britain 'put to an acid test the concepts underlying Soviet policy-making ... [and] ... resulted in a drastic revision of the relations between Comintern and Narkomindel'.[14] In particular the period brought to a head the conflict between two factions, loosely represented by Trotky versus Stalin, and resulted in the 1928 dropping of pretensions to a 'united front', of which the ARJAC episode was one example, and the institution of 'class against class' in the Comintern. The idea held by all Russian partners in the project, whatever the extent of their opposition or support, was that the ARJAC might lead on to greater things; the taking over of the IFTU, for example, by the RILU. Stalin, already pushing his idea of 'socialism in one country', had seen ARJAC in the wider, Russian sense, and was a major supportor of the 'pressure on the government through the TUC' thesis which his great rival Trotsky thought would probably not work.[15]

Stalin also clearly believed that increased Russian influence on the TUC could only strengthen support for the CPGB within the TUC. But most of all Stalin was worried about the increasing hostility within the new Conservative British Government to the USSR after 1924.

In 1925 Trotsky and Zinoviev, representing the hard line in the USSR's official councils, were pushing for a two-fold encouragement of the revolutionary spirit they perceived to be growing within the British working class and a splitting of the 'revolutionary mass' from the right-wing leadership, whose central villians were of course MacDonald, Thomas and Snowden,[16] in order to propel this mass into the arms of the CPGB. Not that Trotsky, in particular, had any sympathy for the left of the TUC or the Labour Party. They were 'left-wing muddlers' or 'distinguished by complete ideological shapelessness and therefore ... incapable of organizationally assuming the leadership of the trade union movement'.[17] This left, according to Trotsky, was allowed to go along with the Moscow appeal by such as MacDonald and the right of the TUC precisely because these leaders regarded 'international matters as a kind of safety-valve for the radical morals of the masses'.[18]

In line with his wider thinking on the future of world revolution, Trotsky foresaw an increasing number of upheavals in British society which would be faced with the same ideological incomprehension by the left of the TUC, the same lack of revolutionary courage so that they would in fact be a brake on the aspiring revolutionary masses that Trotsky saw developing in 1926. The left would propose an 'economic' (i.e. peaceful, compromising, conservative) response (counter to the 'historic process'), which would lead to growing disillusion among all the rank and file with their conservative leadership and the triumph of the 'Communist Party and the best "left" elements'. This was to happen within the next few years, although final victory might have to wait a little while.[19]

Even though future events were to show these analyses and predictions as hopelessly inaccurate, Trotsky ever after proclaimed that the whole ARJAC episode ranked with Stalin's efforts in China as one of his worst mistakes. Trotsky's diatribes against the moderate British leadership and his own colleagues were to have devastating results for his future relationship with Stalin and when trying to enter Britain as an exile in 1929, as will be described in Chapter 7.

Losovsky, General Secretary of Profintern, and one of the main negotiators with the TUC, held no less drastic views on the attitude to take towards the British Labour movement's leaders, as represented by the TUC General Council. As Calhoun comments: 'If the General

Council . . . had been obliged to deal with him, rather than Tomsky, or if it had taken him seriously as an influential leader of Soviet trade unionism, Anglo-Russian trade union rapprochement would have gone no further. Instead, the British considered him a discredited extremist, a joke or a nobody. In any event, they persisted in spite of him'.[20] He seems to have shared Trotsky's view on the General Council which he also described as 'ideologically foggy'.[21]

None the less Losovsky initially seems to have voiced support for the TUC–Tomsky talks as a possible way to take over the IFTU and British Trade Unions. However, he was accused in 1924 by his Profintern colleagues of aiming at the liquidation of their organisation so that he did a partial volte-face and became a hard-line supporter of the critics' abrasive wish to annihilate the Amsterdam-based IFTU. He was not the best man to speak to the TUC about unity.[22]

Tomsky as head of the All-Union Central Council for Trade Unions (AUCCTU) was the only man who seems to have truly approached the proceedings with both a genuine wish for unity and a genuine respect for his TUC interlocutors, and especially for Purcell and A. J. Cook of the miners. In 1924 he got his way, but had it been left to Losovsky undoubtedly the negotiations would never have started. The latter kept looking for ways to destroy whatever progress had been made.[23] And to Tomsky falls most of the credit on the Russian side for keeping the difficult negotiations on the rails, at least until the General Strike of 1926.[24]

The nemesis of ARJAC: The General Strike of 1926

It was the General Strike of 1926, a crisis of major proportions for the British trade unions and indeed for the Labour movement as a whole, which was leapt upon by the Losovsky school of thought with a gross insensitivity and glee that helped shatter the precarious acceptance of ARJAC within the TUC. Gorodetsky and Calhoun make it clear that the Russians were also starting to have second thoughts about collaboration, even with the left of the TUC *before* the General Strike.[25] It was now seen that the initial hope of using the TUC to influence the Foreign Secretary, Austen Chamberlain, was a hopeless one. The Tory diehards were gaining ground, not losing it. One of the very raisons d'etre of the Russian participation within ARJAC was thus seemingly a pipe dream.[26]

There is ample evidence now that the General Council did not wish a General Strike of any length and certainly that they did not wish to bring down the government. But the Russians thought they did and therefore sent vast sums of money to help with the struggle. When the General Council was forced into an embarrassed refusal Trotsky and, especially, Losovsky launched into a tirade of condemnation of their 'cowardice' and the 'lack of determination and faint-heartedness of the General Council'.[27]

Despite the brutality of Losovsky's and others' violent attacks on the General Council of the TUC, Tomsky had had the support of none less than Stalin, as has been mentioned, and was held largely responsible by Trotsky and the opposition for the failure of an 'opportunistic policy', for which he temporarily lost his post. To show to what extent the ARJAC episode was linked to the internal Soviet struggle he was immediately reinstated by Stalin as the 'symbol of the workers, the pride of the party'.[28]

But the subtleties of this struggle were quite lost on the General Council who effectively lost all faith in the possibility of talking to such a divided camp as the Russians were. By early 1927 the General Council all felt confused and humiliated and the official demise of ARJAC was only a question of time. After the General Strike the TUC also realised the great danger that existed of becoming too involved with the communists in Britain. To withdraw from contact with the USSR through ARJAC would be one way of sending a signal to the British communists as well.

The impact of the ARJAC episode on future TUC attitudes

From now on the TUC turned increasingly lukewarm in its attitudes to the USSR as a whole. While condemning the May 1927 Conservative break-off of diplomatic relations, the TUC never again let itself be dupe to Russian manipulation.

They refused to be drawn into the Soviet-inspired 'war scare' when British troops were sent to Shanghai in early 1927. They expressed 'horror and disgust' at a series of trials and executions within the USSR in June 1927.[29] J. H. Thomas made a scathing attack on the Russians' attitude in ARJAC at the National Union of Railwaymen Convention on 8 July 1927.

The TUC was also fighting the Conservative Trades Disputes Bill to limit union power and any relationship that gave the Tories ammunition was a danger. Thomas had said at the NUR Convention: 'A number of people today have a sort of nightmare that every incident, every upheaval, every disturbance and every strike is a preconceived plan originating in Russia and given effect to by dupes in this country'.[30] It demonstrated the end of the TUC right's belief that it was possible to fight domestic battles and pursue a progressive policy of contact with the Russian trade unions. The right of the General Council was to be far more assertive in international questions after 1927.

The TUC was also coming under pressure from its international allies, the IFTU, in the same way as the Labour Party had come under pressure from the LSI. The August 1927 IFTU international congress included a British walk-out over the violence used to attack the ARJAC link – one that in any case was nearly defunct. The IFTU refused to accept the Russia-tainted Purcell, the TUC's candidate for the presidency, and elected the less (but only slightly less) implicated George Hicks. International moderate trades-union unity had almost been broken to pieces by ARJAC. This was doubly galling given the feelings held by the TUC General Council towards the Russians by this stage, that finally showed through in the Edinburgh TUC Congress of September 1927.

So at the Edinburgh Conference of the TUC in September 1927 it was decided to suspend relations 'until Moscow changes its conduct', as Citrine put it in his general report to the Congress.[31] There were, he said, 'fundamental differences', whose resolution 'depends on a more honourable and comradely manner being adopted by the Russians, and a cessation of their dictation of policy to the Council'.[32] The *Daily Herald* editorial expressed regret, but insisted that this was not a break in the Austen Chamberlain sense of the word but rather a way of denying ammunition to the TUC's opponents. Undoubtedly such a feeble defence of a clear decision owed much to the increasing financial dependence of the *Daily Herald* on the TUC, a subject that was raised with increasing frequency in the General Council during 1927 and 1928. 'There is no breach with the Russian working class, no diminution of determination to do all that is possible to safeguard peace and aid the Russian leaders in the great task of reorganising their own country'. But the Russians had no right to 'lessen the authority and power of the General Council' which, whether the Russian leaders liked it or not, was 'the head of the British Movement'.[33] They hoped that all this would be 'rightly understood by the Russian Movement' and that future international collaboration would be possible.

Many readers of the *Daily Herald* did not agree that it would be understood,[34] and indeed even Thomas's own union rather strongly voted against the suspension of ARJAC. For a while it seemed as though a breach in the TUC's position might be caused. To understand how it was avoided we must consider what the Labour Party had been doing during the ARJAC.

The Labour Party and the Soviet Union 1925–7: trade and politics

The general impression one gets of the feelings of the Labour Party leadership towards the USSR during the 1925–7 is one of coolness. The three major issues of the 1924 campaign – the Zinoviev letter, the Anglo-Russian Treaty and the Campbell affair – were directly or indirectly linked to the Soviet Union.

For the Labour Party leadership the 1924 episode had been a bit like the experience of Pandora's box. But how to close it again? It was realised that it could not be closed, but that perhaps benefits could still be had from the experience. Ex-communists, such as Walton Newbold, cautioned that political and economic issues could not be separated as MacDonald had hoped:

> 'There is nothing practical to be gained in an industrial or political struggle with Tomsky's unions or Zinoviev's party ... I am absolutely at one with Thomas in believing this is not the time to force (or to be forced into) a fight. ... With the Russian Workers' state we want trade ... Russia (never mind her government) is today what the Argentine, Canada and the United States was to our fathers and grandfathers, an outlet and a market for manufactures and machinery. Somehow and somewhere we must raise up a food-supplying, raw-material-producing and potentially powerful ally. Russia fits the bill. Only then can we throw off our gold yoke and stand erect, free men and women in Merrie England'.[35]

Newbold's advice, shared by Thomas and increasingly by MacDonald, was the keynote of Labour Party statements on Russia until at least 1929. It was difficult advice to follow for political questions could not be ignored, since they were linked to trade. Indeed it was MacDonald that had linked them in 1924, of which he was often reminded by the Conservatives and his own left in the ILP and other socialists within the party. MacDonald therefore decided upon a pragmatic policy of damage restriction on issues of political contract with the USSR and the stressing of the usefulness of trade links.

For this one man was to act until at least 1929 as almost a one-man Labour Party pressure group. Until the expelling of the Russian trade delegation (ARCOS) in May 1927 a Labour MP, E. F. Wise, was their economic adviser. Wise sent MacDonald several letters with material that he might find useful in his defence of Russian trade in the Commons. Along with the technical details[36] he also wanted to reinforce MacDonald's already clear feelings of the need to encourage moderation within the USSR itself.[37]

The Cooperative movement, which had several MPs and was affiliated to Labour, also continued its close trading ties. Ideologically the Cooperative movement could not be faulted by MacDonald, Thomas or anyone else; there was no doubt of their anti-communist and pragmatic attitude. Their interests were purely practical – the import of grain, timber and other products. This had accelerated since early 1924, when the Midland Division of the Cooperative Society had, for example, agreed to set up with 'three British firms, the Soviet Government's export organisation and certain Russian Cooperative Societies'[38] in a company to export Russian grain. This, it must be admitted, was a commercial contact of fairly limited scale nationally, but Coop involvement inevitably made it loom larger in Labour Party thinking.

Politics: the China crisis and the break

This Labour Party desire to find a modus vivendi with the USSR was progressively less and less evident from the government benches. The sending of a British military expedition to China in early 1927 pushed the diehards into a renewed fury of hatred of the Bolsheviks, who they held entirely responsible for the nationalist upsurge in China and the consequent need for protection of British interests in Shanghai. There is no evidence (as far as the present writer can ascertain) of contemporary Labour movement knowledge that the Politburo, and especially Stalin, was behind the Comintern's machinations in China. But the Labour Party leadership was in no mood to trust the Russians at the end of the ARJAC episode and thus their defence of the USSR's role was in itself defensive. This does much to explain the ambivalence of Labour Party pressure during the crucial months of early 1927.

Baldwin searches for a pretext for a break with the USSR

MacDonald was aware that the danger of the Chinese situation was many-sided – it could plunge Britain into a costly military adventure and possibly war with Russia but it could help the cause of the Third International and the British Communist Party. He was aware that 'Our movement should be careful not to lend itself to action and declarations prompted by Communist intrigue in this country',[39] as he declared in early January 1927. The National Executive of the Labour Party issued a statement followed up by a very moderate *Daily Herald* editorial attacking the 'jingo element' in the country who 'were not unwilling to make enemies of both China and Russia'.[40] Mass meetings and vigorous protests about government action followed.[41]

The government sent a note of protest to the Soviet Government on 23 February. As Gorodetsky says, the note 'remained a pot pourri of pettily vindictive Soviet published material' including a cartoon lampooning Chamberlain in *Isvestya*.[42] The whole affair, in short, reeked of a put-up job to find a pretext for a break-off of relations. This was so clear that MacDonald was forced, perhaps against his better instincts, to put the other side of the argument. He was probably annoyed at the role played by Brailsford (main ILP foreign policy commentator and especially interested in the USSR) who had met Litvinov in Moscow immediately after the delivery of the British note. The ILP had forced MacDonald's hand in the NJC and continued to put pressure on the leadership, asking for further action in the form of demonstrations and much stronger statements.[43] The note, Brailsford said, was 'merely rude', a rather pathetic replica of the bombs the British had used to send. The Soviet Government, secure in its new-found prosperity (that Brailsford had found in his first visit for seven years), had not received the note as 'an earth-shaking event'. There was 'no whining . . . no fear', just a cynical acceptance of Chamberlain playing to his own gallery of diehards.[44] This unofficial diplomacy by Brailsford was typical of the kind of pressure MacDonald was under from the Labour Party left, especially from within the ranks of the ILP.

The sharp exchange of notes between Austen Chamberlain and Litvinov lead to a major parliamentary debate on Anglo-Soviet relations. The debate had a certain wholeness about it that left a centre consensus with diehards and supporters of the Soviet position fairly isolated. Sir Archibald Sinclair (Liberal), who confessed his loathing for Bolshevism, hit the nail on the head when he summed up Britain's interests in Russia as being 'peace and trade' – 'the greatest solvent against Bolshevism any country can have'.[45] MacDonald largely agreed with Sinclair. He did not much like some statements made by the Russians but he put the so-called Russian intervention in China down to 'rumours', and said that to accuse the Russians of propaganda, when one was indulging in the same thing was nonsensical. He would 'not tolerate' Russian propaganda: 'no country can tolerate the interference of a foreign country its own affairs', but that was precisely what the Conservative Government was indulging in itself, towards Russia. What was more, for the Foreign Office to complain of cartoons in the Russian press as 'propaganda' was not a 'legitimate' complaint, those attacking Ministers were. And it was at the ministerial level that the British Government were making propaganda. 'Take our Chancellor of the Exchequer. Put a beard on him, make him talk Russian instead of English and you have Zinoviev. Take the Home Secretary . . . and look at him there to see Trotsky'.

MacDonald's rhetoric led him to a serious distinction that was a continuation of his feelings since at least 1924. The Communist International might be the extremist wing of Russian action but he thought that 'we are all too much inclined to assume hostility on the part of the Russian Government'. The way to weaken the hand of the 'extremists', Trotsky and Zinoviev, commanders of the Third International, was to keep up his party's policy of continual contact. Only by high-level discussions could 'our trade agreement . . . fructify in trade and our diplomatic relations . . . fructify in peace'.[46] The second most important Labour Party parliamentary heavyweight, Snowden, shadow Chancellor of the Exchequer, backed up MacDonald on all of these points as did George Lansbury. The Labour Party's technique in this debate was a confirmation of the leadership's desire to concentrate on the benefits for Britain of the Soviet link and to robustly minimise the problems. It was also one of making a powerful plea that contact would actually minimise and reduce tension rather than maintain or increase it.

The Liberal Party was in agreement with the Labour Party on most of these points, particularly echoing Lloyd George who had stated that trade would civilise these Russians, even if the Conservative Party diehards refused to believe it. If this support was welcome for MacDonald, to hear Lansbury, of the left of the party, agreeing essentially with Snowden, of the right, gave an air of unity to the Labour Party's Russian policy. Snowden had to admit in the debate that: 'It is seldom that he and I [Lansbury] agree about Russia'.[47] In the event Lansbury's remarks did no harm to MacDonald's command of the situation, and he had only to submit to a few sniped remarks from the ILP.[48] He thus had every reason to be fairly pleased with the PLP's united stance even if it had no effect on the Tory diehards. In the build-up to a Conservative break-off of relations the whole Labour Party was sure that the Conservatives had a very poor *casus belli*.

The Labour press was, as usual, used to support the Labour Party line. The *Daily Herald*, in many articles, linked progress of the 'defence force' in China and the risks that this posed to peace with Russia and trade. Huge wool deals with Russia, it was reported on 12 March, had met difficulty 'occasioned by recent political developments' which, said the *Weekly Record and Textile World* 'has not tended to promote a feeling of confidence among those engaged in trade with Russia'.[49]

The ARCOS affair

The debate among historians as to whether Austen Chamberlain was trying to engineer the deterioration in Anglo-Soviet relations and the eventual break-off of diplomatic relations has been described elsewhere.[50] Gorodetsky feels Austen Chamberlain preferred that such a break should not take place but that it was becoming inevitable, and that the 'Labour movement and commercial circles' might have provided the only hope for bringing 'last-minute pressure to bear on the government' once it had reached its decision in the wake of the so-called 'Arcos affair'. The affair was the result of a police raid on 12 May 1927 on the Soviet Trade Delegation and its commercial body, ARCOS Ltd, supposedly to find incriminating evidence of espionage activities.

The Labour Party's reaction to the raid was initially muted. The fear of the government producing incontrovertible evidence of a Soviet plot of some kind was the probable cause of such unusual reticence. This reticence was reduced in the Commons the next day when it was implied by Sir John Simon that the Arcos raid was to find the Russian plan for a British General Strike. This had 'unfortunately' not been found, and never was.[51] However, no official government statement was forthcoming and there were acrimonious scenes the next day when the raid was the subject of parliamentary questions – from Labour MPs Lansbury, Will Thomas and Kirkwood. Kirkwood asked if the raid on Arcos had been expected to reveal a photograph of the Home Secretary. Henderson finally demanded a debate on the ARCOS raid and its implications as a matter of 'very urgent and definite public importance'.[52]

The ILP saw 'darker motives' in the raid; this 'new diplomatic instrument ... the pneumatic drill'[53] was 'engineered behind the scenes as a supreme effort to destroy the Trading Agreement, to bring about the withdrawal of British recognition of Russia, and to create a situation from which war will eventuate'.[54]

Baldwin replied to Labour accusations in the House of Commons on 24 May, when he explained how the office of ARCOS and the trade agreement's terms had been abused, and why the trade agreement was therefore to be terminated. He also made it clear that the government believed that the Russians were in particular using the ARCOS offices to deliberately disseminate misinformation on the British actions in China. He quoted from a Comintern telegram that had been seized (with 'copy to Berlin for Tomsky' written on it) complaining about 'the appalling supply of information and the way in which the wide Labour circles [in Britain] are misled' by official Soviet propaganda.[55]

In any event the Labour Party had its way and a major debate on the ARCOS affair took place in between various readings of the Trades Disputes Bill. The sensitivity of the ARCOS affair was thus reinforced by the sensitivity of an anti-union bill.

All Labour Party speeches agreed that the whole Tory attitude was pointless: Russia would not go away, trade would suffer and 'it may have consequences in future that will be more disastrous than we can appreciate at the present time'. It was clear that this referred to internal problems with unemployment and external ones with the danger of war.

The main debaters for the Labour Party had thus made many of the same points as they did in the previous major debate of March. The link between maintaining contact and trade and encouraging Russian 'reasonableness' had been made in passing. Its chief exponent in this debate was Miss Susan Lawrence. In her view: 'I am quite sure that, as far as Russia is concerned, we have strengthened every bad and dangerous element, and have weakened the influence of every moderate statesman in Russia'.[56] Yet she went further than MacDonald had done, not just stating that there were 'moderates' and 'extremists', but defining what they stood for: 'On the one side were those who pinned their faith to the world revolution; on the other were those who put first the development of this country'. Trotsky, Kameneff and Zinoviev were of the first category, Stalin and Bukharin of the second. The Tory Government had clearly not an inkling of an understanding of what was to her an evident fact, and had proved it by sending the note at the very moment of Stalin's victory. This had given the new Soviet leadership the 'nightmares' of the old, just the kind of nightmares that are normally dissipated by diplomacy. The actions of the government were those of the weak and the stupid, and could well produce the kind of Russia that they said they were fighting, but only towards Britain: 'the only two great underdeveloped markets of the world that are left. In Russia, as in China, the nations of the world will be profiting at our expense'.[57]

Only one dissonant voice range out from the Labour benches against this line of sweet agreement and moderation; he who was to increasingly become MacDonald's *bête noire*, James Maxton, leader of the ILP. That there was propaganda Maxton did not care, for he wanted no delusions about his position:

> My sympathies are absolutely with the ultimate aims and objects of the Russian Soviet Government. Make no doubt about it, that if their powers of propaganda in this country have been injured in any way by this attack on the part of the British Government, I will do my personal best to make up for it . . . I believe that before there is a possibility of world peace . . . capitalism has to be overthrown.

And he hoped it would be done 'with or without Russian stimulation' as soon as possible. Maxton at least admitted that he 'did not claim to be a statesman. I am an agitator'.[58] He had certainly proved it, and in so doing knocked a huge nail into the coffin of ILP–Labour Party relations.

The results of the crises of 1927: 'Au dessus de la melee'

MacDonald was undoubtedly embarrassed by Maxton's outburst. Elections could not be far off, and he and the leadership knew that their position was still far from secure. The party had based its image on one of 'responsible socialism'. This did not mean that rhetoric of a 'new age' could not be indulged in. Ernest Bevin had said in early 1927 that the movement was on the threshold of such a new age. Nevertheless he echoed the leadership when he said: 'It would not be done by loud talk, or by revolution. The revolution they wanted in Great Britain was a revolution of thought and principle'.[59] There could surely be no place, or a limited one at best, for those who proudly proclaimed themselves 'agitators'. The Labour Party under MacDonald continually tried to develop a sense of political style that would entirely distance it from such 'agitators'. The new age would be brought about through the ballot box, not behind any barricades, oral or physical. None the less it would be incorrect to misinterpret the MacDonald leadership's annoyance with its ILP left by confusing it with their real dislike, even hatred, of the Communist Party. The leadership had all, in their time, uttered the same sentiments in the same ways as young Maxton, so their chagrin was more that of a father for an errant son than that of a feud between two clans. MacDonald and Snowden had both come into the Labour movement by the ILP themselves (indeed, MacDonald had been the editor of the ILP-dominated *Socialist Review* until 1923) and their resignations from that body, both in 1927–8, expressed regret and nostalgia.[60]

MacDonald had also to lend succour to his international image within the Labour and Socialist International. In the same way as the IFTU had been dangerously split by the TUC's moves during ARJAC, the LSI was deeply divided about 'united front' tactics (for details of this discussion, see Chapter 3).

With so many bridges to try and rebuild or to make safe for the approaching electoral struggle the leadership therefore wanted a period of reflection without too much intrusion of the Russian problem. They did not wish, as Gorodetsky and others have proposed, to follow Baldwin's line of 'ignoring' the USSR, for as we have clearly seen they felt this was the most dangerous of lines to take. But they undoubtedly did wish a cooling-off period to concentrate on other, more important, tasks. Quite apart from the international situation which could deteriorate at any moment, there were grave domestic problems such as unemployment. Both of these could be partly resolved with Russian cooperation on disarmament and trade, but only if the discussion took place between reasonable partners. The party leadership was pleased to note that some 'statesmen' such as Stalin and Burkharin seemed to be increasingly on top, but the power struggle which was working against the 'extremists' – Trotsky and Zinoviev particularly – needed a while to cool down before further contacts were made. And, in parallel, the British Communist Party must be isolated to ensure that this decontamination was complete. No complete break was therefore contemplated with Russia, but time must be allowed to heal memories and allow the poison of extremism to fully burn itself out.

A clear indication of this new 'au dessus de la melee' attitude was shown by the PLP's decision *not* to call a meeting of the National Joint Council of the TUC and the Labour Party, or even the Executive of the Labour Party, over the diplomatic break. This was in direct contradiction of the NJC's own motion of 18 February 1927. MacDonald thus clearly avoided any possible ILP pressure by refusing to listen. The only official Labour Party statement came in *Labour Magazine* and was a sober statement of distaste at Russian methods but acceptance that there must be accommodation:

> If international relations are to depend on an impartial enforcement of their principles the Labour Party, who do not admire Soviet institutions will have to consider whether a Labour Government should break off diplomatic relations with Fascist Hungary and Fascist Italy, whose institutions, economic and political, are equally detestable to them'.[61]

As to the Labour movement, Soviet propaganda had no effect; they were 'powerless to influence a healthy Trades Union movement'.[62]

The Labour Party leadership's firm attitude was also a declaration of a very new line on the internal organisation of the Labour movement. From now on the leadership insisted that politics be left to the politicians. There are few references, if any, to Russia in the minutes of the General Council of the TUC after 1927. Russia became a 'political' problem and discussion of its internal and external situation was from now on the domaine of the Labour Party's NEC, the International Department and its Advisory Committee on International Questions.[63] Coordination with the LSI became much closer as well. Interest in the USSR as a phenomenon increased, if anything, but there was a growing universal disdain for the remaining extremist ganglions of the early revolution – the Comintern and the CPGB. As we shall see, rare are even the most extreme admirers (within the Labour Party or TUC) of the USSR who had the slightest sympathy for either the Third International or its British subsidiary.

Finally, it must be asked, was there any solid evidence in favour of the

Labour Party's view that a break-off of diplomatic relations would cause irreparable damage to British trade and industry? The Russians had a very positive trade balance in their favour in 1927 (£24,127,900 Russian exports to Britain; £14,401,800 imports from Britain).[64] There was, in 1927, no reason to suspect that this figure would improve or deteriorate to Britain's advantage or disadvantage. The movement of the balance of trade was largely an act of faith, and as such the trade element in Anglo-Soviet relations continued as a leitmotiv of the discussion of the USSR within Britain until the mid-1930s, as will be shown in future chapters.

Notes

1 ULDRICKS, Teddy, J., *Diplomacy and Ideology. The Origins of Soviet Foreign Relations, 1917–1930,* London and Beverley Hills, Sage Publications, 1979, especially Ch. 5. See also EUDIN and FISHER op. cit.
2 Ibid., p. 158.
3 CALHOUN, p. 25.
4 Loc. cit.
5 Ibid., p. 32. cf. also Stephen WHITE, *Britain and the Bolshevik Revolution,* op. cit.
6 See British Labour Delegation to Russia, Report of the TUC and Labour Party Delegates, 1920, p. 150.
7 As Calhoun and others have pointed out, it was difficult to exactly define TUC members, or members of the Labour Party as 'right' or 'left' with any great precision. Theirs was rather 'a point of view identifiable' as 'left' or 'right'. CALHOUN, p. 39.
8 CALHOUN, p. 46. Thomas was very doubtful of the benefits of political contact.
9 His chapter headings were unfortunately followed, as we know, by 'separation' and 'divorce'. Calhoun describes the Russian deliberations to take over the TUC from 'within' in great detail.
10 See CALHOUN, pp. 76–8.
11 Ibid., p. 80. We are still in July 1924.
12 CALHOUN, p. 83.
13 Ibid., p. 86.
14 See GORODETSKY, Gabriel, 'The Soviet Union and Britain's General Strike in 1926', *Cahiers du Monde Russe et Sovietique*, 1976, XVII, no. 2–3, pp. 287–310 (hereafter *The Soviet Union and Britain's General Strike*), p. 287.
15 There seems to be a considerable difference of opinion between Gorodetsky's work and that of Calhoun on Trotsky's position. Calhoun seems to believe that Trotsky was actively for a rapprochement (page 55), although he stated categorically in 1925 in 'Where is Britain going?': 'To assume that trade unions would actually organise revolution was to succumb to "monstrous illusion"' (quoted by CALHOUN, p. 169).
16 TROTSKY, L., 'Problems of the British Labour Movement', in *Trotsky on Britain,* Monad Press, New York, 1973, p. 154 (hereafter *Trotsky on Britain*). Sidney Webb was also often cited in this panoply of evil, and he was accorded a major part of the blame for the 'ideology' underlying the right – the 'conservative Fabian bourgeois politicians', as Trotsky put it in an article of 22 December 1925.
17 TROTSKY, *Trotsky on Britain,* 6 and 7 January 1926, pp. 162–3.
18 Loc. cit.

19 TROTSKY, *Trotsky on Britain*, 5 March 1926, pp. 166–8. This was written during the General Strike.
20 CALHOUN, p. 105.
21 And 'timid and cowardly'. CALHOUN, p. 87. The British communist press also echoed these sentiments.
22 GORODETSKY, *The Precarious Truce*, p. 95.
23 Loc. cit.
24 Gorodetsky notes, in an extremely fine analysis, that Stalin was in fact one of Tomsky's major supporters on the setting up of ARJAC, with Trotsky as one of its main opponents. See *The Precarious Truce*, page 102.
25 See both Gorodetsky and Calhoun, works already cited.
26 ULLMAN, *Diplomacy and Ideology*, vol. 1, p. 162.
27 Losovsky quoted by GORODETSKY in 'The Soviet Union and Britain's General Strike', p. 300.
28 Quoted by GORODETSKY, ibid., p. 305.
29 *Daily Herald*, 23 June 1927.
30 *Daily Herald*, 4 July 1927.
31 TUC Congress, Edinburgh, report in the *Daily Herald*, 9 September 1927.
32 *Daily Herald*, editorial of 9 September 1927.
33 *Daily Herald*, report of 15 September 1927.
34 Ibid.
35 Walton Newbold, a Birmingham MP, in *Birmingham Town Crier*, 15 May 1925, 'Relations with Soviet Russia - Allies, not Dictators'.
36 He sent MacDonald two articles he had written for *Soviet Union Monthly*, 'The Anglo-Russian Trade Agreement of 1921' (15 July 1926) and 'Is the Trade Agreement Necessary?' (April 1927).
37 Wise to MacDonald, 20 May 1927, PRO 30/69/1405.
38 Report in *Birmingham Town Crier*, 4 February 1924.
39 Reported in the *Daily Herald*, 4 January, 1927.
40 'Because the Russian Government has alone of all governments rendered it [the Chinese Government] aid and assistance it is bitterly opposed', *Daily Herald*, 5 January 1927.
41 Cf. WILLIAMS, Andrew, '*The Attitude of the British Labour Party to the Soviet Union, 1924–1934*, Geneva, IUHEI, 1985, pp. 72–5, for more details hereafter WILLIAMS, *The Attitude . . .*
42 Gorodetsky, *The Precarious Truce*, p. 216. The cartoon was published on the cover of the *New Leader* of 4 March 1927, with examples of some British press cartoons. The British papers were, it is clear, far from insulting.
43 NJC Minutes for 5 April 1927.
44 BRAILSFORD, H. N., 'How Moscow Received the British Note: a Talk with Litvinoff', *New Leader*, 11 March 1927, p. 13.
45 House of Commons *Debates*, vol. 203, 3 March 1927, col. 603.
46 Ibid., cols 620–5.
47 Ibid., col. 667.
48 Kirkwood and Wallhead of the ILP both made interruptions, Kirkwood even going as far as to say that Trotsky was a 'better man' than the Home Secretary.
49 *Daily Herald*, 12 March 1927.
50 GORODETSKY, *The Precarious Truce*, pp. 211–31.
51 House of Commons *Debates*, vol. 206, 19 May 1927, cols 1373–7.
52 House of Commons *Debates*, vol. 206, 17 May 1927, col. 1024.
53 BRAILSFORD, H. N., 'In the Cellars of Arcos', *New Leader*, 20 May 1927.
54 BROCKWAY, F. A., 'The Raid on the Russian Trade Delegation: a Summary of the Facts',

New Leader, 20 May 1927.

55 Prime Minister's statement on Russia, House of Commons *Debates*, vol. 206, 24 May 1927, col. 1848.

56 Ibid., col. 2271. Miss Lawrence was undoubtedly an authoritative speaker for the leadership. She was a member of the NEC of the Labour Party continually during the inter-war period and chairperson in 1927–30. She also held minor ministerial posts, in both the 1924 and 1929 governments. The DNB comments that she 'played no small role in shaping party policy'. She had noticed the 'two tendencies' in a visit to Russia in 1924 (*Birmingham Town Crier*, 3 October 1924).

57 Ibid., cols 2267–70: 'So little was this understood or noticed' were her exact words.

58 House of Commons *Debates*, vol. 206, 26 May 1927, cols 2243–52.

59 Bevin made these remarks in a speech at Greenwich, reported in the *Daily Herald* on 4 January 1927.

60 According to Norman Angell, MacDonald had been very annoyed at the ILP from February 1924 at least. He wanted the ILP to 'carry on a socialist propaganda' but not to play as a parallel cabinet (Angell, *After All*, London, Hamish Hamilton, 1951, p. 243).

61 *Labour Magazine*, June 1927, editorial, p. 74.

62 *Labour Magazine*, June 1927, p. 72.

63 However, the TUC continued to have its say in the Joint National Council (TUC and Labour party NRC). The NJC indeed seems to have become moribund until an attempted resuscitation in 1930 (see 6 and 12).

64 Figures given by the President of the Board of Trade, House of Lords *Debates*, vol. 208, 14 July 1927, cols 2323–4.

chapter three

Russia as an element in the power struggles within the Labour Party, 1927–9

Introduction: 'democratic methods and machinery'

When Lansbury took the Russian trade delegation to lunch at the House of Commons as a farewell gesture of friendship and as a slap in the face to the diehards,[1] he was none the less in despair about discussions with the Russians: 'the fault is not all on our side. . . . The main difficulty . . . is to be found in the fact that Russian Communists and trade unionists resolutely refuse to accept any person as honest, sincere or sensible who disagrees with their theories, tactics or policy'.[2]

Lansbury held out no hope for improvement while there was a Conservative Government in control or Communist 'extremists' in Russia. He continued: 'Only a Labour Government will restore the relationship established by Ramsay MacDonald when last in office. This being the case, the Soviet Government and Communist chiefs in Russia will do well to reconsider their present attitude and policy towards British Labour.' Britain and Russia were different yet both could learn from each other, conceded Lansbury. Mainly 'Comrade Stalin and his colleagues in Russia should take stock of the situation and understand their policy has completely failed to win adherents in this country.'[3]

This was one of the first declarations after ARJAC of the Labour Party's key difference with the Russian system. Labour insisted on the need for 'democratic methods and machinery'. The Labour Party was greatly attached to its democratic traditions and it was upon these that the Russians had heaped most insult. Trade unionists in Britain took very seriously the fact that they were making progress in working conditions through non-revolutionary, democratic means. 'Industrial democracy' was at the very heart of their collective mentality. So much so, in fact, that Webbs' book of that title, first written in 1897, was in its ninth impression by 1926 with virtually no revisions.[4]

In this work lies one of the best examples of why the differing views of the 'centralised democracy' of the Russians would be bound to clash with the industrial democracy of the TUC. 'In the English-speaking world institutions which desire to maintain and improve their condition must at all hazards bring themselves into line with democracy'.[5] This was not the case with the autocrat (the Czar was the example given), who would only allow democracy insofar as it did not interfere with his plans, but 'the problem of how far trade unionism is consistent with autocratic government – important to the continental student – is not of practical concern to the Anglo-Saxon'.[6] Given the primacy of the trade-union link with the Labour Party, these attitudes inevitably pervaded the whole movement. It would, however, be too simple to say that the trade union chicken laid the democratic Labour Party egg. Democracy was a subject that pervaded all discussion within the labour movement at all levels during the 1920s and 1930s and was at the centre of all debates on the USSR subsequent to 1927.

Within the movement there was an enormous spread of opinion and the Labour Party had always accommodated this 'broad church', not without some difficulty, because all agreed on the basic definitions of democratic procedure – Lansbury's 'democratic methods and machinery'. ARJAC demonstrated that Leninist methods were not the same as British ones, and had proved that discussion on the same level between Russian and British trade unionists was very difficult. It had long been realised that domestic discussion between the Labour Party and the CPGB was also fraught with difficulty. The Labour Party and the TUC reinforced each other in their refusal of Leninist methods during 1927–9, centred on Trades Union Congress General Council attacks on the communist-inspired Minority Movement within the trade unions, and on Labour Party attacks on the CPGB's infiltration policies. Meanwhile Russia, as a nation, would be accepted into the world system, and even admired for its achievements, as long as it did not interfere in British domestic politics. This dichotomy was a central theme in the period up to the 1929 general election.

Labour attacks the CPGB and the Minority Movement, 1925–8

The Labour Party leadership's theory of there being two tendencies in the Soviet Union that had been developing since 1924 and Lenin's death, which indeed had a great deal of truth in it, has been discussed. The war scare after the diplomatic breach of 1927 had been used by Stalin against his domestic enemies. The most vituperative critics of the British

Labour Party – Trotsky, Zinoviev and Kamenev – had now been expelled from the CPSU. Surely MacDonald's policy had been vindicated, the 'moderates' were now triumphant?

The Labour Party leadership was itself not convinced that this was the case. Stalin had yet to prove his 'moderation' and the 'extremist' British wings of the Communist International, the CPGB and the Minority Movement, were still very active. There had to be a clear distancing of the Labour Party and the TUC from these groups, especially given the probable proximity of elections although the methods of this distancing were a cause of great debate.

The ranks of the Labour Party were full of ex-Communist Party members who had recanted and been fully accepted. Past sins were more than forgotten. Indeed, the continuing influx of those ex-Communist Party members who had seen the light was a major source of hardening attitudes against the communists in the Labour Party as the 1920s wore on. They joined the Labour Party and left the communists because they really believed that unity – also proclaimed by the Communist Party as its aim until 1928 – was only possible within the broad church of the Labour Party. The level of this debate never really progressed from 1920, when a Communist Party 'Unity Convention' had first asked for affiliation. The Labour Party had replied that 'the basis of the affiliation to the Labour Party is the acceptance of its constitution, principles and programmes, with which the objects of the Communist Party do not seem to be in accord'.[7]

When this policy, reiterated in 1924, was reconsidered in 1925, there was a hardening of attitudes. This was partly due to the feeling that Labour Party electoral chances would be compromised by any contact with the CPGB in the wake of the Zinoviev letter, but also partly due to testimonials by ex-Communist Party members. Their intention was largely an exposition of the structure of the Communist Party, but mostly of its methods, which were beginning to be compared to those of the British fascists.[8] They helped in securing an overwhelming vote against allowing the communists to affiliate at the Liverpool Labour Party Conference in October 1925.

What must not be forgotten, however, is that even while denouncing Communist Party methods within the Labour movement, the leadership looked very dimly on any repression of the Communist Party in Britain as a whole. MacDonald made a speech at the beginning of December 1925 condemning 'the acts of the government in initiating the prosecution of certain members of the Communist Party ... a violation of the traditional British rights of freedom of speech and publication of opinion'. This speech was reprinted by the ILP as a pamphlet. 'Labour is opposed to the Communist Party' but this is 'a political trial, inspired by political motives' directly against 'the old liberties'.[9] None the less MacDonald and the majority of the Labour Party NEC had decided to break definitively the links with the CPGB, few as they were, in order to get rid of an electoral albatross and a major source of ideological confusion.

Nineteen-twenty-seven was, as MacFarlane puts it, 'the year of transition'.[10] The Labour Party NEC decided to strike at a moment when CPGB membership was failing, Communist literature selling less well and the entirely Communist Party dominated 'Hands Off China' movement faltering.[11] The line pushed by the ECCI of the Comintern about the 'imminent danger of war' (against Russia) was increasingly viewed with scepticism in all sections of the Labour Party, even if the ILP *New Leader* and a few other excessively ardent pacificists supported the idea.[12] Undoubtedly another element in the NEC decision to move decisively was the rightwards movement of the erstwhile main proponents of ARJAC within the TUC General Council. Even Purcell was now condemned in the communist press, aligning himself with the right of the General Council. Purcell and the 'orthodox left' were also increasingly disappointed with United Front possibilities, at least partly because of the ARJAC experience. Thus, as Martin says, 'The "political culture" of the trade-union movement became increasingly anti-Communist, and anti-Minority Movement'.[13]

The Communist Party was itself pushed in the other direction – to the left – and the break up of ARJAC again played a major role in this. The CPGB, given orders to pursue a 'new line', distanced itself even more definitely from the General Council of the TUC and all its works, culminating in the Comintern Congress of July-September 1928, where 'class against class' was decreed. The TUC reacted to the new mood in a celebrated series of articles penned by the TUC General Secretary Walter Citrine.

Citrine's articles, of which there were four printed in *Labour Magazine* over a period of some months at the end of 1927 and during early 1928, were an attempt to explain the ARJAC episode to a bewildered TUC rank and file and to define a new modus operandi for dealing with RILU and, ultimately, the USSR.[14] They must also be seen as an admission by the General Council that they had failed in exercising any moderating influence over Soviet affairs with a corresponding admission that in future political contact with the Russians had to be carefully coordinated with the Labour Party hierarchy. To confirm this latter point a parallel article by Herbert Morrison, referred to at this period by Ellen Wilkinson as the 'Witchfinder General' for his anti-communist efforts, was also printed in *Labour Magazine* to confirm most of Citrine's arguments and analysis.[15]

These can be briefly summarized. The TUC had been hoist by its own petard, for its belief that it could influence the Russian trade unions and by extension the RILU and Comintern had been demonstrated to be utterly naive. Citrine none the less maintained that the TUC's intentions had been entirely honourable but that it had not fully grasped the nature of the beast with which it had to deal. This was the 'hydra-headed'[16] animal of communism directed from abroad, and more precisely from Moscow. The orders had passed through the Comintern, RILU and the Minority Movement but they had originated with the 'Moscow mandarins' in particular Losovsky, Zinoviev and Trotsky, all of whom where accused by name and all of whom were now in disgrace, Citrine noted.[17]

Citrine's articles were in essence a declaration of war on the RILU and the Minority Movement and were matched by a call for the defeat of the last remnants of Communist International and Comintern influence within the Labour Party's ranks by Morrison in his article for *Labour Magazine*. His light touch contrasted with the forced seriousness of Citrine's complaining tone, the popular politician and the bureaucrat, but they both meant the same thing; the Russians were dangerous partners, and the British communists were pathetic because they tried to be both Russian and British. For Morrison, Moscow had now come to the end of its patience with United Front tactics which had benefited none but the Labour Party. Indeed, wrote Morrison, even Lenin had seen that it was only through the Labour Party that the communists could ever get power. Now that the United Front had been killed off the Communist Party could only go downhill. 'But so far as the British Labour Party is concerned we may thank Moscow for its relative honesty, for its open declaration of war, and for blowing to the winds at last the Tory fiction that the Labour Party is a creature of Communism'. We must 'Pity the poor Bolsheviks'.[18] As far as Citrine, Morrison and the others were concerned, they had declared the end of any possible collaboration between British Communist and Labour parties. In 1928 the Communist Party itself seemed to agree and declared its policy of 'class against class'.

The search for electoral responsibility

Having condemned the Moscow-backed Minority Movement and the CPGB, the leadership of the Labour Party was still left with several Moscow-related problems during the build-up to the general election. During 1928 the one that received most publicity was a renewed discussion as to the veracity of the Zinoviev letter. Some Labour Party members hoped and intended to finally lay low the lie that had cost the movement so dearly in 1924.

Renewed discussion of this issue was, however, a major irritation to the Labour Party leadership during 1928, to the evident incomprehension of some of their less electorally sensitive colleagues. That it had been an explosive election issue in 1924 was denied by nobody. Clynes described it as 'without parallel in modern party warfare'. But he realised why it had been successful, it was 'the electors' fear of alien hostility' that had made the Tory ploy so successful. The letter's resuscitation was a double-edged sword which might work against a Labour victory in the next election. The Labour Party thus wished to avoid all further tarring with the Bolshevik brush.[19] Renewed talk of the letter could only remind voters of the dangers of any contact with Russia, a contact that the Labour Party was convinced was necessary, whatever the risks.

But perhaps the major obstacles to 'respectability' came from within the Labour Party's own ranks and especially from the ILP. The key argument was over how 'socialist' the Labour Party was to be. One is compellingly reminded of the build-up to the 1987 general election. Domestic events, and especially the General Strike, had led some ILP leaders to bitterly complain of treachery by the TUC General Council. The Labour Party leadership saw it differently – they felt the failure of the General Strike proved that a more moderate conciliatory line with an all-powerful capitalism was necessary. This leadership also had less patience with extra-parliamentary activity than before their 1924 experience of government, which they considered had achieved a great deal. They never indulged in the rhetoric of the class struggle. The ILP, on the other hand, did so on every possible occasion, even in foreign affairs.

During the whole of 1928 MacDonald had to wince in Parliament, and at TUC, LSI and Labour Party Conferences, whenever the ILP felt the moment had come for a statement on virtually anything. The ILP carried its concept of democracy almost to the point of anarchy and it was a considerable embarrassment. Egon Wertheimer, generally accepted as a fairly neutral observer, was even more cruel about the ILP.

It had become a 'refuge for all those radical, bourgeois malcontents whose war experience and disillusion had brought them into contact with the Socialist Movement' and who wished to seek 'a platform for the propagation of ideas of the most varied kinds'. These were not the same type of ILP recruit of pre-1914, and had become 'overrun with ex-Liberals, young-men-just-down-from-Oxford guiltless of any Socialist tradition, ideologists, and typical monomaniacs full of their own pet projects'.[20] The pre-1914 ILP, to which both MacDonald and Snowden had belonged, had furnished 30 per cent of the 1924 Cabinet (including MacDonald and Snowden). One hundred and fourteen of the 150 Labour MPs in 1924–9 were ILP. On the other hand most of these MPs and Cabinet members were wholehearted supporters of MacDonald's moderate line against Maxton's tendency to extremist language. A seemingly contradictory situation, to say the least. What had in fact happened, explained Wertheimer, was that the ILP MPs had, in most cases, cast 'neither their votes nor influence ... for ILP issues'. The leadership of the ILP largely outside Parliament had lost touch with its own MPs. The former ILP men of the 1924 Cabinet had even 'undergone a psychological change which did not dispose them favourably towards wildcat ILP schemes'. It was the ILP Executive, the National Administrative Council (NAC), which had gone to the left. Echoing Maxton's speech in the Russia debate of March 1927, Wertheimer wrote that the ILP NAC from 1926, the year that Maxton became its chairman, gave free rein to 'sentimental politics ... and decisions determined by the agitational necessities of the moment'.[21] Some of the ILP's ideas, especially economic, were to see a partial fulfilment in 1945. In 1928 they were an embarrassment.

The final version of the 1928 Labour Party programme, 'Labour and the Nation', on which it fought the 1929 election, was different in tone and approach from that which the ILP would have wished, although every effort was made by the official Labour Party leadership to emphasise what it saw as a 'slight divergence', in public at least. A situation parallel to that being experienced by the British Labour movement in the 1980s was taking place behind the scenes. Henderson and the national agent, Egerton Wake, spent at least some of their time trying to persuade ILP-dominated local constituency parties from ousting official moderate Labour Party candidates in pre-election selection decisions. The Labour Party NEC took these disputes to be part of 'the aftermath of the General Strike', and in successive NEC meetings of 1928 such problems recurred in virtually every meeting.[22]

The ILP in the Labour and Socialist International (LSI)

One of the ILP 'sins' on Wertheimer's list, that of trying to reconcile and unify the Socialist and Communist Internationals, under Fenner Brockway's urging, equally exercised the patience of the Labour Party NEC. Brockway was a leading light on the ILP NAC and particularly influential in international questions, which Maxton seems to have left largely to him while he concentrated on the domestic front. MacDonald had pleaded with him to 'use my influence within the party to encourage an attitude of patience' during the 1924 government on those ILP MPs who wished for more rapid progress.[23] This confidence seems to have evaporated by the 'left turn' of 1926, shortly before MacDonald formally broke his personal links with the ILP.

Brockway became the ILP representative on the Executive of the Labour and Socialist International during 1926. He took with him the informality that was a hallmark of ILP relationships with other 'comrades', which Brockway felt was missing from the 'colder machine-like organisation of the Labour Party'. He found even less of the 'spirit of Socialism' in the vast bureaucracy of the LSI in Zurich, or among the 'heavy, self-satisfied bureaucrats' that ran it. As to his relations with the Labour Party representation on the LSI Executive – Henderson, Gillies (head of the Labour Party International Department) and Cramp, secretary of the NUR (Thomas's union) – Brockway seems to have been even less impressed. He considered Labour Party International Department Secretary Gillies to be a lackey and Henderson himself entirely at a loss out of his native environment. The Austrian and French parties were a particular disappointment to him and only for the Belgians, Vandervelde and de Brouchère, could Brockway find much praise.[24] In this inhospitable climate Brockway said later that he knew that he was 'tilting at the moon' in pushing for 'international unity', especially given the Third International's disdain, but he persevered in his appeals to the ever-mounting exasperation of Adler (LSI Executive Secretary) and the Labour Party delegation.

No sooner had ARJAC collapsed than Brockway and the ILP NAC moved to try some other approach to 'entente' with the Russians, this time within the LSI. Brockway felt his justification lay in the significant minority who had called for continued united efforts at the previous 1926 Labour Party Conference. Adler was surprised and appalled and wrote to Brockway for more information.[25] Brockway wrote back to say that he wanted to try a different tactic with the Russians, that of joining with some of the parties of the LSI and approaching Moscow through the 'Balabanoff International Group'. Adler, understandably, was appalled at what he saw as naive nonsense. It would be a horribly divisive move and 'you will therefore believe me when I say that, in the interests of unity, I regard what you are contemplating as ruinous'. The Balabanoff Group, pointed out Adler, did not really exist in practice, and to drop the SDs and SRs as the privileged Russian interlocutors within the LSI, as Brockway obviously intended, could not work. The basic problem, said Adler was that it was 'out of the question that the communists could just at present be any more inclined towards unity [than] a year ago'.[26] Brockway could not disagree – 'Balabanoff is of no account' – but he believed such groups could be one way to promote unity. He also said, and here his meaning was made transparent: 'I know there is no immediate hope of reunion with the Russians. They are as recalcitrant as any of the parties in the LSI. My clear conviction is that we must stir the rank and file in both internationals and among the "affiliated parties" by an educational campaign to secure the unity we are seeking'.[27] Brockway had raised unity to the level of a fetish. He agreed with Adler on all points (even on the persecutions, which prompted Brockway to boycott the tenth anniversary celebrations in the USSR of October 1927) yet could not go so far as the LSI and break off contact.[28] The Russians rebuffed him completely, and said that the CPSU 'proposes to intensify its counter-attacks against social democracy, inasmuch as the manoeuvre referred to above [Brockway's] is nothing less than a repetition of capitalist manoeuvres'.[29]

The LSI secretariat largely shared the Labour Party leadership's line on Russia and was deeply embarrassed by the independent ILP initiatives. The ILP still refused to drop its wish to 'unity' in spite of Moscow's rebuffs and submitted another request to the Labour Party NEC for collaboration on this point in March 1928. The NEC were sent a 'Manifesto Urging International Unity' by the ILP NAC, which was an embarrassment even to Oswald Mosley, one of the ILP members seconded to the Labour Party NEC. He wanted merely to 'acknowledge' its receipt. But the 'moderate' majority of the NEC went further. Cramp (also on the LSI Executive) moved an amendment declining 'to endorse the manifesto on the grounds that repeated experience had demonstrated the futility of such methods of attempting to secure working-class unity'. MacDonald tried to compromise by substituting 'regrets that the manifesto has been issued' but was defeated.[30]

The ILP claimed that it was trying to find a new way, between that of the Comintern and that of the LSI and Labour Party in the 'Maxton-Cook Manifesto' at the beginning of July 1928, thus 'burn[ing] its boats'.[31] It clearly aimed to do this in foreign as well as in domestic policy. But the fact is that it could not decide on a distinct break with either the Communist Party or the Labour Party to achieve its middle aim in either fields. It fumbled on with its unity programme until after the August 1928 Congress of the LSI in Brussels when it was dropped for the time being.[32] How this affected Labour Party policy for peace will be discussed in the next chapter.

Brockway and the ILP did not limit themselves to these unity attempts. An approach which was to later widen the breach between the ILP and the Labour Party leadership during the 1930–35 period, that through the Comintern 'front' organisations, was also attempted by the ILP. German communist Willi Munzenberg managed to get Brockway to accept the position of International Chairman at the February 1927 inauguration of the 'League Against Imperialism', which was used as a pretext for condemning British intervention in China. The LSI and Labour Party Executives were furious and even the ILP NAC decided to replace Brockway with Maxton in the League so as to answer LSI accusations of implicating them in an affair for which they had the greatest contempt.[33] Maxton was himself quickly evicted from the league's chairmanship by the communists.

Thus the ILP did not heal any breach over international policy but decided to stay within the LSI. It pursued a parallel policy in its relations with the Labour Party, in the role of violent critic. Its attempt to choose a middle path between communists and moderates inevitably ended by bringing it into conflict with both. The Swansea Congress of the TUC at the beginning of September and the Birmingham Conference of the Labour Party in October 1928 were the scenes of violent exchanges on policy, notably towards the 'capitalist class' and the communists. The TUC was attempting joint talks with the Federation of British Industry, attacked by A. J. Cook of the miners as 'Mond Moonshine'.[34] The TUC declared that 'disruptive elements' were to be dealt with in the spirit of Citrine's articles. Criticism of the Mond talks in fact went beyond the immediate ranks of the ILP and Cook. The Mond talks episode can be seen, with hindsight, as the beginning of what led in the end to the 1932 Labour Party/ILP split.[35]

It was clear that the upheaval of 1928 had only created a temporary lull in the quarrel over the greater interests of unity for the elections and facing up to the international situation. The role of Russia in this disturbance was but one element, albeit one that prompted several contemporaries to urge the ILP not to let its feelings for the USSR influence its domestic debates with the Labour Party. Emmanuel

Shinwell, an ILP MP (and a MacDonald protege both before and after the 1926 'left turn' of his old party) put this clearly. He wrote:

> It is true that the Russian revolution disturbed the traditional policy of the ILP and inspired an animated controversy upon the respective merits of the Second and Third Internationals, the problem of whether socialism could be ushered in with speed or must come gradually, and the possibility of conflict with the owning classes; but in the main, public pronouncements and party resolutions – the dedications and manifestos of individuals notwithstanding – have remained faithful to the rigid policy. ... For the purpose of the ILP is to see socialism applied, even if the job is entrusted to others.[36]

Notes

1 *Daily Herald*, 30 May 1927. Lansbury had said at the time: 'I have nothing to apologise for in having representatives of the Russian working class as my guests'.

2 LANSBURY, G., 'A Tragedy of Errors: an Appeal to Russia', *New Leader*, 16 September 1927. In the original all this quote is in italics. This was also repeated in the *Daily Herald* of 16 September 1927. The *Herald* issued a very ambivalent reaction to Lansbury's views, but appears to have reluctantly accepted them. It is possible that either the party or the TUC or both put pressure on the editorial staff not to make adverse comment.

3 LANSBURY, loc. cit.

4 WEBB, Sidney and Beatrice, *Industrial Democracy*, London, Longmans, Green and Co., ninth edition, 1926 (hereafter *Industrial Democracy*).

5 WEBB, S. and B., *Industrial Democracy*, p. 809.

6 Ibid., p. 808.

7 Quoted in DEWAR, Hugo, *Communist Politics in Britain: The Communist Party of Great Britain from its origins to the Second World War*, London, Pluto Press, 1976, p. 37.

8 Particularly at election time when CPGB members would heckle and otherwise indulge in violent or offensive behaviour.

9 MacDonald quoted in *Birmingham Town Crier*, 11 December 1925. It should be noted that the confusion in 1924 as to what should be done to the Communist Party editor, Campbell, was largely due to this kind of crisis of conscience.

10 MACFARLANE, L. J. *The British Communist Party: Its Origins and Development Until 1929*, London, MacGibbon and Kee, 1966, p. 177. This is, in fact, the only really good book on the CPGB in print.

11 MacFarlane says that the Labour Party NEC expressed opposition to this invitation of the 1920 'Hands Off Russia' Committee: MACFARLANE, p. 179.

12 The Minority Movement was also in a state of decline, with membership down from a peak in 1926 of 950,000 to 300,000 (workers represented at national Minority Movement conferences) in 1927. Cf. MACFARLANE, p. 182.

13 MARTIN, J., *Communism and the British Trade Unions 1924–1933: a Study of the National Minority Movement*, Oxford, Clarendon Press, 1976, p. 101.

14 CITRINE, Walter, 'Democracy or Disruption', Pts I-V, *Labour Magazine*, December 1927 – May 1928.

15 MORRISON, Herbert, 'The ECCI's Latest: Why the Life of British Communist Leaders is not Worth Living', *Labour Magazine*, May 1928. *Hereafter*, MORRISON, 'The ECCI's Latest ...'.

16 CITRINE, 'Democracy or Disruption', Pt I, December 1927, p. 344.

17 CITRINE, 'Democracy or Disruption', Pt III, February 1928, p. 438–41.

18 MORRISON, Herbert, 'The ECCI's Latest…'. See also: Morrison's motion to the NEC, 28 May 1928, item 282.
19 J. R. Clynes in a speech at Atherton, reported in *Daily Herald*, 16 March 1928.
20 WERTHEIMER, Egon, *Portrait of the Labour Party,* London, Putnam, 1929, pp. 14–15.
21 WERTHEIMER, pp. 15–17.
22 See NEC, 7 February 1928, for example.
23 BROCKWAY, F. A., *Inside the Left*, London, New Leader Ltd, 1942, p. 151 (hereafter *Inside the Left*).
24 Ibid., pp. 159–63.
25 The call for 'entente' was published in LSI *Bulletin d'Information*, no. 3, October 1927. Adler wrote to Brockway on 9 November 1927: 'Since I know nothing more than what I have read in this Bulletin d'Information, I should be very glad to get information from yourself'.
26 Reported in Circular C19/28 to LSI Executive of 25 February 1928 Adler to Brockway, letter of 24 November 1927 in C 19/28.
27 Brockway to Adler, 28 November 1927, C 19/28, loc. cit.
28 This will be discussed in Ch. 5, 'Russia as Democracy or dictatorship?'
29 Reprinted in (LSI) C 19/28.
30 Labour Party NEC Minutes, 25 March 1928, item 215. For a discussion of some of the implications of CSI-Comintern contacts see BRAUNTHAL, J., *History of the International*, London, Nelson, 2 vols, 1967, vol. 2, 1914–1943, pp. 341–4 and Williams *The Attitude…* op. cit, Ch. 3, (V).
31 Brockway in *New Leader*, 6 July 1928.
32 There was one other ILP proposal for a unity of the 'Balabanoff Group' kind to make a non-patriotic approach to the Russians, reprinted in *New Leader*, 13 July 1928. Nothing seems to have come of it.
33 BROCKWAY, *Inside the Left*, p. 168.
34 So-called because Sir Alfred Mond was Chairman of the Federation of British Industry.
35 See below, chs. 12 and 16.
36 Letter by Emmanuel Shinwell to *New Leader*, 19 October 1928.

chapter four

Russia, peace and the elaboration of Labour Party foreign policy aims, 1927–8

Labour Party foreign policy aims

The impact of the Great War on the collective British memory had made the need for an avoidance of war into an obsession that is clearly reflected in the columns of the labour press, in the resolutions passed by the national governing bodies of the Labour and Independent Labour parties and unions and in the deliberations of the parties' international committees. Egon Wertheimer went so far as to say that 'Labour's international policy – like its economic and social policies – clearly receives its impulse from an ethical postulate, the repudiation of war'.[1] When Russia was added to the equation the mixture was explosive in the extreme.

Nineteen twenty-seven had begun with the diplomatic correspondent of the *Daily Herald* being convinced that the confrontation between British imperial power and the nascent Chinese nationalist movement was 'as considerable as any that has confronted us in our lifetimes ... Nor is the state of Europe reassuring. On the surface all is peace. But there are dangerous undercurrents'.[2] The three dangers were identified as China, Lithuania and Mussolini's expansion in the Mediterranean. China was the field of battle where the British were the most involved during 1927, and also here that the cries from the Tory diehards about 'Bolshevik interference' were loudest.

The leadership of the TUC and the Labour Party undoubtedly felt that it had been to some extent manipulated by the Russians in their internal power struggle with the new issue being used as a tool. Given their deep wish for peace they were thus torn between disgust at so sacred a subject being used for base political motives and a genuine desire to placate Russian worries.

Russia, peace and the elaboration of Labour Party foreign policy, 1927–9

Nineteen twenty-seven saw the production of several major foreign policy studies by key Labour Party foreign affairs spokesmen, or by those who wished to have an impact on labour movement opinion on such subjects. Hugh Dalton, J. M. Kenworthy, H. N. Brailsford and MacDonald were all highly respected commentators within the Labour Party and all saw Soviet Russia as a key touchstone of Labour's foreign policy.

Dalton's 'Towards the Peace of Nations'

The war was a recent memory, as Dalton, future Under-Secretary of State for Foreign Affairs during 1929–31, reminded his readers in his important book *Towards the Peace of Nations.* Horrible though the last war had been, in the next: 'it is foreseen by all who have eyes to see that our civilisation will, quite literally, perish .... Its prevention in the future is by far the greatest task which confronts mankind'.[3] The causes of the last war still remained in embryo and there were 'new factors', some of them happy, some potentially dangerous. The League of Nations was one such new factor and in it Dalton put much hope. Of the other 'new' ones, four were cited: Soviet Russia, Fascist Italy, the 'international Communist movement' (carefully delimited from Russia itself) and a fascist analogue. The 'new frontiers and states of Europe are a new factor' as was the United States, but the world outside Europe would become more important, and here again Dalton mentioned Russia as likely to be a benefactor of the new distribution of power.[4]

The cause of war was considered by Dalton to be primarily economic, although he also considered religious, dynastic and nationalist reasons. His intellectual antecedents were, not surprisingly, H. N. Brailsford and Norman Angell.[5] He took up Brailsford's point (in *The War of Steel and Gold*) about how Anglo-French boundholders' claims were central to friction over Egypt, and the parallels of the Russian bond discussions cannot have been lost on his readers. Trade was the other danger, for when the trader expected his activity to benefit from the support of the country's diplomatic arm he could aggravate the risk of war thus giving no support to the idea of export credits.[6] During 1924 and 1929–31 a major element of the trade with Russia discussion hinged around the starting of export credits to traders. He saw this, however, in a world where trade was to be organised along more rational, 'international plan' lines rather than on a national basis, in a 'socialist' and not a 'capitalist' world. It was also a prelude to his plea for a more efficient League of

Nations. The importance of Russia in all this cannot have been lost on his readers.

Dalton struck a mildly revisionist attitude to the Versailles Treaty, pointing out that many of the 'new' nations were in fact 'old' ones, but that 'revengeful meanness, short-sighted cruelty and economic folly'[7] had been major impetuses in the treaty writers. The experience of this change had had a dangerous effect on Europe's leaders, in both East and West. He singled out the Soviet leadership for particular mention and in so doing echoed many of the Labour Party's pleas in the Commons that 'extremists' would die out given time:

> most of the present leaders have been hunted men, exiles or prisoners ... Such men can hardly escape becoming in some degree abnormal. Their minds have fallen out with thoughts of peace. They see imaginary clouds across the sun. But when this abnormal generation passes, new horizons will be ready to open before their successors. The mere habit of peace, if it endures for a term of years, will count heavily towards the recovery of Europe, like rest and long hours of sleep after fever and debauchery.[8]

But having defined why Russia was important to the future of the planet and especially to ensuring peace, Dalton had thus far not said how he really perceived it. In an illuminating passage of six pages he attempted to do so, 'looking through the naked eye and not through rose-coloured spectacles', seeing 'neither Hell let loose or Paradise regained'. Present relations he likened to a 'broken telephone line ... and official persons at both ends howling hysterical hatred into the receiver'.

But he had to admit that 'much else is misty. Our lack of dispassionate knowledge regarding Russia is only equalled by Russia's lack of it regarding ourselves'. To substantiate the last comment Dalton cited some of the more virulent Comintern insults directed at prominent members of the British Labour movement, including MacDonald, Purcell, Lansbury, Maxton and Brockway, all of whom had been painted in the worst possible light. In common with his party colleagues he emphasised the argument that the breaking-off of diplomatic relations would only serve to bolster Russian 'lack of self-confidence', that it would encourage those in Russia who advocated a revolutionary attitude just when the moderates showed signs of winning. Confidence-building measures were necessary, said Dalton – trade, non-aggressive pacts and arbitration the necessary implements. Russia must therefore be involved in as much as possible in Europe – the League, disarmament talks, trade, economic discussions – all were small but significant blows at extremist tendencies within the USSR.

Dalton therefore felt that Russia had the possibility for civilised behaviour as did many of his colleagues of the Labour Party centre. His book was evidently a bid for acceptance of his foreign policy credentials, for up till about 1927 (and indeed after) he was more thought of as an economic expert. As will be explained later, the economic aspects of the Russian 'experiment' were to interest him more and more during the early thirties, and it was he that coined the phrase the 'exemplar'.[9] In 1927 his views on how Britain could profit from the Soviet experience were rather unformed but he was clearly already looking to it as one possible avenue, one that he explored further as the British crisis deepened. He was representative of the intelligent but guarded approach to Russia that existed within the Labour Party at this stage.

J. M. Kenworthy's 'The Freedom of the Seas' and 'Peace or War?'

Kenworthy, whom *New Leader* was to name as 'one of the best Liberals to join the Labour Party'[10] was far more reserved about the USSR. His political position was definitely to the right of the party, and indeed he was a very recent recruit from the Liberals, in 1926. He had no love for Bolshevism, feeling that the Russian revolution had:

> set up a tidal wave of revolution south, west and east, that threatened to submerge and subvert our political and social structures [and as such was a danger to peace]. At its approach most of us banded together to build dykes to shut it out and to save our property – some few of us set to work building dams to shut it in and use its power.

Among the rather overworked nautical analogies it seems clear that (ex-Royal Navy Commander) Kenworthy was not enamoured of this particular tidal wave.[11] On the other hand he was in favour, with the leadership of his new party, of bringing Russia into more civilised company and dealing with the matters of trade, debts, and allied questions. In 1924, as a Liberal, he had supported MacDonald in almost the same words as used by the then Prime Minister: 'It is necessary to approach this question in a businesslike manner'.[12]

In a book of the same date as Dalton's and dealing with nearly precisely the same questions, if at rather greater length and with embarrassingly purple prose, he agreed with Dalton on economic factors being the most likely new cause of war, with the Russian 'theory' as one of the two combatants. Kenworthy agreed: 'In the present state of the world, the clash between two opposing economic theories is perhaps the most likely cause of a future great war. If this present world state of affairs continues, another great war is inevitable'.[13]

Kenworthy was very much in line with an older, nineteenth-century, British liberal thinking about the strategic dangers posed by an expansive 'asiatic' Russia. He feared the Russian 'drive to the sea', a fear now reinforced through the 'much more powerful spread of ideas'. But he did not draw the same policy conclusions as the Conservative Cabinet. In such circumstances, a breach of diplomatic relations could have no value. Here he rejoined Dalton and MacDonald in believing that a breach would only encourage Russian extremism and propaganda, and it was this propaganda that could well be the seed of war. Not prepared to go so far as Dalton in apportioning blame mainly to the diehards, Kenworthy would not make the ultimate step and become one himself. However, he was evidently close to not believing in the feasibility of the Labour Party's policy of 'civilising' the Russians. For Kenworthy, the 'asiatic' element was likely to reinforce the 'extremist' in a very pessimistic future scenario of Anglo-Soviet relations.

H. N. Brailsford's 'Olives of Endless Age'

If Kenworthy was part of a long tradition, H. N. Brailsford sought to espouse and modernise a different one. Probably the greatest of the Labour press's foreign policy writers, Brailsford was always considered, and considered himself, in the avant-garde left of the movement. In *Olives of Endless Age* this latter-day Voltaire began his major foreign affairs reflection with a re-run of *Candide*, who he situated on a train from Moscow to Geneva. His Candide's search for a land where 'all is for the best' was, as in the original, a hard one.[14]

Brailsford's main aim was to pursue the same fears as those of Kenworthy and Dalton – the fear of a new war. He was, through the columns of the *New Leader*, by far the most strident, during 1927, on the possibility or probability of Britain going to war with Russia. His reasoning was based on his belief, like Dalton and Kenworthy, that the causes of war were economic. This was not so strange in the man who had written, in 1911, *The War of Steel and Gold*, a key inspiration for a whole generation of Labour Party writers. The Versailles settlement had further convinced him of his basic thesis. His new contributions of 1927 painted a picture of Russia itself, gleaned during his 1920 and 1927 visits, as a place of immense hope for its inhabitants and perhaps for the rest of humanity. But he was also wary of the way that such power could be used, of the future that might lie in store for a Russia driven mad by the insensitive dogs of Western incomprehension and encirclement. His Candide encountered as much cruelty at the hands of the Red Russians as at those of the White and had immense trouble deciding which was the worst. He escaped execution many times, the last of which when 'his execution, like that of the surviving hundred million citizens of the Soviet Republic, was postponed to a more fitting occasion'.[15]

Brailsford was greatly saddened by the Soviet purges of 1927, after the Voikov assassination. It was, however, Chamberlain's belligerent attitude that was held responsible for most of the Russian riposte: 'revenge and wrong bring forth their kind', even if 'no calculation, however sound it may be, can excuse the violence which takes life, in a time of peace, without even the formality of a public trial'.[16] *Olives of Endless Age* is clearly not great literature, but a rather self-conscious parody. It is none the less a key text for tracing a growing underswell of even left-wing Labour Party worry about the democratic process in the USSR. This worry will be more fully analysed in Chapter 5.

MacDonald's memorandum on Labour Party policy

Brailsford wrote with a humanitarian concern with which MacDonald could understand and sympathise, but not the preparation that he, as an ex- and probably future Prime Minister, deemed necessary. MacDonald put his fears and hopes into a long memorandum during 1928, on 'Labour Party Policy',[17] in which he considered many aspects of the party of which he was head. The memorandum had three major sections on pamphlets and books, the rise of the Labour Party and foreign policy. The three were clearly linked subjects for reflection.

On foreign policy, that of a 'Labour Government is a subject upon which little requires to be said, so well is it known. It will be directed towards *the double end of democracy and peace*'.[18] What MacDonald felt sure the Labour Party could assure at home he had learnt could not be willed in foreign relations. Objective realities made compromises necessary. Not only were there 'small nationalities' needing to 'find their feet' and 'nations still under tutelage', but 'for some time the British Foreign Office [would] have to deal with nations in a state of revolutionary flux and flow'. The way these should be dealt with was crucial:

> Whilst there are tyrannies and dictatorships in the world, and whilst there are reactionary governments damming up the streams of progress, there will, and there ought to be, revolutions. Until revolutions are completed foreign governments should only be onlookers ... but contact should never be wholly lost, and as soon as they are completed official contacts should be made with them in order to quicken the settling down transition to constitutional and orderly governments, and to relieve the world of inflaming elements. This requires sympathetic but firm handling in every respect different from the feeble confusion of the government treatment of the Russian problem between 1924 and 1927.
>
> After every revolution a country has two parties. One carries on the revolution as propagandists, and seeks to extend it both internally and externally; the other, since the power of goverment has come into the hands of those who during the

> revolution expressed the national will, desires to settle down and use those powers constitutionally to carry out the real purposes of the revolution. It is not only legitimate but necessary that enlightened foreign governments should support that section.[19]

This lengthy quotation shows that MacDonald had by the middle or end of 1928 recovered his equilibrium about the USSR. There was no point being merely shocked or trying to ignore the phenomenon. He wanted the Labour Party to have, as he put it, elsewhere, 'a reputation for enlightenment and good guidance .... Our attitude to Russia is a very good test not only of our democratic and business instincts, but of our insight into politics'.[20]

The central idea put forward by MacDonald, that of directing foreign policy towards 'the double end of democracy and peace', was not fundamentally disagreed with by any of the writers discussed earlier. But as with the debate on the interpretation of 'socialism' on the domestic front, there were divergences over tactics in foreign policy. Once again the ILP tended to push for more rapid progress and the leadership of the Labour Party to stress pragmatic slowness. The discussion on the Russian disarmament proposals of late 1927 are an excellent case in point and can be used as a framework in which to consider the progressive development of a practical foreign policy towards Russia by the Labour Party during 1928.

The Russian disarmament proposals of October 1927

Russian presence at the Geneva preparatory talks for a disarmament conference in December 1927, and their attendance at the May 1927 World Economic Conference (also held in Geneva), meant a first re-emergence of the USSR onto the international conference scene since Genoa in 1922.

The Preparatory Conference opened under the auspices of the League of Nations, to which MacDonald had given his support during 1924. It must, however, be said that a certain scepticism about the League of Nations existed in the Labour Party. MacDonald himself was considered very lukewarm by the major British representative to the League, Lord Robert Cecil, even if he was considered by Cecil to be more in favour of the League than the Conservatives. Philip Noel-Baker, who had been Cecil's private secretary, was a major defender of the League on the Labour Party's Advisory Committee on International Questions (ACIQ), which reported directly to the NEC. MacDonald was thus prone to suggest extra-League agreements (he had supported the Locarno Pacts of 1925, for example), while the ACIQ preferred all discussions about the improvement of international relations to take place within the League.

The Russians seem to have been mainly interested in the League as another partial way out of isolation, and of using it as a propaganda platform. This new policy of contact within a 'capitalist' organisation, such as the League, rather than a 'progressive' one, such as the ARJAC, is in itself a clear indication of a major change of Soviet policy. This is at least strong circumstantial evidence that the Narkomindel was having its policy of diplomatic contracts favoured at the expense of the Comintern-based contacts previously favoured by Trotsky. The Labour Party leadership cautiously took this as a good sign.

MacDonald was particularly worried about the possibility of war on Russia's western frontier, as he made clear in an article at the beginning of October 1927. He suggested the creation of a protocol between the states of the region. In a book on disarmament at the end of 1927, Philip Noel-Baker noted that such a creation had already been suggested by the USSR, but that this had not met with great success.[21] In a mid-November edition of the *Daily Herald* carrying a report that huge crowds were gathering for services in Britain – to pray for peace – Rykov was reported as saying to the Friends of Soviet Russia delegation in Moscow that: 'Peace and the peaceful development of the Soviet Union were the fundamental principles of the foreign policy of Russia'. The day before it had been announced that Trotsky, Zinoviev and Kamenev were to be expelled from the Soviet Communist Party.[22] The links cannot have been lost on MacDonald and the NEC of the Labour Party.

But the Labour Party leadership gave a cool response, evidently doubting whether the Russian proposals were in fact sincere. More concrete evidence of a Russian opening up was obviously needed. The proposals for complete disarmament (made by Maxim Litvinov) to the League after Chicherin's diplomatic 'feeler' towards the League at the beginning of November were cautiously received. Lansbury, the most prominent of the left-wing 'idealists' on the NEC, said that Litvinov's proposals were 'the first commonsense proposals with regard to armaments ... the biggest thing that has been bought into the peace movement'. But among the 'realists' J. H. Thomas and Clynes were more circumspect none the less admitting that 'the League will never fulfil its ideals and work while America and Russia are outside'.[23]

A memo submitted to the NEC by Noel-Baker perhaps summed up the dichotomy facing the Labour Party about this startling Russian bid for League prominence. The 'declared purpose of these proposals is what the Labour Party has always held ought to be the purpose of all civilised governments', and for this reason the proposals were welcomed. But on the other hand, declarations were not enough to end war: 'International machinery for the organisation of peace is required'. If the USSR would join the League they would be better heard and followed in their suggestions. None the less, these proposals 'are a challenge to the present governments of the members of the League to prove that they are sincere' about disarmament.[24]

Typically, the ILP refused to be convinced by this pragmatic reticence. 'This week', said the editorial of the *New Leader* of 9 December, 'Russia had added one more to the services which she has already rendered to the generation. Her magnificent disarmament gesture is an example to the world. Which lead is one to follow? That given by President Coolidge: "More ships, more guns, more war" or that of Russia: "Scrap the lot". Upon the answer destiny rests'.

Brailsford echoed this in the same edition: 'With their habitual want of tact these Russians have taken us at our word, and actively invited us to disarm, totally, instantly .... No wonder they are the most unpopular people on our planet'.[25]

The NEC vacillated in its response to the proposals in spite of some pressure from its rank-and-file constituency parties, but did little. The proposals were discussed again but finally pushed back to the Advisory Committee on International Questions which circulated its findings to the Parliamentary Executive. The keynote was caution. The Borah Kellogg proposals for the outlawing of war of the same era seem to have got a better response, but only slightly.[26]

As might be expected, there were differences of opinion as to whether the Russian or the American proposals should be treated with trust or suspicion. The main fear was that the total insensitivity of the Conservatives who were, naturally, conducting the negotiations in Geneva, might destroy whatever hope lay in the Russian proposals.

The Conservatives' effective refusal to deal with the Russians in Geneva gradually pushed the Labour Party into more open sympathy for the Russian case. Ponsonby commented that many Conservatives believed 'that it does not very much signify if Russia remains an outcast nation'.[27] Declarations of good intent by the Conservatives were not believed. A prominent member of the Labour Party International Committee, Noel Buxton, asked Sir Austen Chamberlain in July 1928 what he thought of the Russian peace proposals to which the Foreign Secretary replied that 'he could not support neither could he object to it'.[28]

The Labour Party was slowly coming out of its hesitancy over Russian commitment to disarmament, and increasingly underlining the need to ensure peace through diplomatic and trading contacts with the USSR, having no wish to have its policy of reticence to Russia confused with that of the Conservative Party. The NEC meeting of 25 July confirmed this new feeling and situated it firmly in the build-up to the next election. The occasion was the discussion of the manifesto 'Labour and the Nation'. A specific motion about Russia was discussed and a hesitant minute accepted: 'That reference to Russia be included in the final paragraph of the section on page 16'.[29]

The decision was treated with delight by the ILP, and even such a mild statement over Russia did much to re-cement the Labour Party at a moment when ILP/Labour Party relations had never been worse over the issue of the Maxton–Cook Manifesto.[30] The 1927–8 disarmament proposals had created a new populist feeling for peace and were beginning to overcome the leadership's reticence towards Russia, at least over the issue of disarmament.

The position of the Labour Party leadership at the end of 1928

The final manifesto of the LSI's Brussels congress, issued in mid-August 1928, reflected that the rest of the LSI were not prepared to accept Russian sincerity as was described in the last chapter. Russia had not been the only bone of contention for the British delegation for the LSI had passed some very embarrassing motions on British imperialism in Egypt, questions that had been dealt with by the 1924 Labour Government. On Russia however, the LSI, obsessed understandably given its SD and SR Russian sections, both overestimated the horror felt by the British Labour Party leadership at the trials and persecutions in Russia, and underestimated the central importance of peace above all to Labour Party foreign policy. To further emphasise this point the British delegation to the Brussels meeting was a very heavyweight one, especially on disarmament, where MacDonald and Henderson were given special responsibility (Henderson was now also President of the LSI). Lansbury, the greatest pacifist of all, was made overall head of delegation. Now that it had been more or less decided to give Russia the benefit of the doubt on at least this issue (as we shall see the leadership of the Labour Party largely agreed with the LSI on the internal persecutions) the line was held wherever the Labour Party was represented, at home or abroad.

There was probably also another issue that influenced the leadership's seeming change of heart. This issue, that of growing unemployment and the consequent need for better trade, will be considered more fully in Chapter 6 for it is a large subject in itself. The rise of interest as expressed through the columns of the *Daily Herald* and the new speeches about a Russia which had been largely ignored for many months was more than palpable. It could probably also be speculated that the new Comintern line of 'class against class' had finally convinced the leadership of the party that since the United Front was dead the movement had nothing more to fear from the Communist Party or from the Minority Movement. As Morrison had said, the declaration of war by the Third International had cleared the air, defined the moderates and made dialogue once again possible with the Soviet Union itself with no real fear of domestic disruption or overspill.

Nineteen twenty-eight thus drew to a close on this note. Disarmament had been made a major platform of the coming electoral struggle. The Russian proposals had done much to highlight Labour's emphasis on peace. Nevertheless, the old reticence engendered by the events of 1924–7 were still there in MacDonald's mind. In a speech in late December the future Prime Minister said that 'Russia could not remain where she was now, and the sooner we recognised Russia diplomatically the better' but 'diplomatic recognition would not mean recognition of the Russian internal government'.[31]

Notes

1 WERTHEIMER, E., *Portrait of the Labour Party*, London, G. P. Putmans and Sons, 1929, p. 158 (1930 edition).

2 *Daily Herald*, 1 January 1927.

3 DALTON, Hugh, *Towards the Peace of Nations*, London, Routledge, 1928, p. 1. Henry R. Winkler, in his article 'The Emergence of a Labour Foreign Policy in Great Britain, 1918–1929', comments that Dalton's book: 'Presented as a personal statement, was nevertheless the most carefully worked out argument for the policy which was emerging as that of the Labour Party to appear in print during this period' (p. 257).

4 DALTON, pp. 5–6.

5 Although he finds Angell less convincing than Brailsford.

6 DALTON, p. 21.

7 Ibid., p. 27.

8 Ibid., p. 35.

9 Ben PIMLOTT's *Hugh Dalton*, London, Jonathan Cape, 1985, page 186 also makes this quite clear. *Hereafter* PIMLOTT, *Dalton*.

10 NEVINSON, H. W., 'The Devil's Vat: Will Civilisation Crash?', *New Leader*, 2 December 1927.

11 KENWORTHY, J. M. and YOUNG, George, *The Freedom of the Seas*, London, Hutchinson, 1928. Both had naval backgrounds, both were Labour Party MPs, and both had a great interest in foreign affairs.

12 House of Commons Debates, vol. 175, 7 July 1924, col. 1874.
13 KENWORTHY, J. M. *Peace or War?*, New York, Boni and Liveright, 1927, p. 35. This book was called *Will Civilisation Survive?* in the British edition, London, Ernest Benn, 1927.
14 Brailsford published a whole series of 'Candide Revisited' articles in *Socialist Review*, during January, February and March 1928, reprinted in *Olives of Endless Age*, New York, Harper and Bros, 1928.
15 BRAILSFORD, *Olives of Endless Age*, p. 26.
16 BRAILSFORD, 'Revenge and Wrong: Commentary on Murder', *New Leader*, 17 June 1927, p. 57.
17 The document is undated, but the probability is that this was written in 1928. MacDonald Papers, PRO 30/69 1054. The exact group title is 'Articles on Labour Party Policy' (hereafter 'Labour Party Policy'). I have found no trace of their publication so far. For more details see WILLIAMS, *The Attitude . . .*, op. cit, pp. 131–4.
18 'Labour Party Policy' p. 1, section on 'Foreign Policy'. My underlining.
19 MACDONALD, 'Labour Party Policy', pp. 1–3 (each section was renumbered).
20 *Daily Herald*, 31 October 1927.
21 MACDONALD, 'The Pursuit of Peace', *Daily Herald*, 3 October 1927, and NOEL-BAKER, Philip, *Disarmament*, London, Hogarth Press, second edition, 1927.
22 *Daily Herald*, 11 and 12 November 1927. Among the FSR delegates was Barbusse. John Jagger, later a Labour MP, was also there as one of the three British delegates.
23 Lansbury and Thomas reported in *Daily Herald*, 2 December 1927.
24 NOEL-BAKER, 'Russian Soviet Government's Proposals for Disarmament', Labour Party Advisory Committee on International Questions (ACIQ), December 1927, p. 1-2. cf. also NJL Statement, *Daily Herald*, 9 December 1927.
25 *New Leader*, editorial 'Russia Again', and BRAILSFORD, 'The tactless Russians', *New Leader*, 9 December 1927.
26 NEC Minutes, 6 February and 2 May 1928. For more details on these feelings see WILLIAMS, *The Attitude . . .*, op. cit., pp. 137–41.
27 PONSONBY, Arthur, MP, 'Politics and Peace', *Daily Herald*, 8 May 1928.
28 Reported in *Daily Herald*, 31 July 1928.
29 NEC Labour Party Minutes, 25 July 1928.
30 Editorial 'What We Think', *New Leader*, 10 August 1928.
31 Speech by MacDonald to the 1917 Club, an informal and ad hoc Labour Party foreign policy pressure group to which J. H. Hobson, Pethwick-Lawrence and other prominent political figures belonged. *Daily Herald*, 15 December 1928.

chapter five

'Russia the enigma': Labour Party opinion leaders' analyses of the USSR, 1927–end 1928

Having defined the doubts about Russia in the upper reaches of the party leadership, the question must now be posed as to what was the opinion held by those lower down the political hierarchy, who might none the less have opinions that could normally be treated with respect. In any other context but Britain these would be called the 'intellectuals'. In Britain they may perhaps be termed the 'opinion leaders'.

The aim of this chapter is to analyse the major elements of how Russia was perceived as a phenomenon in itself. At the level of party decision-making and policy we already have some elements of this: the principal preoccupation of peace and employment made Russia a major issue in domestic politics. But there was also further investigation pursued at other levels of the party to put these central concerns into better perspective by trying to define what it was one was dealing with.

There was an almost mystical need to find something that would wash out the horrors of war and industrial decay with white-hot optimism. And scarcely a British intellectual, and especially those who considered themselves 'progressive' did not have a try at penetrating the new phenomenon that was the USSR, the only really new thing in an old, old world.

The saviour of Western civilisation?

A cynical deputy editor of the *Socialist Review*, C. R. de Gruchy, commented in early 1928:

> There are two ways of acquiring a party reputation as a foreign affairs specialist in the present-day political world. If one is conservative one goes to America, spends three hectic weeks being pump-handled by enthusiastic Americans and then comes back and writes a book proving that capitalism is the only possible

> system, etc. etc. In the other political camp one goes either to Russia or to Geneva.[1]

But intellectual opinion on the Russian 'enigma' tended to oscillate between two poles. As has been described, there were those who felt that the growing power of the USSR was a threat to Western civilisation, such as Kenworthy, and those, like Dalton, who at least gave the impression that such was only a danger if the West treated Russia badly by isolating it. The Dalton thesis was the one largely held by the leadership, and particularly by MacDonald and Henderson. Both broad tendencies were often portrayed in all the labour movement periodicals, and often within the same person. The reason for this ambivalence is clear from the most cursory examination of writers on foreign affairs. The single-minded pursuit of peace that had made it such a vital Labour Party policy, also made rank-and-file Labour MPs eager to discuss why it was that Russia was so seemingly devoted to this cause.

An extreme version of this thesis came from Wilfred Wellock, a Labour MP passionately devoted to the cause of peace. He visited Russia in late 1927, for the tenth anniversary of the Revolution. His motive was simple: 'despite all our pretences the Russian Revolution of 1917 is still the outstanding event of modern times, and of even greater importance than the World War'. He found in the USSR the promised land or a near approximation: 'a sort of Book of Revelations. The impossible has happened. The things of which prophets have spoken have come to pass. The mighty have been pulled down from their seats, and those of low degree have been exalted. Not that I wish to imply that everything is ideal and rosy in Russia, far from it'.[2]

The dichotomy is clear. How, it may be asked, can there be such a land of biblical promise where all is not well? The answer lies in the general direction. It would be easy to merely laugh at the exaggerated exuberance of Wellock, but the cause of it is clear. He was seeing something that was so *different*. The things that worried him, the anti-democratic nature of the Russian regime, the physical appearance of Russia and the Russians, were not of crucial importance. Wellock looked almost entirely at Russia through his own obsession, that of peace. However he saw not a trace of 'imperialist ambition' in the land of the Soviets; the main threat imputed to the Russians was one that was a product of the 'capitalist mind'. If Russia was not pushed into violence, or did not let herself be pushed, the vast resources of the USSR could be devoted to domestic expansion in all fields and by so doing 'she would do more to protect herself against foreign invasion than the biggest of armies could do'. If the traditions that had created Tolstoy were to be thus fostered 'Russia might yet save Western Civilisation'. There was not a trace of the 'asiatic' in Wellock's analysis of Russia even if the mystery still remained.[3]

This theme of 'civilisation in danger' was becoming almost generally accepted and was a main driving force behind Labour Party writers' obsession with the need for peace. The celebrated philosopher and Labour Party fellow traveller, C. E. M. Joad, was less sanguine about the possibility of saving 'Western civilisation' from itself. It had, he said, to face up to the fact that decay had to set in, for 'biological', economic and psychological reasons, a belief shared by many of the cultural giants of his age.[4] Western civilisation, many intellectuals were echoing, was in need of revitalisation. Shaw had seen such revitalising power in Mussolini's Italy. The majority of the British labour movement could not agree with Shaw's analysis, but Russia did hold out one possibility.

Wellock had not been alone in visiting the USSR for the tenth anniversary of the Soviet Republic. Commenting on this event, the Chairman of the ILP, James Maxton, MP, wrote of the immense task that had faced Lenin and the Bolsheviks in 1917: 'lion-hearted heroes, who deserve praise and honour from the rest of the world'.[5] The *New Leader* for that anniversary week had eight such articles.

Nor was it only the ILP that was eloquent with admiration. A British workers' delegation also went to the celebrations, twenty of the hundred being ILP members, the others either Cooperative Party or trade unionists. A presumably incomplete list of those that went was published at the beginning of a report on their return. Only four claimed CPGB membership, although the report was (probably) published under CPGB auspices,[6] and reflected the stalinist line on the war danger very strongly.

Dorothy F. Buxton's *The Challenge of Bolshevism* claimed that Russia could serve as an example of real vitality in a world confronted with failure.[7] The *Daily Herald* reviewer seemed to agree: 'This little book is one which should have a wide appeal to those who, conscious of the failure of our Western Civilisation, when judged from moral standards, yet shrink from the contemplation of the Communist alternative because of the violation of moral standards which, it seems to them, Communism implies'.[8] Buxton found a far higher moral standard – 'the ideal of life' not the 'ideal of wealth'. The *Socialist Review* reviewed her book even more enthusiastically than the *Daily Herald*. So by now there were those who found examples of a biological, economic and even moral regeneration in the USSR. However, it must be stressed, most had reservations about the methods being used to achieve this regeneration.

The editor of *Socialist Review*, John Strachey, was drawn towards the USSR as a source of ideas, ideas that he, and many others, felt lacking in the Labour Party. The whole ILP/Labour Party quarrel was in a sense about this. What distinguished 'new' intellectuals like Strachey from Brailsford was the attempt to take 'emotional' issues out of the debate on Russia. Brailsford saw the misery on his visits to the USSR (especially in housing in the new cities) – Strachey tried to look 'even higher'. Brailsford looked back on the problems of the past, Strachey always to the 'next ten years'.[9] Strachey was progressively giving up on the Labour Party as it was constituted as a way out of the crisis of ideas and looking elsewhere. This was to end with his joining the CPGB in 1932. In this sense Brailsford was far more at one with Lansbury and Dorothy Buxton in his assessment of a basket of moral and physical issues. Strachey started a new tradition of ruthless appraisal that was to find its apogee with the Webbs, and was in fact a denial of the humanitarian democratic basis of the British Labour movement.

We can date Strachey's conversion to this line to during his early 1928 visit to Russia, in the wake of the trials and the expulsion of Trotsky. He was manifestly extremely impressed by the changes that had taken place, and here he differed significantly from most of the Labour Party leadership, not because he thought that Stalin's 'Thermidor' would mean a 'return to sanity'[10] – or to a growing moderation. He felt the new age that had dawned with the end of the first ten years would organise the country to socialism of a new kind. He was significantly the first Labour Party theoretician to have the dubious distinction of praising the growing cult of Stalin's personality. Strachey's subsequent articles dealt with the enormous economic difficulties faced by the USSR and the peasant question, all of which would be 'settled' by Stalin.[11]

He and the other fellow travellers of the 1930s have all been condemned by British (and other) writers for their refusal to see the bad sides of the Soviet experiment. Strachey in 1928 was an early version of this intellectual blinkering and more can easily be found to prove the point. But if there is an attempt to put them into what they thought was the context of Britain and the world (with the emphasis on Britain, which they knew by far the best), a twinge of understanding creeps into the most democratic heart.

Strachey saw an insouciant Britain heading, with probably the rest of the Western system, for economic disaster. He was not wrong, even if he underestimated the powers of this system for intellectual and physical recovery. Oswald Mosley made the same analysis. Indeed, he and Strachey were close friends in the 1920s and joint authors of the

'Birmingham proposals', the essence of which closely resembles the Keynesian demand policies finally accepted as the salvation of the West.[12] The Liberal Industrial Inquiry said very similar things in 1928. But the time for such ideas was not ripe. It should be noted that even the Liberals mentioned Russia, though as an 'extreme case' where unemployment had been abolished, even though 'no mere unemployment statistics – even if they existed – could give in cold print any real measure of the human suffering involved in the economic upheaval of Russia'.[13]

Strachey wanted an economic upheaval for the whole planet and had very sophisticated reasons for this. To be fair to him, he did not advocate the same measures in the USSR as in Britain. The 'difficulties' were not the same, the crisis existed in both places. What Russia needed and what Stalin was trying to do was to 'spend a heroically high proportion of a fixed capital development', to sacrifice current consumption for future production; what the economist of today would call 'inter-temporal substitution'. Brailsford, Buxton and many of the other 'moral socialists' looked at the Russia of 1928 as a vision of victory over oppression. Strachey went further and said it was a new approach to wider problems of economics. Thus he felt able to shrug off the 'moral' as secondary. The truly great 'moral' problem of the next three to four years, what happened to the peasants, was early dealt with by Strachey as well. He saw them as the main obstacle to the new economic order (much as did Stalin and Trotsky) and was to start a whole tradition of explaining away the 'liquidation' of 'kulaks' as disfunctional to the sacred 'Smitchka' (the unity of workers and peasants).[14] Collectivisation and its horrors were still to come, but he had prepared the grounds for excusing it.

Others had attempted the difficult task of analysing these latter developments. Labour Party militant and trade unionist, Mark Starr, in a book review entitled 'Whither the Soviets' had commented: 'the easiest and safest thing to say about Soviet Russia is that it is an experiment about which an open mind must be kept, and from which a definite result will be expected later'.[15]

It is not difficult to find evidence of frustration and annoyance with the intellectuals among those who ran the real risk of political responsibility. In the immediate aftermath of the ARJAC break, in late 1927, Charles Roden Buxton, prominent member of the ACIQ, felt that he knew quite a lot about Russia – it was no 'enigma' to him. His 1920 comments were still of 'considerable value .... When people talk of sending further delegations to Russia, I wonder sometimes if they have ever realised the amount of knowledge which the party has already accumulated about Russia at great trouble and expense'. His findings are less important than the way he looked at them. He distrusted all the accoutrements of the intellectual, especially statistics: 'I base myself on casual observations of my own, and on the opinion of people whose judgement commended itself to me as likely to be solid'. A similar article by him in the *New Leader* none the less admitted that lack of knowledge about the USSR and Soviet ignorance about Britain was widespread. He bewailed, in a phrase later to be made famous by Churchill, the 'iron curtain' that falls 'when hostility is deliberately fostered by the Press on both sides, when prejudice grows and ignorance deepens in the absence of free intercourse and reciprocal knowledge'.[16] Buxton however joined Dalton in his condemnation of the Soviets for their part in encouraging this mutual ignorance far more than lauding their 'new civilisation', as did Strachey and others.

So even within the ranks of the 'intellectuals' there was some disagreement and some disquiet as to the implications of an overenthusiasm for the 'experiment'. C. R. de Gruchy, Strachey's deputy editor, seems to have been directly attacking his boss when he printed a review of three books by Wells, Shaw and Stalin. He acknowledged the need to examine the outside world, for only thus could the Labour Party intellectuals provide 'the new ideas and outlooks which we badly need'. But he found Wells 'futile, precious and snobbish' and Shaw even more absurd with his talk of Italy. As to Stalin's book, his model of Russia is of no use to British observers; 'Its scope is purely Russian ... Mr Stalin's book has roughly the same value as, say, a book by Herr Hilferding on the problems facing German Socialism; no more and no less'. The analogies were 'ill-considered'.[17] Strachey was clearly in a minority in his wholesale approval. Even the ILP had doubts, which will be examined in the next section, about internal Russian democracy.

The majority of the Labour Party would definitely have stressed in 1928 what Russia could learn from Britain as much as what Britain could learn from Russia. Lansbury wrote that:

> The Russian nation needs us, needs the benefit of our centuries of experience in cultural, national and municipal development. We need to get from them the inspiration of working in a conscious manner for a great ideal of national ownership and national administration. Above and over everything else, Russia, ourselves and the world need peace.[18]

After all, as he might have said, Lenin himself had studied the Webbs well before the Webbs came to study Lenin.

Russia as democracy or dictatorship?

A recurring theme of previous chapters has been the debate over the nature of Soviet democracy. It should be stressed that the crisis of Western democracy so widely perceived after 1929 as a result of the Wall Street crash and after 1931 in the Labour Party was not so present in 1928. Harold Laski, for example, in spite of what he wrote about Russia, still retained a firm belief in 'pluralism' until at least 1930.[19] The reflection of this chapter must not therefore be seen as essentially the same as that of the later period of the 1930s.

In 1927, as later, prominent members of the Labour Party NEC were often to be heard making speeches attacking non-democratic practices in the USSR. The deaths of socialist victims from fascist or bolshevik bullets often led to high-level expressions of bitterness and anger. At the unveiling of the Matteoti monument in 1927 the victims of both fascism and bolshevism were deplored by Henderson. Socialism, he said, stood for democracy and equality and the recent events in Italy, Russia and the United States (a reference to Sacco and Vanzetti) had shown the drawbacks of repression and violence. The door was left open, the door of good old British democracy, to show that other methods were possible.[20]

The particular bitterness of Henderson's remarks was undoubtedly due to the moment at which they were uttered – at the end of ARJAC but before the Russian Geneva proposals – but they are none the less indicative of deeply felt dismay. The vast majority of the British Labour movement outside the ranks of the CPGB rejected the idea of Soviet communism as a democratic structure, because it did not measure up to British standards.

However, Susan Lawrence, who was close to the leadership of the Labour Party in 1927–8 and who had formulated the two elements of the power struggle that she had seen in her 1924 visit to the USSR, was impressed by the Soviet Union in spite of reservations: 'A great experiment of socialism; and that is not a fact to be forgotten, however we may rightly deplore the want of liberty'.[21] On this point in 1927–8 nearly all in the Labour Party were in accord. The wave of explaining away excesses was in some ways only on the rise in 1927, to peak in or around 1936, although in different hands. What remains clear are the elements of differentiation based on different 'starting points' for Britain and Russia in the level of *initial democracy* and the way that this initial level was improved. Until the crises of the 1929 government there was little discussion of a decrease in the vitality of British democratic institutions, as had been shown by the Labour Party's rise to power and gradual evolution. Thus the perception of Russian democracy was one of regrettable aberrations that would disappear as Russia became one of the 'comity of nations' or, for Maxton, when it stopped being 'isolated from the socialist movements of the world'.

The first step in the late 1920s analysis, as later, was always one of observing what the internal political system was like and searching for metaphors that the Western reader could understand. A key question must be 'How was the Russian internal political system perceived?'

The Russian system of government was clearly a major factor in the theory of a 'new civilisation'. Both opponents and proponents or mere observers were of one mind that the way Russia was run was a new phenomenon, confusing for the average reader in the West. Some writers went to extravagant lengths to explain what it was like, the Americans being the worst. Ivy Lee, a 1927 visitor, described Stalin 'the man of steel' as 'the political boss of Russia.... The government of Russia is in some ways organised like that of New York City ... [Tammany Hall] ... Stalin, as the head of the Communist Party, is the 'Charlie Murphy' of Russia' etc. He was also 'the man to watch in Russia'.[22]

Brailsford's book, *How the Soviets Work*, also tried to put Russian practice into a British idiom and was written somewhat before the shock that he and others were to receive over the Voikov reprisals of early June 1927 (a shock which does not seem to have induced him to change the text for a second edition). Brailsford went to great lengths to explain that, in relative terms, Russia was a far better place than it had been before the 1917 revolution, the current 'dictatorship' portrayed as a necessary phase not a permanent reality. 'Fundamental change' necessitated the centralised power of the party, and 'would it be reasonable to expect of any party, which had done what this Russian party did in its first months and years of power, that it should jeopardise the very basis of the new system by risking elections, which might bring its adversaries to the helm and result in the undoing of all that it had achieved'. What in any case, he asked the British observer, does the average voter in the West have to decide upon: 'Whether a Zinoviev letter is a menace or a forgery?'[23] Indeed, he found real democracy at the factory level (one whole chapter on the subject) and in the party. Unfortunately for Brailsford, he used the example of Trotsky's opposition: 'An "opposition" exists within the party, which includes some of its ablest men. It may be wrong-headed [Trotsky's opposition]; it may represent no coherent view. But it is strong enough to force a thorough debate on every issue that emerges ... In short, the party lives, for it continues to combine democracy with discipline'.[24]

The explanation of this structure was couched in terms designed to appeal both to the hard-headed Labour Party and the TUC anti-intellectual. The workers were portrayed as being in total control of their factories and therefore of the state. Intellectuals indeed were frowned upon since they formed the bulk of the Socialist Revolutionary Party to which the 'Russian Social Democratic Party arose by way of intellectual reaction', with a 'steely resolution and a stern faith in their cause which often recall the temper of the Puritan Ironsides of the seventeenth century ... This party would hear of no shortcuts to Utopia'.[25] He explained later that the intellectual in Russia, so important in his revolutionary role, was rather superfluous now that the revolution has been achieved. For unlike in the West the intelligentsia's 'ideas do not percolate down to the mass ... [for] it enjoys no economic influence'. Liberals, he reiterated, have no place among vast 'fundamental changes'. The 'candid observer' who crops up throughout the work, must understand that this state of affairs, regrettable though it may have been, and limited as it probably would be, was none the less necessary for the time being and 'he will recognise that the Russian Communists are, by devious ways, attaining some of the advantages which democracy ensures'.[26]

Brailsford's early 1927 appeals to pragmatic latter-day puritan Ironsides of the TUC and the Labour Party leaderships clearly fell on some stony ground as E. T. Whitehead's article in the very official *Labour Magazine* shows. Whitehead had found no evidence of democracy in the Russian trade unions and, by extension none on the factory floor. Unimpressed by numbers, he claimed (rightly) that the Russian Communist would obey 'the dictates in his trade union work of the local Communist Party Committee'.[27]

Once the full extent of the Stalin purge of 1927 became evident, there grew up a genuine feeling of alarm, even among the ILP, up till now the greatest defender of the USSR. The Voikov reprisals shook Brailsford (*after* he wrote his book, as has been noted); they shocked the rest of the ILP as well. In fact, during 1928 Brailsford pulled back somewhat from the eulogistic accounts that he had expressed in *How the Soviets Work*. The stalinist 'revolution', so remarked upon by Strachey, seems to have rather reminded Brailsford of a step backward. Brockway even went so far as to boycott the tenth anniversary celebration (which Brailsford did not), a boycott which was closely remarked upon and approved of in the LSI. Stalin's defence of the imprisonment of large quantities of Social Democrats as 'counter-revolutionaries' was received by the ILP leadership with astonishment; perhaps thinking of their own attempted collaboration with the communists they commented: 'What is the use of talking about the united front when the Bolsheviks politely intimate that if it is successful those with whom they have cooperated will, as early as possible, be put in prison?'[28] In an attempt to squirm out of their own dilemma the ILP had to go to great lengths to justify this Soviet policy.

Hence the first news of Trotsky's and Zinoviev's expulsion from the Soviet Party was greeted cautiously. The sentence was seen as mild, analogous to the treatment of the CPGB and Minority Movement by the Labour Party. The ILP did not really like this either but they could just about accept that 'all parties and groups, if they so desire, have a perfect right to exclude from their fellowship those whose speech and action hamper the effective carrying out of a majority policy'. But at the same time the ILP felt the manner of Trotsky and Zinoviev's going was not quite fair play and would set a bad example for the right of the Labour Party, 'the bureaucrats of Eccleston Square' who wished to exclude anyone who did not agree with their opinion. The arrests were, in short, seen more in the ILP as a blow against the vital plurality of the Bolshevik Party in Russia, and direct parallels drawn with the campaign being waged by Citrine and Morrison in Britain. Trotsky and Zinoviev were even referred to as 'the left wing' and 'Minority Movement'[29] of Russia, persecuted, thought the ILP, as much for their ideas as for their actions.

The ILP increasingly allowed the 'democracy' debate to overwhelm that of interest in the 'new civilisation' during 1928. This rendered the whole debate incoherent for Strachey: 'Few of us, I would think , are in a position to form any judgement on this point', and he explicitly condemned others for so doing. A definite split had developed in ILP thinking. Strachey was almost alone in this in the columns of the *New Leader* and *Socialist Review*, but he reflected many other readers' beliefs. His main argument was that democracy was being raised to the level of a fetish.

Here he found powerful intellectual allies in 1928 (George Bernard Shaw and H. G. Wells), but both of them were on the fringes of the Labour Party, even if well known by most within it. Both of them, and particularly Shaw, were taken as commentators of interest, generally read and respected, but were felt to be too far removed from political reality to be really important.[30] But on this one subject of democracy they hit some very raw nerves in the British Labour movement.

However, Shaw went too far when he said that he understood why Mussolini had had to get rid of Matteoti. This statement met with a particular disgust from Adler, General Secretary of the LSI. The *Daily Herald's* comment, one that would have been shared by the left-wing critics of internal Labour Party repression such as the ILP, but equally by Henderson, in spite of his emotion over the killing of Matteoti, was that 'there is a world of difference between bolshevism and fascism'. Bolshevism, for all its faults, was on the right track, 'based on a theory not of Capitalism, private property, competition, but of Communism and co-operation'. The *Herald* hated the rule of dictators but was not prepared to accept that Russia had one like Italy. But there is an uncomfortable truth in Adler's comment that Shaw's attitude was 'dangerously near to the attitude of the British ruling class to "natives"'.[31]

In their urge to be as objective as possible there had to be a blurring of issues and a generous dose of optimism. They did not know very much about the phenomenon they were trying to analyse and the very object of their analysis was in continual flux so as to make things even more complicated.

Only the LSI had a definite view of what Russia represented within the Labour Party orbit and they were largely considered as slightly excessive in their judgements even by the leadership. The great 'voyages of discovery' to Russia for the Labour Party were in many ways yet to come, especially after 1930. The impetus for inquiry already existed but was only at a primitive stage. Impassioned debate and emotional discourse was still rare. When domestic issues were touched the debate could get quite hot, but never dramatically so.

But most of the seeds of the attitudes of future travellers and observers had been sown by the end of 1928. The industrialisation of Russia had been noted, if little understood, the social innovations examined, if not too closely, and the beginnings of a disquiet over persecution born, if not too vehemently. To push these negative and positive feelings into greater clarity a domestic British crisis was necessary, that was provided by the 1929–31 Labour Government and its awful end.

Notes

1 C. R. De Gruchy, assistant editor of the *Socialist Review* until 1930 when he became editor after John Strachey left, was writing a review of Dalton's 'Towards the Peace of Nations' in the April 1928 edition of the Review. He went on to comment: 'Mr Dalton has been to Geneva, hence the present book'.

2 WELLOCK, Wilfred, 'Soviet Russia Today', *Socialist Review*, January 1928, pp. 23–30, p. 23.

3 Wellock went even further on this thesis of the incomprehensibility of Russia in a November 1928 article in *Socialist Review* entitled 'On the Need for a Balanced View of

Russia': 'It is impossible for any unbiased observer, whatever be his political views, to step into present-day Russia without at once realising that he is in the presence of something new - an atmosphere, a spirit, and methods of carrying through every-day transactions that are strikingly unfamiliar .... One is confronted with changes so colossal that one falls back bewildered. Thus of it one can truly say: "The first time in history".' (p. 31).

4 JOAD, C. E. M. 'Fears and Hopes', *Socialist Review*, February 1928, pp. 14–23. He gave this talk to a No More War Movement rally, an organisation given the backing of the Labour Party.

5 MAXTON, James, 'Labour and Russia', *New Leader*, 4 November 1927.

6 British Workers' Delegation Report, *Soviet Russia Today*, London, Twentieth Century Press, December 1927.

7 BUXTON, Dorothy F., *The Challenge of Bolshevism*, London, Allen and Unwin, 1928.

8 J. W. Brown in *Daily Herald*, 28 July 1928 and 'A Quaker on Communists', *Socialist Review*, August 1928.

9 Cf. BRAILSFORD, 'Ten Years of Soviet Rule', *Daily Herald*, 7 November 1927 and STRACHEY, 'Russia: The Next Ten Years', *New Leader*, 2 March 1928.

10 STRACHEY, John, 'Russia: The Next Ten Years: I - Stalin and the New Leadership', *New Leader*, 4 March 1928.

11 STRACHEY, John, 'Russia: The Next Ten Years: II - Her Economic Difficulties', *New Leader*, 9 March 1928 and 'III - The Peasant Question and Smitchka', *New Leader*, 18 March 1928.

12 For their relationship see SKIDELSKY, Robert, *Oswald Mosley*, London, Macmillan, 1975.

13 Liberal Industrial Inquiry, *Britain's Industrial Future*, London, Ernest Benn, 1928, p. 268.

14 See his subsequent article 'The Peasant Question and "Smitchka"', *New Leader*, 16 March 1928.

15 STARR, Mark, 'Whither the Soviets', *New Leader*, 10 February 1928.

16 BUXTON, C. R., 'Russia 1920–1927: A Comparison', *Labour Magazine*, November 1927 and 'Behind Russia's Curtain', *New Leader*, 21 October 1927.

17 Cf. *Socialist Review*, August 1928, pp. 14–15.

18 LANSBURY, G., 'A Tragedy of Errors', *New Leader*, 16 September 1927. Already cited above.

19 See DEANE, Herbert A., *The Political Ideas of Harold J. Laski*, New York, Columbia University Press, 1955.

20 Henderson at LSI meeting, *Daily Herald*, 12 September 1927.

21 Susan Lawrence in an article in the *Birmingham Town Crier*, 3 October 1924.

22 LEE, Ivy, *Present Day Russia*, New York, Macmillan and Co., 1928, p. 99.

23 BRAILSFORD, H. N., *How the Soviets Work*, Vanguard Press, New York, 1927, pp. 142–7.

24 Ibid., pp. 127–8. As to elections, '"Election" may be the only name for these singular formalities which the dictionary allows. The Russian language has its idiosyncracies' (p. 31).

25 Ibid., p. 115.

26 Ibid., pp. 145–8.

27 WHITEHEAD, E. T., 'The Problem of the Russian Trade Unions', *Labour Magazine*, August 1928, p. 157.

28 'Stalin's Reply', *New Leader*, editorial of 18 November 1927.

29 'Trotsky and Zinoviev', *New Leader*, editorial of 18 November 1927.

30 A typical comment was that made by Gerald Gould in the *Daily Herald* of 26 November 1927: 'It is easy to see how good and wise men like Wells and Shaw are led astray into believing that there is, or can be, a short cut'. The tone is slightly patronising but respectful.

31 *Daily Herald*, editorial, 13 October 1927, and front page story.

chapter six

Russia and the Labour Party during the 1929 election

Russia in the general context of the 1929–31 government

The disasters that befell both Britain and the Labour Party during the years of its second attempt at power (1929–31) has led many writers to try and explain the reasons for these disasters.[1] The aim here is primarily to show in some detail the links between domestic problems, especially the economic ones, and the 'Russian element', both as an 'exemplar' and as a possible palliative for British problems.

In some ways it becomes even more difficult in 1929–31 to divide Russia into a 'domestic' and 'foreign' problem and focus of interest. The year 1929 marks a watershed for both the Soviet Union and the British Labour Party. The latter was given its first real attempt at government, if we accept that the conditions of 1924 had not allowed the Labour Party a free hand. Soviet Russia embarked on a new and dramatic phase in its revolution. A prominent commentator later remarked (in 1934) that a book he had published in 1929 on the Soviet Union seemed five years later to be of 'purely historical value' for since 1929 'the whole quality of Soviet life has been transformed'.[2]

The Five Year Plan and collectivisation had barely begun, and the power struggle for political dominance in the USSR had only just ended (and its later ramifications were not even imagined). In Britain the problems of a chronically ill economy had not yet defeated the credibility of long-held truths, and the 'great betrayal' had not yet happened. This made the Labour Party's attitudes at all levels significantly different pre-circa 1930 and after this date.

Britain's economic problem and the 'Russian trade card'

The 1929 election has been described by Skidelsky as the 'major missed opportunity of the inter-war period'.[3] There is much justification for this view, because a major new approach to Britain's continuing problems of de-industrialisation and its attendant unemployment was overlooked by the British electorate. The Liberal 'industrial report' of 1928 proposed a major new approach to government intervention in the economy, one that was not far removed from Mosley and Strachey's 'Birmingham proposals' (also known as 'Revolution by Reason') of 1925. Keynes was one of the co-authors of the Liberal report.

Recent research seems to confirm Skidelsky's point in that the Conservatives under Baldwin appear to have been rather worried by the liberal challenge to their orthodox 'safety first' doctrines, but not necessarily for the same reasons.[4] The Liberal proposals were not taken seriously, except by Baldwin, even when Lloyd George promised to 'conquer unemployment' in a speech of 1 March 1929. But Lloyd George's statement was seen as the kind of reckless promise that might just bring down a government, unless the Conservatives simply refused to engage in battle, which is what they did. Hence the slogan of the election chosen by Conservative Central Office: 'Safety First'.

The alternative to 'Safety First' and the Conservatives was therefore a radical Liberal Party which advocated dramatic new economic policies. Skidelsky demonstrates that the Labour Party had very little idea about how to tackle unemployment in a radical way, having rejected ILP 'socialist' alternatives. He explains this by saying that the Labour Party was a 'parliamentary party with a Utopian ethic. It was not fit for the kind of power it was called upon to exercise'.[5] If such is the case, neither, by his own token, was the Conservative Party, whose policies so resembled Labour's in practice, if not in theory. It goes without saying that the debate on the required economic policy when faced with a major depression is far from settled. It is clear that the key issue of the 1929 election was unemployment and that it continued to be the main issue of British politics until the storm clouds on the international scene brought renewed fears of war. A measure of the power of this single issue lies in the formation of Mosley's New Party in 1930 and the Labour Party/ILP split of 1932.

Stimulation of the internal economy by the external boosting of trade had long been (with minor exceptions) the English way of creating prosperity and especially of increasing employment, the major aim of the new Labour Government. But unfortunately MacDonald's Britain had not the same dominant world trading position as had the Britain of Palmerston or even that of Lloyd George. Britain had been in relative decline since the 1870s compared with its continental rivals, and its attempts to increase a flagging share of new world markets was by no means assured. Its industry was archaic and structured better to suit the nineteenth than the twentieth century. Many of these problems and contradictions were to see their most devastating effects during 1929–31.[6] Of the new markets, Russia had been touted throughout the 1920s by all sections of political and business opinion as the one most likely to prove of worth. Until 1928 this new prize for the British buccaneers of industry had seemed a modest one, and Baldwin did not suffer too greatly by his boycott of Russian trade. However, reports of the crock of gold at the end of the Russian trade rainbow evidently were numerous enough to provoke intense official discussion.[7]

New developments in Russia made this non-committal stance increasingly difficult for even a diehard anti-bolshevik administration to sustain. For the Labour Party it tipped the balance firmly in favour of a renewed relationship with Russia. The Labour Party leadership was openly linking trade with Russia and the pursuit of peace (see Chapter 4). This was essentially a continuation of its policy of 1924, when the MacDonald Government had clearly seen trade as the major benefit of contact with Russia, along with the correlated 'civilisation through trade' feeling held by even those who totally disagreed with domestic Soviet policies.

Labour MPs such as Wilfred Wellock spoke for many backbenchers of his party when he wrote in November 1928 'No government with any regard for fruitful cooperation and healthy trade could avoid making a serious endeavour to establish mutually advantageous trading relations with Russia'.[8] Naturally the Conservatives too appreciated that trade would also help Russia, as Strachey and others pointed out.

By early 1929 official figures were drawing a moral that was not lost on either side of the House of Commons. Britain had dropped from first partner in 1924 to third partner with the USSR in terms of its export trade, and drastically so, largely to the benefit of Germany.[9] During the build-up to the election, this manifest sacrifice of British jobs at the altar of ideological Tory purity was a major factor in presenting the Labour Party as a pragmatic and sensible alternative to a tired, unimaginative Baldwin Government. MacDonald and the leadership pursued a campaign in which they carefully stressed commercial contact with Russia while also stressing the Labour Party's alienation from all things communist or 'extreme'. The Liberals, meanwhile, were portrayed as 'Tweedledum' to the Tory 'Tweedledee'.[10]

Frank Wise MP was able to present the reduction of trade as 'sheer madness' both for economic and political reasons.[11] The argument used by Wise and others was always that *diplomatic* recognition of the USSR by Britain was a necessary corollary of better trading relations. It should be said that both sides produced figures to prove their case, but that the truth of the argument was buried beneath the quicksands of faith. It must be explained why MacDonald and the NEC of the Labour Party were to put so much emphasis on the benefits of Russian trade for British recovery. After all, the evidence for it being a universal panacea was pretty thin.

The reason seems to have been a mixture of rank-and-file pressure and the chance happening of a major corroboration of Wise's views from an unexpected and eminently respectable source. This source – one that must have been of great embarrassment to Baldwin – was the visit, in early 1929, of a powerful group of British industrialists, mainly from the depressed north, that relied extensively on exports for its industrial survival.

This reasoning was in fact widely accepted by early 1929, and the *Daily Herald* could therefore feel free to unleash a veritable campaign in support of increased Russian trade without much fear of being daubed with any bolshevik brush. What was more, the leadership could give this campaign its full approval and support in the knowledge that no major section of moderate or even most of the diehard opinion would stand out against it. As long, that is, as the discussions were confined to financial and commercial matters where, since the revolution, there had been no complaints about Russian perfidy. But it must have been clear to the Labour Party leadership that such an ideal relationship with Russia was not going to be easy to achieve or maintain.

What is perhaps most surprising about this is the sight of the Labour Party defending big business against the Conservative Party. MacDonald presented himself as the defender of 'British engineering and other manufacturing concerns', the only flash of socialism being in an attack on 'banking and financial considerations' (there being no such creatures in the delegation that was going to Russia). One important proviso was included, persumably to mollify the City, the assurance that no loans would be accorded to the Soviet Union: 'Actually the Labour Party does not stand, and never has stood, for any such thing', a rather extreme bending of the record.[12]

How can such behaviour be explained? The most obvious reason was the desire by MacDonald to win the election. He was still haunted by the 'Red Letter' election of 1924, and wanted it to be quite clear that any involvement with the USSR was for purely pragmatic reasons. This conviction he undoubtedly succeeded in conveying. He also wanted no doubt to be left that he was none the less set on re-establishing relations with the USSR on his own terms. These terms, he made clear, included an agreement on political questions, both domestic and within the Empire. Hence, a 'linkage' was established for the benefit of the electorate and the Russians from the outset of the campaign.

The political and industrial side

The NEC of the Labour Party was convinced that the Tories were going to attempt another 'stunt' as in 1924, since virtually no one in the party believed that the Zinoviev letter had been genuine, and even those that did were convinced that its 'discovery' was a crude electoral ploy mounted by the Tory diehards. A perfect document did in fact exist, in the Leeds convention of May 1917, 'To Follow Russia', signed by many of the Labour leadership, including MacDonald and Snowden. Labour Party headquarters informed its candidates 'that the Tory Party may be impelled, before the poll, to issue garbled accounts of the Convention'.[13]

During the election campaign MacDonald was sent several letters reminding him of the painful side of contact with Russia as well as the positive gains that might be had. A major landowner in his constituency of Seaham, Lord Londonderry, reminded him in April that there was even communist subversion among the miners during an ongoing strike in Durham, aided and abetted, it was implied, by 'the left wing in your party'. Londonderry attempted to turn the knife a few days later with 'I think you will agree that it is a pity that the Communists, aided by money from Moscow, are subsidising your men to be idle'.[14]

Another letter highlighted another major possible source of embarrassment for a future Labour Government: a letter passed to MacDonald by Ponsonby, who clearly wanted the Foreign Secretaryship after his thankless task in dealing with Russia in 1924. This related how Ponsonby had investigated a report from *The Times* correspondent in Cairo about a 'bolshevik plot'. The activities of the Third International in the Empire might have been weakened by 1929, but were far more potentially dangerous than the CPGB within Britain. Ponsonby's source reassured him that the story emanated from a source within the 'European Department Ministry of the Interior' (sic) and '[no] doubt the publication of news about a Bolshevik plot in the British press will have influence on the British elections'.[15] Such letters probably did much to stimulate MacDonald's conservatism and persuade him to stress Labour's opposition to political influence from Russia.

It is, of course, impossible to ascertain whether such rumours were at all founded on reality. The Leeds Convention document was indeed used by Labour opponents, but at the 1931 election, and by the 'British Empire Union'.[16] That whole election was marked by a far more tense atmosphere and considerable bitterness on all sides. In contrast, the 1929 election was marked more by apathy, the kind of campaign where 'good riddance to bad rubbish'[17] was the strongest insult bandied about by Labour, and the epithet 'socialist' by the Tories.

The net result of such scares was to force MacDonald into making a clear definition of the Labor Party's policy towards the Soviet Union. A letter that his personal secretary, and perhaps closest confidante, Rose Rosenberg, wrote to an important inquiry sums up this policy with the greatest simplicity and clarity, a clarity that MacDonald seemed curiously loth to use most of the time. The letter reads:

> He [MacDonald] is determined – if the chance be given him at the next election – to tackle the problem of Soviet Russia both on its political and its industrial side. He thinks it is both a disgrace and a folly for those responsible for the government of this country to pretend that Russia does not exist. They are only throwing it into the hands of its most dangerous extremists, creating tremendous world problems (especially in the East), and depriving British workmen and capital of sources of income which, in the national interests, should be open to them.[18]

Thus on the industrial side of domestic policy Russia was a card MacDonald had to play. But on the other hand he could not allow this card to introduce the 'joker' of political interference by the USSR within Britain by the CPGB or of the Comintern in the Empire. Equally, on the foreign policy side the letter reiterated the long-held MacDonald and Labour leadership belief that the 'moderates' in the USSR must be encouraged, rather more with the carrot than with the stick.

The first point in the Labour Party's electoral arsenal was that the Russians were essentially replying to Tory provocation. The Conservatives, according to this line, had fired the worst, if not the first, shots with the false 'Red Letter', the ARCOS fiasco and the suspension of diplomatic relations. Russian dissatisfaction had then been demonstrated partly by releasing the minor irritant of the CPGB, but mainly by doing far more trade with Germany and less with Britain.

The second point used by the Labour Party was to minimise the importance of the Communist Party's activities, which were almost exclusively of the rowdy speech variety. The *Labour Speakers Handbook for 1929* therefore issued a blanket recommendation that both minimised the danger and suggested a simple remedy. Once again it was an eminent businessman whose words were used to justify such an attitude, one that reiterated the linkage with trade: 'In any trade agreement . . . we should leave out any reference to subversive propaganda by the Soviet on the workmen and institutions of this country and leave this to Scotland Yard to look after'.[19]

Was it possible to do the same with propaganda directed to British interests outside Britain, notably in the Empire? The Conservatives were particularly able to point to Comintern activities in China and India, to which a whole section was devoted in their *Election Notes 1929*. But they also had to admit that such activities were 'illegitimate' in the very words of James Ramsay MacDonald, and could not find a single instance of a Labour Party leader expressing support for such activities.[20]

The Conservatives were on fairly shaky ground about China in a recent period, since the trouble there seemed to have died down, at least that caused by Communists. British intervention in Shanghai had not been particularly popular, for there was no desire to get involved in another war about anything at all, and dwelling on such a subject gave the Labour speaker an ideal chance to say that it was the Conservative Party that were the war-mongers in that theatre. In the Far East, Russia had largely succeeded in making itself look like the victim of aggression, particularly from the Japanese.

India was more difficult. Here it was the ILP that had been giving MacDonald his most uncomfortable moments. Comintern activities had been publicised through two channels, the early 'Front' organisations and an increasingly famous legal case in Meerut. Luckily for MacDonald this case, where a large group of Indian and a few British citizens had been arrested for crimes of subversion on 29 March 1929 did not really attract attention until after the election, in June 1929, when a 'Meerut Prisoners Committee' was set up. The first letters that were received by Transport House arrived in April 1929, a month before the election. International Secretary, William Gillies, merely acknowledged the 'protests against the action of terrorism which is being used by the government against the Indian workers'. To other inquirers Gillies replied that there were other facts in the case that 'are not commonly understood', the main one being that 'all the arrested men were communists'.[21] But there is evidence of extremely high-level concern in the Labour movement that the Communists could use the Meerut case to damage other aspects of Labour Party support,[22] especially among the growing section of the community that wanted freer government in India, a principle that was conceded partially in the Simon Report of 1930.

This was reinforced by the source of one complaint that had been received by Walter Citrine, which came from the League against Imperialism. Such organisations had long been condemned by the LSI as Communist Front organisations, feelings shared by Citrine and Gillies and most of the Labour Party leadership. Although the attacks on such organisations by the Labour Party, usually through Gillies himself, were to really only fully develop after spring 1930, there was already an unofficial policy of non-communication before May 1929. This became systematic during the latter part of the year, when Gillies took to marking on letters from communists 'Communist. No reply', even when the correspondent was writing in another capacity, as a trade union or trades council official, for example.[23]

Understandable as this policy may or may not appear, it was pursued for electoral reasons before May 1929. But one unanswered and crucial question is how such an attitude towards communists could be squared with dealing with, and wanting closer ties with, the USSR. The answer lies in essentially the same line of reasoning that had been used by Labour Party commentators over the previous period. The USSR, it should be remembered, was divided, in the MacDonald leadership's mind at least, into 'moderates' and 'extremists', with Stalin as a moderate and Trotsky and Zinoviev as extremists.

Stalin had shown himself a moderate by his action against the extremists, and hence the expulsion of Trotsky was followed with almost manic glee in the columns of the *Daily Herald* as he made his sorry progress to exile. Of Stalin himself, precious little was really known in early 1929, but the *Herald* could note that he was far more interested in building up Russia on the inside than on the outside, which was essentially the case. Not much speculation was allowed or suggested in the Labour press of what he intended to use this power for, but a lot of emphasis was put on the logical and rational nature of the changes being implemented. Since one of the major changes was the purge of the trotskyites, an argument was often suggested that Stalin was doing to his party what the Labour Party was doing to its communists. The Communist Party and the Communist International on one side and the Soviet Goverment on the other, were therefore clearly separated.

However, since so little was known about Stalin, a careful distance was taken from his methods of operation. Bolshevism was continually condemned for that most heinous of Labour Party crimes, being 'anti-democratic', but a tacit exception seems to have been made for Stalin's treatment of the Trotsky group. 'Fascist Blackshirts and Bolshevik Redshirts are both detestable to the democrats of the Labour Party',[24] said the strongest (and more pre-electoral) of official Labour Party texts.

The emphasis throughout was not one of showing 'moral solidarity' with bolshevism, but of contact with the Russian Government, who could not be treated in the same way or dealt with as were the 'amateur revolutionaries of the CPGB', wrote Morrison.[25]

The likely future of Anglo-Soviet relations as presented by Labour

So how would a Labour Party fare where the Conservatives had not? This was the ultimate question that tied together the whole Labour Party campaign on 'Russian linked' questions.

Sufficient stress has already been put on the hoped-for benefits from trade with Russia as a way of improving production and employment prospects. Since trade improvements were the only way that anyone, except Keynes and the Liberal Industrial Report group or certain sectors of the ILP, could see for improving employment prospects, trade with Russia was primordial to Labour's election platform.

The other half of the 1928 manifesto, apart from calls for more employment, was for a world at peace. The Labour Party was able to point to the position of Russia in the two key areas of tension, Eastern Europe and the Far East. In both these areas it was a quasi-fascist regime that seemed to be acting the mostly aggressively, Poland in Europe (with a little help from the Baltic states) and Japan in Asia. The only threat from a Soviet organisation to international tensions, the Comintern, was being reduced in importance. Propaganda, it could be hoped, might become a thing of the past in dealing with a more sensible USSR. All that was required for all this wishful thinking to come true was encouraging noises from the Russians themselves. These did not tarry in arriving.

On the subjects of trade, peace and even more delicate matters, they made several statements that could be read as promising. The Russians only made one distinct precondition, one that the Labour Party was perfectly willing to grant, that of diplomatic relations being speedily re-established. MacDonald was able to quote the speech of Mr Piatakov, President of the Russian State Bank, whose words to the British business delegation had aroused 'widespread interest ... in London political and business circles'. He promised 'orders to the value of £150,000,000 to £200,000,000 on the condition of a resumption of normal diplomatic relations'.[26] Diplomatic relations would thus lead to an increase in trade and a 'clearing [of] the air'.[27] Such minor details as the need for a loan to Russia were largely ignored in the desire to believe in Russian goodwill.

Pravda announced Labour's victory in the polls well before it happened: 'the presence of the British delegation in Moscow is evidence of Labour's victory, which will lead to a revival of Anglo-Russian trade and help to reduce the number of unemployed in England'.[28]

As to the prospects for peace, the Russians were equally obliging with their confrontation of MacDonald's remarks, or so it appeared in the columns of the *Daily Herald*. The culminating point in the whole campaign came in a speech by MacDonald to his faithful in the Albert Hall in which he linked Russia, employment and peace in as clear a way as could have been possible. To knock the point home the *Daily Herald's* editorial made the same linkage as MacDonald: 'a primary essential of trade revival is real peace between the nations. To that end Mr MacDonald declared, without equivocation, in favour of an immediate return to diplomatic relations with Russia', even if this 'is only part of a wider international necessity'.[29]

Notes

1 SKIDELSKY, Robert, *Politicans and the Slump: the Labour Government of 1929–31*, London, Macmillian, 1967, is the best summary. For a discussion of the 1930s, see HOWKINS, Alan and SAVILLE, John, 'The Nineteen Thirties: A Revisionist History', *The Socialist Register*, London, Merlin Press, 1979, pp. 89–100.

2 CHAMBERLIN, William Henry, *Russia's Iron Age*, Boston, Little, Brown and Co., 1934, p. (viii) and p. 3.

3 SKIDELSKY, *Politicians and the Slump*, p. (xii).

4 WILLIAMSON, Philip, 'Safety First: Baldwin, the Conservative Party and the 1929 General Election' in *The Historical Journal*, vol. 25, no. 2, 1982, pp. 385–409.

5 SKIDELSKY, *Politicians and the Slump*, p. (xii).

6 The literature on this is, of course, vast. One useful summary can be found in Sidney POLLARD's *The Development of the British Economy, 1914–1980*, third edition, London, Arnold, 1983.

7 e.g. a discussion about German credits to Russia in 1927; B.D. IA/IV, No.71. Chamberlain to Lindsay, 29 November 1927.

8 WELLOCK, Wilfred, MP, 'On the Need for a Balanced View of Russia', *Socialist Review*, November 1928.

9 The figures given by the *Daily Herald* of 11 January 1929 were Great Britain (exports to USSR) £9,700,000 in 1926–7; £4,500,000 in 1927–8. In the latter year Germany had exported £24,000,000 and the USA £18,000,000. Source: Board of Trade.

10 For example, *Daily Herald*, 22 May 1929.

11 WISE, E. F., 'The Anglo-Russian Trade Agreement of 1921', *Soviet Union Monthly*, 15 July 1926 and W. & Z. COATES, *Why Anglo-Soviet Diplomatic Relations should be Restored*, Anglo-Russian Parliamentary Committe Nov. 1928.

12 MacDonald in an interview entitled 'Russian Orders and British Goods', *Daily Herald*, 9 April 1929.

13 'For the Information of Labour Candidates', leaflet attached to *Notes for Speakers*, limited distribution, Labour Party 1929.

14 Londonderry to MacDonald, 23 April and 25 April 1928, MacDonald Papers in PRO

30/69/1174 (Party Correspondence: 1929, Foreign and Domestic).
15 Hamed Mahumud to Lord Ponsonby, 8 May 1929. Copy to MacDonald.
16 See copy of B.E.U. facsimile in Labour Party Archives, 'Election Files'.
17 *Daily Herald*, 11 May 1929.
18 Rose Rosenberg to A. Ash, 16 April 1929. MacDonald Papers, PRO 30/69/1174.
19 *Labour Speakers Handbook 1929*, pp. 175–80. H. E. Metcalf in *Manchester Guardian*, 16 February 1929 is quoted here.
20 Conservative Party Election Notes 1929, p. 322.
21 Watford Divisional Labour Party to William Gillies, 17 April 1929. Reply of 24 April 1929 and other replies. 'India Overseas Correspondence', Labour Party Archives.
22 T. F. Richards (General President of the National Union of Boot and Shoe Operatives) to Middleton, 16 March 1929. Answered by Gillies (no date) and Citrine to Henderson, 16 May 1929. Replied to (probably by Gillies, but over Henderson's signature) on 22 May 1929, 'India Overseas Correspondence', Labour Party Archives.
23 This will be described in some detail in Ch. 8.
24 'Blackshirts and redshirts', 'Notes for Speakers', 22 May 1929, published Labour Party, Noel-Baker Papers, NBKR/4/63. This is by far the strongest language I have come across in this pre-election period.
25 Morrison in *Daily Herald*, 15 May 1929.
26 'Russian Orders and British Goods', *Daily Herald*, 9 April 1929.
27 Interview with MacDonald, *Daily Herald*, 9 April 1929.
28 *Pravda* comment report in *Daily Herald*, 9 April 1929.
29 MacDonald speaking in the Albert Hall, reported in the *Daily Herald* of 29 April 1929.

chapter seven

The Russian element in the Labour Government's politics June – December 1929

Restoration of relations: but how and when?

MacDonald now saw for the first time the reports of the Anglo-Russian Delegation of 'big business' that had figured so strongly in the electoral campaign. The key passage of the discussion lay in the solving of 'political difficulties', with Litvinov specifically mentioning 'Far Eastern matters', and diplomatic recognition of Russia by Britain. The delegates had clearly been impressed, and talked of the likelihood of orders in the range of £150-200 million.

Foreign Office officials were not so positive agreeing only with the link between trade and renewed diplomatic relations. The other points suggested by the businessmen – on debts being soluable, the effective provision of guarantees on propaganda and the findings of the necessary credit facilities to pay for these exports to Russia – were largely rejected as unrealistic and as 'hardly appear[ing] justified'. The five-year plan, it was pointed out, allowed for the total of all foreign trade with the USSR not to be increased by more than £200 million in the five-year period. In any case, credits would not be forthcoming until the debt problem was solved. These remarks were endorsed by a handwritten comment from MacDonald's then PPS, Sir Robert Vansittart. The latter announced that he proposed sending the report to the Foreign Office, so that Henderson would see the negative comments.[1] His future actions show that the Foreign Secretary largely agreed.

It is difficult to know exactly what impact the demolition of such a report had on MacDonald, but it is known that the proposed previous timetable for re-establishing relations was now considerably modified. A diary entry by Dalton, by now Under-Secretary of State at the Foreign Office, tells all about Henderson's feelings at this juncture:

> As to Russia there is no question of recognition. That endures since 1924. One problem is the method of resumption of diplomatic relations. Ewer and other pro-Bolshies [i.e. Labour MPs] say nothing short of an immediate exchange of ambassadors will soothe Soviet pride, suspicion and inferiority complex. Uncle [Henderson] is not prepared for this. He proposes an invitation to Moscow to send a special representative to discuss all questions in dispute. If they refuse he will have no hesitation in telling Parliament so.[2]

The pro-Russian Labour Party parliamentary lobby, Ewer and Wise, believed they could help to maintain the impetus for Russian trade built up during the past six months. Ewer – even though he was Foreign Editor of the *Daily Herald* – was a great political naive, in the sense that he did not understand the way such negotiations should be conducted and concerted. Dalton was furious at his efforts 'to settle the Russian Government for us', which he had done right over Henderson's head to 'his Russian friends in Paris' – presumably Russian Ambassador Dovgalevsky. As Dalton pointed out in the privacy of his dairy: 'He has probably done more harm than good, having aroused suspicions as to our intentions and expectations *and* his ability to interpret, or even to modify them ... He is a tiresome busybody'.

E. F. Wise had a professional interest as advisor to Russian trading organisation Centrosoyuz in the UK, but his actions were no more appreciated than those of Ewer. He also was 'busy-bodying' although at least this was 'to be expected'. Wise had a whole series of suggestions, all of which reflected his belief that the restoration of relations and the extension of trade was imminent. Wise's main suggestion was that Russia should be granted adequate trade facilities (that is, export credits) and that the Russians should be put directly in contact with the City, bypassing the Foreign Office.[3] Such unofficial intervention by Labour Party backbenchers was to plague Henderson and Dalton throughout the proceedings and probably slowed them up. The fact was that the 'political and the industrial sides', as MacDonald had called them in April 1929, were proving to be inextricable.

From King's speech to recognition: July 1929 to December 1929

Delay and guarantees

The Russians had clearly sent the message that the first step of any new Anglo-Soviet relationship should be the restoration of diplomatic relations. The King's speech, one of the shortest on record, promised them this in a penultimate paragraph dealing with the USSR: 'My Government are examining the conditions under which diplomatic relations with the Government of the Union of Soviet Socialist Republics may be resumed and are in communication with My Governments in the Dominions and the Government of India on the subject'.[4] The King's distaste for the Soviet regime was well known, so to make him say such words was a great trial. Various drafts were considered by both Cabinet and monarch.[5]

The rank and file of the party could have been forgiven for thinking that relations would be far more rapidly re-established. Even the *Daily Herald*, which acted throughout this period as the voice of patience, had leaked its interpretation of what the King's speech would contain on Russia the day before the speech: 'On Russia it is known that the Government intends, at the earliest possible moment, to resume full diplomatic and trading relations with that country. And here again ... some of the preliminary steps have already been taken'.[6] Two days later, after the speech, the *Herald* had to plead for patience, and hopefully suggest that 'unemployment and world peace were the dominant notes of the first meeting [of Parliament]'. Maxton and Wallhead, our 'ILP hotheads', were 'not enthusiastic' and especially not about the reference to Russia which was 'extremely vague, in the light of the definite pledges made by every member of the Labour Party during the election'.[7]

MacDonald clearly thought he had good reason to delay, and the rest of the Cabinet with him. Guarantees had first to be obtained. The Russians were particularly to be informed that they could not hide behind the excuse of the Comintern not being under the control of the Soviet Government. The Labour Party wanted trade, trade that the Cabinet at least now realised was likely to be far less than anticipated, but the *quid pro quo* of this lessened trade must be even less Soviet propaganda. As Lammers says, MacDonald and the Cabinet also had to continue 'the carefully constructed image of British Labour as a hard-headed party definitely capable of keeping Communism at arm's length'.[8] Reduced expectations of benefit and the desire to maintain a minority government in office with the minimum fuss therefore prompted a cautious attitude.

The 'undertaking' of 15 July 1929 and pressure from the Labour backbenches

There were 'vigorous protests' by Labour MPs to MacDonald's 15 July undertaking not to formally resume relations without the approval of Parliament. Henderson protested that even he and the Cabinet had not been consulted about this decision. This was no doubt due to MacDonald's excessive worry about what his Liberal allies and

Conservative opponents might do should such a consultative precaution with Parliament not be taken, but it was not lost on his Labour Party colleagues that their views seemed to come last. It was, as Carlton says, 'somewhat inept' of MacDonald,[9] even if the result was to make Moscow realise that the new government would not be a 'push-over' in negotiations. The domestic Labour Party effect was to make any move by the government suspect where Russia was concerned and to give ammunition to the very 'disruptive [and especially ILP] elements' that MacDonald wanted to discourage, without any corresponding reciprocal understanding from the diehard Tories who used Russia against MacDonald on every possible occasion.

MacDonald's vacillation was all the more strange since it had already (by 10 July) been decided to make official contact through the Norwegian Government. Dalton reveals that other events were threatening to turn the whole enterprise into comic opera. The Dominions were dragging their feet about their commitment to the Russian *pourparlers* but Dalton felt that 'we need not take too much notice of those'. On the other hand he could not get rid of Wise, who continued to put pressure on Henderson to speed up the resumption of relations, spending his days at the Foreign Office and his nights in 'Uncle's room'. Dalton's view of Wise's reliability was 'he's alright if you *want* him to leak to the Russians . . . but not otherwise'. The message that Henderson wanted transmitted to Moscow was one of continuing genuine interest in diplomatic and trading contacts, but *only* if there was agreement on propaganda. Until then 'we have let a little grass grow here', to put it in Dalton's words.[10]

In the event, rumours of Wise's antics clearly reached the ears of some Conservatives and it was at this point that MacDonald made a speech undertaking not to resume relations without Parliament's approval. It is likely that he panicked in the heat of cross-questioning in the Commons, perhaps after a word with Henderson that the 'rumours' were true. Although Dalton was as usual scathing about MacDonald's attitude, the ghost of 1924 had undoubtedly whispered in MacDonald's ear at the crucial moment, a frisson Dalton could not possibly imagine. Henderson reminded Dalton of this three days later, when he said 'Russia has brought us down once. We can't afford to let it happen twice'.[11] MacDonald nevertheless immediately realised his own mistake and wanted to retract the undertaking, a course he was discouraged from since it would have suggested total confusion.

The episode augured very badly for the future, if only because feelings now ran very high. MacDonald felt aggrieved, even if it was largely his own fault. Henderson had been overruled and not informed on a matter that was entirely his business. Wise was rushing around Europe with the vaguest of mandates that he had practically forced on Henderson. Much of this was undoubtedly the result of inexperience in government generally; 'terribly like bad staff work in the war' in Dalton's words. But it could not be ignored that it was Russia that was at the root of this first crisis. It made everyone even more wary, like Henderson and MacDonald, or more intransigent in their insistence for relations, like Wise and a great many other backbenchers and trade unionists.[12]

First contacts

Wise's travels coincided with the sending of a note to the Soviet Government via the Norwegian Government on 17 July.[13] Much to general surprise, the Russians accepted to talk on the basis of an invitation to negotiate 'outstanding questions' before the actual resumption of relations. The receipt of this acceptance of 24 July was the first real sign of tangible success in the midst of a sea of criticism.

Dalton could only explain it by saying: 'This decision is thought to be a victory for Stalin'[14] that is for the Soviet 'moderates', of whom Stalin was considered the leading member, thus vindicating the hard line taken by MacDonald and Henderson. It does indeed seem to have greatly stilled ILP criticism. Not another word of reproach is recorded in the columns of the Labour press of whatever persuasion until the exchange of ambassadors in December.

MacDonald may have wanted to make amends to Henderson and Dalton for his intervention in June and now left the whole matter to the two men. MacDonald had in any case got his hands full with vital discussions with the United States over reductions of naval forces, that culminated in the London Naval Conference of 1930. MacDonald clearly did much to polish his domestic and international reputation with these American discussions, leaving the less glamorous, and far more difficult, Russian negotiations to the Foreign Secretary. Such a clear division of labour did however make Henderson's task an easier one.[15]

There are divergent views on the success of the first official meetings. According to Carlton, the first meeting between Henderson and Dovgalevsky in July 'was not very successful and indeed was the cause of a serious breakdown in negotiations'. Dalton felt the opposite at the time, that it was 'apparently a good start'.[16] Dovgalevsky did indeed go straight back to Paris, but probably not in anger. He went because

Henderson had now made it clear that some sort of agreement on propaganda had to be signed before an exchange of ambassadors took place. The Russian therefore needed instructions.

Temporary suspension and reassessment

The *Daily Herald* feared a reaction, to be sure, and hoped that the 'temporary suspension of the Anglo-Soviet conversations will be calmly assessed'. The *New Statesman* saw no problem in this explanation. Henderson was taking a steady course, ignoring alike the murmurs of his friends who wanted him to prostrate himself on the Soviet doormat, and of opponents who would like him to be another 'Jix', the previous Conservative Home Secretary. 'There may be some hitches before the Anglo-Russian Treaty is signed, but we do not think they will be of Mr Anderson's making' said the *New Statesman*.[17]

MacDonald had now realised that he could not ask too much of the Russians on propaganda, and wrote a letter to Dalton setting out 'a reasonable version of our requirements on Russian propaganda and debts'. This letter insisted only on a 'reiteration of the 1924 pledge that they would refrain from it' [i.e. propaganda]. On the other hand, he did not insist that the said propaganda 'must cease *before* recognition', but rather give 'good evidence that it recognises its obligations and gives us assurances satisfactory to us that it is to face them with a genuine desire to settle them'. On debts MacDonald would be satisfied by an 'official acceptance of the fact that they exist' and, should that be agreed, that there should be 'an agreement to appoint representatives to have them examined'.[18]

Resumption of negotiations and the decision to resume relations

The interlude in official contacts was none the less becoming rather extended, with Henderson in The Hague and most of the rest of the Foreign Office dealing with either the talks on the Young Plan or the Optional Clause, plus the fact that August was a traditionally slow month. September saw movement on the Russian question. Henderson certainly came under pressure, at the TUC Belfast Congress in early September, and he did make a new invitation to recommence talks in Geneva on 4 September.

All the speeches at the TUC Congress urged that the issue of trade was 'non-political', but they were divided on the importance of guarantees on propaganda. J. Hill of the Boilermakers Union was particularly scathing on this point and said that the 'Foreign Secretary's lack of courtesy' in not exchanging ambassadors 'has been approved by every reactionary diehard'.[19] Henderson refused to be swayed by this insult, however, since he made his statement in Geneva the day before. The statement was in any case very brief and reiterated the need for Parliament to ratify any agreement that was reached with a 'responsible representative' on 'the procedure and programme for subsequent negotiations'.[20]

The Russians accepted within a week and were back in London by 24 September. Propaganda and debts were still the only major unresolved items on the agenda. Guarantees of the cessation of propaganda proved impossible since the subject of who controlled the Comintern remained taboo, but then Henderson had never promised to obtain them, whatever the Conservatives might claim. Nor must all questions be 'settled' – 'a misunderstanding'.[21] The *Daily Herald* rejoiced in a geographical metaphor to explain how the proceedings progressed. Henderson went from Brighton to Lewes and Dovgalevsky from London: 'Each, as it were, came some distance to meet the other'.[22]

Many issues remained to be resolved. In fact nothing really was resolved since the propaganda question could not be settled without reference to the Comintern. Debts, a commercial treaty, and several minor matters were to be referrred to specialised committees. The 'pledges' given to Parliament had been completely 'fulfilled' said Henderson. Ambassadors would therefore be exchanged. Probably the only real victory was with his own side. They had the diplomatic relations that they wished. It was not to prove as simple as had been hoped in the balmy days before the election. Henderson's success was none the less portrayed as such and he was 'quite happy . . . to await any attempt to prove that there has been any repudiation of pledges given either by myself or Mr MacDonald', he told a cheering Labour Party Conference, which was going on while the agreement was being signed.[23]

The 'Trotsky case'

As if one major Russian problem was not enough for the Labour Party in 1929 another, much stranger, one arose. Leon Trotsky requested political asylum in the UK. Trotsky had made a particular impact on the British public consciousness, probably far more than any other post-revolutionary Russian, with the exceptions of Lenin and Zinoviev. He had posed a particular problem for the Labour Party, in that he had made many widely publicised statements about the party, especially during the ARJAC episode of 1924–7. Norman Angell's *Must Britain Follow the*

Moscow Road? had been a reply to Trotsky's insulting remarks about the Labour Party, and it is clear that Angell's remarks were widely accepted in the Labour Party as a whole. MacDonald's numerous remarks about extremists in the Russian leadership were largely directed against Trotsky and Zinoviev in the 1924–8 period, as we saw in Chapter 2.

Balancing this attitude was a widespread respect and admiration for the founder of the Red Army: his physical and intellectual achievements were widely acknowledged. In 1930 Harold Laski was able to enthuse about Trotsky's *Autobiography* in the most glowing terms: 'This I beg you to read. Nothing even approaches it either as explanation of Russia, its strength and weakness, or as a great and dramatic narrative. The book pulsates with excitement and I know nothing of the kind for years that has moved me so much'. Laski's feeling were extremely important because he had seen himself, and been widely accepted, as one of the most influential Labour intellectuals since about 1920. During the 1929 government he frequently prepared memoranda and made policy suggestions to MacDonald, Henderson and Sankey (Lord Chancellor, and a great personal friend of Laski).[24] Neither must his close assocation with Dalton be forgotten, who Laski claims owed his Under-Secretaryship to his intervention with MacDonald.[25] Dalton was Laski's colleague at the LSE, as was Sidney Webb. All played important roles in the 'Trotsky debate'.

To further complicate the attitude towards Trotsky was the British tradition of extending political asylum even to political opponents, a tradition from which it might have proved dangerous to depart without at least exhausting all the possibilities for solution. The affair was therefore dealt with at the highest levels of government.

Trotsky had been exiled within the USSR at the beginning of 1928, being closely followed in the Labour press.[26] He assumed more immediate importance when he was finally expelled from the USSR in January 1929 to Turkey – not the place he wanted to stay. His presence was barely tolerated by the authorities and he immediately put out feelers to go to Germany or to England. The former country was reported to have turned him down because of hoteliers in the Spa areas 'feeling that such an unusual advertisement might frighten away wealthy visitors'.[27] He must have known that he had no hope of entering Britain while Baldwin was still in power.

The arrival in Turkey therefore coincided almost exactly with the election campaign. It was realised by the party leadership that it was extremely likely that Trotsky would apply to come to Britain, so a 'coincidence' seems to have been arranged. Sidney and Beatrice Webb suddenly arrived in Turkey, ostensibly on a short holiday. Webb was not standing as an MP, although he was to be awarded the Cabinet posts of the Colonies and Dominions in the June 1929 government, as well as a baronetcy (he became Lord Passfield), so it is probable that he had some kind of Labour Party mandate to find out if Trotsky was 'safe'.[28] Whatever the exact nature of their conversation, after the Webbs' return to England Trotsky wrote to Beatrice thanking her for the gift of her latest book *My Apprenticeship*. Two versions of this letter exist, the original draft by Trotsky and the copy received by the Webbs, both in French. The crucial line is that referring to the differences in their 'points de vue'. In Trotsky's original these are described as 'irréconciliables', in the final version 'irréductibles', neither one being too hopeful. He had none the less indicated to the Webbs his 'sympathie déjà ancienne pour la British Museum'. This rather subtle phraseology was more blunt in the earlier draft: then it was a question of 'pour ce qui me concerne personellement'. Pride clearly made him substitute the lesser request. The Labour Party victory in the elections – 'encore plus grande que vous ne l'escomptiez vous-même' – had made him draw some hopeful conclusions.[29]

The differences, according to Trotsky, were the old ones of different 'conceptions historiques', but they were clearly deep enough for Sidney Webb not to recommend Trotsky's admission. Even so, Trotsky obviously held out some hope and sent Sidney Webb a telegram once he was installed in the Colonial Office: 'Me permets vous rapeller necessité pour moi aller en Angleterre. Raisons santé et travail. Espère decision favourable nouveau gouvernement'.[30]

Why were the Webbs not more forthcoming with their support? Two major clues exist. The first can only be termed 'cultural'. On the copy of the letter Beatrice received she had written 'snobishness'. A more concrete reason is one expressed by Beatrice in a letter to Trotsky the next year. Here she wrote:

> My husband and I were very sorry you were not admitted into Great Britain: but I am afraid that anyone who preaches the permanence of revolution, that is, carries the revolutionary war into the politics of other countries, will always be excluded from entering these other countries. The right of asylum, if there be a right – only relates to rebels against their own [underlined by Trotsky] governments – not to rebels who try and upset the government of the country into which they wish to be permitted to come.

She ended: 'I am afraid this sounds rather involved; but perhaps you may catch its meaning'.[31] Trotsky undoubtedly did. The Webbs were not prepared to take any risk on his behalf.

Once the election had been won Trotsky immediately made an official application to come to Britain. Normally such an application would have been dealt with exclusively by the Home Secretary – in this case Clynes – but there were other issues involved that made the decision a Cabinet one. These issues can be categorised as those of raisons d'etat, both domestically and in foreign policy and that of the reaction within Parliament and the country in the Labour Party. The aspects that concerned raison d'etat were presented to Henderson as soon as he took over his new post. He and Dalton were told by Sir Ronald Lindsay (Permanent Under-Secretary of State at the Foreign Office and highest ranking civil servant) that Trotsky's entry would not be a good idea: 'from our point of view [the Foreign Office] there is no advantage in letting him in; from the point of view of the HO [Home Office] there are obvious objections'.[32]

The 'obvious objections' were partly those that had always been put forward by Home Office and Labour Party leadership alike about the risks of contaminating 'propaganda'. Trotsky had been the most prolific producer of this commodity in the past, the architect of 'permanent revolution' and a major inspiration of the now largely defunct Minority Movement that had given the Labour Party such trouble in 1927–8. The problems of militant communism were now the problems of the government, personal animosity doubled by the needs of state.

On the foreign policy side, Trotsky being welcomed in Britain could only compromise the delicate, and not yet operational, talks with the USSR. Yet Henderson was not prepared to follow Lindsay's advice, at least until the Cabinet had discussed the affair. His reply to Lindsay was to say 'that is a new way of approaching the matter to ask if there is any advantage to us letting him in. What about the right of asylum?' Dalton applauded this stand against what he saw in these first weeks as typical bureaucratic cynicism – had they not just distributed 'Labour and the Nation' to show that policy was from now on to be determined by moral and socialist principles?[33]

It was on these principles that Trotsky relied, on the sense of history that underlay it. It is probably for this reason that he chose to send a supplementary private plea to George Lansbury: 'I hope to be able soon to return you the kind visit you paid me at Kislovodsk' (presumably in 1920, when Lansbury had last visited the USSR).[34] The refusal that was delivered to Trotsky was inevitable, given a minority government and the problems of government itself. But it was not an easy decision to make, and its making was undoubtedly a major source of disappointment and anger in large sections of the Labour Party. The

Cabinet fully realised this in its discussions of 10 July.[35]

The decision to refuse Trotsky was announced in the House by Clynes; the reaction was swift and dismayed. His statement can be summarised as follows: although 'assurances' were offered on Trotsky's behalf, the Government did not believe them; even if he had the intention of merely seeking medical treatment, writing his 'life' and doing research, 'persons of mischievous intentions' would exploit his presence. Moreover, once he was in England it would be very difficult to get rid of him again. As to the question of the 'right of asylum', Clynes said that no such right existed. He denied any suggestion that the decision had in any way been influenced by the USSR's intervention. When asked by Colonel Wedgewood (a Liberal MP) whether the decision had anything to do with the delicate business of restoring relations with Russia, Clynes did not deny it. This was, in fact, undoubtedly the main reason. In the words of Clynes' memo to the Cabinet 'the admission of Trotsky into this country might be regarded as an unfriendly act by the Soviet Government'.[36]

Pressure within the Labour Party outside the House of Commons came from two major groups. Those that considered themselves 'socialist' (or more so) were one group, the 'intellectuals' another. John Strachey in the *Socialist Review* felt the 'instinctive reaction of nine-tenths of the socialist movement is "Why on earth shouldn't he [be admitted]?"' Fenner Brockway was equally adamant that he could do no harm, and that his admission would do much to polish the image of Britain as the home of freedom. Both Strachey and Brockway poured scorn on the idea that his entry would compromise the rapprochement with Russia, or that he would encourage the enemies of the Empire and 'revolutionaries' within Britain. Brockway did admit that the entry of Trotsky might have some effect on the re-establishment of relations, but he did not think so. He himself 'profoundly disagreed' with Trotsky, but it could not be denied that 'he has been one of the most powerful creative forces of this generation'.[37]

On this point his other supporters were agreed, from the editors of the *Manchester Guardian* to men of letters. One series of letters that could not be ignored came from Shaw, H. G. Wells and Augustine Birrell. They essentially repeated what Brockway had said in his article, Shaw being characteristically the most longwinded. They dwelt on the glorious liberal past, on the fact that Trotsky was a great man of letters, however much they personally disagreed with him. Shaw dropped into his letter the point that 'some of the signatories of this letter may claim as English writers to be considerably in advance of Mr Trotsky, and that

England is traditionally the home of so-called dangerous opinions as well as of lost causes',[38] all to no avail.

'Alas, poor Trotsky' announced the *Daily Express:*

> It looks . . . as though, in spite of the national pride in Great Britain as a refuge for the rejected of other lands, Trotsky's request will be refused. The government is bound to consider the Prime Minister's predicament and susceptibilities: it is bound to spare him the exquisite discomfort of Trotsky's neighbourhood.[39]

The result of the Anglo-Russian contacts of 1929

It is inescapable that the efforts undertaken to renew relations with the USSR, and the way in which it was done, created a gulf in the party or rather, perhaps, re-opened old wounds that had partly healed during the election. By the end of 1929, after six months of negotiation, there were no tangible results except the promise of an exchange of ambassadors. This was all the more serious because such enormous hopes had been built around the 'Russian card', especially over trade. But it was already clear that no progress could be realistically made until the question of debts and credits had been solved in some form of commercial negotiations as yet not decided. Propaganda could never be guaranteed to be excluded, since the question of the Third International's relations to the Russian Government had not been accepted. In fact little could be said to have been achieved.

Even if the government's policies on other subjects had not been as yet called seriously into question, the seeds of a future and far more serious doubt had been sown. As the government moved into 1930, the mounting economic crisis and the increasingly indecisive measures to deal with it were noted. Russia played its part in this, both as an example of a country where decisions were made, even if they were not always the right ones, and as a source of ideas and practical solutions for unemployment.

MacDonald should have conducted his first contacts with Russia in a far more open manner, which would have saved much of the ensuing disillusion in Labour Party ranks. Since any demand for information was treated with impatience by MacDonald, if not by Henderson, MacDonald lost much of his personal appeal in the party, especially among intellectuals (Dalton and many others among them), who were absolutely essential to ensure cohesion and the production of ideas in a crisis. It is therefore no exaggeration to see the mismanagement by the Labour leadership, and particularly by MacDonald himself, of the Russian question in 1929 as the first in a long line of disillusions that were to see their culmination in late 1931.

The Trotsky affair only reinforced this, since it invalidated in many eyes the claim that MacDonald's Government would be different from that of the Conservatives. Principles were paramount to many Labour Party members; they had been trampled underfoot with much publicity in the first weeks of a government that had been greeted with such idealistic enthusiasm. Even among his loyal supporters, MacDonald had sown the seeds of doubt. Henderson was in a state of some annoyance over his treatment, although not to the extent of his deputy, who was furious with MacDonald. 'Damn his slow caution' Dalton announced to his diary about the Prime Minister in July. By the end of December he doubted that the government would last until 1930: 'All the powers of Hell have not prevailed against us – although they came bloody near it'.[40]

Notes

1 Attached note by J. H. Seymour, 24 June 1929, 3 pp. PRO 30/69/266 with annexed memo from Vansittart to MacDonald.
2 DALTON, *Dairy*, entry for 17 June 1929. The diary is a source of major importance in the 1929–31 period on foreign policy matters, given Dalton's post as deputy to 'Uncle' and his evident acccess to his boss's innermost feelings. Dalton's biography *Call Back Yesterday. Memoirs 1887–1931*, London, Frederick Muller, 1953, is a rather more dubious, if useful source.
3 DALTON, Diary, entry for 29 June 1929.
4 House of Commons *Debates*, vol. 229, 2 July 1929, col. 48. CARLTON, pp. 147–8.
5 Tom Jones (PPS to MacDonald) to Lord Stamfordham (Private Secretary to King George V), 25 June 1929, PRO 30/69/365. Successive drafts are in the same file.
6 *Daily Herald*, 1 July 1929.
7 *Daily Herald*, 3 July 1929.
8 LAMMERS, Donald N., 'The Second Labour Government and the Restoration of Relations with Soviet Russia (1929)', *Bullėtin of the Institute of Historical Research*, vol. XXXVII, 1964, p. 65.
9 See David CARLTON, *MacDonald Versus Henderson, The Foreign Policy of the Second Labour Government*, London, Macmillan, 1970, pp. 148–50.
10 DALTON, *Diary*, entry for 10 July 1929.
11 DALTON, *Diary*, entry of 17 July 1929.
12 DALTON, *Diary*, entry for 18 July 1929. For more details see WILLIAMS, *The Attitude . . .*, pp. 227–34.
13 Decided in Cabinet, 10 July 1929, CAB 23/61.
14 DALTON, *Diary*, entry of 24 July 1929.
15 See CARLTON, Chs. 5 and 6. It must be said, however, that Foreign Office officials continued to go behind Henderson's back to MacDonald. There are extensive references to the Anglo-American talks in CAB/23/61 and 62.
16 CARLTON, pp. 150–51 and DALTON, *Diary*, entry for 29 July 1929. Lammers quotes Mary A. Hamilton, a close intimate of Henderson, as saying the same thing in her *Arthur Henderson: A Biography*, London, W. Heinemann, 1938, p. 311. This, for Lammers, is 'misleading', cf. pp. 68–9.
17 *Daily Herald*, 2 August 1929 and *New Statesman*, 3 August 1929.

18 DALTON, *Diary*, entry for 7 August 1929 and MacDonald to Dalton, 7 August 1929, FO 800/290. For much greater detail on this episode see WILLIAMS, *The Attitude* . . ., pp. 234–7.
19 *TUC Congress Report*, Belfast, 3–6 September 1929, pp. 392–5.
20 *Daily Herald*, 5 September 1929.
21 *Daily Herald*, 14 September 1929. This was repeated to Lord Stanfordham in a letter of 1 October 1929. FO 800/280.
22 *Daily Herald*, 2 October 1929. The correspondent was none other than Ewer.
23 *Daily Herald*, 2 October 1929.
24 *Holmes-Laski Letters. The Correspondence of Mr Justice Holmes and Harold J. Laski, 1926–1935*, Harvard University Press, 1953, vol. II. Laski to Holmes, 7 June 1930, p. 1257 and DEANE, pp. 85–6.
25 *Holmes-Laski Letters*, Laski to Holmes, 11 June 1929, pp. 1155–6.
26 See *Daily Herald*, 11, 12, 17 and 19 January 1928 and WILLIAMS, *The Attitude* . . ., p. 241.
27 *Daily Herald*, 21 March 1929.
28 Letter from Sidney Webb to Trotsky, 29 April 1929, Trotsky Archives, Harvard, 5838.
29 Trotsky-Beatrice Webb draft (undated), Trotsky Archives, T.A. 10791, copy of final typed letter, also in Trotsky Archives, and original in Passfield Papers, L.S.E. correspondence file.
30 Telegram from Trotsky to Webb, 11 June 1929, Trotsky Archives 10792.
31 Beatrice Webb to Trotsky, 30 April 1930, Trotsky Archives 5837.
32 DALTON, *Diary*, entry for 10 June 1929.
33 Loc. cit. He continued: 'A good opening. Uncle will stand firm on simple principles and won't let them put it across him'.
34 Trotsky to Lansbury, 14 June 1929, Trotsky Archives 8802.
35 Cf. CAB 23/61, conclusion 5. The decision was made on the basis of a document written by Clynes (CAB 24/204 of 24 June 1929).
36 CAB 24/204, 24 June 1929, p. 2.
37 STRACHEY, 'Why Exclude Trotsky?', *Socialist Review*, July 1929 and BROCKWAY, 'Should Trotsky Come to London?', *New Leader*, 14 June 1929.
38 The letters were found in the Trotsky Archives at Harvard. They were sent to Trotsky by Ivor Montagu on 12 August 1931. Archive reference 3379, 15432 (Shaw draft), 15613 (Wells), 13791 (Birrell).
39 *Daily Express*, 19 June 1929.
40 DALTON, *Diary*, entries for 15 July 1929 and 19 December 1929.

chapter eight

The Russian element in the Labour Government's domestic politics, January 1930 – August 1931

Economic problems got worse in 1930, and continued to deteriorate until the end of the government. Unemployment rapidly went through the two million mark and stood at nearly 20 per cent of the working population by the end of 1930. Far from adopting a radical economic solution, Philip Snowden, with the full backing of the Bank of England, was set on an even more traditional economic policy. An increasing section of the Labour Party began to look for new ideas wherever they might be found. As Skidelsky says, by the end of 1930 'underlying everything was a growing pessimism about the future of world trade, a greater willingness to toy with unsound expedients as a way out of depression'.[1]

One of the unsung elements in this realisation was the dismal progress made in the talks with the Soviet Union over commercial links with Britain in 1930–31. They failed essentially because the financial actors could not agree with the industrial ones. The government had to try and represent the wishes of both groups, the first by recovering their lost debts from pre-1917, the second by providing the necessary credits to allow exports to be sent to the USSR. Snowden's insistence on a 'sound' budget meant that the second became impossible. The Russians refused to pay the Czar's debts. This failure provided further fuel for those who believed that capitalism was doomed, for it seemed to prove that a divided economic system could not even mobilise to save itself using the most widely accepted remedy for slump, an increase in trade.

The crisis over religious persecution: January – March 1930

However, the initial problem was political. Reports started reaching Britain during the middle of 1929 that part of the new five-year plan might involve a certain 'criticism' of the traditional role of the Orthodox Church in the USSR. It rapidly became clear that rather more than this might be intended. The Conservative Party saw a welcome opportunity to harass the very recently renewed relations with Russia. They probably cannot have initially foreseen just how embarrassing their campaign was to prove. Neither would it have been possible at the outset to imagine perhaps the major crisis between church and state in the inter-war period.

The Labour Party and religion

Many Labour Party members felt a need to define their faith in quasi-religious terms. The ghost of 'christian socialism' still haunted the party and at times it remained a part of its distinctive style. The physical links with this evangelistic past still remained and provided an important element in the legitimation of the Labour Party's position in the movement as a whole. Outside the House of Commons, in the myriad of weekend speeches reported in the Labour press, the evangelistic style remained undiluted.

In the eternal debate about the decline of religion, the Labour Party leaders were always presented as true believers. The *Daily Herald* asked 'were not the best men in public life those who had come from the Chapel and the Sunday School?'. Of course these men were MacDonald, Henderson and Snowden.[2] Those who claimed a direct descent from the freethinker school (for example, Brailsford), were also at pains to state that they came from a deeply spiritual tradition, direct descendants of Blake and William Morris, knights of purity to build the new Jerusalem. Herein lay part, a growing part, of interest in the 'new Russia'.

Of course faith was not to be equated with religion, either for the traditional Chapel and Sunday School leadership or for the freethinkers. In domestic, and even more so in foreign politics, religion was generally used to denote the 'Tory Party at prayer', the Church of England. However crude this stereotype might seem, its perennial attraction is shown in the many bitter passages about the anglicans in, for example, Robert Tressell's *Ragged Trousered Philanthropists*. The crisis over religious persecution of early 1930 did much to highlight this feeling, since the major weapon on the conservative side was the aid of the Archbishop of Canterbury, William Gordon Cosmo Lang.[3]

The unfolding of the crisis

The Times correspondent in Moscow had reported the institution of an 'anti-God' campaign back in June 1929.[4] During the slow rapprochement in Anglo-Soviet relations there had been further occasional reports with a first question in Parliament on 17 July. The Labour press initially minimised these allegations. A report in the *Daily Herald* two weeks later, at about the time the diplomatic negotiations were suspended, said the demolition of the 'Shrine of the Iberian Virgin' in Moscow was 'the most sensational blow at the Church since the Soviets came to power', but that 'under the Tsarist regime anybody passing the shrine (whatever his religion) *was compelled to bare his head*'.[5] The demolition was thus presented as a blow for reason. A series of articles during August, by the temporary *Daily Herald* correspondent in Moscow, Michael Farbman, made no mention of any religious problems.[6] Nor was there any reply to increasing coverage in *The Times* during the period until the beginning of December.

In the inevitable debates in the House of Lords at which the diehard Tories so excelled, there was none the less an undertone to the debate that showed indignation to be at a low level. The Archbishop expressed sympathy with MacDonald during January 1920: 'Lest my silence be misunderstood' he did feel outrage at the treatment of Russian christians, but none the less felt that 'there is more chance of procuring some alleviation of their most difficult position if representations could be made on the part of this government by ordinary diplomatic means ... than if we were at present to involve the cause of religious people in Russia with denunciations of the Soviet Government'.[7]

It was not until February 1930 that the problem of religion again really hit, but it hit very hard once it did. Rabid anti-Russian attacks in the diehard press in December rose to hysteria when the accusations became international with a fierce papal condemnation of Soviet religious persecution and then by an anglican statement. Both the Archbishops of Canterbury and York now agreed that 'no words can be strong enough to express the indignation with which we have heard day-by-day news of the revival of persecution such as is incompatible with the elementary principles of civilisation'.[8] The Archbishop of Canterbury now declared that he had been wrong to be patient with the workings of diplomacy. The attack on the government had become far more than a diehard criticism.

The change in atmosphere was palpable. Even the new Russian Ambassador in London noticed it. As Sokolnikov said to Sidney Webb (now Lord Passfield and Minister for the Colonies) and Philip Noel-Baker: 'he had left Russia in the middle of December unaware that there was any such thing as Religious Persecution ... he arrived in England to find the question becoming to be one of burning political importance'.[9] He was not the only one to be surprised. The questions were: why and in whose interest had this campaign been mounted, if indeed there was a conspiracy and were the charges true?

The clear leader of the campaign was Church of England Prebendary, Gough, who set up a Christian Protest Society and launched a tirade of letters in the columns of the *Manchester Guardian*. It was largely his information that seems to have persuaded the Archbishop of the need for an inquiry.[10] Defenders of the USSR immediately took up the challenge in the same columns. Zelda Coates (joint editor of the *Anglo-Russian Parliamentary Committee Weekly Bulletin*) was one prominent letter writer. No one could conclusively prove or disprove the allegations of persecution. Lang said that he felt an enquiry would at least clear the air, for: 'satisfactory diplomatic relations must depend not on material advantages only, but also and even more on the common acceptance of those principles of justice, liberty and humanity which are the basis of all international discourse'.[11]

Therein lay the formula that made it impossible for the government not to respond, for the honour of the party was now at stake, as it had been to a lesser extent over Trotsky. Baldwin, of course took some delight in the government's discomfiture and used the opportunity immediately to draw the lesson that it was impossible to deal with the Russians.[12] So it was clear who would benefit most from this affair – the Conservative Party, whether they were behind it or not. Dalton told his diary:

> Religious Persecution Stunt is worrying Uncle a great deal. Ovey and the officials (Foreign Office) want us to do nothing. But the Wesleyan and the Politician combine to make him try to do something. In the last resort, we may have to choose between sending Sokolnikoff away or seeing the Govt. go down. If that wretched choice comes, we shalln't willingly choose the latter. But we aren't there yet'.[13]

The question was discussed in the Cabinet and it was decided to take top-level dissuasive action.[14] In public the leadership therefore pretended that they would take stern action against the USSR should the allegations turn out to be true; in private they tried to dismantle the campaign. An official Foreign Office inquiry was announced, to be conducted by Ambassador Ovey in Moscow, and other measures taken to ascertain the facts.

Ovey had only just arrived in Moscow, and had travelled little as yet. Henderson therefore asked his Ambassador in Berlin, Sir Horace Rumbold, if he had any views about the truth of the allegations. Sir

Horace believed that the Pope, whose letter had really unleashed the campaign, was shocked at the response it had received. The papal Chargé d'Affaires in Berlin believed that 'accounts of religious persecution in Russia were somewhat exaggerated'.[15] The Pope had not intended the complaint to be a political declaration, the Chargé had told Sir Horace.

Noel-Baker and Sidney Webb had also asked the new Soviet Ambassador what he thought of the charges. He enumerated all the religious freedoms that were allowed: 'he would be very surprised if 1 per cent of all the Churches in Russia had been closed', the only possible exception being that sects were not much appreciated. On being pressed on this he said that one of these sects, the Baptists, 'were a special case because they were an international organisation and therefore brought in foreign influence which was regarded as being anti-Soviet'. Noel-Baker noted that 'perhaps this amounts to an admission that special measures against Baptists had been taken'. The two most important points he made were that the report that Ovey had been asked to make would be impossible to write, since neither Soviet Government nor private sources would be available, an astonishing admission. Moreover '[his] conviction, after studying the facts, was that the agitation had been manufactured by the newspapers with the help of Conservative politicians, and that it was designed to embarrass not the Russian Government but the British Labour Government'.[16]

Henderson and the government came under more pressure from the Coates, who tried their utmost to persuade the Cabinet that there was no truth in the allegations. From the beginning they were highly active, husband disseminating information, wife replying to Prebendary Gough in the press. An issue of their *Bulletin* in early February printed a lengthy rebuttal, quoting extensively from official Soviet decrees. It also stressed the awful record of Czarist religious persecution. Priests, it said, were unfortunately sometimes also full-time counter-revolutionaries 'under the guise of religious activities'. It pointed out that the main organs stirring up trouble for the government were also those who had opposed restoration of diplomatic relations from the beginning. A more detailed document sent by Coates to Henderson in mid-February pursued this line even further.[17] Such was the insistence of Zelda Coates in the columns of the *Manchester Guardian* that Gough in the end broke off the discussion.

While they and others argued about the facts, MacDonald admitted that the facts were not really known. In a letter that was reprinted in its entirety in both the *Labour Magazine* and in the *Daily Herald*, he said that he received a lot of mail about the persecutions, but he felt that 'a good part of the statements which have done duty from time to time have proved to be false'. However he admitted that reports such as these emanating from Russia had proved true in the past, 'and the revolutionary mentality which generations of oppression have created has all the characteristics of narrowness and violence of purpose'. What was more his own background, and that of his colleagues, meant that he had inherited a hatred of religious persecution. But he did not believe that the truth was 'the question of issue. Rather we have to consider what we can do'.

This pragmatic line had been confirmed for him by the Russian reaction to the campaign. 'To outlaw a country is not to make it amenable to world opinion but the opposite'.[18] The Russians took it as yet more proof of conspiracies against them. Litvinov had already signalled to Ovey his dislike of the campaign even though he went to extraordinary lengths, for a Soviet Foreign Minister, to calm the waters by allowing an interview with Metropolitan Sergius of the Russian Orthodox Church which was widely reported.[19]

Given his uncertainty about the facts, Henderson was largely at a loss as to how to react to the attacks in the Commons. However, once the report written by Ovey arrived from Moscow on 3 March, he had new ammunition. Dalton seems to have had the opportunity to read the report first, feeling that it was a 'first-class document, blowing up all the atrocity stories'. Henderson declared his immediate intention to publish the latest Russian decree of 8 April 1929 on religious associations, which was done in the form of a Command Paper in April.[20]

The Conservatives quite rightly asked about the veracity of Ovey's sources, a worry that we can now understand, but the report seems to have convinced some of those who saw it. One impressive support came from the King himself, not one to be soft on bolsheviks. As Dalton commented: 'pretty good, this particular Royal intervention'. The King felt that 'Sir Esmond Ovey would be irreplaceable'. In fact, the only problem was whether the report should be published. Henderson himself and Dalton wanted to publish it; the King's Secretary, Stamfordham, Vansittart and the Foreign Office, including Ovey himself, did not wish to, on the grounds that this would create a bad precedent and 'make Ovey's position in Moscow untenable'. It remained unpublished.[21]

The report also arrived in time to defuse what could potentially have developed into a major constitutional crisis. The Archbishop of Canterbury had ordered 'prayers of intercession' for foreign Christians to be said at Sunday parades of the armed forces. MacDonald forbade their use and unleashed a new storm at the beginning of March, before the report arrived. MacDonald complained to the Archbishop that 'As things turn out your day of intercessions will be much more profitable for the party in opposition to us than it will be for the promotion of religious toleration in Russia'.[22] Lang replied that he had harboured no intention to embarrass MacDonald or the government. He had not realised that the services would cause 'any difficulties' and claimed to have seen both Henderson and Vansittart to be sure. MacDonald seems to have cooled down somewhat by the time of his second letter, but still urged the Archbishop to realise that 'We are undoubtedly having some good influence on the better minds of the Russian Government, and I do not want that to be lost'.[23] The fact is that MacDonald probably agreed that religious persecution was widespread in Russia, and that he was not convinced by Ovey's report. He felt that it was still not worth upsetting his wider plans for European peace over a relatively minor matter. He was at his angriest with Lang when he considered the political capital that the opposition was making out of the affair.

Dalton was not alone in finding the continuing campaign 'very vexing'.[24] There was a dialectic between those in the Labour Party who believed the allegations might be true and those who only concerned themselves with the domestic impact of the campaign. Snowden and MacDonald broadly speaking found themselves in the second category. Henderson was in the first and he probably went through agonies of conscience until he persuaded himself of the lack of truth in the allegations. A lot of people fell into both categories.

The ILP freethinkers were divided along similar lines, with the important proviso that they felt that they themselves were the victim of religious persecution in Britain as Brailsford asserted in an article in *New Leader* in late February. He furthermore accused the Conservatives of hypocrisy, for they had not complained about Czarist excesses and called for understanding of an alien culture: 'one must envisage the scene with some broader attempt at comprehension'. This was coupled with an explanation; the Russian peasant had for centuries been kept in bondage by the church. Religious repression had gone hand in hand with a desire by the rich kulaks to resist beneficial progress, for example, agricultural cooperation. The Soviet state had been guilty of pointing this out in a rather ugly manner, that is visually ugly, with demonstrations and other events designed to ridicule. But the Archbishop was being 'grossly misleading' in suggesting anything worse. Other ILP literature clung to the same line. Magda Gellan in a later edition of *Socialist Review* explained that the violent attacks on God in posters, for example, were 'to explain and emphasise the design of the government to the worker', an alien method for a different environment, but harmless none the less.[25]

Henderson had received much the same argument from Ovey, minus the socialist rhetoric. He considered the accusations being made in the Tory press and Party as exaggerated and suspect. Undoubtedly this is the clue to why so many intelligent people refused to believe what was in fact happening in the USSR in 1930. World War One had left the major intellectual sequel of a disbelief in 'atrocity stories' from the right-wing press. Kingsley Martin observed this about the very crisis of 1930 in an article in *Political Quarterley*. He collected some of the worst excesses of *Morning Post* anti-Soviet rhetoric: how one Christian Father was 'first beaten and dragged by the feet through the garden. Then his arms and legs were broken' (I spare the further details that Martin did not spare his audience). His point was that such overkill, for such it seemed to him evidently to be, had been backed up by no evidence, and served only those who sought to denigrate the USSR. He concluded that the

> motives for the renewal of anti-Soviet propaganda are mixed. They are compounded of sincere religious feelings, genuine horror at a regime deliberately founded on a materialistic and communist philosophy, the desire to discredit a Labour Government and to strengthen the cause of reaction in Europe. Finally there is the inducement to discard the dullness of peace talks in favour of more profitable fare.[26]

Of all these reasons only the first found favour with any section of the Labour Party or with Kingsley Martin.

Most important of all, the result of the diehard overkill in this affair seems to have made a very deep impression on 'progressive' public opinion, and particularly that of the Labour Party which now had almost a monopoly on such opinion. Kingsley Martin was after all the editor of the *New Statesman* and co-editor, with Keynes and others, of the new *Political Quarterly*: 'Red Atrocity' stories were simply not believed by such opinion leaders from now on. The Great War's atrocity stories had started the rot, it had 'deadened our sensibility and also made us sceptical of reports of cruelty ... It is part of the general debacle of that Liberalism which belongs to no Party but which is synonymous with civilisation. It was the most serious of the casualties of the war'.[27]

When further information about collectivisation came in it had to fight the total disbelief formed in the Great War and reconfirmed in the early months of 1930. The war myths about German behaviour were now believed to have been transferred to Russsia. The first had been proved foundless, no doubt the second would as well. This is not to say that wider public opinion in Britain did not believe in the stories just a little, or even that the Labour Party entirely discounted them, but the experience meant that the USSR would be generally given the benefit of the doubt for at least the next four years.

The trade issue during 1930 and 1931

Henderson hoped for some counterpart to the aggravation that Russian proximity was causing him. He still tried to fulfil the trade pledge of the electoral campaign. The task was no easier than any other contact with Russia. Trade had indeed increased by 1931, although not in the proportions originally expected.[28]

The negotiations over commercial relations and debts

These negotiations must, of course, be seen in the context in which they took place. In the mounting atmosphere of crisis since about October 1929 and the Wall Street Crash, the government was under increasing pressure to do something to alleviate growing unemployment and reduced production. Between June 1929 and June 1930 unemployment went from 1,163,000 (9.6 per cent of the insured population) to 1,912,000 (15.4 per cent). This total, which continued to rise to 2,500,000 or nearly 20 per cent of the insured population by December 1930, was a huge embarrassment to the government. For years the Labour Party had been blaming 'capitalism' and the 'system' for the unemployment figures, now they *were* the system, or at least in charge of it. Moreover, most Labour Ministers could not think of how to implement any new system. Both Snowden, as Chancellor of the Exchequer, and William Graham, as President of the Board of Trade, upheld socialism in theory but were financial conservatives in practice. As Skidelsky comments, 'In Snowden's mind socialism and public finance existed in two entirely separate, watertight compartments'.[29]

The implications for the commercial negotiations were crucial. As Supremo for Trade, Graham had a large word to say in how the negotiations were to take place. As Treasury head, Snowden could insist on 'sound finance' in the negotiations, which meant that he could block anything thought of as excessive, such as extended export credits. Henderson and his two deputies, Philip Noel-Baker and Dalton, were therefore outnumbered. To add to this, they were forced to accept a nonentity from the Board of Trade, the Secretary of the Overseas Trade Department, Gillett, as the main spokesman in the Commons, and chief negotiator when Henderson could not be available, which was much of the time. An added obstacle was that of a worsening of other problems with Russia. The negotiations took place during almost exactly the same period as the religious persecution crisis, to the point where the two issues often came up in the same speech, the embarrassment of the first often being counter-attacked with the promise of the second.

The Conservatives had wished all issues with Russia to be dealt with as a 'basket', and this from 1917 onwards. The Russians had always refused this principle. The Labour Party compromised, partly through fear of an outraged public opinion, and the loss of City support. Hence the insistence by Henderson that the 1924 propaganda pledge be renewed, but that the other issues – commercial, debt and fisheries (the last of these will be ignored for reasons of space) – could be negotiated to some extent separately after an exchange of ambassadors.

It was not until January 1930 that serious talks began. The embargo on Russian trade in oil products, against which prominent Tories like Sir Henry Deterding of the Anglo-Persian Oil Company (now BP) had led a major war, was lifted in late August. This was not without a fight within the Cabinet for although the War Office, led by Tom Shaw, favoured much increased contact with the USSR as a way of promoting peace, asked for a withdrawal of embargo in July, Graham asked for a delay. Graham pointed out that the Russians might use this strategic product as a bargaining counter or cut supplies, as they had in 1926. He therefore suggested that since the Russians might *want* to sell oil, the British might use the embargo to exert pressure. The Russians would have been furious, and MacDonald obviously thought it not worth the risk, for he approved the lifting. There were two influences on him: the first was Henderson, who minuted the Graham comment: 'The Foreign Secretary does not regard this point as an important one', thus setting the tone for a Foreign Office/Board of Trade enmity on the Russian question for the rest of the negotiations. The second was Snowden, who also disagreed with Graham but for a different reason – he wanted government departments to buy 'wherever they want', i.e, wherever it was cheapest.[30]

Another reason for Henderson wishing the issues to be kept separate was because, as Noel-Baker noted for his own clarification in late 1929, there was 'no reality in their [the Conservatives] argument re debts – only by resumption can debts be dealt with'. What was more, they had not objected to Romanian or Mexican non-payment, 'this is because of regime'.[31] In fact, as the Graham intervention showed, Henderson had more to worry about from his own colleagues than from the Conservatives.

Of course, the other problem was that of how much trade, and consequent alleviation of the unemployment figures, could be expected? It was candidly admitted in February 1930 that the government did not really know how much could be expected. Talking of the sending of a commercial attaché to join Ovey in Moscow, Gillet stated that he was to be sent because business interests in Britain had asked for it (the Anglo-Russian delegation), and due to the growing investment of firms like Metropolitan-Vickers. But mainly he felt that 'it is a distinct advantage to have men on the spot who can give us information as to what is passing in that great and mysterious country'.[32]

This admission of ignorance held another problem which complicated still further the internal discussions within the Cabinet. The clue lies in the distinction between trade and finance. A member of the Anglo-Russian delegation volunteered his views to Noel-Baker in late 1929, saying that he wished to tell him some of his misgivings about the wild claims made by the delegation. Without credits for the export of British goods and the import of Soviet goods, 'Russia is at present only *potentially* a market for this country' without some form of export credit system.

The problem lay in the fact that the delegation had intended to have financial representation but 'owing to differences of opinion in England the delegation did not represent finance to say considerable extent'.[33] This 'difference of opinion' could not be got over as easily as this delegation member obviously hoped. Gillett's placing of the commercial attaché was intended to give information to the Department of Trade that Ovey of the Foreign Office might not be qualified to give. Ovey could not be trusted to see things in their proper financial aspect. The attaché was working for Snowden and Graham, Ovey for Henderson. The former only cared about the financial 'bottom line', the latter only, or mainly, about the political aspects. It was, in short, a renewal of the problem of keeping the political and industrial sides apart, translated into an internal Cabinet difference.

Ovey did his best to keep Henderson informed about the likely concrete benefits of trade in a series of lengthy despatches throughout the negotiations.[34] His analysis confirmed the feeling that British business optimism was greater than probable returns. Ovey was clearly impressed by the scale of the five-year plans, which dazzled the delegation of businessmen, but he felt that conversations he had had with such businessmen might be over-optimistic. Litvinov had spoken, said Ovey, 'for the purpose of producing a good effect' but, and this was important, he did not deny that optimism may be correct. But he also stressed repeatedly that without finance there was no hope of a really large order-book for Britain.[35]

The vicious circle therefore continued. Whenever Sokolnikov or Litvinov asked their respective interlocutors to speed up the financial side of the discussions, as opposed to the political which were being dealt with by Dalton, Henderson and the Foreign Office, Henderson or Ovey had to refer the Russians to Graham's department. What must have made it even more infuriating for Henderson was that Litvinov, through Ovey, was continually promising millions of pounds worth of trade in 'options', which of course meant in return for credits. Ovey was himself well aware of the problem of financing, and seems to have shared the view of the need for extensive credits. He also seems to have seen the later 1929 report from the member of the Anglo-Russian delegation, and felt that 'of course, were his Majesty's Government in a position to extend greater credit facilities, there is no question as to the advantages that would accrue'.[36]

A showdown between the Foreign Office and the financial ministries headed by Snowden and Graham therefore became inevitable. The event was precipitated by a memo from the Board of Trade at the beginning of March 1930. Graham made two objections to the proposed commercial treaty. The first which he admitted was 'not primarily my concern', related to the diplomatic status of the Russian delegation in London, and Henderson cannot have appreciated this evident poaching on this territory. The second objection was financial, the granting of export credits, and was a direct challenge to Henderson. Credits were a:

> question to which there is reason to think that the Russian negotiators are likely to attach almost as great importance [as us] and if they are to be told that no reference whatever to this matter can be included in the temporary agreement . . . there is every possibility that the whole negotiation will prove abortive

'As you will see, added the Board of Trade civil service memo attached to Graham's memo, 'the course and indeed the fate of the negotiations . . . is vitally affected by any decision which is arrived at'.[37] The Cabinet was asked to decide on whether the political or the financial argument would prevail.

The Cabinet meeting of 5 March came up with the inevitable compromise cobbled together by MacDonald. There seems no doubt that he would personally have liked to grant all the credits Henderson wanted, if only because he entirely backed the idea of 'civilisation through trade' and his fear of more propaganda if the deal didn't come off. But he was too scared of Snowden's prophesies of doom if he were to throw state money into the coffers to pay for credits. In a growing climate of crisis even the naval estimates had been cut by £5,000,000 and the best that could be obtained were a grudging twelve months of limited credits, after which there would be no more state money.

Dalton told his diary of other efforts being undertaken by E. F. Wise, but 'nothing materialises there'. In the battle with the Board of Trade, Gillett remembered where his first loyalty lay, to Graham, and he 'won't seriously try to move them'. The Foreign Office was by now isolated on this (and other) matters.[38] Economic nationalism was finding increasing support in the country and even in the Labour Party, where the passing of a tariff truce was meeting more and more opposition. The best that could be obtained in these circumstances was a Temporary Commercial Agreement, signed by 16 April 1930 amid much publicity and rejoicing.[39] But in fact the hopes never came up to the realities precisely because there was no general agreement to follow the idea through with cash in any reasonable quantity.

The question of debts had also to be solved before a more permanent agreement could be signed. Henderson tried, setting up the required 'joint committees' on debts and claims.[40] Once set up, the Prime Minister was assailed with requests to help the running of the Committee or asking for their money back (from Russia), Vansittart protecting his boss from such requests.[41]

In this sorry story of inter-departmental rivalry we should ask if there were not other factors within the Labour Party that had an impact on the decision-making process, especially over the question of trade credits. The only section that eventually dared to speak up about the government, and especially its handling of the economic situation, was the ILP contingent, in particular Oswald Mosley. But even he did not speak until November 1930 in the NEC, although he had most eloquently outside it, by resigning his Cabinet post in May 1930. In his Commons speeches, while he still remained a member of the Labour Party and ILP, his *bête noire* was the 'treasury view' held by Snowden, Graham and others. His remarks were at least related to Russian policy, a Russia where he greatly admired the 'constructive fury' of the five-year plans. But in the NEC it must be said he was a lone voice even if they all agreed that there 'was grave concern and dissatisfaction which exist within the party' on the economic situation.[42]

The TUC also had an angry word to say about the handling of this situation, and more particularly on the precise question of Russian trade. As early as 17 March the General Council had written to MacDonald to voice its concern over the non-granting of 'trade facilities' which the TUC had demanded should be extended to Russia at its 1929 Belfast

Congress. The extension of 'export credits', but only for a maximum of twelve months, was also felt by the General Council to be insufficient, because the Advisory Committee which dealt with such matters 'appeared to be prejudiced against trade with Russia'. Graham and Gillett were also approached with the same argument (so the General Council must have realised exactly what was going on), during May 1930. By the Nottingham TUC Congress in September 1930 no progress had been made. By the next Congress the TUC seemed better pleased with progress and revealed that the government had been finally persuaded to 'consider' credits for £1,300,000 with £2,739,000 of orders actually placed by Russia in British factories.[43] But this was no triumph considering the hopes of 1929.

Trade-related issues until the end of the government

Unsatisfactory as this agreement was, Soviet trade was to continue to pose problems for the rest of the government's life. Accusations principally turned around 'dumping' and 'slave labour'.

Although there was certainly an element of a continuing Tory hostility to Soviet Russia, the main reason for the conservative accusations of Soviet dumping, particularly of wheat, were part of a general movement by the Conservative Party and large elements of other parties and industry towards the policy of 'safeguarding' or tariff restrictions. *The Times*, and even Keynes and some prominent Labour figures, including Bevin, moved towards 'Empire preference' during the 1929-31 government with important implications for trade with the rest of the world, Russia included. The Labour Party continued, officially at least, as a convinced free trader, but they were consequently all the more vulnerable to accusations of malpractice by their chosen trading partners, and Russia had been very consciously chosen.

At the beginning of his stay, Ovey told Henderson that he felt certain 'special features' of the trading relationship might cause trouble, by which he meant dumping, but that this would diminish as time went on, and which 'incidentally ... may possibly be somewhat exaggerated'.[44] But by August William Strang (based in Leningrad) was actually warned by the Russians that they would have to dump about 50 per cent more grain because of the slump in prices, an astonishing admission.[45] Conservative accusations started in March 1930 in the Commons, and were refuted by Henderson. The press got hold of the idea and Coates felt obliged to swing into action in successive editions of his *Bulletin* to defend Soviet honour. It was 'misrepresentation and insinuation to prevent would-be customers from purchasing Soviet goods'. This was, in short, another 'baseless' campaign.[46]

The same applied to accusations of the use of forced labour in the timber industry in the USSR. Britain had to import most of its timber and Russian timber was well priced. The USSR was using these exports to pay for the imports of manufactured goods, a market the British were of course very interested in. To attack Russian practices in such an important export industry was therefore the same as attacking the very principle of trade with Russia, a fact that Bron of the Russo-British Chamber of Commerce never tired of pointing out.[47]

Questions on this in the Commons and Lords became almost as frequent as Henderson's 'PQs' (propaganda questions). They were deflected in much the same way. Either there had been no such complaint on the matter reaching HM Government, or the British worker and his need for trade were invoked.[48] The TUC gave the impression of thinking the whole campaign was diehard rubbish. Coates was able to reprint a whole series of letters, all to the *Manchester Guardian*, from four trade unionists of impeccable moderate political stances, certainly not communists, led by John Bromley of the ASLEF. He said: 'Frankly we are naturally suspicious of those who are leading the campaign against Russian timber .... When have these diehards ever helped organised labour in this country?' What was more he didn't believe the accusations: 'It is a matter of common knowledge that, as in this country, convicts in Russia have to work. It is possible that they are employed on felling timber for home purposes. Is that any worse than making mailbags in His Majesty's prisons in this country?'[49] The use of the words 'home purposes' perhaps shows a certain moral qualm in Bromley's words. Citrine, by now General Secretary, did not follow them. His 1925 visit had not filled him with unmitigated love for Russian work practices, but of course he could not have said so at this juncture, although he later did.[50]

Notes

1 See SKIDELSKY, *Politicians and the Slump*, p. 203.

2 'Is Religion Dying?', *Daily Herald*, 2 January 1930.

3 The Church of England had, of course, a complex relationship with the Government of the day. As the Church of *England* it was also the Church of state with certain presumed responsibilities for the stability of that state. It was and is (cf. Runcie on the Falklands issue) the conscience of the government, especially in moral and religious matters. William Cosmo Gordon Lang was made Archbishop of Canterbury by Baldwin in 1928, cf. *Dictionary of National Biography*, 1949, vol. IV, Oxford University Press, 1959, pp. 474–8.

4 *The Times*, 12 June and 18 July 1929.

5 *Daily Herald*, 31 July 1929 (their emphasis).

6 *Daily Herald*, 19, 29, 30 August, 3 and 4 September 1929.
7 House of Lords *Debates*, vol. 75, 1929–30, cols. 888–97.
8 Reported in *Daily Herald*, 10 February 1930 and 13 February 1930.
9 Typewritten report by Noel-Baker, sent to Henderson 19 February 1930. Noel-Baker Papers, Churchill College, NBKR 4/631.
10 *Manchester Guardian*, 4 February 1930. He was Prebendary of St Paul's Cathedral, London and therefore of some importance.
11 *Manchester Guardian*, 13 February 1930.
12 Baldwin speaking at Belfast University, report in *Manchester Guardian*, 15 February 1930.
13 DALTON, *Diary*, entry for 18 February 1930.
14 Cabinet Conclusions, 12 February 1930, Conclusion 2, CAB 23/63.
15 H. Rumbold to Henderson, 19 February 1930, B.D. 2/VII, no. 65.
16 Noel-Baker on Sokolnikov conversation, report sent to Henderson, 19 February 1930, Noel-Baker Papers, Churchill College, NBKR 4/631, pp. 1–3.
17 Anglo-Russian Parliamentary Committee *Bulletin*, no. 13, 6 February 1930 and Coates to Henderson, 13 February 1930, FO 800/281.
18 'Russia and Religion', *Labour Magazine*, March 1930. Original of letter in MacDonald Papers, February 1930, PRO 30/69/266.
19 Cf. Ovey to Henderson, 22 February 1930, B.D. 2/VII.
20 DALTON, *Diary*, entry for 3 March 1930. Decree of the All-Russian Central Executive Committee and the Council of People's Commissars 'respecting religious associations', Cmd 3511. 'Certain legislation respecting religion in force in the USSR', Cmd 3641.
21 DALTON, *Diary*, entry for 3 March 1930.
22 MacDonald to Lang (Canterbury), 7 March 1930, PRO 30/69/1175.
23 Lang to MacDonald, 8 March 1930, PRO 30/69/1175 and reply, 10 March 1930; for more details see Williams, *The Attitude . . .*, pp. 263–5.
24 DALTON, *Diary*, entry for 3 March 1930.
25 BRAILSFORD, 'Russia and Religion; Exploiting the Primary Passions', *New Leader*, 21 February 1930 and GELLAN, Magda, 'USSR', *Socialist Review*, December 1930.
26 MARTIN, Kingsley, 'The Influence of the Press', *Political Quarterly*, vol. 1, no. 2, April 1930, p. 171.
27 MARTIN, Kingsley, 'Public Opinion', *Political Quarterly*, Janary-March 1931, p. 120.
28 Exports to Britain from the USSR in 1931 amounted to about £15 million and imports to the USSR came to about £9 million. For a discussion of these figures see ch. 15, pp. 429–31.
29 SKIDELSKY, *Politicians and the Slump*, p. 395.
30 Graham to MacDonald, 17 August 1929, with Snowden's and Foreign Office annotations, PRO 30/69/415.
31 Handwritten notes by Philip Noel-Baker, Noel-Baker Papers, end 1929. Probably written during a debate. NBKR 4/631.
32 Parliamentary *Debates*, 20 February 1930, vol. 235, cols 1733–4.
33 Typewritten report addressed to Noel-Baker by unnamed member of Anglo-Russian Delegation, late 1929. Noel-Baker Papers, NBKR 4/631, 5 pp.
34 See B.D. 2/VII, ch. II 'Anglo-Soviet Relations in 1930: Temporary Trade Agreement of April 16 1930 . . .' for full details.
35 B.D. 2/VII, no. 52, Ovey to Henderson, 4 January 1930.
36 B.D. 2/VII, no. 60, Henderson to Ovey, 3 February 1930 and no. 71, Ovey to Henderson, 4 March 1930.
37 Graham to MacDonald, 4 March 1930, accompanying memorandum by C. P. Duff (Board of Trade Permanent Secretary), MacDonald Papers, PRO 30/69/266.
38 Cf. DALTON, *Diary*, entry for 3–9 March 1930 and for 9 April 1930: 'Vansittart says the

F.O. have a very bad reputation now, with the PM and Chancellor of Exchequer and Tory Party and in Fleet Street.'

39 Temporary Commercial Agreement, Cmd 3552, Treaty Series no. 19 (1930), published HMSO, London, 16 April 1930.

40 See, for example, Henderson to Goschen, 13 June 1930, FO 800/284.

41 Cf. correspondence from Birch Crisp (industrialist) to MacDonald 8 July 1930. Vansittart recommended no action, since 'it would be an intolerable burden on his time'. 12 July 1930, PRO 30/69/676.

42 See SKIDELSKY, *Oswald Mosley*, pp. 209–17 and Labour Party NEC Minutes, 25 November 1930 and MOSLEY, Oswald, 'Will the Cabinet Act?', *New Leader*, 14 February 1930.

43 TUC Nottingham Congress Report, September 1930, p. 114 and TUC Bristol Congress Report, September 1931, p. 337.

44 B.D. 2/VII, no. 71, Ovey to Henderson, 4 March 1930, p. 109.

45 B.D. 2/VII, no. 94, Strang to Henderson, 18 August 1930, p. 149. (Strang was Ovey's temporary stand-in and usually head of the Leningrad station at this time).

46 Anglo-Russian Parliamentary Committee *Bulletin*, 8 May 1930.

47 See, for example, Anglo-Russian Parliamentary Committee *Bulletin*, 19 March 1931, 'Mutual Advantage'.

48 See, for example, House of Commons *Debates*, vol. 236, 26 March 1930, cols 559–64. Henderson may also have been swayed by a comment by E. F. Wise in a speech on 13 November 1930: 'Russia is much more interested in building up foreign trade than in propaganda, but if the situation changes propaganda would increase', Noel-Baker Papers, 4/631.

49 John Bromley in the *Manchester Guardian*, 12 February 1931, reprinted in Coates's *Bulletin*, 26 February 1931: 'Some Authoritative Views on "Forced Labour" in the USSR'.

50 See below, Conclusion, and CITRINE, W., *I Search for Truth in Soviet Russia*, London, George Routledge and Sons, 1936.

chapter nine

The Labour Party's foreign policy and Russia, 1929–31

The Labour Party and the Foreign Office view of Russia

After the 'red letter' scare of 1924[1] the suspicion remained that it would be impossible to pursue an authentic socialist foreign policy with a capitalist Foreign Office. Dalton was of the view before getting into government that there were two schools of Foreign Office thought on Russia. The first, exemplified by Eyre Crowe, who had published the 'red letter', was convinced that the letter was genuine and 'attached no importance to improving Anglo-Russian relations'. This school had triumphed under the Austen Chamberlain domination of the Foreign Office until the 1929 election. The second school hoped for 'and believed in the possibility of improving relations'.[2] Dalton linked these two schools with their different views on the trade agreement, the first not concerned about it, the second wanting it to work properly and 'take up firmly and in detail' breaches of it – in other words, to take the trade relationship very seriously, but not let the Russians get away with too much.

MacDonald accordingly appointed Henderson as Foreign Secretary in June 1929 to ensure that the second school of thought triumphed within the Foreign Office, which Henderson did to the best of his ability. He concluded the agreement to resume relations with guarantees of a sort on propaganda and restarted trade with the Temporary Commercial Agreement of April 1930. By the end of 1929 Henderson was evidently relatively convinced of the loyalty of his Foreign Office staff, on the Russian question as on all others, since he rejected many Labour Party suitors for the post of Ambassador in Moscow and selected a career civil servant, Sir Esmond Ovey, rejecting Ponsonby, who had led the 1924 talks with the Russians for the then Labour Government, a source of great indignation to the latter. Henderson had decided he wanted a diplomatist and, in particular, a Russian speaker, hence his choice of Ovey, being strongly supported by MacDonald in the Cabinet,[3] a rare example of MacDonald's support for Henderson on this or any other issue. In domestic policy MacDonald totally supported the Treasury view of Snowden and Graham. Henderson was no better treated or supported in foreign policy by his Prime Minister.

Carlton asserts that 'in a sense, Great Britain had two foreign policies from 1929 to 1931'.[4] Henderson was to receive little support from the rest of the Cabinet and to be progressively isolated from his Cabinet colleagues. This was what later saved his reputation from being sullied by the crisis of October 1931. In retrospect his reign as Foreign Secretary was always looked upon as a lonely success in a disastrous government.

By remaining active as Secretary of the Labour Party throughout his Foreign Secretaryship he never lost contact with the party's grassroots in the way that MacDonald, Snowden and the others did. MacDonald never bothered to turn up to Labour Party NEC meetings: Henderson nearly always did. As a result he never came under the often open attack in the Commons that the Prime Minister was increasingly to experience from his own supporters.

On the Russian question, Henderson was loyally followed by the Foreign Office and kept to the initial policy of accommodation, and we have seen the battles that this entailed for him in the Cabinet. But he was clearly obeying the mood of the party base in so doing, a base that was ignored by MacDonald as irrelevant or a nuisance. MacDonald was moving rapidly away from his own party on many fronts. His leaving the ILP in February 1930 was but one symptom of his breaking with the past, as was his giving up the purely nominal post of Treasurer of the Labour Party in late June 1930.

The problem as it had been envisaged before the election, that is as one of socialism versus the Foreign Office had turned into one of Foreign Office, Foreign Secretary and much of the rank and file against its own Cabinet.

India, the Comintern and the ILP problem in foreign policy matters, 1929–31

It has been noted that there were major differences between the Labour Party leadership and the ILP over various issues in foreign policy. These included disarmament and, particularly, the Empire. Once in government these disagreements assumed great importance, especially given that Maxton, Brockway and others used Parliament to express the disagreements with MacDonald, Sidney Webb (now Lord Passfield and Colonial Secretary) and Wedgewood Benn (as Secretary of State for India) that they could not express elsewhere. Here the breakdown of inter-party communication was to have extremely embarrassing consequences for the government.

It has already been indicated that Henderson was prepared to spend long hours with ILP MPs, such as Wise, who wished to put pressure on the Russian negotiations in 1929. He was not over-criticised for his handling of the various propaganda campaigns orchestrated by the Tories or the religious persecution campaign. But he was included in the general stricture of Brailsford's 'too much safety' on the various Russian questions. And he did not escape ILP wrath on the Indian question simply because of his office and his Cabinet post, although his name was spoken with far less animosity than Lord Passfield's or Wedgewood Benn's in the hard debates on India of 1930–31. In these the ILP were the main supporters of Gandhi's Congress Party against a Labour Government that was hesitant to grant any of Gandhi's wishes.

It is outside the scope of this study to analyse why the Labour Government was so disinclined to grant independence to any of the Empire except the 'white' areas. Gupta clearly believes that it was due to racist attitudes being as deep in the Labour Party as they were in the Conservatives. Tales of 'White Men and Coloured Girls' were common shock-horror stories in the Labour press. Even the *New Leader* carried what must be deemed racist remarks and reasoning. One 1931 article in praise of a book on 'Race as a Political Factor', concludes that 'the desirability of segregation is stressed, since the interbreeding of the three primary races of mankind produces general inferiority'.[5] Sidney Webb had no major objectors when he talked about 'natives' as if they were inferior beings in White Papers published by his office. No doubt this also had something to do with his disregard for 'Mujhiks' in Russia during his 1932 visit. The point is that he was by no means isolated in this kind of prejudice.

Where there was a truly 'Russian' element in the Indian question during 1929–31, and indeed after, lay in the allegations of Comintern interference in Indian affairs. A Foreign Office memorandum to the Cabinet made great play of the efforts by Henderson to make British displeasure over Dominion and Empire propaganda clear to the Russians. India was 'specially mentioned in the note which Sir Esmond Ovey [was] to present in Moscow .... The Soviet Government have accepted the draft of this note ... and therefore have, or will have, given a specific undertaking to desist from propaganda in India'.[6]

The Conservatives, of course, took every possible opportunity to claim that the Russian promises were being systematically broken. Although it was difficult to accuse the Indian Congress Party of subordination to Moscow, the Tories nevertheless tried to say that this was so on occasions. The Simon Commission Report of 10 June 1930 probably had far more to do with the upsurge of Congress discontent, delaying as it did any hope of Dominion status for India. The civil disobedience campaign had little of the hallmark of the Comintern. In its handling of this crisis the Labour Government fell in between several stools, so it set up a 'round table conference' to try and calm matters.[7]

The government could not take a position critical of British presence in India and MacDonald was particularly scared at the prospect of annoying the armed forces. More concretely, with the economic situation deteriorating, the government desperately needed the markets of the Empire and could not antagonise the Empire lobby, which included a growing number of trade unionists, Ernest Bevin and Ben Tillet among others. Gupta quotes a Treasury Minute on one of Sidney Webb's colonial schemes which was criticised as being 'for the most part quite unrelated to the problem of providing direct and immediate relief of unemployment in Great Britain'.[8] The Empire trade debate was thus part of the same debate in which trade with Russia figured. And the same indecision was a major feature here as well. It was not until the Ottawa Imperial Conference of 1932 that the Empire was finally chosen as the area of concentration, and by then the Labour Party were no longer in power.

It was not, however, on commercial grounds that the ILP assailed Government policy on India during 1929–31 or why Maxton declared himself the 'Member for India'. The policy of non-interference in the Meerut trial of Indian and British communists pursued by Transport House meant that the official Labour Party line became synonymous with the government line after the arrests of May 1929. An India Office statement was sent to all inquirers after February 1930. This stated that there were 'procedural problems' holding up the trial and was forced to admit that there was no 'universal right to trial by jury in India'. This damaging assertion was followed by another. There was no intention to prosecute the accused as 'trade unionists or at least [sic] as communists ... nothing is further from the intentions of the Government of India than to place obstacles in the way of the development of a healthy trades unionism in that country'.[9] To back up this government line the TUC also published a statement that was reported in full in the *Manchester Guardian* on May Day 1930.[10] This was intended to prove that all allegations of persecution of trade unionists in India were the work of communists or those under their influence.

The Meerut prisoners themselves appealed directly to the Labour Party Conference at Brighton in 1929, and the Meerut Prisoners' Committee could claim several Labour MPs as members or supporters in its pamphlet of August 1929.[11] These were all ILP MPs of course, who equally lent their support to Bridgeman's League Against Imperialism, an organisation which had a suspiciously similar address to that of the Meerut Prisoners' Committee, as Gillies never tired of pointing out.[12] The Labour Party NEC took longer to condemn the Committee, probably in the interests of conserving unity.[13] This was particularly important because at the very same moment (late 1929) a major row was developing over respective Labour Party and ILP representation on the Executive of the Labour and Socialist International. Bridgeman was interviewed by the NEC and a decision on his organisation postponed. The writing was on the wall, however, and at the same meeting a whole series of communist-backed organisations were forcibly disaffiliated from the Labour Party, including the Friends of Soviet Russia, and the Minority Movement. The Meerut Prisoners' Committee was given another chance, if not for long.

The embarrassing fact persisted that Labour MPs, be they ILP or not, were supporting an organisation of which the Labour Party leadership disapproved. These MPs continually spoke against and voted against official policy, forcing the government into the unusual position of being kept in office by conservative votes on these occasions! The Conservatives, of course, did not give this support without making political capital, and in questions on propaganda often bought up bolshevik propaganda in India. They also loved to point out the differences within the Labour Party about India. Some ILP members did not hesitate to compare the current (1930) situation with that of 1917 in Russsia.[14] If Gandhi was Lenin, did this not leave the Labour Government as 'Tsardom'?

The Comintern poured fuel onto the fire by announcing that it was contributing greatly to the disturbances. Whatever Rusian interference there was never even remotely approached the levels of 1925–7 in China. This crisis over India was far more damaging for the internal solidarity of the Labour Party, for it led the ILP one more step along the road to disaffiliation.

Peace and disarmament 1929–31

In an increasingly fragmented and disillusioned party only one issue still made the whole membership glow with simultaneous passion and that issue was peace. Yet at this moment no one really hazarded as to exactly where the threat lay geographically. The main potential dangers had not been redefined since the mid-1920s, and were not to be so until the 'Mad Dog of Europe', to quote Beatrice Webb on Hitler, came to disturb the dreams of the 1920s in 1933. The only potential dangers lay in the inexorable rise in armaments, or rather their maintenance at what many thought were dangerous levels. As to actual national state menaces to peace, the only candidates remained fascist Italy, difficult to take too seriously, and the Soviet Union.

Henderson felt the key lay in diminishing the political tensions with Russia by diplomatic recognition and increasing positive economic contact through trade. The latter was proving difficult. What else could be done by Henderson? If the national British arena could not be influenced, he must try elsewhere. There is a well-documented drift by Henderson away from British interests towards the presidency of the League of Nations disarmament talks in 1932 after the fall of the Labour Government, until his death in 1935. Dalton tells us that the League became a progressively increasing obsession for Henderson as 1930 wore on. His disaffection with London politics must have had some basis in his lack of real progress over the Russian issue in Cabinet.

One memorandum identified several key areas for action by the ACIQ and International Department of the party. The most important of these was disarmament. And the only really drastic proposals were those of the Russian delegation, presented in 1927. However 'Our party have [sic] all been agreed that there were serious practical difficulties in accepting this draft as it was first put forward, but we have also been agreed in holding that the purpose of this draft was that for which our parties have always stood'. None the less this offer, which the author believed and 'we all believe' to have been a 'most serious proposal' had been 'treated with absolute contempt' by all the delegations attending the Preparatory Commission in February 1928. A second Russian proposal, one that had proposed partial disarmament 'in progressive stages' had got even shorter shrift, 'but without question it was one which should have had the most serious and sympathetic consideration'. Since then the Preparatory Commission had not met, and had only just agreed to do so again: 'Rather than discuss this new Russian proposition they have brought the whole work of the Preparatory Commission to a standstill'.[15]

Now there was a chance to reverse this policy. Lord Robert Cecil, the Conservative Government's representative at the League had stayed at his post during 1924 upon MacDonald's invitation and had become progressively convinced that the best hope for peace stood not with the Conservative Party that he had served so well, but with the Labour Party. It was in many ways a strange coalition of forces. MacDonald had led the pacifist UDC during the Great War, Cecil had been Minister charged with the blockade of Germany. MacDonald was the illegitimate son of a Presbyterian mother, Cecil a pillar of the Anglican Church.

MacDonald was very flattered at being able to work with the noble Lord, his sycophancy for the aristocracy being an open secret. Although Cecil was undoubtedly honest in his praise of MacDonald's party, it is not so sure he felt the same about MacDonald himself. Cecil was a profound believer in the League, MacDonald was not, even if Cecil had once written to MacDonald: 'I feel the peace of the world depends on disarmament ... and that your government is the only British Government within sight that is in a position to carry through that policy'.[16] When MacDonald switched to the National Government, Cecil resigned as British representative to the League soon after.

However, in 1929 the fires of hope at the Preparatory Commission had been rekindled by the advent of a Labour Government committed to disarmament policies. Cecil renewed his close acquaintance with Philip Noel-Baker, who had been his Private Secretary during 1924, and with Arthur Henderson. Both were now in positions of real power within the Foreign Office. Cecil wrote to Henderson upon arriving in Geneva: 'I cannot help feeling that we have a great chance now ... if we let this opportunity slip it may well prove a serious blow to all for which this government stands. As to the reaction on Home Affairs, I will not venture to express an opinion'.[17] He knew that it could prove fatal for the Labour Party, such was its reputation as the party of peace.

Significantly for Cecil the great unknown factors remained Italy and Russia, providing a close parallel between the Labour Party's and Cecil's own thinking. Later in the slow-moving negotiations Cecil was writing, 'What European country, unless it be Russia, can afford to quarrel with us?'[18] However, it was not from this quarter that he was having trouble, but rather from the French, whom it is evident he could not stand, and whose delegates spent most of their time retarding any progress lest Germany be given any concessions or France's security threatened. France indeed needed to be brought down a few pegs, by using Italy and Germany against her, said Cecil.[19]

On the Russian front he felt optimistic: 'I am myself not without hope that Russia may come in [to the League]'.[20] Russia's presence in the League would help both the League and Russia itself by decreasing tension in both areas. Cecil was encouraged in this course by Labour Party member Konni Zilliacus, a member of the League Secretariat. Zilliacus's presence was clearly important to the Labour Party. Cecil was informed by Noel-Baker before the talks really began that: 'As I think you know, both Dalton and the Secretary of State [Henderson] attach considerable importance to Zilly's views'.[21] How he was viewed by the League Secretariat is more difficult to ascertain, since his file is still under a fifty-year embargo. We can guess that it was a rather difficult relationship. The most important fact is that Zilliacus became an almost fanatical supporter of Russian entry into the League as the 1930s progressed (see Chapter 17).

The disillusion with the Soviet Union that became apparent with Henderson during 1930 also soon hit Cecil as well. It does not seem that Cecil was particularly shocked by the religious persecution crisis of early 1930, although he might well have been given his very close friendship with the Archbishop of Canterbury. What seems to have put him off the Russians was their negotiating manner. In a letter to Noel-Baker, to whom he was far more frank than to Henderson or MacDonald, Cecil wrote: 'I have done my best to get into relations with the Russians as far as I can bring myself to do so, but I must say they give me a shiver down my back every time I look at them. I don't know whether Litvinov or Lunatcharsky [the two main Russian negotiators] has the more repulsive countenance'. As to their behaviour: 'they are behaving quite well . . . It is rather like the man in the pantomime rehearsal, if you ever saw that work, who is always throwing up his part'.[22] The rather obscure literary allusion is to a character who is continually changing his own lines to the general confusion of the rest of the cast.

Noel-Baker tried his best to change Cecil's mind. 'I have a strong feeling that there is now a big opportunity to modify the policy of Russia both towards us, towards the League, and towards international cooperation in general'. He was sure, and had been so informed by Zilliacus, on good terms with Litvinov, that the Russians were now keen to emerge from their isolation, at least partly to be able to better concentrate on the five-year plans. Could not Cecil therefore use his immense influence to persuade the other diplomats also to extend the hand of friendship and to 'try and treat Litvinov as if he were a human being?'[23]

When Cecil actually saw what the Russians had to propose as their passport to acceptance he was not amused. The actual issue was rather technical, Land Budgetary Limitation, i.e. the amount at which the national partners might be allowed to limit their expenditure on land-based weapons. The Americans seem to have been a rather more important real obstacle to this issue being settled, but Cecil was clearly not of the opinion that they did so from any perverse motives and he was in constant and frank touch with them. The Russians, on the other hand, were actually declaring themselves in favour of the limitation, a far more radical measure that Cecil confided to Noel-Baker was 'impracticable'. He therefore had voted against Litvinov, not because of disagreement, but because he feared such wild demands as were being made by the Russians would make the Americans and others even more intransigent, which they in fact proved to be.[24]

Cecil was even more infuriated three days later when Litvinov now voted *against* Land Budgetary Limitation. The vote was 15–1, 'one being Litvinov as usual though he explained that he was not against budgetary limitation in itself. (However reasonable I may desire to be, I am afraid I am convinced that as a practical force he only exists to obstruct and to make propaganda speeches on every possible occasion)'. What was more, Litvinov took the same opportunity to attack the London Conference (also on disarmament) 'which may or may not be true but is certainly irrelevant to anything we are trying to do here'.[25]

Perhaps the most flagrant example of the obstructionism of which he was now convinced the Russians were guilty came in another committee. A 'Soviet amendment A' was put to the vote 'and no one voted for it, not even Litvinov, who abstained as a protest'.[26] By the end of 1930, Cecil had lost nearly all hope of progress. Russia played its part in this disillusion, especially because he had by now lost all faith in her sincerity. The whole of 1931 did nothing to change this view, and the next time that Russia became a source of interest at Geneva was during 1932 and the Manchurian crisis, which will be dealt with later. It would be fair to say that Cecil had not really changed his mind about the Russian contribution at Geneva. His experience in 1930 does not seem, however, to have made him completely despair about the Russians and he was clearly a man that believed leopards could change their spots. His later contribution to Labour Party efforts to strengthen the League through Russian entry was important, especially as he and the party were prepared to try anything by 1934. But during 1931–2 he probably contributed towards the growing dissatisfaction in Labour foreign affairs circles with the renewed relationship with the USSR. This will now be examined from its London end.

The Foreign Office and the USSR during the latter part of the 1929–31 government

The great hopes invested in the renewal of diplomatic relations with the Soviet Union had been dashed from the point of view of their domestic benefit by mid-1930, as has been seen. It remained open whether any other benefits might be obtained in the field of foreign affairs or at least in terms of information, a main function of any representation in a foreign country, which Britain now had in Moscow and Leningrad. Ovey's and William Strang's despatches from Moscow and Leningrad were for the eyes of Henderson and his staff and some of the Cabinet only. They thus had an impact on very few people, but some of these people continued in very influential positions after 1931, be it as party officials or opinion leaders in the Labour Party, except of course those that defected to the National Government. These latter, notably MacDonald himself, Snowden, and Thomas also retained important posts, for a time at least.

There was only one important exception to this general rule: Beatrice Webb shared her husband's access, 'one of the advantages of being a Cabinet Minister's wife is that Sidney shows me interesting despatches' and especially Ovey's, whom she considered to be an 'acute diplomatist'.[27] He clearly had a great impact on her drift during 1930–31 towards the Soviet Union, as will be seen later. The fact is that Ovey, whom Carlton dismisses as a virtual nonentity,[28] was in an almost unique position for feeding information to the Labour Government. There is no evidence that Henderson doubted the truth of his despatches. Dalton went to the Soviet Union as soon as he could for confirmation (see Chapter 12). Even Beatrice Webb was convinced!

We have already alluded to and quoted some of Ovey's reports on the progress of the five-year plan. For a country like Britain proposing to export its way out of recession this was obviously a task of paramount importance. On this level Ovey's reports seem to have been quite level-headed. A typical remark went thus: 'Although the magnitude of the scope of the Five Years' Plan should provide a considerable market, particularly for machines of various kinds, for some years to come, I cannot help fearing that, finally, the export trade from Great Britain to Russia can hardly permanently increase'.[29] He continually harped on about the need for credits and, from the end of 1930 on, linked the need for these with a change in Soviet foreign policy which he, Ovey, put down to the need felt by the Russians for peace in order to pursue their economic development.

Thus the Russians' interest in the Geneva talks was more than to have a propaganda platform, as Cecil had thought when Litvinov first spoke in October 1930 at the Preparatory Commission. Cecil was told by American visitors to Geneva that Russia desperately needed peace to ensure the success of the five-year plans.[30] Simultaneously, Ovey told Henderson: 'All attention is concentrated on the industrial plan. "Credits, credits, credits!" is the cry and to utilise credits requires peace'. As the possibility of these being made available waned as Britain fell into financial crisis in July 1931 (with the rest of Europe and America), Ovey suggested that a withdrawal of credits might encourage Russians who wished to go 'fishing in troubled waters', who would argue that 'they might just as well go the whole hog even at risk of endangering the Five-Year Plan'.[31]

It would clearly be too easy to blame the disappointing results of Anglo-Soviet contact on the narrow-mindedness of the British Cabinet. A suspicion of the Soviet regime lingered that was no doubt fully justified. One of Ovey's first despatches had indeed expressed dismay that Litvinov 'appeared to be more innately fanatical than I had expected', even if genuinely inclined to be cooperative. Kalinin had also appeared to be 'a simple and sincere fanatic'. But Ovey had from the beginning come to the conclusion that the Russians were 'more sinned against than sinning',[32] naturally suspicious because of past injuries and needing to be carefully wooed back to the fold. Henderson clearly believed this himself, and he certainly was a pillar of patience throughout 1930, never openly indulging in polemic against the Russians. Henderson was not at all sure that he knew where the Soviet Union was heading, an opinion also shared by the perspicacious William Strang, one of Britain's most famous diplomatists.[33]

Ovey did not hide the unpleasant side of the Soviet regime, and kept Henderson as up-to-date as he was able to on the latest trails and the progress of collectivisation, as well as on material conditions, especially in Moscow and Leningrad. On the all-important issue of collectivisation, Ovey was at a distinct disadvantage in being based in Moscow: 'It is not often that one has ocular evidence of this process'.[34] The same despatch included a very clear account of peasants being loaded into goods wagons for shipment to Vologda concentration camp, a sight that one of the embassy staff saw while 'during the course of a walk'. Deportation of Kulaks was well known to Ovey and therefore to the Foreign Office.

Yet this dislike of 'bolshevik methods' did not restrain Ovey's enthusiasm for the 'experiment in itself [...] one of the most important and far-reaching that has even been undertaken'. His June 1930 report, a six-monthly progress report on Russia itself and Anglo-Soviet relations in general, was very 'bullish' about Anglo-Soviet trade, less optimistic about propaganda and mainly concluded that:

> we are face-to-face with a going concern. If we are to trade with them, we must trade with them as they are. One cannot destroy the cake of Bolshevism and still have the cake of trade with Russia. Evolution can only be gradual .... This process of constant self-searching and re-experiment is a part of the Bolshevik method.

In short, economic and political facts dictated a continued and growing contact between Britain and the USSR from which Britain could learn much. There was, after all, as Ovey perhaps rather tactlessly pointed out, no unemployment in the Soviet Union which was, strictly speaking, true. In a final and lengthy conclusion, he wrote that Russia was changing under the 'rod of iron' of the bolsheviks. 'The customary criticism that Russians are useless and feckless human beings' may no longer prove to be quite so true, although he 'did agree with this criticism generally'. Only the bolsheviks were a new race, bringing a new 'Mahometanism' to an essentially backward people. But then, finished Ovey, 'Mahometanism introduced an improved state of affairs among the Arab and negro races, and remains, after more than half a millennium, a factor to be considered'.[35]

This rather long quotation is necessary to show the now rather neglected fact that the British elite, brought up on a diet of undiluted cultural superiority and imperial pride, actually rather admired another partially backward country trying to 'civilise' its peasant elements. There was never a suggestion that the British would be amenable to similar methods, because they were of quite another moral and physical type, even the wilder among them. As has been said, to study such a phenomenon would be a book in itself, but it is impossible to ignore the widespread appeal of Ovey's statements. They would have been considered normal in the Britain of the 1930s, and in no way extreme. An alien and therefore incomparable phenomenon was being examined.

One important mind in which Ovey's remarks found full echo was of course Beatrice Webb. She read the above-mentioned despatch and was deeply impressed. She quoted him in her diaries almost word for word:

> Soviet Communism is firmly established and increasing its hold day by day ... Autocracy is indigenous in Russia and will survive in the Soviet Republic as a political constitution. What has been revolutionised is the *purpose* of Government – to bring about a millennium, a transformation of the motives of man – only in *this* world and not in a mystical after life.[36]

The Labour Government and Foreign Office of 1929–31 therefore seem to have had a fairly accurate picture of the progress of Stalinism, at least in its more obvious aspects. But undoubtedly the degree of repression and liquidation was not known. The evidence for this is, in a sense, difficult to define. Henderson got very upset about the trial of the 'Industrial Party' in late 1930, a group whose sabotage, it was discovered, had led to certain problems with the five-year plan targets.[37] An enormous number of despatches passed between London and Moscow on this issue. Had he known of the much worse real liquidation of the Kulaks, would Henderson have restricted himself to such indignation about what was, by Stalinist standards, a minor event? What upset Henderson the most was the implication of a few British subjects in the trial, and the accompanying usual denunciations of Western capitalist imperialism in the Russian press. For this alone Ovey was to 'lodge a strong protest with the Soviet Government'.[38]

The domestic situation in Britain once again goes some way to explaining this attitude. The Labour Government was under severe pressure by the end of 1930. It desperately needed some successes. The Foreign Office had in fact made quite a good showing over Egypt, in talks with Europe, etc. Only Russia really gave problems, especially the ever-present propaganda questions ('PQs'). These evidently gave Henderson much pain and contributed to a mounting exasperation with the Soviet Union. By the end of 1930 Dalton was confiding to his diary: 'Russia is a bloody hair shirt! As Uncle said, if only it wasn't for Russia, we should be having quite a good time at the FO . . . . Uncle has got a Soviet complex at the moment'.[39] But this complex was almost exclusively because of the embarrassment of Soviet propaganda, not because of disgust at bolshevik practices.

The experiment of contact had therefore been less than totally successful in foreign relations, tied in so intimately as they were with hopes of a domestic economic recovery. As the crisis in Britain deepened during 1931, Henderson devoted his energies elsewhere, as is evidenced by a marked slowing of diplomatic traffic between Moscow and London. The financial crisis also hit the USSR, which had less foreign currency to pay for its imports of machinery as the price of raw materials plummetted. Dumping was undoubtedly a wild attempt to save a deteriorating situation by the Russians, but of course this was unacceptable in Britain. Hence MacDonald's 'This is bad' on a despatch at the end of 1930 by Strang to Henderson.[40]

Russia therefore became a side show and was allocated only enough interest to salvage the few positive elements of the rapprochement. A close friend of Strang wrote to him in March 1931 to say 'I lunched with Vansittart and Leeper the other day, but we did not discuss Russia at all I must confess. This shows you the sort of backwater you have become politically'.[41]

Notes

1 See, for example, the Swanwick memorandum where she says that questions will not be 'understood or sympathetically treated by Foreign Office officials', ACIQ, Labour Party, November 1929.
2 DALTON, *Diary*, entry for October 1928.
3 Loc. cit., entry for 31 October 1929. See also CARLTON, *MacDonald Versus Henderson*, pp. 156–7.
4 CARLTON, *MacDonald Versus Henderson*, pp. 23–9. For more details see WILLIAMS, *The Attitude* . . . , pp. 283–6.
5 'Some New Books', *New Leader*, 9 October 1931.
6 Foreign Office memorandum, dated 9 December 1929 and Memorandum to the Soviet Government by the Norwegian Minister in Moscow on 28 November and draft note to be delivered by Ovey. B.D. 2/VII, no. 33, 3 December 1929.
7 For details, see GUPTA, ch. 7, pp. 201–224 and CAB 27/470.
8 Treasury comment by A. W. Waterfield, T.161/297/34609, quoted by GUPTA, p. 137.
9 India Office, February 1930, letter signed by Wedgewood Benn, Labour Party Archives, WG/IND/1929–30.
10 *Manchester Guardian*, 1 May 1930. First published in the TUC's press sheet, 'Industrial News', 29 April 1930.
11 Telegram to Labour Party Conference, 25 September 1929, 'India Overseas Correspondence', Labour Party Archives, WG/IND/1929–30. The pamphlet was called *The Meerut Trial: The Facts of the Case*, London, Meerut Prisoners Committee, 1929, 16 pp.
12 Gillies to M. Crout of Woolwich Labour Party, 2 December 1929, WG/IND/118(i).
13 Labour Party NEC Minutes, 27 November 1929.
14 House of Commons *Debates*, vol. 239, 26 May 1930, cols 911–14 and 946.
15 'Letter from Mrs Swanwick to the Secretary regarding the work of the Committee', Labour Party International Department, November 1929. Noel-Baker Papers, Churchill College, NBKR 2/3, pp. 14–15.
16 Cecil to MacDonald, 18 October 1930, Cecil Papers, Add.Mss 51081.
17 Cecil to Henderson, 21 December 1929. This long memo reviewed the whole disarmament process. Cecil Papers, Add.Mss 51081.
18 Cecil to MacDonald, 18 August 1930, Add.Mss 51081 (another long memorandum).
19 A typical comment was to Noel-Baker: 'All Frenchmen are liars', 3 August 1929, Add.Mss 51107.
20 Cecil to MacDonald, 18 August 1930, Add.Mss 51081.
21 Noel-Baker to Cecil, 14 February 1930, Add.Mss 51107, Cecil Papers. Caute in *The Fellow Travellers*, reserves some of his best venom for Zilliacus, although he does acknowledge that he was an 'outstanding fellow traveller', p. 2.
22 Cecil to Noel-Baker, 11 November 1930, Add.Mss 51107/Add.Mss 51154.
23 Noel-Baker to Cecil, 13 November 1930, loc. cit.
24 Cecil to Noel-Baker, 14 November 1930, Cecil Papers, Add.Mss 51107.
25 Cecil to Noel-Baker, 17 November 1930, Cecil Papers, Add.Mss 51107.
26 Cecil to Noel-Baker, 17 November 1930, loc. cit. (two letters seem to have passed on this date).

27 WEBB, Beatrice, *Diary*, 13 September and 30 June 1930.
28 Cf. CARLTON, *MacDonald Versus Henderson*, pp. 156–7.
29 Ovey to Henderson, 4 January 1930, B.D. 2/VII, no. 52.
30 Cf. interview between Cecil and Harold Butler, Jacobssen and Hambro February 1931, Cecil Papers, Add.Mss. 51099.
31 Ovey to Henderson, 30 June and 26 July 1931, B.D. 2/VII, nos. 138 and 139.
32 Ovey to Henderson, 23 December 1929, B.D. 2/VII, nos. 40 and 47.
33 Strang to Henderson, 11 August 1930, B.D. 2/VII, no. 93.
34 Ovey to Henderson, 21 April 1930, B.D. 2/VII, no. 81, with enclosure on kulaks.
35 Ovey to Henderson, 3 June 1930, B.D. 2/VII, no. 88.
36 WEBB, Beatrice, *Diary*, entry for 30 June 1930. This despatch seems to have played a significant role in her 'conversion'.
37 Strang had been particularly insistent on the slowing of progress on the five-year plan, cf. despatches during his replacement of Ovey during the Summer of 1930, especially 8 September, B.D. 2/VII, no. 97.
38 Cf. despatch Henderson to Ovey, 3 December 1930, B.D. 2/VII, no. 118. This note was delivered and announced in the House of Commons on 15 December 1930, cf. *Debates*, vol. 246, col. 797.
39 DALTON, *Diary*, entry for 4 December 1930.
40 Strang to Henderson, 3 November 1930, in MacDonald papers, PRO 30/69/325.
41 Poliakov to Strang, 8 March 1931, Churchill College Archives, STRN 4/2. Leeper and Vansittart were of course top Foreign Office officials.

chapter ten

Looking at the Soviet Union through Labour Party eyes during 1929–31

The Information Problem

It has been stressed that during this period major changes were taking place in the Soviet Union about which even the Foreign Office had only a vague idea. Malcolm Muggeridge, who took up a post with the *Manchester Guardian* in 1931, recounted later that 'the life of a foreign correspondent in Moscow was even then largely detached from the land, the government and the people whose affairs we were supposed to be reporting'. How was information gathered? According to Muggeridge: 'out of the [local] newspapers we managed to extract items which could be made to appear like news. The newspapers were our only source of information'. All despatches were censored by the Russian authorities and 'the truth is that the Soviet authorities despised us, and not without reason'. Most correspondents, he implies, did not like this treatment, although there were some, 'like Louis Fischer all the time, [who] felt bound to defend the regime'. Muggeridge was equally scathing about British diplomats.[1]

It should be said that the major Labour organs of information did not have full-time correspondents in Russia, and during 1929-31 most reports came from temporary correspondents, mainly based in England. Such was the case of Michael Farbman, who did a series of important articles for the *New Leader* and the *Daily Herald* in early 1930. He had the advantage of speaking Russian. The Glasgow *Forward* had a correspondent in Moscow, Alexander Wicksteed, who also seems to have spoken Russian, but it is not clear if he was permanently posted. He was almost certainly there for most of 1931.

Muggeridge's strictures must be given some credence, but they must also be put in the context of his later development, and that of his society. His complaints are but rarely echoed in comments of the time, except by the right-wing press. The Labour Party's press clearly did worry that the whole truth might not be known, but then that was true of many other places, and the public had already been trained to look on Russia as an enigma. Somewhat later William Strang, wrote that 'in the thirties, the truth about the Soviet Union was still a subjective phenomenon'.[2]

We are therefore faced with two major categories of observer, the professional journalist and the occasional visitor. As MP or member of a delegation, the visitor had only a passing interest in the USSR, one that needed to be classified with other experience. Of this experience, the major element was his or her domestic political interests, with their usual emphasis on social conditions or, possibly, some broad foreign policy interest, usually the maintenance of world peace. The main drift of Soviet studies, in 1930 a new field, has been in the direction of political analysis. But does it follow that this was the main interest of those who went to Russia in the 1929–31 period, or for some time before or since? They were no 'Kremlin watchers'. The distinction has been underlined most ably by Roger Pethybridge who distinguishes 'political dynamics' from the 'motor of social change'.[3] The Labour journalists were indeed interested in the 'political dynamics' but the usual visitor was not. They were interested in lessons that could be drawn from a society without unemployment, the position of women, the cost of living and factory conditions. These two groups will now be examined in more detail in order to build up a composite picture of how the Soviet Union was viewed by the Labour Party observer.

Labour Party press reports of the USSR during 1929–31

Early reports on the "New Russia" 1929–31

During 1929-31 collectivisation and the first five-year plan were widely discussed in the Labour press. They were discussed with an almost pathological desire to be fair, to avoid 'atrocity stories'. When ILO Secretary-General Albert Thomas visited the USSR in early 1929 he was quoted as saying:

> One no longer believed the stupidities of those journals which for ten years have been prophesying regularly the downfall of the [Soviet] Government . . . Has not the time come for a scientific, calm, serious, objective study of the real facts with the help of the Soviet Government itself? . . . Can we not find the men who can rise above mere polemics?[4]

The *Daily Mail's* 'Fairy Tales' were regularly exposed by the Coates' *Weekly Bulletin*, showing misquotes as normal and accusing the diehard press of 'specialising in highly spiced but wholly unreliable news from their Riga correspondents'.[5] But never were Labour press organs, or the *Manchester Guardian*, ever questioned by the Coates. The emphasis was always on stressing their 'commonsense' approach as opposed to the blind prejudice of the diehard press, even if the quotations were, of course, sometimes rather selective. The underswell of sympathy for the USSR in Labour Party attitudes was exploited to the full by the Coates. Whether this was on orders from Moscow can only be guessed and a guess would probably be libellous.

Labour press comment in 1929 on the subject of the Soviet Union was largely confined to the problems of the renewal of diplomatic relations. But some preliminary reports about the USSR itself did emerge in late 1929 and especially in early 1930. This coincided with two important domestic British developments that have already been developed at some length. These were the religious persecution crisis, in effect the first real intimation of the nature of Stalinism, and the rapid deterioration of Britain's employment problem.

There was a gradual suggestion that Russia may have had some major lessons for Britain. Michael Farbman, who sent back a series of reports for the *Herald* and *New Leader*, found that '[t]he Russia of 1929 has indeed very little in common with the Russia of 1924'. He noted that the New Economic Policy in 1924 had seemed practically the 'Thermidor of Bolshevism' because it had at last seemed that Russia was being accepted by international capitalism largely, he implied, under the promptings of the 1924 Labour Government. The hardening of the new Conservative Government had then meant a drastic rethink of this liberalisation, so the story went. Furthermore, the NEP had clearly benefited the richer peasants and led (sic) to the 'expropriation of the poorer peasants on a large scale'.[6] This imbalance had now been realised and the combination of foreign pressure and inequality had led to major changes, starting in 1927, of collectivisation and 'industrial revolution'. The NEP had led to widespread disillusion among the workers, but industrialisation had 'succeeded in seizing the imagination and arousing the imagination of the urban workers'. The NEP was the '*antithesis*' of revolution, 'Russia's present stage [was] the synthesis'. Its inauguration had renewed optimism, channelled through the five-year plan.[7]

As Farbman himself admitted, this would mean big changes for the countryside, and economic dislocation at the very least. Was it all really necessary? It was, he said, since an inevitable result of the Revolution had been the opening up of internal markets that could not be satisfied by a level of production such as had existed in Czarist times. The one hundred and twenty million peasants had then only been a market for vodka, now their 'deeply-rooted individualist nature' was a positive barrier to change. Primitive techniques in the countryside were the main obstacle to increased production, linked to very small individual plots that made technical improvements difficult. In his words: 'It was only when the problem of utilising tractor energy was solved and the idea of *Colhos* [collective farms] became familiar and indeed popular in the villages, that the government concentrated all its energies on the policy of developing collectivist agriculture'. Only a few NEP men and Kulaks now obstinately stood in the way of enormous prosperity for the mass of the peasants who would become 'one of the most extensive markets in the world'.[8] Even here the British worker was made to see his possible personal interest.

The *Daily Herald* clearly took most of Farbman's comments at face value since he was used for a book review during February that is one of the best of the 'peasant as mindless savage' genre. The book, by Dr E. J. Dillon, portrayed as one of the world's greatest experts on 'the Russia of yesterday' with 'eyes . . . still undimmed', was at his best on the peasants, says Farbman. Indeed 'to keep the soul-spark of these semi-savages from being utterly extinguished, to make them active members of the human community, was the work to which the Bolsheviks set their hands'. And they had partially succeeded when Dr Dillon visited Russia in late 1928. But Dillon doubted that they could wholly succeed against the 'stubborn Moujiks', having seen the very beginning of the *Colhos* movement. Now, said Farbman, his opinion would be different, now the 'peasant is wide-awake and superlatively self-conscious' and the 'initial success' of the *Colhos* had only come in the past year. But these were disagreements of detail. Dillon and he both had the same feeling about the USSR. 'I realised that I had witnessed nothing comparable to this spectacular array . . . It was unique and symbolical . . . Nowhere is life so intense, so volcanic, so all-absorbing'.[9]

But obviously one journalist, however respected and believed, does not make a press campaign. Farbman's themes were further developed by himself and others who have become more (in)famous since. Two of these names have come in for particular criticism, those of Anna Louise Strong and Louis Fischer. Caute in *The Fellow Travellers* is particularly scathing about these two, with some justice. Fischer later renounced his faith in the Soviet Union but 1930–31 was the period of perhaps his greatest love. He generally worked for American papers, but produced several articles for the British Labour press in 1930–31 generally stressing Soviet desires for peace. Anna Louise Strong had arrived in

Russia in 1922, edited the English-language *Moscow News*, married a Russian agronomist in 1932 and was, according to Caute, 'one of nature's fellow-travellers, a woman who had fallen in love with the biggest Sunday school of them all'.[10] She was certainly an enthusiast, and she wrote for the British Labour press during this period, especially for *New Leader*.

Fischer, Strong, Wicksteed and Farbman produced the bulk of professional Labour journalists' work on the Soviet Union during the rest of 1930 and 1931. They were the ones who attempted to show what the 'new Russia' was and did much to lay the basis for the interest shown increasingly by individuals (of note or not) and groups that was to continue throughout the 1930s.

The presentation of the new Russia during 1930–31

The Labour press was full of articles suggesting this and that remedy, for the worst depression since the 1870s. The more they were ignored, it seemed, the worse the situation got. It is therefore perhaps not surprising that the most virulently pro-Russian articles appeared in the *New Leader*. The Russians were the very antithesis of 'fatalistic Mr Thomas'.

The film columns played a primordial role in this process of implicit comparison. Russian films had of course always been followed by a certain intellectual elite. Unfortunate rulings by the local authorities in London, generally Conservative it must be said, had led to the banning of a number of films of Soviet realism. The *New Leader*'s film critic, Benn, was able to call these films 'magnificent' and 'amazingly fine'. Why, even a bourgeois audience at the London Film Society, '[a]s the film swept to its climax ... rose from their seats and applauded; cheer after cheer, hand-clapping and stamping in honour of a most wonderful film'. Bernard Shaw also lent his authority to Benn's plaudits.[11]

All the films, with the possible exception of Gorky's work, were, of course, along the approved lines of the new Soviet film. They are now generally seen for the propaganda that they were, but compared with the vast majority of romantic trash then being produced in Hollywood, these films were found refreshing as the thinking man's western. *Turksib* by Victor Turin, and Eisenstein's *The General Line* came in for particular eulogy.

Given this created atmosphere, such writers as Benn and Strong were able to portray collectivisation as a spiritual necessity. *Turksib* was 'remaking the lives of nomad tribes and of ancient settled cultures'. This was their 'awakening'. The 'Agrarian Revolution' was a magnificent success and all those who had contributed 'wanted every one to know it'.[12]

In its fight for development, the USSR was quite simply inspiring to watch. But compared with it, the British scene was ever more depressing. A typical sign of this depression can be found in the aside of a Labour MP in a debate on unemployment in the House of Commons: 'Russia, I believe, will be on its feet long before this country'.[13]

The failure in Britain was widely analysed in the *New Leader* as one due to lack of imagination and, by extension leadership. The *Daily Herald* naturally found this very difficult to repeat. None the less a kind of code can be detected that has a very Russian element. This was the gradual introduction of the personage of Josef Stalin. Until 1930 he had, of course, existed for the Labour press, but always as a shadowy figure, a good solid moderate. Now his image became more polished, the moderate assumed a new energetic face. The *Daily Herald* was just as much a contributor to this process as the ILP papers.

The most obvious manifestation of this was in the use of photographs. The pictorial level of the British daily press being rather crude, the usual adjunct to any article concerning a key personality was a small passport photograph. Hence Pius XI would figure on an article about the Vatican, MacDonald on one about the Labour Party, and Stalin now started to appear on virtually every story about the USSR. This was first really noticeable during Farbman's articles in the *Herald* and *New Leader* at the beginning of 1930.

Stalin was pictorially represented as an avuncular figure, often with a pipe, the 1930s mark of the thoughtful man. The articles themselves identified him as the bringer of good tidings, usually 'Gosplan' figures, or as the moderating brake on excessive enthusiasm. In this last role he was widely quoted during the religious persecution crisis and collectivisation. One example of mixing the former with the latter is a headline in the *Daily Herald*: 'New Soviet Policy Easing Up of The Anti-Church Campaign – Stalin's Order No Extermination of Private Trade'.[14]

On the other hand, Stalin could be presented as tough, as wanting progress at a reasonable pace. There could of course be no retreat on the 'Koolaks', already presented to the British public as a weird sub-breed. His defence of the small peasant was indeed now being presented as adulation. 'Stalin – Idol of Russia, Popularity Among the Peasants, Little Father' announced an article about his 'new popularity' in the *Daily Herald*, with not a comment on the reuse of the hated Czar's familiar patronymic.[15] The *New Leader* printed an early Anna Louise

Strong article at this period which went much further. 'Stalin United Russia – The Revolution in the Countryside', she wrote. It was now 'evident that he has suddenly stepped to an equality with Lenin'. This was the entire explanation of the Western 'campaigns' against the USSR, for they now rightly feared a vast upsurge in patriotic revolutionary pride and production as a result of Stalin's leadership in the five-year plans and collectivisation,[16] said Strong.

Labour MP John Strachey was even able to use a review of Trotsky's *My Life* to say that the 'miracles' predicted by Lenin and Trotsky were now being seen under Stalin. Was this his 'justification'?[17] The 'right-wing campaigns' against Stalin were faithfully reported in the *Daily Herald*, one even accusing Tomsky and Lenin's widow, Krupskaya. As the CPUSSR Congress drew near in June 1930, the difference between Stalin and the right were portrayed as 'caution fights with enthusiasm' with the whole argument being merely one of 'pace'. This view was even given the imprimatur of the *Daily Herald's* chief foreign editor, W. N. Ewer. On a later date Stalin was proclaimed 'Soviet Premier?' by Ewer. What was more, '[i]t would surely be a clear gain, both for Russia and the world generally, if he now takes the position which publicly corresponds with his real authority'.[18]

But by far the bulk of press comment was about the new found 'enthusiasm', the 'spirit of sacrifice' and the results of this. One key word came to be mentioned more and more – planning. With Bevin and Keynes talking ever more about a new kind of protection of home industries,[19] Louis Fischer wrote about 'SACRIFICE according to PLAN – How the Soviets are building up "Home Industry"'.[20] This, of course, was in strict intellectual conflict with the free trade ideas behind the Labour Party's policy and the urgings for Russian trade. But it shows how Russia was portrayed as providing something for all economists. It should be said that the idea of planning itself really assumed importance in the Labour Party only after mid-1931, (see below) but it did now make its Russian entry.

The five-year plans were now being portrayed, especially in the ILP press, as almost biblical texts for study. Reports of the ILP summer school in 1931 used this exact wording.[21] But it was really the non-existent unemployment that amazed observers most. Alexander Wicksteed in the Glasgow *Forward* seems to have coined the phrase 'The Communists have solved the problem of unemployment'. The USSR, said Wicksteed, had converted itself into a 'vast economic laboratory' where such waste became much more difficult. It was now almost impossible to find a good domestic in Moscow! On the *quality* of life, Wicksteed was even more eloquent. The British worker needed no reminder of the degradation of unemployment. He echoed the belief of many 'men in the street' as well as official Labour Party policy when he asked: 'Why on earth can't people who make shirts set to work on the wool and cotton and make work for the shirtless?'[22]

One problem caused friction between outright supporters and sceptics in the Labour Party. This was the mention of 'dictatorship'. Strangely enough, this element that had caused so much anguish in 1924–9, and was to again after 1931, was much less discussed in the interim. Press reports did mention the occasional differences in the CPUSSR, as has been noted, but Stalin's 'moderation' was seen as actually encouraging healthy dissent. There was some Labour press comment about trials of saboteurs and socialists, especially during the trial of fourteen Mensheviks in February 1931.[23] It is known that the Labour Party and LSI were perturbed by these occurrences, but no trace of this appears in the Labour press at this point. The main worries were speculations about dumping, always refuted, presumably in the wider interests of fostering Russian trade. The *Daily Herald*, after the beginning of 1931, seems to have been almost ordered to be cheerful come what may – the situation in Britain was so awful.

It can thus be concluded that the British Labour press had effectively built up a dazzling picture of a 'new Russia' by 1931 that contrasted starkly with a Britain in decline. Clearly this vision attracted visitors, if only out of curiosity, a phenomenon that will now be briefly examined for the years 1929 to mid-1931. For the purposes of analysis, this will be done in three parts, one for groups, another for individuals or small unorganized groups, and one for 'opinion leaders'.

Labour Party visitors to the USSR, 1929–31[24]

Small groups and individuals

Given the practical problems of being a minority government, there were no Labour MPs, of whatever persuasion who could visit the far-off USSR during this period, except during the parliamentary recess. The daunting nature of the Russian climate also played a part. They had, with a few notable exceptions, to travel under the guidance of Intourist, both because of Soviet policy and because of linguistic problems. There is little evidence of linguistic ability, with the possible exception of Magda Gallen, who travelled in one group of largely ILP MPs. Frank Wise MP, who mixed his activities with that of working for ARCOS in Britain, was a constant visitor and must have spoken Russian. Jenny Lee

MP (ILP), who later married Aneurin Bevan MP (Labour Party) and who visited Russia in 1930 commented that 'Fascination with all things Russian still had a strong hold on Socialists, whether left, right or centre'.[25]

The group that is probably the most interesting comprised John Strachey MP (Labour Party, later to defect to the CPGB), Bevan and Lee and George Strauss MP (Labour Party). The latter was a close collaborator of Herbert Morrison on the London County Council, Morrison being Minister of Transport and the 'hammer of the Communists'. As such, Morrison combined great MacDonald-like orthodoxy with an openness to new ideas, and especially planning. They were accompanied by Magda Gallen, who wrote several articles upon her return on Soviet wheat exports, a burning question due to the 1931 International Wheat Conference[26] and Celia Simpson. Their itinerary was typical of what Caute calls 'conducted tours', where all accounts begin and end with the Soviet ship to Leningrad, the visit to a Kolhoz and one or more factories. There is very little point in describing these. I shall concentrate on their reactions, where a record exists.

Bevan kept a diary, which is unavailable to historians, but which has been used by his biographer, Michael Foot. Foot comments that '[it] curiously at first sight seems valueless; it is stuffed with pig-iron statistics and contains not a single Bevanite flash of comment or insight'. Foot explains this away as Bevan always being 'ready to apply the test to a nation's industrial or military strength: how much steel does it produce?', referring back to Bevan's origins as a miner and forward to his wartime activities. The key point for Foot was that Bevan 'in 1930, apparently ... came away from Russia with his Marxist faith neither diminished nor greatly fortified. What he did learn – or rather what he confirmed in his mind – was the doctrine ... that "freedom is the by-product of economic surplus"'. Another impression that he recalled later was 'whereas in Britain we were slaves to the past, in Russia, they were slaves to the future'.[27]

Jenny Lee also recalls the same feelings. For her, the Comsomols were 'widely excited about the future. The hardships around them were inevitable: they would pass'.[28] These hardships included travelling in a train, for long periods, across famine areas. The train itself was a 'physical endurance test', and Jenny Lee was the youngest Labour MP; what the peasants had to suffer was far worse. She wrote this in 1980. In 1930 an article she published in *New Leader* upon her return told the same story, with a rather different emphasis. What struck her most then was the incredible pace of change, 'a century in four years'. But the 'hardships' were presented as both less and more explicable. Shortages are described in detail, although 'the grain problem has been solved and there is no shortage of bread'. What became clear was that all these shortages were the fault or 'partly due to the resistance of the kulaks, or richer peasants, who slaughtered a large proportion of the livestock throughout the country rather than take it into the new communal farms'. Another key point for Lee was the fact the 80 per cent of the population as a whole were peasants: 'even the slightest variation in their standard of living is sufficient to dislocate the entire market and cause havoc in the towns until a new equilibrium is reached'.[29] Can we detect a certain unease in these words?

The most striking of their mutual observations were on the Russian ability to survive and its manifestation in the five-year plans. They were all extremely impressed by the sheer energy and enthusiasm of those they were allowed to meet, and the size of the undertaking. This is reflected in Bevan's statistics, as well as in Strauss's and Lee's descriptions. There were lessons as well. Russia was 'sacrificing present needs for future prosperity'. It was 'a challenge to the world's industry' in its coming efficiency. This was both a warning to inefficient capitalism and a huge possibility for future markets.[30]

In 1930 Lee railed against a 'certain type of visitor who sees and understands nothing except that there are queues in the streets of Moscow'.[31] These visitors were given space to explain themselves to the Labour Party. One who went at the same time as the above group, was Labour MP, J. Toole. His account in the *Daily Herald*, where he told that he had always been 'pro Russian', now told that he 'could see nothing but incompetence, insecurity, insanitation, disease and want'. He saw prices and conditions that no English worker could have supported, and political repression and factory discipline that no trade unionist could have accepted. This element worried him most of all: 'The "boss" class still exists, but its form has changed' and 'The fact is that Russia has shed one despotism for another. The colour has changed: Red has superseded Black'.[32]

Another small group, this time not MPs but still trade unionists and Labour Party Members, had a similar feeling. They were miners from Tilmanstone in Kent, who visited the Donetz Basin in August-September 1929. The two miners, Mr Roome and Mr Crane, were sent by the colliery owner, Mr Tilden-Smith, who hoped to introduce more up-to-date methods in the mine. They therefore set off and, due to an administrative mistake in Moscow, travelled entirely alone to the mining area. Their account is one long tale of woe. Subtitles include 'a revolting street scene' and a 'never ending stream of beggars', 'a boy and a bone' to quote but three on the first page.[33]

The *Daily Herald* reacted to both these reports. Toole's comments had not been presented 'of course, as the ultimate truth about Russia, nor would Mr Toole himself make that claim ... Other observers have returned with accounts as lyrical as Mr Toole's are gloomy'. On the miners' report the paper had a similar line. 'Surely we in the Labour Movement desire the truth, even if it should be unpalatable?',[34] it reported the chairman of the local branch of the Kent Mine-Workers Association as saying in defence of the report. A. J. Cook of the TUC General Council had evidently accused the men of being in the pay of the bosses, as had many other less-eminent members of the British Labour movement. The miners' comments had been doubly unpalatable at that crucial moment in the re-establishment of relations with the USSR. But they would probably have elicited the same response at any moment in the next few years. The defenders of the USSR were far more vocal than the attackers.

Some group visitors from the Labour Party

The most interesting and best-documented groups to go to Russia in the course of the 1929 government were two groups of 'cooperators', who went in August 1929, and again in July and August 1930. They were ordinary people who went to look essentially at ordinary things. They observed the condition of the people, educational facilities, housing, factories, farms, etc. Anecdotal narrative make up most of the reports' substance. The only truly analytical part, in the first 1929 report, called 'Miscellaneous Notes' discussed the proposition 'you only see what they want you to see'. This homely approach was answered by the affirmation that 'we had abundant opportunity to speak to all kinds of people, and met several who were bitterly critical of the Bolshevik regime'.[35] All the members of the delegation expressed similar feelings, one even writing to the *Daily Herald* to refuse J. Toole's complaints.[36]

A great deal of these reports, as with those of the individual travellers, concentrated on organisation, conditions and what can be called 'anecdote'. Nowhere is there any mention of the political struggle in the USSR. One small section in the 1930 Coop Report does deal with the state and religion, but here again the analysis largely consists of 'what the Captain of the Ship told us' and similar comment. Only Emrys Hughes, one of the group, approached a political statement, when he postulated that the Communist Party had become 'the alternative religion': the members of this new religion who venture into the interior, for example Turkestan, 'face dangers as real as any that Christian missionaries have faced in Central Africa, and among the head hunters of Borneo'.[37]

In short, the report spoke (1) about what the visitors thought would interest the people at home, and this at a fairly low level; and (2) in terms of how Russia had been presented to them in the press at home. There was some mention of the 'new Russia', with the five-year plan being briefly described. But the implementers of this plan, the Comsomols, etc., were likened to Barnsley men spreading the word of God among a heathen and alien race, not suborning their own countrymen, which was the truth of the matter.

If we can none the less forgive what were essentially ordinary working people for not having an analytical approach to their subject matter, other groups of educated persons did not have the same excuse. But evidence of such groups is rare. It was not until after 1932 that there was, for example, an organised mass visit of British journalists. However, some Labour Party representation did exist on a late 1929 trade delegation of businessmen.

Malcolm MacDonald MP, the son of the Prime Minister, spoke in a debate in mid-1930 in which he admitted having gone to Russia incognito with this group, of Canadian businessmen. He admitted that he could 'claim no authority at all' as an expert, had written no articles on his return nor a 'book entitled the "Real Russia As I Saw It"'. The Russians he had met had 'not any idea that I had any relations sitting on the Government Front Bench'. He had come back convinced that renewed Anglo-Soviet relations would have a 'tremendous effect' on ordinary Russians and 'has created a new feeling of friendliness and trust towards this country'. A great deal of 'patience' was necessary before this would be wholly the case with the Russian Government because distrust was so deeply embedded, but there his analysis stopped. It was no doubt very difficult for a man in his position to express any deeper opinion in the House of Commons.[38]

Some other visitors of great influence on the Labour Party

The most celebrated of all visitors during this period is difficult to classify, but he cannot be left out of any analysis: George Bernard Shaw has been cruelly attacked in recent literature for his flippant remarks about Russia, but as founder of the Fabian Society with the Webbs and others he still had a role as 'opinion leader' in the Labour Party. The same Emrys Hughes who went to Russia with the Cooperators in 1930 described him as having a 'bigger audience than anybody else on

Earth'.[39] He was certainly treated as such in Moscow. Stalin gave him a two-hour interview during his July 1931 visit and his comments have become classics of 'fellow travelling'. It is very difficult however to ascertain to what extent Shaw was taken seriously within the Labour Party, and to what extent he was seen as the court jester.[40]

When Shaw did finally visit the Soviet Union in summer 1931 he thoroughly lived up to his eccentric manner. He went with Lady Astor, a major critic of the USSR, firmly on the right of the Conservative Party. He gave speeches that equated Soviet communism with fabianism. Emrys Hughes, in his article about Shaw's visit, asked 'How much of the new dictatorship is to be Stalin; how much Mussolini, and how much Mrs Sidney Webb?' He could not answer his own question, since neither his own visit, nor what he had read in the Labour press was likely to give him an answer. All he could say concretely about Shaw was that it 'will all help to make the world think a little more and understand more about Russia, and help break down the mood of suspicion and hostility'.[41]

Russia viewed through Labour eyes, 1929–31

Emrys Hughes' conclusions on Shaw's visit demonstrate the contemporary Labour Party thinking about Russia during this period. If Dalton's 1929 'much else is misty' had been superseded by a somewhat more sophisticated mystery, mystery was still the word to use. Change had been so rapid, that there was a great lag between event and the understanding of that event. Moreover, reports were sketchy and isolated, and generally emanating from a very small group of committed Labour or Soviet journalists.

Visitors mainly went as passive observers armed either with their life experiences and beliefs and/or a reading of reports in their press. One distinct cleavage remains to be explained, however. How could some of the visitors come back shocked and disillusioned and others not? The answer lies, for this period and for others, outside the normal categories or left and right, or is at least inadequately explained by them. Bevan was not particularly impressed, but he was to constitute the far left of the party in the late 1930s. His future wife, Jenny Lee, was impressed. Malcolm MacDonald, to join the National Government in October 1931, also expressed admiration. Two Kent miners, not a generally conservative breed, were appalled. Walter Citrine, who visited in 1925 and 1935, perhaps gives a clue to this dilemma. He and the other critics had the common feature of basing their judgements on the living conditions of the working class. This linkage was by no means as simple as Lenin's denunciation of the 'trade union mentality' would lead us to believe. Equally there were those who had seen and excused such horrors in Russia, such as Jenny Lee. But this identification of domestic and Russian conditions in some and not in others does seem to have been a major factor in these initial reactions. And it must be stressed that these were often initial reactions modified by reflection over the next few years.

Another tempting explanation is to say that those who liked what they saw in the USSR were the intellectuals of the Labour Party, whereas the rank and file were more mitigated in their enthusiasm. The attack on the Webbs and other British 'fellow travellers' has this continual implicit accusation. To say the least, it seems that the evidence for this is incomplete for the years 1929–31. However, what is increasingly true over the next period is the linkage of impatience with the Labour Party and its tactics and personnel with a growing admiration among intellectuals for strong government. Mosley's defection to fascism, John Strachey and others to the communists (via the New Party) are all evidence of this.

These reflections must be made, since they have become a major historiographical obsession in the last few years. But in 1929–31 'fellow travelling' was only a proto-movement, Shaw being an important but fairly lonely forerunner. Beatrice Webb was still giving the same speeches that she always had to ILP summer schools. But in private she was already railing against 'intellectual hollowness' in the Labour Party. She was also asking herself: 'Will a new party arise to start afresh the struggle for the equalitarian state? Much depends on the success or failure of "Sovietism" in Russia. If it were to succeed . . .?'[42]

For in spite of everything there was no guarantee that it would succeed for the observer of 1930. Only when it was well entrenched, for good or for bad, did the 'fellow travelling' or enthusiastic attitude really take hold, and then by no means everywhere in the Labour Party or outside it. This had to wait for a major domestic crisis in the Labour Party and far more information about the 'New Russia' itself.

Notes

1 MUGGERIDGE, Malcolm, *Tread Softly for You Tread on My Jokes*, London, Collins, 1967, pp. 25–7. One comment about Ovey is that he 'had a plan for abolishing unemployment, but somehow I could never get the hang of it', *ibid.*, p. 32.

2 STRANG, Lord W., *Home and Abroad*, London, Andre Deutsch, 1956.

3 Cf. PETHYBRIDGE, Roger, *The Social Prelude to Stalinism*, London, Macmillan, 1974. See discussion pp. 1–21.

4 Anglo-Russian Parliamentary Committee *Weekly Bulletin*, 28 February 1929.
5 Ibid., 14 March and 5 December 1929.
6 FARBMAN, Michael, 'Soviet Russia in 1929: I – Reconstruction Begins', *New Leader*, 10 January 1930.
7 FARBMAN, 'II – The Industrial Revolution', *New Leader*, 10 January 1930 and 'III – The Five Years' Plan', *New Leader*, 24 January 1930.
8 FARBMAN, 'IV – The Turning Point in Agriculture', *New Leader*, 31 January 1930.
9 FARBMAN, Michael, 'Giving Soul to Savage Peasants', a review of Dr E. J. Dillon's *Russia Today and Yesterday* (London, J. M. Dent, 1930), in *Daily Herald*, 26 February 1930.
10 CAUTE, *The Fellow Travellers*, op. cit., pp. 74–5. Fischer's *The Soviets in World Affairs* appeared in 1930 and was serialised in *Socialist Review*.
11 BENN, 'Storm over Asia – Another Censored Film' and SHAW, G. B., 'The Latest Index Expurgations', *New Leader*, 28 February 1930.
12 STRONG, Anna-Louise, 'A Russian Triumph: The Turk-Sib Railway' and 'The Agrarian Revolution' *New Leader*, 20 June and 25 July 1930.
13 Mr Sandham in House of Commons *Debates*, vol. 236, 13 March 1930, col. 613.
14 *Daily Herald*, 12 March 1930. See also *Daily Herald*, 27 February 1930 (agriculture figures), 17 March 1930 ('Relaxing the Iron Hand Policy – No Forced Closing of Church', 'Worshippers Desires Must be Restricted', 'Communist Order').
15 'Our Own Correspondent', *Daily Herald*, 8 April 1930. Again the obligatory picture of Stalin appeared.
16 *New Leader*, 21 March 1930. Again the obligatory picture.
17 STRACHEY, John, *New Leader*, 6 June 1930 and *Daily Herald*, 29 May 1930 (author unknown).
18 EWER, W. N., 'How Stalin Will Face His Critics', *Daily Herald*, 6 June 1930 and 'Stalin – Soviet Premier?', *Daily Herald*, 18 July 1930. Trotsky also gave interviews to the *Manchester Guardian* and *Forward* that confirmed great successes in the first five-year plan.
19 Keynes' article 'Proposals for a New Revenue Tariff' first appeared in the *New Statesman and Nation* on 3 March 1931. Bevin announced a new direction for the TUC in autumn 1930, rather prematurely.
20 FISCHER, Louis, 'Sacrifice According to Plan', *Daily Herald*, 14 October 1930 (the capitals are his) and another article on 15 October 1930 on the wonders of collectivisation.
21 GREENRIDGE, Terence, in *Socialist Review*, July-September 1931.
22 WICKSTEED, Alexander, 'The Labour Shortage in Moscow – Where There is No Unemployment', *Forward*, 3 January 1931 and 'In Moscow Now: Things You Cannot Buy For Money', *Forward*, 18 April 1931.
23 Cf. reports in *Daily Herald*, 9 and 10 March and 15 April 1931. The last report was perhaps the most serious since it ended in ten death sentences on kulaks. The sentences were without comment. Karl Radek also published four articles in *New Leader* justifying the repression of 'saboteurs' (Jan.-Feb. 1931).
24 I cannot pretend that this list is totally complete. I have gone through all the Labour Party-linked press of the years concerned and mentioned all the visits found therein. There were not many to be reported. An exhaustive list not seem possible.
25 LEE, Jenny, *My Life With Nye*, London, Penguin, 1981 (first published 1980), p. 86.
26 GELLAN, Magda, 'Breakdown of Wheat Exporting Countries Conference', *Socialist Review*, July 1931 and 'USSR', *Socialist Review*, December 1931.
27 Cf. Michael FOOT, *Aneurin Bevan*, vol. 1, New York, Athenaeum, 1962.
28 LEE, Jenny, *My Life With Nye*, p. 89.
29 LEE, Jenny, 'A Century in Four Years: Russia's Will to Survive', *New Leader*, 7 November 1930. See also STRAUSS, George, MP, 'Soviet Russia: Some Impressions of a Short Visit', *The London News* (published monthly by London Labour Party), December 1930 edition, which confirmed the other findings.

30 STRAUSS, loc. cit. and 'How the Five Year Plan is Affecting Russia', *London News*, July 1931.
31 LEE, Jenny, 'A Century in Four Years: ...'
32 TOOLE, J., MP, 'What I Saw in Russia', *Daily Herald*, 28 August 1930.
33 *Tilmanstone Miners' Report on Russia*, Dover, St George's Press, 1929, 32 pp.
34 'The Truth About Russia', *Daily Herald* editorial, 28 August and 4 October 1930.
35 *Report of a Group of Cooperators on a Visit to Russia, August 1929*, Manchester, Co-operative Union Ltd, 1930, and *Report on Visits to Russia by Members of Two Groups of Cooperators, July-August 1930*, Manchester, Co-operative Union Ltd, 1931. Quote from 1930 visit, pp. 63–4.
36 *Daily Herald*, 30 August 1930.
37 *1929 Coop. Visit*, p. 62.
38 House of Commons *Debates*, vol. 239, 6 June 1930, cols 2610–12.
39 HUGHES, Emrys, 'Bernard Shaw as a Bolshevik', *Forward*, 15 August 1930.
40 SHAW, *The Listener*, BBC publication, 23 October 1929. For Beatrice Webb's reaction to this see WILLIAMS, *The Attitude* ..., pp. 333–4.
41 HUGHES, Emrys, 'Bernard Shaw as a Bolshevik'.
42 WEBB, Beatrice, diary entry for 16 April 1930.

chapter eleven

The Labour Party in crisis and reconstruction 1931–4: Russia the 'exemplar'?

'Annus terribilis 1931'[1]: the categories of problem facing the Labour Party

The setting up of the National Government was largely due to the banking crisis of early 1931 and the subsequent run on the pound sterling. The differences in the Labour Cabinet were about where to make cuts in public expenditure, not whether to make them. Unable to persuade his colleagues of what he had himself been persuaded by Snowden, MacDonald went to the King, resigned and then became Prime Minister of an essentially Conservative 'National' administration until 1935. Snowden and Thomas were the only prominent Labour minsters who joined him and have shared the condemnation meted out by Labour Party biographers.[2] The Labour Party appeared momentarily to disintegrate and then slowly recover in the years up to 1935. It survived by effectively changing its character from a very tolerant into a relatively disciplined party. It also spent a long and agonising time deciding about its future role and policy, a process which was completed in its real essentials by 1935.

There were three major categories of problem facing Britain in the years 1931–5. They were the economic, the domestic political and the external threat of war. In all of these the USSR was able to intrude sometimes as an important, and sometimes as a minor, factor. To these categories should be added a crisis that mainly affected the intellectuals and that has usually been referred to as one of 'modernism'.[3] The West had come face to face with its own ambiguous industrial and social past as a result of war and then depression. Whether the date of 1929, 1931 or 1933 is taken as the point of conversion to intellectual 'depression' on a vast scale is relatively unimportant. What really matters here is that the phenomenon was widespread and that the USSR formed part of the focus in the search for new ideas.

The new emphasis in power relationships within the Labour Party

As the advent of government had meant a shifting of power in the relative direction of the Parliamentary Labour Party (PLP) in 1929, the defeat of 1931 meant a reversal of this trend. Only fifty-five Labour MPs retained their seats in the holocaust of the 1931 election, and only Lansbury was left of the old leadership. Clement Attlee, a minor minister in 1929–31 now had prominence thrust upon him.[4] Sir Stafford Cripps, a lawyer whom MacDonald had almost forced onto the party, now became the leader of the left. Cripps's importance has perhaps been exaggerated by historians, but he was certainly a very loud voice from the Labour left throughout the 1930s. His relationship with the USSR is less clear, except during the war.[5]

The focus of power was temporarily deflected from the PLP to the other organs of the party, partly as a result of this dramatic fall in electoral fortunes. The Labour Party headquarters, Transport House, became the physical and metaphorical embodiment of Labour Party power. Built in 1928 as the home of the biggest and most influential trades union, the Transport and General Workers' Union (TGWU), and its General Secretary Ernest Bevin, Transport House also provided offices for the Labour Party that it retained until the late 1970s. In the early 1930s this physical proximity was naturally echoed in an alliance of the moderate wings of the political and trades union sides of the labour movement. The communists were of course strictly excluded from this cosy relationship, as they had been since 1926. Any other group that was deemed unworthy of consultation, such as the ILP after 1932 was also rigorously excluded.

MacDonald had semi-encouraged a new generation in the persons of Hugh Dalton, Herbert Morrison, Cripps and Attlee. Of the four, only Dalton and Morrison had an existing power-base on which to build. Morrison's was most solid, in the London Labour Party, which he continued to build up during the 1930s, culminating in the Labour group's control of the London County Council in 1935. Dalton was in no such position of geographical superiority, but he made up for it with a flair for the political game and a rare intelligence that made him indispensable in the 'blueprint writing' that followed 1931. Morrison and Dalton in fact became staunch political allies and dominated the

NEC throughout the whole of the 1930s. Rare was the decision that did not have their approval. Those that didn't were usually pushed through by another body, the National Joint Council (NJC).

This body was revitalised in 1931 to impede any repeat of the cult of the personality that had grown up around MacDonald. The NJC comprised representatives of the Labour Party NEC, the PLP and the General Council of the TUC. Its aim was to 'endeavour to secure a common policy and joint action' on all matters affecting the 'workers as producers, consumers and citizens'.[6] It could also call for joint conferences with the TUC, which had a built-in majority. Its limits were defined in early 1932 as being a 'vehicle for dealing only with matters concerning the Labour movement as a whole'. This was to ensure that domestic problems of the three bodies were not overly discussed to avoid overlapping and to underline that 'There are matters upon which it will be necessary to preserve a definite Trade Union or Labour Party point of view'.[7]

During the period covered by this study, subjects of joint concern were notably those of international tension and of internal discipline. The 1930s included the period of the communists' attempts at a 'united front' and a great deal of discussion took place about the Labour movement's attitude towards this (see Chapter 15). For the first two years after 1931 the communists themselves excluded real contact. It was only after 1933 that new conciliatory moves were made by the CPGB.

In the light of these joint concerns it is perhaps not surprising that certain administrators should receive greater prominence than before. Until 1930 at least, Arthur Henderson had managed to keep control of the NEC through his position as Secretary of the Labour Party, a post that he never neglected. With his nomination to Geneva to the Disarmament Conference of the League of Nations, 'Uncle Arthur' could no longer balance so many roles, and gave up effective administrative dominance to J. R. Middleton, who Pimlott dismisses as 'loyal but ineffective'.[8]

One figure of under-estimated importance during our period is William Gillies, Secretary of the International Department. The evidence points towards a major role for Gillies not only in the International Department, but also in the fight against the communists and their 'front' organisations. As such he was a key figure in that he had a direct role in the consideration of Labour Party policy towards the USSR in its several manifestations.[9]

Gillies seems to have satisfied the introspective mood of the Labour

Party of the early 1930s. By all accounts he was a man of great capacity for hard work and a polemicist of some skill. He was also – curiously perhaps for a secretary of the International Department – reputed to dislike foreigners or at least to distrust them. His dislike of Russians is clear from everything he ever wrote. But it must be said that such xenophobia in the Labour Party was far more common than it would like to admit. The whole atmosphere of England in the 1930s tended in this direction and the Labour Party was by no means exempt from the influence.

The new Labour Party and its immediate reaction to the crisis

With MacDonald's passing into opposition a series of mental as well as operational changes were necessary in the Labour Party. Leadership has been correctly analysed as the primary problem by Pimlott. The new importance of the National Joint Council gave the trade unions a far greater say in party affairs than before, particularly Walter Citrine and Ernest Bevin, who dominated the TUC throughout the 1930s. They reversed the previous policy of leaving politics to the politicians and played a major role in the elaboration of economic and social policy in an often uneasy partnership with Dalton and Morrison, the latter hated by Bevin but with whom he was forced to work. This conflict was probably not a bad thing in the long run for the policies developed.[10]

The other tendency that has been noted by Pimlott and others is that of a furious new effort to develop new ideas through institutionalised research and the setting up of ginger groups. Within the party structure this meant the inauguration of a Policy Committee in December 1931. This was proposed by the Head of the Research Department, Arthur Greenwood. Dalton and Morrison were both members, as was Lansbury as head of the PLP.[11] Ad hoc committees were immediately formed, on the 'wheat quota' and the 'means test', and more permanent bodies followed to discuss 'finance and trade', 'reorganization of industry', 'local government and social services' and 'constitutional' questions. These committees show extremely well the overall concerns of the party. Outside Transport House, a similar tendency can be detected, which was vital to Labour Party attitudes to the USSR in the 1930s. Several bodies were formed, of which the most important were the XYZ Club, the Society for Socialist Inquiry and Propaganda (SSIP) and the New Fabian Research Bureau (NFRB). It is not necessary to tarry over the XYZ Club too long. It was a shady body that seems to have met in pubs and discussed mainly domestic financial problems such as the abolition or reform of the City.[12] The other two have a distinct Russian element and are therefore of great interest.

The Society for Socialist Inquiry and Propaganda (SSIP)

The SSIP was the first physical expression of the need for a drastic rethinking of the Labour Party's role in British politics and society during the 1929–31 goverment. In spite of MacDonald's disapproval, by the time of its official launching in June 1931 its founder, G. D. H. Cole, had managed to get Ernest Bevin of the TUC General Council to be its chairman. The SSIP was a potentially radical force within the Labour Party for it combined the best of the intellectual force of the left with the industrial power and realism of the TUC. Its first months were very promising and the fact of its existence in October 1931 probably had a deal to do with the ability of the Labour Party to pick itself up from defeat so fast. The SSIP felt that it reflected the 'crying need for disciplined realist thought within the Labour movement'.[13] Again the parallels with the late 1980s are perhaps striking.

The first two SSIP debates underlined the atmosphere of crisis. The second pair put all their emphasis on ways out. Planning was to do the trick. This was the first major indication and reflection of a growing awareness of the possibilities of this new approach to economics which was to become an obsession (see Chapter 14). Russia was also featured and managed to attract some of the biggest audiences.[14]

The SSIP's activities were given full Labour Party backing after December 1931. C. M. Lloyd's speech on Russia was even delivered at Transport House. The Labour Party never lost its almost visceral distrust of rival research organisms, however. The SSIP never asked for official affiliation to the party, and was never offered it. The vision of the Labour Research Department, which had been taken over by the communists, was no doubt still a fresh memory. Membership of the Labour Party was, however, a prerequisite for joining the SSIP.

Its contributions to the future of the Labour Party were both positive and negative before it wound up in late 1932. It certainly stimulated Labour Party discussion of a previously unheard of intellectual level on very complex subjects especially economic ones. Negatively it did much damage to long-term party unity by the method of its passing. This was because when it merged with the later-formed Socialist League, Bevin was asked to stand down as chairman. This had the universally recognised result of antagonising Bevin, and by extension much of the TUC, against the intellectuals, who were generally on the left of the party.[15]

It made one very important contribution to our subject. In its short search for a policy to emulate, no country was considered as a possible exemplar other than Russia. In June 1932, Bevin prefaced his remarks by saying 'No country outside Russia appeared to have a policy today', whereas Britain was in a terrible mess largely because it had no policy of any kind.[16] Bevin's views give rise to the conviction that he believed very strongly in the necessity of tough measures being taken to bring about socialism and that Russia was the only place that seemed to have done anything along these lines. He was often accused in the latter part of his career of having 'stalinist' tendencies and Bevin indeed did express understanding and sympathy for Stalin's efforts on more than one occasion. Thus we have the paradox of a man who was very insistent on democracy in politics but could tolerate its apparent opposite in economic endeavour, especially at a safe distance in Russia.

The New Fabian Research Bureau

This body's famous antecedents are well known. The brainchild of the Webbs had been allowed to fall into disrepair in the MacDonald-dominated 1920s. His departure heralded its revival in the 1930s. It was in effect an entirely new organisation, with none of the old presuppositions about permeation of other parties. The old Fabian Society continued to exist and gave its blessing to the new undertaking while remaining independent. Like the SSIP, the NFRB did not affiliate to the Labour Party, but was loyal to it and tried 'simply to influence Labour opinion without pressing their ideas on the movement in any organised way' in the words of G. D. H. Cole[17] and many of its members, such as Leonard Woolf, were prominent on Labour Party international committees.

Its 'Panel on International Research' was particularly star-studded, at least in Cole's original list. The forty-one names included Attlee, Noel-Baker, Bevin, Kingsley Martin, William Mellor, Dalton, Citrine, Leonard Woolf and Gillies, all of whom were to loom large in the elaboration of Labour Party foreign policy in the next few years in different capacities. There are a few absences of note. Henderson was not there, presumably because of his work in Geneva, and neither was E. F. Wise. But virtually all the different shades of Labour Party opinion figured on the list in 1931, a sign of the desperate need felt by Cole and others to reunite the party, although the left was to later form its own grouping in the Socialist League.

As was the case with the SSIP, a widespread belief existed in the

NFRB of the need for a 'thorough re-examination of socialist theory and practice ... in the fields of both economics and politics'. International relations was a field in which this concern was felt most strongly. 'Interdependence' was not a word used as yet by the NFRB, but a similar phrase, 'intricately internationalised', was. National policy was therefore meaningless without international policy.

This was all discussed very early in the life of the NFRB in a document entitled 'Memorandum on a Plan of Research into International Relations and Policy'. Some of its main points were those of traditional Labour Party foreign policy concerns. The question of open diplomacy and the role of the Foreign Office, progress towards the elimination of war and more general concerns about the role of the League of Nations all came in this category, even to the point of postulating the eventuality of a super-state and the building up of the international civil service and organisations as an essential preliminary. Many areas for study followed, primarily in the field of economic cooperation.

But the only nation-states that were seen as being of particular interest for study were the USSR and Sweden, principally the former:

> How far does the USSR fit into a scheme for an international society? The reactions of the militant Communist movement upon present and future political relations. In what spheres of international activity does the USSR cooperate with other states? The problems of recognition and membership of existing international organisations.
>
> How does the policy of a nationally-planned economy affect the economic relations of the USSR with other states and with international public and private organisations and regulation? The proposal for an economic boycott of the USSR[18]

These notes formed the basic themes around which not only the NFRB, but also the Labour Party itself, looked at the USSR until at least 1935. They implied both domestic and foreign policy initiatives for the Labour Party, and also internal party concerns, mainly that of how to deal with the CPGB and the Comintern. The basic distinction between the militant communist movement and the USSR as a state in its own right was clearly made. But how could the Labour Party stop talk of a possible economic boycott of the USSR becoming reality? And how could it ensure the entry of the USSR into the League? All of these questions were to receive an answer before 1935. In the meantime it was recognised in 1931 that the answers would take an 'indefinite time', as would the answers to the wider questions posed in the document.

The only countries seen as having progressive integrated political and economic systems were essentially the USSR and the Scandinavian countries. A pamphlet was circulated about a 'Proposed Mission of Inquiry to Russia 1932', for it was 'the only country where a large-scale socialist experiment is being carried out . . . where under the dictatorship of the proletariat the whole economic life is being changed from a capitalist to a socialist basis'. Whereas the 'Memorandum' had stressed the USSR as a foreign policy interest, the brief of the 'Mission' stressed its domestic interest for the Labour Party and Britain: 'While it is recognised that conditions in this country would require a policy very different from that at present pursued by the Soviets, it is obvious that over a very large range of subjects . . . valuable lessons can be learnt from the Russian experiment'. The direct interest of the NFRB and Labour Party lay in the fact that in no instance has there been a thorough-going inquiry conducted by members of the Labour Party into Russian economic developments in the last few years with the definite objective of using the results to assist in the working out of a Socialist policy for Great Britain'.

Now was the moment to do this research, because not only was the first five-year plan near completion, 'but the economic crisis in the capitalist world is turning the attention of everyone to the planned economy of Russia'. Other visitors, of whatever political persuasion, had confirmed this, said the circular. And in the party itself 'the thoughtful part of the Labour movement is intensely alive to the importance of the Russian experiment, and anxious above all things to avail itself of Russian experience as soon as this can be made clearly and intelligibly available for it'. Such a report would 'do more at the present time to concentrate and clarify Labour thought and Labour energies than any form of propaganda'.[19]

This still stands as the most clear declaration of interest in the USSR expressed at this period by what was essentially a broad cross-section of the Labour Party. The best available experts were asked to go by Cole, who it seems drew up this list, as so many others. The Annual Report, dated the same month as the circular, had fifteen names, allocated to various fields of interest. Dalton and Pethick-Lawrence (a junior Minister of Finance in the 1929–31 government) were given joint responsibility for the key areas of finance, banking, capital movements and prices. Dalton also had to look at economic planning. Other areas to be examined were industry and transport, agriculture, labour, the social services, political life (which was largely 'legal') and cultural life.[20]

Going on the mission was obviously considered a great honour and of immense importancce in the Labour Party. Bullock relates that Bevin had been asked but had 'to his regret . . . to give up the place which Cole wanted him to take'. Planning had been given pride of place in the original mission brief. It was believed that in Russia alone was 'economic life being conducted on scientific and up-to-date lines'. The emphasis that planning was given in these early documents of the revival of the Labour Party in 1931–2 is the clearest sign of the major changes that were taking place in the party as a whole.[21]

The ILP's disaffiliation from the Labour Party in 1932

The desire for change that was so important in the setting up of the SSIP and the NFRB was also evident in the ILP. They had warned against MacDonald throughout the 1929–31 government, with a determination that had nearly destroyed the Labour Party. It might have been expected that with his passing the ILP would make its peace with the rump of their colleagues. Such was not to prove the case. The NEC of the Labour Party did in fact hold out the pipe of peace in late 1931, but when the conditions were known they were rejected by the ILP. The conditions were to finally obey the party whip in the House of Commons and to obey the Standing Orders of the party as voted in the Annual Conference.[22]

This long-standing quarrel had a strong Russian element. The ILP was made up of firm supporters of the USSR. Its members – Brailsford, Brockway, Maxton, and Wise in particular – had been most vociferous in their condemnation of MacDonald's 'non-respecting' of the 1929 election promise to bind the two countries together. Indeed it had nearly always been ILP MPs who had attacked the government's Russian policy during these difficult years of 1929–31. Support of Russia had been for the ILP a true litmus test of the Labour Party's socialism, and this continued to be the case. Linked with the even more critical ILP reaction to the 1931 debacle, it was enough almost in itself to drive many ILP members into exile from the Labour Party. The ILP was by no means united in the need for disaffiliation. A series of votes from early 1930 on had always rejected the course finally taken in July 1932. Brockway became the leading proponent of withdrawal from, and Brailsford for remaining in, the fold.[23]

The division was over the degree of disgust felt over the Labour Government's performance and whether it could now be trusted to mend its ways in opposition, even if they be only on certain issues. A major difference subsisted in that many in the ILP believed that the Labour Party's leadership may have been changed but its guiding ideas had not. Lansbury, as Pimlott points out, was extremely 'moderate' in the MacDonald style. Bevin was now more powerful than ever, and Henderson had never ceased to be the Secretary of the Labour Party, where he had waged merciless war on ILP indiscipline. (Dalton and Morrison were certainly no friends of the ILP either).

Even this might have been excused but for the fear in certain quarters of the ILP that a belief in the basic soundness of the capitalist system as a whole was still held by the vast majority of the Labour Party and TUC leadership, whatever they may have said to the contrary. Bevin's remarks about Russia to the SSIP had clearly indicated that he believed capitalism might in fact save itself. The ILP only spoke about the 'approaching collapse' of the capitalist system as if it were ordained, and more important, imminent. In this alternative scenario the USSR was given an even more prominent, indeed obligatory, place.

An early 1932 ILP pamphlet (i.e. before the official break with Labour which took place in July) made this link. Produced by Poplar (London) ILP it sandwiched 'The Success of Soviet Russia' between 'Approaching Collapse of Capitalism' and 'The Coming Crash'. The USSR was not presented merely as a successful experiment and a source of inspiration but as being a system that would inevitably succeed capitalism. This would be brought about either by industrial upheaval (strikes, lockouts, etc.) or 'inter-capitalist war' (between the USA and Britain, for example) or 'anti-Soviet war, broadening into international civil or class-war'. Such statements were never forthcoming in any Labour Party literature.[24]

The hardening of the ILP line was due to the birth of a new ginger group within its ranks, the Revolutionary Policy Committee. Poplar ILP particularly favoured this line. The Committee considered itself marxist and it seems to have dragged a lot of the leadership along with it, Maxton and Brockway notably. The marxism in question included a large and growing measure of belief in the USSR. The *New Leader* published numerous articles essentially confirming the Poplar line. The threat of war with the Soviet Union was given particular emphasis.[25] To confirm the other points there were continual reminders of the 'impending' collapse of capitalism and a major new monthly series, the *New Russia*. This latter four-page supplement continued for years to come, and is one of the most explicit examples of uncritical admiration for the USSR in the British press of the 1930s.

Not that criticism of the USSR did not appear in the *New Leader* at this crucial point in the ILP's fortunes in early 1932. The urge for 'democracy' that had so infuriated the NEC of the Labour Party made the ILP on occasion a fierce denouncer of undemocratic tendencies in the USSR, even if they were mostly excused.[26]

Unfortunately for the ILP it was increasingly dismissed as an irrelevance since it spoke to the heart, not to the head. It remained as a reminder of youthful folly, a fond memory, losing membership steadily until it finally went from 653 branches in 1932 to 233 in 1937, and from an income of £1,445 13s. 3d. in 1931 to £221 2s. 6d. in 1938.[27] Certainly it was possible to argue, as did Brockway, that a 'revolutionary socialist' party did not need a mass membership, but he later realised his mistake.[28]

The ILP continued in its adulation of the USSR in the *New Leader* after its disaffiliation in 1932. It also tried to continually renew ties with the Communist Party, which treated it with unconcealed contempt. The USSR figured large in this so-called relationship, in that the CPGB had explicit orders to push the changing lines of Comintern and Soviet foreign policy.

Simultaneously the ILP tried to build up its position within the LSI as an alternative British member with the Labour Party. This had the sole effect of enraging the Labour Party and the LSI. The latter also did not appreciate ILP attempts in the 1930s to form an alternative, revolutionary, international with some of the small continental parties. Trotsky tried to use the ILP as his English base.[29] The effect on the CPGB of such activity can be easily imagined. The net result was a progressive breakdown of morale and cohesion.

The Socialist League

Although the disaffiliation of the ILP necessarily removes it from this continuing analysis of the Labour Party, a very important group of the ILP preferred not to go with Maxton and Brockway but to remain in the Labour Party. They formed themselves into the Socialist League in September 1932.

Pimlott is particularly emphatic about the progressive marginalisation of the left as a whole in British Labour politics during the 1930s. Whereas the left had come up with some of the most practical suggestions in the 1920s (the ILP's emphasis on planning being one) in the 1930s the ILP and the left in the Labour Party, the Socialist League, became increasingly obsessive and out of touch with reality. As Pimlott says: 'The Socialist League was Socialist first and radical second; like the ILP and the CP its approach was fundamentally utopian'.[30] The Labour Party became solely interested in the 'art of the possible' and left its socialist rhetoric increasingly for the wastepaper basket, a tendency which essentially continued until the later 1970s.

Was there any reason for the new Socialist League to think otherwise in 1932? After all, some of the best brains in the ILP joined it – E. F. Wise and H. N. Brailsford to name but two – and it was led by Sir Stafford Cripps who was universally admired for his penetrating intellect (or at least his reputation for having one). As for the atmosphere in the Labour Party, one of its most visible signs was the desire for change.

The problem was that the Socialist League misjudged the direction that this change was taking in the Labour Party in the 1930s. Although it is recognised that the Leicester Conference of the Labour Party in October 1932[31] did in fact pass a good many of the Socialist League's resolutions, none of them could be described as extreme. They reflected a widespread indignation at MacDonald and all his works rather than a swing to the left. This feeling was soon subordinated to practicality and the Socialist League was left stranded with its obsessions, as will be seen in subsequent chapters.

On foreign policy the initial Socialist League position was very pro-Soviet, and continued to be so. The First Annual Conference of the League at Derby during Whitsun 1933 passed a series of resolutions that put a rather different emphasis on relations with the USSR than was then, or ever, suggested by the NEC of the Labour Party, or indeed by its conferences. This conference was greatly overhung by the threat of Nazism in Germany. The Socialist League, like the ILP, felt that the Labour Party and the masses should look for allies in the coming struggle. On the internal level they followed the ILP into dreams of a 'United Front' with the CPGB. The outside saviour was to be the USSR.

A resolution passed at Derby had as item 14, on international policy, the advocation of 'establishment of closer economic and political ties with the Union of Soviet Socialist Republics based on the fullest possible interchange of goods and services and on the closest possible political collaboration'. At this stage the individual member of the Socialist League or wider Labour Party might have seen no particular difference of emphasis. This was suggested in the supplementary motion by Charles Trevelyan objecting to National Government proposals to stop Anglo-Soviet trade.[32] But it is clear that the Labour Party had never advocated the 'closest possible political collaboration' with the USSR. Moreover, it would never have agreed with the sub-clauses of other motions that its continued membership of the League of Nations and ILO should be conditional on, among other things, 'any attempt to use the League as an instrument for the preservation of world capitalism necessarily involves resignation from the League'.[33] This would never even have occurred to the vast majority of the Labour Party leadership as possible.

Both left and right of the party agreed that the necessary corollary of any new attempt for power lay in searching for new ideas. Russia provided the best experimental testbed around, and all the more so because it was far from Britain and could be examined without too much harm. It is proposed to show in the following chapters how the Labour Party simultaneously discovered its new road in domestic and foreign policy while discovering its disillusion with the Soviet Union. In many fields the USSR acted as a midwife for new ideas and attitudes that went far beyond the framework of Anglo-Soviet relations. This was certainly true before 1931, but after it was very obvious indeed. Of course not all was new in the Labour Party. There was reaffirmation of some older fundamental beliefs, such as in parliamentary democracy, that were reinforced by observation of the USSR.

Notes

1 Chapter heading of Arnold TOYNBEE's *Survey of International Affairs, 1931*, Royal Institute of International Affairs, London, 1932, p. 2. See also SIEGFRIED, Andre, *England's Crisis*, London, Jonathan Cape, 1931.

2 A certain revisionist approach has developed in the last few years with David Marquand's *James Ramsay MacDonald*, and Ben Pimlott's *Labour and the Left in the 1930s*, as prominent examples of the trend. There have been non-Labour defenders of MacDonald's action, of course, cf. BASSETT, R., *Nineteen Thirty-One, Political Crisis*, London, Macmillan, 1958 and NICHOLSON, Harold, *King George V: His Life and Reign*, London, Constable, 1952 as prominent examples of the genre.

3 Cf., for example, HYNES, Samuel, *The Auden Generation: Literature and Politics in England in the 1930s*, London, Faber and Faber, 1976; SYMONS, Julian, *The Thirties: A Dream Revolved*, London, Faber and Faber 1975 (revised edition) and BERMAN, Marshall, *All That Is Solid Melts Into Air: The Experience of Modernity*, London, Verso Editions, 1982.

4 For good biographical sketches of Labour Party leaders during the 1930s see PIMLOTT, *Labour and the Left in the 1930s*, pp. 21–35.

5 GORODETSKY, Gabriel, *Cripps' Mission to Moscow*, Cambridge University Press, 1984.

6 NJC Minutes, 27 May 1930.

7 NJC Minutes, 21 January 1932 and 26 April 1932.

8 Cf. PIMLOTT, *Labour and the Left in the 1930s*, pp. 71–108. As one might expect, most of this activity took place between 1934–7 when the Comintern permitted 'Popular Front' tactics.

9 I have Stephen Bird, Archivist of the Labour Party, to thank for both the origins of this insight and the sorting of the documents.

10 For details of these quarrels see BULLOCK, Alan, *The Life and Times of Ernest Bevin*, London, Heinemann, 3 vols, 1960, 1983, vol. 1: *Trade Union Leader 1891–1940*, pp. 459, 510, 574, and WILLIAMS, Francis, *Ernest Bevin*, pp. 183–7.

11 Labour Party NEC Minutes, 16 December 1931. Also PIMLOTT, p. 36. Pimlott does not discuss this Committee at any length.
12 Cf. PIMLOTT, *Dalton*, pp. 223–4.
13 *SSIP News* Bulletin, December 1931, p. 2. This became 'Zip News' from its March 1932 edition.
14 The 'hall was packed to hear C. M. Lloyd on Russia' on 27 November, *SSIP News* Bulletin, December 1931.
15 See PIMLOTT, pp. 45–6 and BULLOCK, p. 515.
16 SSIP Policy Session, June 1932, SSIP Papers.
17 COLE, G. D. H., *History of the Labour Party*, p. 283.
18 'Memorandum on a Plan of Research into International Relations and Policy', Cole Papers, Nuffield College, 16 June 1931, 6 pp., pp. 4–5.
19 NFRB 'Proposed Mission of Inquiry to Russia 1932', 4 March 1932, 3 pages, unpublished.
20 NFRB, *Annual Report*, year ending 28 February 1932, p. 4.
21 BULLOCK, page 505 and NFRB, 'Mission to Russia 1932', p. 1. Chapter 13 will be devoted to the findings of this visit. The intention here is to explain the context of its inception.
22 Labour Party NEC, 27 August 1931. See also DOWSE, Robert, *Left in the Centre: The Independent Labour Party 1893–1940*, London, Longmans, 1966, ch. 12.
23 Cf. BROCKWAY, *Inside the Left*, ch. 4, pp. 237–47.
24 CULLEN, C. K., (Poplar ILP and major leader of the 'Revolutionary Policy Committee'), no apparent title, published Poplar ILP, 1932, 11 pp.
25 Cf. DOWSE, pp. 180–83; e.g. SLOAN, Pat, 'Moscow is Waiting; Will Japan Attack?' and editorial 'Russian War Threat' in *New Leader*, 11 March 1932 and 22 April 1932. This coincided with the major period of RPC influence.
26 For example, MURRY, Middleton, 'Why I Joined the ILP', *New Leader*, 1 January 1932, and BROCKWAY, *Inside the Left*, chs. 25 and 26.
27 ILP NAC Minutes, end 1938, Item 25, LSE Archives.
28 Cf. BROCKWAY, *Inside the Left*, pp. 18–19. His regret was, in 1942, only partial.
29 Some elements can be found in UPHAM, Martin, *The History of British Trotskyism to 1949*, PhD thesis, Hull, 1981 and in ARCHER, J., *Trotskyism in Britain 1931–77*, PhD thesis, CNAA, 1980.
30 Jupp, in his *The Radical Left in Britain, 1931–41*, is rather more positive. PIMLOTT, *Labour and the Left in the 1930s*, p. 65.
31 LPACR, Leicester, 3–7 October 1932. Published Labour Party 1932.
32 Socialist League Annual Conference, Derby, 3–5 June 1933, especially Item 20, 'Russia and Germany'.
33 Ibid., item 14. I am grateful to Mr Reg Groves for letting me look at his papers on the Socialist League (he was Secretary of the London area from 1935–7).

chapter twelve

Gathering evidence for the blueprint: Labour Party visitors to the USSR 1932–3

The National Government and Soviet-based Western journalists' knowledge of the internal situation in the USSR during 1932–3

The major sources of information about the USSR that found their way to the Foreign Office during this period continued to be the reports sent by Ambassador Ovey in Moscow and his Chargé d'Affaires in Leningrad, Strang. Their sources continued to be largely limited to the area around their respective offices, and to a more or less reliable system of informers among the local population, as well as contacts with journalists. As has been noted previously, most journalists also confined themselves to Moscow and with a few honourable exceptions did not look too deeply at events outside the Soviet capital. Muggeridge's strictures about diplomats and journalists in Russia remained valid throughout the 1930s.

Only the very rare Western observer managed to escape the information straitjacket enforced by the OGPU such as William Chamberlin, correspondent of the *Christian Science Monitor* among other papers. His findings were not published until 1934 in *Russia's Iron Age* after which he was definitively expelled from the USSR. His visit to Karelia in 1931 led him to believe that he had found 'abundant confirmation of the general impression in Moscow: that Karelia has been used as a place of exile and forced labour on a gigantic scale', although 'one's freedom of travel and investigation has a very definite and concrete limitation in the shape of the barbed wire which surrounds the Gay-Pay-Oo concentration camps'. He was not able to publicly declare these findings but they fuelled his disgust when he and his wife met George Bernard Shaw during that summer. Shaw declared that there was no food shortage in the Soviet Union, and that he had thrown his hampers out of the window of the train. He [Shaw] seemed 'quite oblivious of the really superb histrionic efforts which are being made for his benefit'.

Chamberlin was noting the spread of a new harshness in the Russian countryside, one that had not existed in 1929 or even 1930. His next trip was not until October 1933, when he travelled to the North Caucasus and the Ukraine in response to 'rumours of wholesale starvation among the peasants there during the past winter and spring'. The authorities had forbidden all travel for several months to these areas. He found the rumours to be true.[1]

The National Government had similar information to that gleaned by Chamberlin, but had not his journalist's vocation to reveal it. The Cabinet merely wished to define what they were dealing with for internal Government use at a time when British policy was being redefined in a number of fields. As a general rule, and as had been shown in the religious persecution crisis of 1930, successive British governments made great efforts to maintain the secrecy of Foreign Office despatches in order to protect the integrity of their ambassadors. Any information received was therefore kept within the official channels. Even during the highest point of Anglo-Soviet tensions, during the Metro Vickers trial in 1933, this remained the case. Strang's 'Notes on Conditions in the Leningrad District', for example, was extremely detailed on many subjects, from building to scientific advance. It noted widespread typhus epidemics, the development of what seemed very much like a class system, abuse of minorities, very high infantile mortality rates and a whole host of failures in the agricultural and fisheries sectors.[2] Ovey had a similar message: "There is a grave shortage of food ... In the North Caucasus, where results were very bad, large bodies of OGPU agents have been brought in to search for grain, and there has been a good deal of shooting'. In short, the bulk of the horrors of collectivisation were known. Duff had annotated Ovey's report with 'PM [i.e. MacDonald] You should read this desperately gloomy account by Ovey of the present picture and outlook in Russia'. The increasingly resigned MacDonald had merely written 'File' on it.[3]

Other very reliable information came to supplement this kind of report. Yet again this was not released for public consumption. The Empire Marketing Board sent one of its agronomists, Canadian Andrew Cairns, on a particularly successful industrial espionage mission in 1932. the Board was particularly worried about the effects of collectivisation on Soviet wheat production, since should the USSR achieve even its

1913 export totals the North American wheat producers, especially in Canada, would have been badly hit. Cairns was able to reassure these interests for he discovered a complete production disaster in the Ukraine, Crimea, North Caucasus, Volga region and Western Siberia which he visited in three separate trips.[4] The correspondent of the International News Service, Deuss, had told him 'vivid stories about his travels through agricultural Russia – hungry people, gross mismanagement, cattle farms far removed from supplies of fodder, wholesale acceptance by the Russians of a lot of advice from 'bum' engineers and now bitter disillusionment'.[5] Apart from Chamberlin, who seemed to be 'the best posted of the many people I have met so far', he only met one person who had much idea on the subject, Dr Otto Schiller of the German Embassy, and it was with him that he travelled.

Although his reports were totally damning on all aspects of the five-year plans and collectivisation, it is his asides on the presentation of Russia in the West that perhaps interest us most here. While Deuss, Chamberlin and Duranty had all been ruthless in their oral condemnation of the USSR to Cairns, they never said so in their reports. They all wished to keep their visas, and one is left with a very poor view of the gentlemen of the press in reading his copious notes. Similarly, he was very effective in his condemnation of other expert bodies in the West. Seeing a prison he commented: 'I thought of the nice little speeches I had heard about Russian prison life (holidays, freedom, etc.) in Chatham House'.[6] But he could not really believe that these journalists would not eventually start to tell the truth about what they saw.

At one point he met a group of visiting British journalists who included Kingsley Martin of the *New Statesman*. One of Cairns's friends, Lyall, went up to Martin who had just witnessed a starving man being thrown out of a restaurant: 'Martin was sure he must have been an ordinary beggar'. Other journalists were more condemnatory. Mencken, of the *Economist* and a professor at the LSE, had said to Cairns: 'I can't get over the infernal cheek of these people wanting us to adopt their system. Look at these thousands of hungry people sitting in worse than oriental filth and squalor'. Cairns concluded: 'I am afraid the journalists' visit is going to be one more communist experiment gone wrong due to lack of adequate control. I'll be surprised if at least some of the guests don't fairly roast their hosts when they get home'.[7] Of course some of them did. Kingsley Martin did not, as the future record was to show. Martin, as has clearly been noted, was one of the journalists who had most made it his business to quell the 'atrocity' stories emanating from the diehard Tory press which were often backed up by very little and were wildly inaccurate. The result, said John Maynard Keynes, publisher of the *New Statesman*, was that the account was 'A little too full of good will. When a doubt arises, it is swallowed down if possible . . . This is the right spirit to visit Russia, if one wants to enjoy oneself'.[8]

Cairns's letters were initially sent to Strang in Leningrad, who sent them by diplomatic pouch to the British Government, to the Canadian Government and to the heads of the Canadian and Australian 'wheat pools'. MacDonald definitely saw them, for there is a copy in his papers. The report was also later quoted by Ovey in a meeting of the Committee on Anglo-Soviet Relations of the British Cabinet.[9] It was thus a major source of information for the government, and there is some indication that the Labour Party was also informed of Cairns's findings.[10]

The NFRB visit to the Soviet Union in 1932

The much heralded NFRB 'mission' mentioned previously has left us with one of the best documented visits by a Labour Party-linked delegation to the USSR in the early 1930s. The only other visit that has such evidence is that of the Webbs, which will be discussed in the next chapter in some detail because of the widespread comment it has attracted, especially from the school hostile to the 'fellow travellers'. The NFRB trip has in stark contrast attracted virtually no post-facto comment. Margulies' book on the visits of 1924–37 has no mention of the resulting major publication, *Twelve Studies in Soviet Russia*,[11] in its bibliography whereas Citrine's 1935 publication is mentioned, as are some far more obscure English visitors of the left of the post-1931 period.[12] Caute only gives the NFRB a passing mention, although he seems to think that the Webbs went with them, which they of course did not. In this case it seems only too evident that they were ignored as not really fitting the argument being exposed. Caute himself had to admit, in one of his few non-critical remarks about 'fellow travelling', that: 'If Clement Attlee and Hugh Dalton could admire Russia's productive vitality during the era of the plans, we certainly have no cause to sneer'.[13] It is perhaps a pity that he did not take his own advice more often. The most recent book on the Anglo-Soviet phenomenon, by Northedge and Wells, also has no bibliographical or textual mention of the NFRB trip.

The nature of the evidence that exists lies in the publication mentioned above, as well as at least three biographies or autobiographies of two of the key participants, Hugh Dalton and F. W. Pethick-Lawrence. The first needs no introduction; the second was one of the key financial experts of the Labour Party and, after 1935, on the executive of the PLP. He had a somewhat ambiguous friendship with Dalton who it must be admitted was ambiguous about most of his political allies. Dalton and Pethick-Lawrence also left very extensive unpublished details of their immediate impressions, Dalton in his diary and Pethick-Lawrence in two typewritten accounts that he circulated to the Labour Party NEC and the TUC General Council and a selection of friends.[14]

Dalton's diary is of particular use in deciding upon the development of his attitude during the visit in that it was written in two parts. The first part is a diary in the conventional sense, written up immediately and thus in a somewhat chaotic form. The second part is a far more logical categorisation of impressions. Both were written while still in Russia. Taken together they provide many clues to both what Dalton himself saw and thought and also to how the group gathered their information.[15]

The areas investigated reflected a broad range of subjects of interest to the Labour Party. Dalton's introductory article confirmed that the 'General View of the Soviet Economy with Specific Reference to Planning' remained the principal interest. Pethick-Lawrence followed with 'Finance'. The economic essays concluded with T. G. N. Haldane on 'Power and industrial development', G. R. Mitchison on 'The Russian worker' (of great interest to the TUC) and John Morgan on 'Agriculture'.[16] Other essays (in order) dealt with the political system, the legal system, women and children, architecture and town planning, the press, archaeology and the intellectual worker (sic) and the film in Russia. It is very tempting to see this published order as a priority list for the Labour Party. A great majority of previous interest had been in economic issues, with political affairs coming second. This is not to say that other features of the Soviet system were not of interest, but one of the things that is striking about this book is how the economic aspects of the system were continually stressed.

The overall motive for the visit, as stated by Cole and Attlee in the introduction, grew organically out of the conviction explained in Chapter 11 that national Labour Party policy had to draw on different types of experiences, especially international. It was none the less stressed that they went as individuals, 'each participant preparing themselves by special study for the particular field of investigation which they were to undertake'. A healthy English generalism was allowed to float over the published papers, probably to parry any accusations of remote control. As a result there was a great diversity of opinion expressed, none the less dominated by Dalton's first chapter,[17] and a great variation of modesty.

H. L. Beales and D. N. Pritt were particularly lacking in this virtue and wrote on the political and the legal systems respectively. The most modest of all was John Morgan, a farmer, who affirmed: 'Six weeks in Soviet Russia. Time enough to see a good many things, but hardly time enough for an agriculturalist, however expert, to do more than form a few general impressions of what was taking place'.[18] Such refreshing modesty was the introduction to what was probably the best and truest account of Russian agriculture published before 1934. Beales and Pritt's lack of any such modesty lead into the most embarrassing chapters of the whole book. In a private memo Pethick-Lawrence followed a line much more akin to Morgan's but was more optimistic about the possibility of accurate findings.[19]

Dalton lent the experience in private his usual bitterly accurate eye, whereas in the published account he studiously avoided all mention of the reliability or otherwise of impressions and sources. In private he was scathing about the enthusiasts who made up a large proportion of those he met visiting the USSR: 'those who come hoping most fall furthest'. This apparent imbalance was smoothed by the general intelligence of his remarks and the lack of hyperbole. He slips through the fingers of the potential critic by providing an account into which one could read virtually anything while at the same time making some very clear points, especially about planning.[20]

His private notes demonstrate very clearly what the main sources of oral information were, as opposed to what could be seen with the naked eye. He spent some time talking to various members of the British Embassy staff. It should not be forgotten that as a recent parliamentary Under-Secretary of State he was well-known by the staff of the embassy, at least by name, and in Ovey's case, personally. He would thus have been let into far more confidences than many other visitors, no matter how important, as an accredited, if former, member of the closed club of British diplomacy. He recorded long conversations with Ambassador Ovey, Consul General Ballard and another staff member, Ridley.

Ovey's position was, of course, crucial. Dalton thought 'Ovey is as good as I remember' and was particularly impressed by his efforts to meet Russians. Ovey told Dalton that his despatches back to London were often criticised for not giving 'more adverse reports' by some members of the government. Dalton could, however, see the limits of these contacts with diplomats: 'The diplomatic community is apt to be a little self-contained island'.[21]

Generally the excessive claims of the few were buried among the modesties of the most important contributors. The publication was thus a slick public relations exercise. The reasons for this seem obvious – Dalton and the two introducers of the volume had also heard that Pethick-Lawrence had been told that the Russians would select what was to be seen. They were also aware that the Soviet Union was in a transitional stage and did not want to be seen as accepting a frozen picture of Soviet reality. Some of the accounts which are the least convincing as writing or as truth made just this mistake and can thus be analysed as interesting aberrations of the Western intellect. Dalton and several others were clearly near to a truth that still appears balanced.

It seems appropriate to start with the extremes, in that they demonstrate two very important currents in Labour Party thinking that are none the less not entirely typical. The true 'fellow travellers' in this volume are Beales and Pritt, particularly the latter. Beales started by pouring scorn on the British parliamentary system, comparing what a similar Russian observer would deduce of our system had he been in a Russian NFRB. He would have experienced far worse obstruction than the NFRB: 'no access to our Department of State or to our more important officials with the freedom that is possible in Russia'. Any research would have had to be skin keep since quite simply no information existed on the British system. In a brutal and stupid aside which must have cost him a few friends in the Labour Party he wrote: 'The only Party which ever get analysed in the same way as the Russian Communist Party is the Labour Party: there is an almost statistical exactitude about the extent of Labour mugwumpery and the percentage in Parliament of superannuated trade union officials'. These bilious comments ended by saying that in the Soviet Union all was different. 'To go to Russia is to be reminded of the social contract beloved of our political philosophers, and to find it actual reality. That truly is a disconcerting experience'.[22] After this inauspicious beginning it is difficult to take any of the rest seriously, and it must be said that no other contributor took the same virulent tack.

Pritt, a lawyer and KC, was more measured in his blindness. A lawyer who was to make a fully deserved reputation as an exposer of the legal crimes of the Nazis, he was a well-respected figure and his opinions carried weight outside the Labour Party. But his account of Soviet justice is almost a parody of the truth. His 'straightforward description of the system' describes the law in the USSR as 'not generally dissimilar from that of England', prisons in Russia were 'reformatory and not in the least punitive' in the 'old-fashioned type of prison' and the 'open or semi-open camp is in many ways better than this'.

The Russian system was thus the ideal of the English writ large: 'everything that Russia has recently done is what English reformers have preached for years'.[23] The Pritts and Beales of the Labour Party used Russia as but one more whip to push their conviction of the decline of Britain. They were in the same class of critic as the ILP disaffiliationists and those who believed that massive change must be imminent. In so doing they ignored the reality of what they looked at, or allowed themselves to be misled.

Morgan's passage on agriculture was conspicuous in the opposite direction. He used the freedom of his experienced eyes to go from an initially very well inclined observer to one who was very disappointed by the end. His preparatory reading about Soviet agriculture had impressed him. However, in the three weeks that he spent in the Ukraine, 'the largest lump of good food-growing land it has yet been my lot to look over' his enthusiasm slumped. What was more, he 'established a conviction, which grew with every day on, that Russia's agricultural troubles have arisen for other reasons than lack of natural resources, or the failure of seasons'. For Morgan the peasant, in general or in his Russian particular, was 'intractable, recalcitrant, suspicious'. When he got land for the first time, as in 1917, he wanted it for himself alone. Hard experience had not taught him the need for cooperation. This had meant a head-on collision between peasant and central authority when collectivisation had started. The peasant had, Morgan rightly surmised, obstructed this process by refusing to sow crops and killing cattle and the result had been, and still was in 1932, chaos. The kulak had been the major actor in this drama, since he had most of the breeding stock and 'held out against the changes like a wolf with his teeth showing'. The kulak had been spoken about wherever he went: 'I did not meet this fearsome creature as such, though I found him still warmly regarded as a creature of horror by the folk, mostly urbanised, with whom I discussed him'.

Morgan was told quite openly that the kulak had been 'liquidated' – 'he was a marked man anyway. Communist theory had no use for him'.[24] But if Morgan had no great sympathy for his plight, he seems in common with most observers of Russian agriculture or society not to have seen 'liquidation' as physical. The skating over of such terms as 'liquidation' rightly makes us uncomfortable, but it is a theme constantly found in British accounts of collectivisation, whether they be by the Labour Party or anyone else. The reasons no doubt lie deep in the British psyche, a people who had 'liquidated' their own peasants several hundred years before in order to have an industrial workforce. The Labour Party had of course a long tradition of harking back to a 'Merrie England' which had strong rural undertones. The seeming contradiction is to be found in the differentiation that is and was often made between the 'yeoman', and the 'free-born Englishman' as against the 'downtrodden peasant' of the continent. The British, and particularly the English, could therefore almost sympathise with the Soviet need to 'liquidate' the kulak.

But the Labour Party's main interest was in industrial and economic matters as they affect an industrial state. The accounts of Russian economic progress were unremittingly descriptive for most of their lengths. Given the little knowledge of the five-year-plans among the rank and file of the Labour Party, both within and outside Parliament, this is not surprising. Dalton summed up all the economic chapters conveniently when he wrote that the USSR had created 'a formidable material apparatus of heavy industry and electrical supply, and ... it has set going a unique type of industrial revolution, unique both in its speed, its geographical extension and its planned Socialist basis. On the other hand ... this material apparatus is not yet organised and handled with any degree of efficiency'.[25]

All of these points stressed differences with the then current Western European experience. They recurred constantly in all accounts. Dalton himself was most interested on the role of planning. His main sources for this were the interviews he was accorded with the architects of the second plan (1933–7). Pethick-Lawrence also met these officials. He had thought them 'very able men'. In private, Pethick-Lawrence also said that the figures given 'broadly represent the facts'.[26] Dalton seems to have agreed, for nowhere did he mention in his private notes any hesitation in accepting proffered figures, and the plan spokesmen impressed him with their 'ability and drive'. The whole planning system was put into the positive column by Dalton. He praised, in private, not in public, which is even more telling, the 'fluidity of communism v. rigidity of capitalism. Readiness to learn from experience and change direction. Fertile in expedients. Trial and error v. error without trial'. This particular key outburst ended with 'Ernest May said to me: What did Spengler say? Didn't he spot these people as winners?'[26]

However, he was amazed that there seemed to be no theory about what was going to happen. In private he wrote: 'Not much theory, disappointingly little behind it. "Our practice has always gone ahead faster than our theory" they told us under pressure from cross-examination'. His self-explanation of this was that under any government objectives had to be adapted to experience. In the published text he was or 'disappointed' by this lack of theory at all: 'The method of trial and error had been courageously applied'.[27]

There were, however, negative aspects in Dalton's summary and elsewhere in his writings. These can be summarised as inefficiency, low living standards and lack of freedom. All were probably introduced to Dalton and the others by members of the Embassy. Ovey had intimated to Dalton that the 'experiment' was not without its drawbacks, expecially inefficiency. Ballard had been harsher on the other categories of failure. Dalton was initially well-disposed towards Ballard as one who had been at Cambridge with him, an ex-Fabian 'and one of my admirers'. Dalton now found him 'rather a sad creature, living a lonely life', and very negative about the USSR. Ballard was particularly critical about 'the tyranny and the lack of freedom', later about 'the humbug of much Communist propaganda'. In all Ballard was 'too pessimistic, undoubtedly, but a useful antidote'.[28]

In another meeting with Ballard, Dalton was told that he thought 'the outstanding qualities of the Russians are their physical hardiness and their submissiveness'. Admitting that there was no unemployment in the USSR due in part to a 'high mobility of labour brought about by industrial conscription', Dalton commented to himself: 'here submissiveness is, no doubt, an important quality'. Even if he had not entirely agreed with Ballard, Dalton was definitely awakened to some realisation that all was not roses in the experiment.

This ambivalent feeling was accentuated by experiences outside Moscow. Dalton could 'fall in love with Kiev' but be all too aware that he was in 'Asia' in the trains. At one point he recorded another member of the party as saying 'in an exasperated moment ... "Well, this is a lousy civilisation"'. Inefficiency was the key to this exasperation, a leitmotiv of all the economic accounts. Haldane found that it was *the* problem, as did Pethick-Lawrence. But they all stressed in their written accounts that the base from which Russian industry started excused much of this inefficiency. Mitchison was particularly clear about this when he wrote that 'the actual standard of efficiency is production up to or beyond the figures of the plan ... In practice it does not work'.[29]

This standard of comparison became even more important in the section, again by Mitchison, that was of most interest to the average labour voter and to the TUC, that on working conditions. Citrine's 1925 visit had led to his critical position on the benfits to the worker of Soviet Communism. But he was not to visit again until 1935 and so Mitchison's account was glowing about the seven-hour shifts with two or four weeks paid holidays in state resorts and homes. The level of wages, always a thorny problem in British industrial relations, was more difficult to assess, as many other writers found, due to the difficulty of comparison between the rouble and the pound sterling. Mitchison solved this by taking a typical unskilled worker and family using cooperative stores for their purchases: 'my own view is that he [the worker] is more than contented, but rather less than prosperous',[30] and that in the future the plans would redress any balance that existed. The reader was left to review a contented and, most importantly, an unemployment-free working class in Russia. Other writers added to this impression with homely comparisons. The workers lived in flats 'similar to those built in London by the London County Council',[31] in themselves wonders of the 1930s, if horrors of the 1980s. Margaret Cole made very approving noises in favour of childcare facilities, and so on.

But what comes over most strongly as a criticism in Dalton's private, but yet again not public, feelings is his hatred of the methods and mental results of the Soviet system: 'The British Socialist's mixed feelings and conflicts of impressions'. He was shocked by the 'unintelligent uniformity of opinion. Ignorance of the world ... Excess of communal over personal elements in life', as well as the aforementioned inefficiency. Even he put this down to the 'heritage of past', an excuse he could not find for the lack of freedom. He was definitely in two minds about his trip. He could have sat down:

> after an interval and writt[en] two strong briefs – one each way. It wouldn't be hard ... Sometimes one was exalted ... At other times I shared the view that this was a lousy civilisation, and that this ugly, lumpy, slow-moving people, which neither gesticulates nor runs about grinning consists, as has been suggested, of the descendants of the stupidest of the Aryans, who got left behind in the great trek westward (c.f. Trotsky's *History of Revolution*, vol. 1. opening chapter).[32]

A Summary of the results of the NFRB trip to the USSR

So did the NFRB come away from Russia with a positive or a negative view of the USSR? Dalton's remarks of ambivalence are probably as near as we can get to the truth of the NFRB's reactions to Russia in 1932. The only ones who felt no ambivalence were Beales and Pritt. Even they took what can only be seen as a patronising tone towards the Russia they saw. How amazing that such a backward race could achieve so much! On the other hand there was a genuine admiration and even envy that crept into all the accounts, private and published, that cannot be ignored. They came away with descriptions that pose almost as many questions as they answer, not least about the future of the USSR.

If an analysis is attempted of minus and plus points the older 1920s categories seem to emerge yet again as those that guide the participants' own analysis. All that which was 'asiatic' was bad and that which was 'modern' (or dare we say it, european) was good. Hence all that can be put into the column of despotic feudalism was to be regretted. This could include both kulaks and the central authorities' efforts to suppress freedom but not its efforts, necessarily, to suppress the freedoms of kulaks, in themselves a feudal hangover. On the positive side, Soviet industry impressed as a general rule, with the proviso of inefficiency. Any real doubts that this was not leading to an appreciably higher standard of living for the Russian worker was repressed. These doubts remained as a source of future problems. More crucially, since this was the major aim of the trip, what were the lessons for a British socialist? Only Pethick-Lawrence openly hazarded a suggestion:

> Why should not we in this country travelling along an entirely different road from that which Russia has pursued also reach in the same period a somewhat similar position where the haphazard vagaries of our present individualistic system have given place to ordered economic planning and where with a sufficiency for everyone of all that is required for a full life there are added some refinements to reward those who show greater skill or who take greater responsibility in furthering the common weal?[33]

This sentence, which does much to explain Dalton's periodic infuriation with Pethick-Lawrence, none the less sums up the main problem of learning lessons from the USSR in 1932 viewed from a capitalist democracy. How could the experiences of an 'asiatic' nation be transferred to that of a european one with a very different tradition?

Other visits in 1932

Having examined the Russian visit of a Labour Party satellite organisation in some detail, it seems appropriate to examine what other material was available to the reader of Labour publication. The *New Clarion* set up a sort of travel bureau that encouraged readers to go to Russia, for 'readers of the *New Clarion*, of whatever political shade, will be interested in what is going on in the country of the five-year-plan'.[34] But there were very few printed accounts in the Labour press, with the notable exception of the Webbs' accounts and extracts from the NFRB visitors. *Daily Herald* readers did not even get this, and had to be content with the odd article such as that of June 1933, by 'the noted woman traveller' Rosita Forbes. This was a particularly nonsensical account, full of breathless gushings about the Soviet Union.[35] It is difficult to believe that the *Herald's* editors took such rubbish seriously, but perhaps a good proportion of their readers did. It perhaps also illustrates the new downmarket *Daily Herald* at its worst in its attempts to increase distribution. The *New Clarion* was now the main source for intellectual Labour movement journalism, even if regrettably short-lived.

The few brief authoritative accounts that are available were not widely diffused but are none the less instructive. The trade union veteran A. A. Purcell, a visitor to Russia in the first 1920 fact-finding mission of the TUC and a previous chairman of the General Council, went back in August 1933. He seems to have spent a lot of time in cars and thus used them as a gauge of progress. They showed a 'new Socialist Civic Spirit ... inconceivable in the towns of capitalism'. On the other hand, talking of a trip into the countryside from his Leningrad base, 'to reach this place we travelled in a high-powered car over roads – and sometimes landed in a field – which are behind our own in their surfaces, but it gave a fine opportunity of viewing crops and the harvesting'.[36] Such howlers convey much the same message as the NFRB travellers, an admiration for the enthusiasm and an awareness that very much remained to be done.

The President of the Shop Workers' Union, John Jagger, left a fifty-six-page account that seems to have been circulated in roneotyped form. Most of the text was an attempt to clarify his own ideas about the statistical nature of the phenomenon. He was particularly interested in the cooperative system, and especially the production and distribution of essential products. He seems to have found nothing but praise for these processes, and their description shows the depth of importance given by the Labour movement to their cooperative branch. This interest was very similar to that of the Webbs. Yet again it is obvious that Jagger put most emphasis on what he could see with his own eyes or glean from official figures. As with Purcell's account the only hint of inefficiency came from his contact with the roads, and what he could see from his motor transport. Hence 'the best proof of the excellence of the buses turned out by the Soviet factories is that they can be run on these roads day after day without resolving themselves into their component parts' or 'Onwards we bumped, rolling and rattling through an occasional village'.[37] From this bus he derived some bad impressions of dry rot in the houses(!) but very positive ones of urban building.

The most rigorous other piece of Labour Party-linked research of this period before 1935 was that of the 1932 visit by the Cooperative Union. It followed the same pattern as the others mentioned so far, in that the main interests were those of impressions of a general nature, the Soviet economy and Russian life. Collectively they are impressed by Russia, but not as a comparison with Britain: 'A much more appropriate comparison would be with India, and such a comparison we have included in our reports'. But they were none the less (again) impressed by the energy of the Russians in their 'war ... to establish the basic industries of the country in an incredibly short time'. The war analogy also served to explain the excesses for the group. Seen in this way, the Communist Party did not subject the population but led it magnificently. Did the people of Britain want the conditions that prevailed in India to be allowed here? The TUC report on India of 1928 was amply quoted to make the point more forcefully. In India the five-year plans might also do the trick.[38]

Some conclusions about the visits of 1932–3

The temptation to read a massive commitment to the Soviet system is inevitable in the accounts published by Labour Party visitors in the period 1932–3, but it must be resisted. All of the accounts stressed that they are examining a process, not the finished product. Provisos of the style 'whither Russia?' still abounded, particularly over the problem of urban/agricultural relations. No one was quite sure what their base of comparison should be, but all agreed that Russia's base was a very low one from which to start. Multiple excuses are made linked explicitly to the problems of the early 1920s, for which many Labour Party members had a feeling of residual guilt, coming as they did from the country that had helped in the Allied intervention, as well as one that had consistently (with the exception of 1924 and 1929–31) tried to freeze out the USSR in international politics. A groundswell of basic sympathy therefore existed, mixed with a certain disappointment.

The USSR's five-year plans were lauded as the efforts of a people to free itself from 'asiatic' bonds. What exactly this 'people' was is fudged throughout. The expression 'communist', for example, even in its Russian context, was rarely mentioned in the published texts by Labour Party members, even if it was in the private texts, such as Dalton's. The nature of the system that was leading the Russians to industrial development was thus left fairly vague and was in 1932 still a major gap in Labour Party appreciations. The NFRB trip did not solve the problem of what stalinism was; it hardly seems to have been noticed. This was because the Labour Party visitors were entirely in their old research traditions. They saw the USSR almost exclusively through their own lenses. The comparisons made by Beales and Pritt are the worst examples of this, but all the rest showed the same style of approach. In their efforts to describe in what they felt were truly empirical ways, the Labour Party visitors thus left many of the questions we would now ask, in the light of 1956, unanswered. It would also be tempting, to say that the 'intellectuals' of the left were the ones who were wrong and the 'realists' of the TUC and the Labour Party leadership were right about the USSR. The one, concentrating on 'efficiency' was able to dismiss the inhumane realities of the Soviet factory and society. In its extreme forms this version makes sense but even Citrine the 'realist' was always impressed by the Russians' 'energy', found much to commend in their individual leaders and found at least as much fault in his system as in theirs. The approach to the USSR in the British Labour movement varied from individual to individual, and no blanket judgement can be made, but only a careful case by case analysis.

To this reflection must be added the domestic climate that has been stressed throughout. In 1932–3 the disgust with the results of British capitalism was at its height in the Labour Party and in other sectors of British society. What Dalton had expressed as the desire for an 'exemplar' was at its height in 1932–3, especially as the political situation seemed to give no way forward for the Labour Party by conventional political means.

This may charitably do much to excuse the excesses of the Labour Party visitors of 1932–3 in that it places their enthusings in the context of a fierce internal political battle within Britain. The early 1930s were a most ungentlemanly epoch in British politics. In such a battle any ammunition was useable, often grabbed off the barricades and flung without too much thought at the exact moment of throwing. Given a National Government that had become adept at its own propaganda, as in the 1931 election, with Snowden accusing the Labour Party of being 'Bolshevism gone mad', the party sometimes used the same dubious rules of exaggeration. But the question is, did those in positions of power in the Labour Party really believe their own enthusings, for example about Soviet Russia, in their entirety? The answer, it seems, must be no. Dalton was demonstrably as much concerned about the negative problems of the Soviet regime as about the positive achievements. He never again made such a positive contribution to literature on the USSR. But on the other hand he could not give ammunition that could in any conceivable way be used by his opponents. Dalton preferred published half-truths in this atmosphere to the fully documented doubts that he and his colleagues mostly harboured.

In fact, the only ones of the NFRB group who did continue to enthuse about the USSR were those who have come down to us with the epithet 'fellow travellers' firmly afixed to their reputations. D. N. Pritt has particularly suffered from this due to the truth being known about the Soviet legal system in the purge period after 1934. Pritt kept steadfastly to his beliefs about the system until long after it was obvious that he was wrong.

He was one example of a small but vocal tradition in the Labour Party that can only be described as 'idealist'. The Webbs, the subject of the next chapter, also fall into this category. But after 1932 these people had very little real influence over the elaboration of actual policy in the Labour Party, be it towards the Soviet Union, except in 1941–5, or over wider domestic questions. The 'realists' – Dalton, Morrison, Bevin and Citrine – dominated here, with their proteges in Transport House. The 1932–3 visits must be seen in the context of a progressive return to political self-confidence by the new leadership and a growing realisation that to tie the party too closely to the USSR would be to tar oneself with the same brush.

Notes

1 CHAMBERLIN, William Henry, *Russia's Iron Age*, Boston, Little Brown and Co., 1934. Diary entries (reproduced as Chapter XVIII) for March 1931, p. 365 and July 1931, pp. 266–367 and October 1933, pp. 367–9.

2 Strang to Simon, 28 December 1932, PRO 30/69/325.

3 Ovey to Simon, 28 December 1932, N 7653/39/38, PRO 30/69/325, 3 pages.

4 A full copy of his unpublished letters is on deposit in the BLPES in the papers of Edward Mayow Hastings Lloyd. The relevant sections for the three trips are (LSE code) 4/33 'Description of a tour in Western Siberia', June 1932, 60 pages; 4/34 'Description of a tour in the Volga Region', 24 pp.

5 Andrew Cairns to Lloyd, 26 June 1932, Lloyd Papers, 4/32.

6 In a letter from Western Siberia (4/33), p. 18.

7 CAIRNS, Andrew, 'Description of a Tour of the Volga Region', August 1932, pp. 14–15. Martin went with Low, the famous cartoonist. See MARTIN, Kingsley Basil, (ed.), *A Second Volume of Autobiography 1931–45*, London, Hutchinson, 1968. The trip was recorded as *Low's Russian Sketchbook: 56 Drawings by Low*, with a text by Martin.

8 KEYNES, John Maynard, *Collected Writings*, vol. XXVIII, Macmillan and Cambridge University Press, 1982, pp. 15–16. Also published in the *New Statesman*, 10 December 1932.

9 Cabinet Committee on Anglo-Soviet Relations, 3 April 1933, CAB 27/550.

10 Dalton was told about some of Cairns' evidence in Russia by members of the Embassy. Exactly what he was shown is difficult to estimate.

11 NFRB, *Twelve Studies in Soviet Russia*, London, Gollancz, 1933 (Introduction by Attlee and Cole); MARGULIES, *The Pilgrimage to Russia*, op. cit.

12 CITRINE, Walter, *I Search for Truth in Soviet Russia*. Also mentioned is MANNIN, Ethel, *Forever Wandering*, New York, E. P. Dutton and Sons, 1935. Mannin wrote a column for the *New Leader*.

13 CAUTE, *Fellow Travellers*, p. 70.

14 PETHICK-LAWRENCE, F. W., *My Trip to Russia – General Impressions*, 9 August 1932, 8 pp. (hereafter *My Trip to Russia*) and paper of same title 'On the Way Home', end July 1932, TUC Archives.

15 These sections of Dalton's diary are filed under the numbers 53 and 54, the day to day reactions being under 53 and the more ordered categories under 54. 53 is 75 pages long, 54 is 44 pages.

16 The full list (with actual or future functions) was Dalton (NEC), Pethick-Lawrence (PLP Executive 1935–9), T. G. N. Haldane, G. R. Mitchison (SSIP Executive), John Morgan, H. L. Beales, D. N. Pritt (SSIP Executive, NEC 1937–39), Margaret Cole, Geoffrey Ridley (NEC 1936–40), R. W. Postgate, Naomi Mitchison and Rudolph Messel. M. Cole, Postgate, N. Mitchison and Messel were to become famous in their own right, of course.

17 NFRB, *Twelve Studies in Soviet Russia*, p. 8.

18 Ibid., p. 107. Cairns (see above) saw a great deal more because of his refusal to be bound by Intourist guides.

19 PETHICK-LAWRENCE, *My Trip to Russia*, op. cit.

20 DALTON, *Diary*, vol. 54, p. 2 of Russian diary.

21 DALTON, *Diary*, vol. 53, 9 July 1932, p. 18 and vol. 54, p. 5.

22 NFRB (H. L. BEALES), *Twelve Studies in Soviet Russia*, pp. 125–6.

23 Ibid., (Pritt), pp. 156–72. The quotes are typical of many others.

24 NFRB, (Morgan), *Twelve Studies in Soviet Russia*, pp. 109 and 114–5.

25 NFRB, (Dalton), *Twelve Studies in Soviet Russia*, pp. 15–18 and 37. PETHICK-LAWRENCE, *My Trip to Russia*, p. 2.

26 DALTON, *Diary*, vol. 54, p. 1.

27 DALTON, *Diary*, vol. 54, p. 34 and *Twelve Studies in Soviet Russia*, p. 19.

28 DALTON, *Diary*, vol. 54, p. 5 and vol. 53, p. 53.

29 DALTON, *Diary*, vol. 53, pp. 16, 45, 56, 70 and 84.

30 NFRB, (Mitchison), *Twelve Studies in Soviet Russia*, pp. 84–102.

31 Ibid., (Ridley), p. 214.

32 DALTON, *Diary*, vol. 54, pp. 1, 3 and 18.

33 PETHICK-LAWRENCE, *My Trip to Russia*, p. 8.

34 'Russia: Why Not See for Yourself?', *New Clarion*, 11 June 1932.

35 FORBES, Rosita, 'Russia', *Daily Herald*, 20 June 1933. One typical statement is: 'It is so easy to travel to Russia. There is the mildest pretence of customs'.

36 PURCELL, A. A., *Days in Leningrad*, published by Manchester and Salford Trades Council, Manchester 1933, 4 pps. pp. 1 and 4.

37 JAGGER, John, *Russia Re-Visited*, (notes compiled), June-July 1933, 56 pp., TUC Archives (unpublished), p. 6.

38 Cooperative Union Limited, *Soviet Russia 1932*, (summer 1932), Manchester, 1933, pp. 60, pp. 7, 8 and 20–22.

chapter thirteen

The Webbs' visits to the USSR in 1932 and their impact on Labour Party thinking about it

Writing on the Webbs' visit

Unlike the NFRB visit which, it has been noted, has attracted virtually no adverse comment, the Webbs' *magnum opus*[1] of 1935 has called down the vengeance of history, or at least that of historians. Perhaps the most striking example of this is to be found in David Caute's *Fellow Travellers*.[2] This was undoubtedly a necessary counterweight to accounts very favourable to the Webbs, which seemed to gloss over their apparent inability to see the full horror of Stalinism.[3] Since all of these accounts were written more documentary evidence has come to light and it is worthwhile to attempt a new analysis.

Many writers stress the Webbs' role as intellectual leaders of the Labour Party, and the links between their fabianism and what they saw in the Soviet Union, or rather what they thought they saw. The question remains as to why their new positive attitude did not penetrate deeper into the party that they had helped to create? It also poses other problems to the historian in that the criticism of the Webbs is, in spite of its claims to 'context' placing, supremely ahistorical in that assumes the knowledge of 1962 or later, not that of 1932–4 when the research was done. Thus the questions that must be asked here are 'What was the mental background for the Webbs' visits?', 'What sources of information did they rely upon?', 'What results did they obtain?' and finally 'What was the reaction of the Labour Party organisation to thier findings?', at least in the period up to 1935 when the book was published.

The Webbs' 'mental background' in 1932

After October 1931 the Webbs had a lengthy intellectual odyssey behind them and could normally have looked forward to a well-deserved retirement. Indeed, a contemporary account exclaimed 'The Webbs! But they must be dead, they cannot still be alive!'[4]

The Webbs had spent much of their 'partnership', as Beatrice often termed it,[5] in acting as the contemporary historians of the onward march of labour. They had been major contributors to a belief in social engineering planned and carried through by an elite devoted to the idea of efficiency.[6] The Webbs' emphasis on efficiency and its corollary of planning can even today be seen clearly imprinted on Labour Party philosophy. But this 'cult of efficiency over amateurism' was by no means an exclusively Webbian domain, or even a Fabian one.

It appears that they had a rather mitigated enthusiasm for the new Russia in the 1920s. Liebman stresses that during the war itself Sidney was hostile to a separate peace, even wanting an Allied intervention in Russia in 1918. But Liebman's postulation of an enduring hatred for the Soviet Union throughout the 1920s seems somewhat of an exaggeration.[7] The Webbs did share a hatred of the Communist Party and the Comintern with many in the Labour Party and in the trade unions, not of the USSR itself. The ARCOS raid of 1927 had been blamed by the Webbs (in typical Labour Party fashion) on the extremists of both sides, British and Russian. Preaching revolution in such a situation was likely to have the opposite results to those intended: 'I have not the slightest fear of revolution in Great Britain. What I fear is the reaction, even among the workers, against any organisation which seems in the slightest degree to be revolutionary in its objects and methods',[8] wrote Beatrice.

The meeting with Trotsky in 1929 had not shown any change in this attitude. There was, however, a growing disquiet about the team that the Labour Party had to forward progress in Britain itself. 'In home affairs I doubt the zeal of the PM and Snowden and the capacity and courage of Thomas, Greenwood and Margaret Bondfield. In foreign affairs it may be that this Cabinet is vastly superior to the last.'[9] There is very little to disagree with in this analysis, if it is not for the over-exaggeration of Sidney's skills at the Colonial and Dominions Office. By late 1929 Beatrice was convinced that the Labour Party within Britain was mainly distinguished by its 'intellectual hollowness'. The civil service was reported on 23 November 1929 as spending most of its time 'keeping Ministers out of trouble' (Sidney, for example?) and, worst of all, 'the governing class' seemed to have 'lost its intellect – even its horse sense'. In looking round for possible 'virility' in government abroad, she came across very few possibilities.[10]

The main ones she found were those of the United States and Soviet

Russia. Neither seemed all that attractive at the beginning of the 1930s, and she derisively compared the 'secular and the ecclesiastical dictatorships' of Moscow and Rome. Her ever-present moral sense was presented with a choice between a 'USA, with its cancerous growth of crime and uncounted but destitute unemployed', in the middle of the worst recession in living memory, and 'Soviet Russia, struggling with fanatic fervour, to bring about for the first time in the history of the world, an equalitarian state, based on an uncompromising scientific materialism'. As for the rest of the world, Germany and Italy, the first 'hanging over the precipice of a nationalist dictatorship' and the latter 'boasting of its military preparedness', confronted a France 'in dread of both'.[11] She thought nowhere presented a wholesome picture, in line with most other Labour thinkers. It should be noted that much as the disillusion with Britain was growing, there was no corresponding praise for the political alternative of Soviet-type communism: 'Russia is sure of itself – and that by suppressing all other opinions. What a world!'[12] This was more a period of generalised despair at all political systems for the Webbs.

The discovery of new sources of information in the midst of this despair was to be the crucial factor in the beginning of a conversion to the Soviet Union. As has already been stressed, the atmosphere of defeat made many, if not most, members of the Labour Party look elsewhere than Westminster for inspiration in late 1931. The Webbs were by no means unique, and in consequence it would seem foolish to assume that their interest was thought other than fairly normal at this point by their colleagues and friends.

Sources of information about Russia

This especially important stage of the Webbs' conversion is rather neglected by their critics. One is left with the impression that their new enthusiasm was born without much encouragement, except from the Soviet Ambassador, of course.[13] The Webbs indeed spent much of 1931 and early 1932 talking to anyone they could about the Soviet Union, as well as doing a lot of reading. To be sure, at this stage they did not express many doubts, but they did consider adverse comments.

Yet again the key element that must be stressed is the domestic atmosphere in which they worked. The pessimism that they felt from late 1930 on about the state of Britain and of the Labour Party in particular reached crisis proportions. The world seemed quite literally to be falling apart. 'Will a new party arise to start afresh the struggle for the equalitarian state? Much depends on the success or failure of "Sovietism" in Russia. If it were to succed . . .?', Beatrice wrote in her diary in April 1930. This was only two months after she had first met the new Russian Ambassador, Gregori Sokolnikov. He and his wife made a mixed initial impression but 'in their simplicity and unpretentiousness the two of them made an attractive couple and we shall see them more often'.[14] The were indeed to meet frequently in the next two years, and it was the Sokolnikovs who first urged the Webbs to go to Russia.[15] Their liking for Sokolnikov was not unique, and even the difficult Philip Snowden expressed the same liking.

In this early period of conversion such reinforcements of opinion were obviously crucial, especially coming from critical observers such as Snowden. The Labour Party seemed to be giving its blessing. And Snowden was one member of the Cabinet that the Webbs felt had considerable intellectual and moral weight. Other official confirmation also came from Ambassador Ovey in Moscow, in despatches mentioned in Chapter 9. This reinforcement became even more crucial in 1931 and 1932. The Webbs were visited by other intellectuals close to the party, expecially Elie Halevy who agreed with her analysis about the impending crash of civilisation. Only Russia remained as a candidate for study.[16] That this conversation had a great impact is without doubt, for it was written out in full by Beatrice.

As the crisis of capitalism continued into 1931 the Webbs, as has been shown, were not alone in seeing the end of an era. Beatrice was particularly impressed by even the *Times* now seeming to agree that Russia showed the only signs of success. That she had radically changed was seen after a visit by George Bernard Shaw, just before his trip in the summer of 1931. In 1929 Beatrice had greeted his radio broadcast about the wonders of Soviet Russia with scorn. Now she was prepared to share his enthusiasm up to a point even if it was 'a little discounted by his equally demonstrative admiration of Italian fascism, three years ago'. In this new sympathy she felt the support of 'the majority of Fabians',[17] newly reorganised in the NFRB. Beatrice obviously felt she was part of a new and widespread feeling about the USSR, not out on a limb.

The flow of Labour Party intellectuals to visit the Webbs in 1931 swelled to a flood in 1932. R. H. Tawney was one very important visitor. The author of *Equality*, written in 1931, had also visited the Soviet Union. He was now 'converted to the equalitarian state in practice as well as in theory, but frightened at the lack of personal freedom . . . and not an admirer of communist mentality. All the same he and we find ourselves in agreement on world affairs'.[18] His approbation is significant on several levels. He was becoming and has remained one of the key writers of a new generation of Labour Party authors. His approach took what is a recognisably Webbian approach, talking of the 'religion of inequality' at a time when the Webbs were redefining their own beliefs in similar terms. And the disagreement on communism was exaggerated by Beatrice. She herself had recently attacked the CPGB's *Daily Worker* as 'absurd'[19] and the Webbs never lost this dislike for the Communist Party in Britain, or indeed for the Comintern. What was already emerging in their thought was an admiration for the Russian communist, not his British counterpart.

The Webbs had nothing but admiration for the NFRB and SSIP. Yet again she turned the same way as Tawney and Dalton and so many others: 'What little intellect there is, be it noted, is in the Fabian Society and is swinging towards Soviet Communism – to the horror of continental Socialists. Dalton, another of their visitors at this time, reinforced this faith in reborn fabianism when they discussed their forthcoming respective trips to the USSR. Dalton had been one of the few who, in the Webbs' eyes, had retained credibility after October 1931 as a junior minister in the Foreign Office. Now he and they were following exactly the same intellectual course. The diary recorded: 'Dalton's attitude towards the future of the Labour Party is very much ours and like the Webbs he has his eyes fixed on Russia as the exemplar'. He even went some way to answer Tawney's only major criticism about freedom – Dalton told her: 'Stalin thinks that the Regime is sufficiently successful to be able to tolerate a little more freedom and allow of a little less suspicion and suppression. But for how long?'[20] These meetings all went a long way to reinforce a belief of common interest by the 'good element' in the Labour Party in the Webbs' visit to the Soviet Union. They were in a small way being reinstalled in their older role as guides and grandparents of the young and upcoming generation.

The only ones in the party who had doubts were those who were descredited for the Webbs or in disarray. Transport House came into this category, as did 'continental Socialists'. A prominent member of this band was the secretary of the International Department, William Gillies. He was peripherally involved in the Webbs' trip preparations through his dealing with 'continental Socialists' such as Friedrich Adler and was obviously being used to gather information for them. In this context he replied to a letter from A. V. Baikaloff, an exiled Russian socialist, by suggesting the Russian send the Webbs a copy of his book on slave labour in the Soviet timber industry, once again making minor headlines in 1932. This was intended by Gillies to soften the blow of not setting up a TUC/Labour Party Committee of Inquiry. Baikaloff seized Gillies' suggestion and sent his book, and told Gillies he would try and get an interview with the Webbs before they left for the USSR.[21]

Gillies had his own very definite reason for putting the Russian emigre onto the Webbs for he was dismayed at their approach to the Soviet Union. His frequent visits to the LSI in Zurich and his friendship with Alder had given him an almost 'continental Socialist' approach to the USSR, i.e. one of deep distrust. Indeed, emigre German socialists were amazed by 1932–3 at the neutral attitude of the British left to both communists and the USSR, a distinction that they did not make. To Alder Gillies wrote that he should send the Webbs a copy of a very hostile pamphlet entitled 'Stalinism and Socialism'. He followed this with 'What do you regard as the recent really authoritative and reliable books in French and German which he [Sidney] ought to read, or ought to be made to read? I am afraid that he is already infected. I have already said, after a conversation with him yesterday, that he knows, before he goes, what he will write on his return'.[22]

This remarkable letter was the forerunner for the later Labour Party slow disavowal of the Webbs' views on the USSR. But for the moment Gillies kept his views for himself and Adler. The latter was not nearly so negative about the Webbs. In a mild implied reproach to Gillie he wrote: 'I suppose, however, that the Webbs will be primarily interested in genuine scientific work and that they will probably have all that is necessary at their disposal'.[23] The implication is that Adler could not believe the Webbs guilty of what Gillies accused them. To prove it to him, Gillies sent a copy of a letter from Beatrice that he had just received. She thanked him for Adler's pamphlet, but said that 'stories about the treatment of prisoners are very difficult to test . . . it is difficult, even with the best intentions, of getting (sic) the right people as warders'.[24] In another echo of the disbelief in 'atrocity stories' that was so widespread among English intellectuals at this period, she went on to recount a report she had read in the *Moscow News* about Dartmoor prisoners being tortured when in fact they were just 'making themselves disagreeable' by howling, which Beatrice thought showed just how the truth could be distorted. Gillies sending the letter to Adler was all the more significant in that Beatrice had attacked him in person: 'He [Adler] seems to have changed his opinions about Soviet Russia, in his attempt to explain Otto Bauer's approval'.[25] Her putting Alder's increasing disquiet down to an intra-LSI power struggle cannot have done her standing with Adler a lot of good.

The Webbs not only spoke to people in the Labour Party before going to Russia. They did a large amount of research, aided by Margaret Miller ('I think that it is a wonderful experiment, most *thrilling*; but I don't like the restrictions on freedom of opinion') and spoke to not a few Russians, although there is no trace of Baikaloff having had his wish to see them fulfilled. Sokolnikov does not seem to have directly influenced them as to content, which the next ambassador, Maisky, was to do. They met a balanced sample of other Russians, Baron Meyendorff (an LSE lecturer), no lover of the Bolshevik regime and especially of its record on human freedom, but who seems ironically to have reinforced the already noted propensity, shared by the Webbs with many other labour intellectuals, of a disdain for the qualities of the Russian peasant. Mirsky, a 'Bolshevik', obviously gave no such negative report.[26] Michael Farbman, also communicated his enthusiasm most effectively, and was perhaps the single greatest encouragement of their attitude at this crucial juncture.

So in what frame of mind did they embark for the USSR? The answer must be that of most visitors of 1932, with bated breath, and a willingness to overlook problems, such as lack of freedom, to see how an experiment was working in one of the most genuinely backward nations on earth. But there was one additional factor that may or may not have affected other visitors, but for which the Webbs could at least claim a long and respectable heritage: 'It is the invention of the religious order, as the determining factor in the life of a great nation, which is the magnet that attracts me to Russia. Practically that religion is Comteism – the religion of Humanity .... How can we combine religious zeal in action with freedom of thought? That is the question which we want to solve by studying Russia.[27] Beatrice Webb felt she spoke for the long moral tradition of humanistic socialism, the kind that Lansbury as leader of the Labour Party still espoused. The Webbs went to Russia for all the same reasons as the other Labour Party visitors except that they felt their mission with a greater depth for having seen that mission over a far longer period than virtually anyone else in the party. But, and it must be repeated, they were in no way really out of step with general Labour Party sentiment other than in their intensity in May 1932.

The Webbs in the USSR

They were running the danger, as Sidney Webb suggested to his wife on 14 May 1932, of becoming 'monomaniac' about the USSR and it is perhaps to their credit that they realised this was the case. That the Webb team was not monolithic in its approach to the subject in hand, comes through fairly clearly from comments like this made by Sidney

Webb. It is difficult to say whether they are really on their guard against the drawbacks of their 'monomania' – one cannot take their saying that no one would care too seriously.

They were certainly aware that they were going to the 'Russian show',[28] as Beatrice Webb says in her description of the passengers aboard the ship. They also had a fairly clear idea of the model they had come to examine and wished to make their visit show them its various aspects. They summed this up shortly before departure as the three-fold Constitution of the Soviets (political democracy), the factory committees (vocational democracy) and the 'consumers' democracy' of the cooperative socialists of an agricultural or artisanal nature. To guide all this there was the religious order of the Communist Party giving to the nation 'its distincitve character' and pervading all its activities.

The outward passage to Leningrad gave the Soviet authorities a preliminary opportunity to influence their guests. A speech was made at the ship's Soviet praising their monumental tomes on the trade unions in Britain (read by Lenin), and their having been among the founders of the Independent Labour Party. They were treated to two receptions in Leningrad: on 28 May with the foreign editor and the chairman of the editorial board of the *Moscow Daily News*, the English language newspaper, as well as Radek, Bron, and two members of Gosplan and Centrosoyuz, the cooperative organisation. On 29 May they were dined by Petrov, the head of VOKS, the Society for Cultural Relations. They lost no time in asking him about their idea of the 'three-fold Constitution' and the leading role of the party. They also showed their belief that the party leadership was very flexible, that it was 'unique that the ostensibly national figure did not always hold the same *office* (contrast Stalin with Lenin)'. This was apparently 'a new idea' for Petrov 'but he did not demur, except to add that Stalin was not *only* General Secretary'.[29]

They continued their search for the 'soul' of Soviet Russia in their talk with Ambassador Ovey on 2 June, who confirmed their idea of the party being a 'sort of religious order'. As for their search for the 'consumer cooperative', he had never heard of them and felt the 'state' was the only employer. As will be explained, they were forced to progressively diminish their emphasis on 'consumer democracy' but it was a factor in 1932.[30]

The Webbs were witnessing vast changes in the USSR which gave rise both to great enthusiasm and great confusion in their analysis. They had arrived in the middle of the most inchoate part of both the industrialisation and collectivisation process. They saw, for example, residual elements of new economic policy (as in the private sales of fish on some of the collective farms) and took these to be fundamental government policy, something which, again, gravely damages their arguments about the cooperative system. When taken round the industrialising area of the Lower Volga, Sidney was led to flights of an almost biblical fantasy as he observed how the Russians are 'creating a veritable Manchester in this desert of Volga sand'. But when taken to see Autostroy, the Russian equivalent of Henry Ford's Detroit, he was forced to admit the 'outstanding failure of the Nation' was before him: 'Inside the machinery looked as if it had been dumped anyhow, with broken floors and dust everywhere'.[31]

Their observations of agriculture were extensive, based on the few examples they saw. Given their views on the Russian peasant, they were ever-eager to find how much of the old habits had been eradicated, and how it had been done. At the Gigant collective farm in the Lower Volga region, Sidney Webb could not believe the collectivisation process had been forced: had not '*whole* villages [taken the] decision to become Comsomol whatever their age?' Were not they repeatedly told: 'Nobody cares for [religion] here'. Exceptions were always allowed to reflect on their folly, and only some had to undergo the final step of being deported – Sidney was told one such recalcitrant was shot as an English spy.

There are several references to the not always smooth passage of collectivisation. They tried at least twice to find out who had been responsible for the process taking place. This resulted in a tragi-comic episode when a Foreign Ministry official from Kharkov, in the Ukraine, when asked who was responsible, 'seemed not to know and implied the Kholkoz was an old form in some places'. Anna Louise Strong, the American working for the *Moscow Daily News*, on the other hand, told Sidney Webb he was 'right in ascribing to Stalin (substantially) the idea and the decision to spread the Kholkoz system all over Russia . . . letting it develop into communes where it would, incidentally, "liquidate" [their punctuation] the Kulaks'.[32]

There is a similar inexactitude as to the precise meaning of 'liquidation' in the Webbs' notebooks as we have seen elsewhere. Beatrice later wrote that 'Of course, the dominant impression is of the complete liquidation of the former governing class and the extraordinary enthusiasm of the new'. There was an almost complete acceptance in these comments of the party line of 'the extermination of a *class*', prevalent in official literature until much later than 1932.[33]

As to whether they saw any evidence of any other kind of 'liquidation' other than the metaphoric kind, there is some reason to believe that they did. In the Ukraine, Sidney Webb saw '[t]rains of box cars – full of families – what was this?' He was told (or chose to believe) that they were either 'seasonable workers' or people benefiting from Narkomtrud's 'mass movements of agricultural peasants rendered locally surplus by mechanisation through [the] Kolkhoz'. They were, he noted with approval, sent 'fares paid by employing industry – sustenance on journey provided'.[34]

Beatrice Webb came back from Russia an ill woman and she remained so for the major part of the writing of the book. But whereas she may not have done the actual writing, it is clear that she was a major guide, not confining herself to organisation and corrections. Given the Webbs' habit of working as a team, it can safely be assumed that they were largely agreed on what was finally written. However Beatrice expressed more doubt at this stage than Sidney.

Articles that came out shortly after their return illustrate this very well. Sidney Webb was extraordinarily prolific during the several months that followed, producing nearly a dozen articles on Russia, all favourable. Beatrice Webb took a rather different line. Whilst convinced that the Soviet Government 'is perhaps the most firmly established in the world and the least likely to be radically altered in the next few decades', the system was still 'immature'; 'the plan is superior to the execution' to the extent that 'some features of Soviet Russia will be and remain, repulsive to more developed races'. The 'new civilisation' was only partial and set against the 'disappearance of unwanted persons', and 'the dark side' (reminiscent of the Middle Ages). For Beatrice only the Comsomols seemed wholly admirable. On their subject she waxed lyrical and was very impressed by their 'passion for self-improvement and self-discipline' and their 'hygienic self-control'. They had returned from the USSR with a mission: Russia *must* be investigated and explained because it was the only alternative to 'the surrounding darkness of capitalist civilisation in Europe and the USA'.[35]

Her doubts did not disappear and the immenseness of the task, reflected even in the preface to the finished book, evidently became too daunting at times. The most extreme despair at this difficulty often coincided with her worst periods of illness, as on 27 March 1933 when she wrote: 'Regarded from the standpoint of research, it is an illegitimate venture – neither our equipment nor our opportunities suffice ... Anyway, it will give zest to our declining years ... All the same I shall be glad to be quit of the vast and incomprehensible USSR'.

Given this feeling of the difficulty of getting reliable material, expressed less forcefully in other places, the Webbs attempted the portrayal of the major features of the 'new civilisation' rather than a thorough explanation of the details. When such details include the question of the 1932–3 famine we are left with an extremely unsatisfactory opinion upon reading the sections dealing with this human catastrophe. In the final version they argued that an Indian who had visited Russia in 1933 had told them 'he had no evidence of their being or having been anything like what Indian officials would describe as a famine'.[36] But here again she echoed the comments of many other visitors.

The Labour Party's reaction to the Webbs' research

What the Webbs recorded in their private diaries during their 1932 visit is not so very different from the thoughts that can be found in *Twelve Studies in Soviet Russia* or the private jottings of Dalton and Pethick-Lawrence on that trip. However, even during the respective contemporaneous visits there were differences emerging. Dalton met the Webbs in Kiev and cuttingly remarked that when Sidney was 'brought up [the Cathedral tower] to see the admirable view [he had said] "I had no idea of the existence of the River Dnieper ... at any rate I have of the Thames!"'[37] But this admission by Sidney was not so different from the confusion shown by any visitor of the period, Dalton included. The more important issues, collectivisation, the role of Stalin and the very nature of the regime and its policies, were all but dimly understood after the 1932 visits. Everyone was left with impressions that took years of digestion.

However, whereas the NFRB published its account very rapidly, the Webbs were to wait another three years. They used these years to exorcise their doubts for the publication of *Soviet Russia: A New Civilisation?* The NFRB presented its account as just what is was, impressions, not the absolute truth. They thus escaped the subsequent fall from favour in a way the Webbs did not. The Webbs were warned by their friends in the party that this was exactly what they were risking. It cannot have been easy to tell Beatrice Webb that she was mistaken! The first to do this was possibly the interviewer for *New Clarion* in October 1932. He 'suggested that a number of people, sympathetic to Russia, who had visited that country this summer, had returned disappointed, finding instead of idealism materialism'. Beatrice retorted that 'that's too easy a criticism to make. It is probably inspired by the almost superhuman concentration on the industrialisation of the country'.[38]

William Beveridge at the LSE rapidly became incensed by the route he now saw the Webbs taking. Beatrice's favourite nephew, Malcolm Muggeridge, also bombarded her with warnings about the true nature of the Soviet regime which he had seen close-up as a reporter with the *Manchester Guardian*. These and other attacks gave rise to periods of doubt but ultimately seem to have had the opposite effect. In any case, the Webbs got quite a lot of positive agreement from others, such as Arnold Toynbee.[39]

Within the Labour Party the Webbs sided with the left, and particularly with Stafford Cripps and his Socialist League. This body rapidly divided itself off from mainstream Labour Party thinking on most issues, as will be seen later. But for most of the period when they were writing their book the Webbs were convinced that they were in the mainstream of Labour Party thinking on both domestic and foreign matters in general and the USSR in particular.

Their blindness to the truth extended to ignoring evidence of the horrors of collectivisation from other quarters. The Soviet authorities did their very best to ensure that the Webbs continued in their ignorance and in particular that they kept believing in their 'three-fold structure', in the face of evidence to the contrary. Sidney was despatched to Moscow to find out about this and other, more minor, points. The notebook for the September 1934 visit holds little clarification, apart from some rather naive comments about shoes in the Leningrad cooperative shop being 'very expensive by English standards', and that there were 'apparently more shop assistants than one normally sees in Selfridge's', Their investigation of the 'details' led Sidney to talk to the 'Editors of the Publication Department of the Commissariat of Agriculture' on 27 September. The editor had read the 'chapter on agriculture and was especially enthusiastic about the explanation as to why the Kulaks received the treatment they did and the difficult conditions of 1932–3: in the latter he detected a note of "English calm"'.[40]

Back in Britain the Russian Embassy put all its possibilities at their disposal. Each of the chapters was read as they were written, usually by Maisky himself. The list of other Soviet officials who helped is too long to enumerate, as are the various ploys attempted by the Soviets to influence what they wrote. One particularly striking and macabre example is contained in a postscript from Maisky in a letter of 29 October 1935, just before the book was printed. He asked if they would send him the proofs 'of the last part of your book [the new civilisation] as well as the chapter on "Liquidation", together with the contents'.

Maisky was clearly showing what he considered important. The Russians did not much care for their emphasis on the party as a sort of jesuitical brotherhood, and the Webbs' disdain for official propaganda about the dictatorship of the proletariat. There was a dispute over whether to call the chapter on the party 'Man as an organiser', rather than their preference for 'Man as a believer'. The eventual compromise was 'The vocation of leadership'. But the Russians, going along with the Webbs' fear of 'not having enough information' obviously persuaded them to keep their attention focused on the 'philosophical and ethical content of Communism'. A 'gentle and subtle Soviet philosopher', Dr. Julius F. Hecker, was sent to talk to them about this, in spite of warnings that he was an OGPU agent: he was thanked for his help in the preface.

In the face of what must be described as blatant attempts to influence them we can only ask if this influencing did not arouse suspicion. It does not seem to have done so and, in an inverted turn of logic, Beatrice wrote that it was probably better to talk to Russians outside Russia because 'Soviet citizens are far less afraid of saying what they really think here than they are in their own country' (21 October 1933). She seems to have believed that she was talking to average Russians.

Unfortunately for the Webbs, doubts about the USSR were already beginning to polarise many in the Labour Party and the TUC away from support for the Soviet Union even in 1933, even if they were not yet generally voicing these doubts in public. As will be shown in the next chapter, interest in the Soviet Union as an exemplar was far from being as fresh in late 1933 as it had been in mid-1932. The party was definitely beginning to change, the Webbs were not. In this atmosphere even a visit from Walter Citrine to warn them went unheeded. He did not pluck up enough courage to do it until mid-1934. Beatrice's account of the meeting is characteristic: Citrine is 'the autocrat of the Trade Union Movement ... in fact an honoured member of the British governing class and is treated as such by the bigwigs of the industrial, political and financial world ... He is an embittered enemy of the USSR and mightily indignant with us for being in favour of Soviet Communism. He threatened us with "the loss of your influence"'. Citrine never bothered to try and convince them again.

By mid-1934, before the book even emerged, they had also lost many of the NFRB. Cole was 'too much of an individualist'[41] to really like Soviet rule by then. Others stayed faithful, Laski for one. The Webbs tied themselves to the USSR by their intransigence when all but a small sect, the Socialist League, were beginning to lose faith. It must be concluded that they went the same way as Shaw, to become 'yesterday's thinkers', still obligatory for radio programmes and as evidence of the longevity of Britain's socialist dream, but no longer relevant to its politics.

Among the Labour Party elite after 1933 and, especially, among the top leadership of Attlee, Bevin, Citrine, Dalton and Morrison, too many incertitudes remained about where the USSR was going or even what it was really doing. The previously mentioned split between the party's left intellectuals and the more realist leadership remains one that must be treated with caution. On at least two points all were agreed: a stand had to be made against Hitler and fascism, and an economic policy developed.

However, the process of assimilation of the material and experience gained by these visits was one characterised after 1933 by a growing awareness of the limits of the Soviet experience for the British context. The leadership of the party that emerged after 1932 was almost entirely in the camp of those who searched out an authentic British path to industrial, and therefore social and economic, progress. This is by no means to say that the Soviet exemplar did not play its role in inspiring these policy decisions, but rather that the USSR was not to have nearly the influence that the Webbs and others hoped it would. The process was also characterised by a new realism in Labour Party relations with the USSR. The Soviet Union was seen more and more as just another nation state, certainly no saint on the international scene, but none the less one that could not be ignored and which might still be a force for peace. The next chapters will therefore explore this changing relationship, showing the USSR's influence on the Labour Party in both domestic and foreign affairs until the end of 1934.

Notes

1 Sidney and Beatrice WEBB *Soviet Communion: A New Civilisation?* 2 vols, London, Longman, 1935.

2 Cf. David CAUTE *The Fellow Travellers*, op. cit., and CLARKE, Peter, *Liberals and Social Democrats*, Cambridge University Press, 1978, pp. 262–3. Both Caute and Clarke feel that the reaction of the Webbs to the USSR was mainly one of 'projecting their positivistic rationalism onto Russia' (CLARKE, p. 329). Also LIEBMAN, Marcel, 'Fabianisme et communisme: les Webb et l'Union soviétique', *International Review of Social History*, in two parts, vol. V, 1960, pp. 400–423 and vol. VI, 1961, pp. 49–73 (hereafter 'Fabianisme et communisme'). Also published in *Survey*, April 1962, no. 41 as 'The Webbs and the New Civilisation'.

3 For example, in COLE, Margaret (ed.), *The Webbs and Their Work*, Hassocks, Harvester Press, revised edition 1974 (hereafter *The Webbs*). She also edited a series of Beatrice Webb's *Diaries*, London, Longmans, 1956, of which the volume 1924–32 is of the most interest here. cf. also MACKENZIE, Jeanne and Norman, *The Letters of Sidney and*

Beatrice Webb, 1912–1947, London, Cambridge University Press, 1978. Hereafter MACKENZIE, *Letters 1912–1947*...

4 WEBB, Beatrice, 'What I Think of Soviet Russia – in an Interview', *New Clarion*, 8 October 1932.

5 As in WEBB, Beatrice, *Our Partnership*, Cambridge, George Feaver, 1975.

6 WEBB, Sidney and Beatrice, *A Constitution for the Socialist Commonwealth of Great Britain*, London, Longmans, 1920, and *The Decay of Capitalist Civilisation*, London, George Allen and Unwin, third edition, 1923.

7 LIEBMAN, 'Fabianisme et communisme', p. 40. For a full discussion of this point cf. WILLIAMS, *The Attitude*..., pp. 401–2.

8 Beatrice Webb to J. L. Hammond, 15 July 1927. MACKENZIE, *Letters 1912–1947*, p. 290.

9 WEBB, Beatrice, *Diary*, 26 July 1929. Quoted in MACKENZIE, *Letters 1912–1947*, p. 312.

10 WEBB, Beatrice, *Diary*, 9 November and 23 November 1929.

11 WEBB, Beatrice, *Diary*, 30 October 1930.

12 Beatrice to Sidney Webb, end February 1931, in MACKENZIE, *Letters 1912–1947*, p. 348.

13 LIEBMAN, 'Fabianisme et communisme', p. 414.

14 WEBB, Beatrice, *Diary*, 16 April and 20 February 1930.

15 Cf. WEBB, Beatrice, *Diary*, 12 November 1930.

16 WEBB, Beatrice, *Diary*, 6 June 1931.

17 WEBB, Beatrice, *Diary*, 24 and 28 June 1931.

18 TAWNEY, R. H., *Equality*, London, George Allen and Unwin, 1964. First published 1931. WEBB, Beatrice, *Diary*, 1 February 1932.

19 WEBB, Beatrice, *Diary*, 10 October 1931 at the Labour Party Conference.

20 WEBB, Beatrice, *Diary*, 7 March and 27 January 1932.

21 Baikaloff to Lansbury and Middleton, 6 April 1932, Labour Party Archives, WG/RUS/7, with reply by Gillies 22 April 1932, WG/RUS/9 and Citrine to Baikaloff, 7 April 1932, WG/RUS/8. Baikaloff to Gillies, 24 April 1932, WG/RUS/10.

22 Gillies to Adler, 22 April 1932, WG/RUS/13.

23 Adler to Gillies, 3 May 1932, WG/RUS/16.

24 Beatrice Webb to Gillies, 12 May 1932, WG/RUS/20(ii). Gillies to Adler (enclosing this letter), 30 May 1932, WG/RUS/20(i): 'Her trend of thought will interest you', wrote Gillies.

25 Beatrice Webb to Gillies, 12 May 1932, WG/RUS/20(ii).

26 WEBB, Beatrice, *Diary*, 19 April and 28 February 1932.

27 WEBB, Beatrice, *Diary*, 4 January 1932.

28 WEBB, Beatrice, *Diary*, 23 May 1932.

29 Russian Notebook A, 2 May and 29 May 1932. References to notebooks in Sidney Webb's handwriting A, B and E will be made to date, not page, to avoid confusion.

30 WEBB, Beatrice, *Diary*, 2 June 1932.

31 Notebook B, 7 July 1932.

32 Notebook B, all June 1932. The Webbs report Strong 'admiring general success of the regime, but critical of much of its administration'.

33 *Diaries*, probably 10 June 1932. cf. also the famous 'Short Course', *History of the Communist Party of the Soviet Union (Bolsheviks)*, New York, International Publishers, 1939.

34 Notebook B, 22 June 1932.

35 Article published in *New English Weekly*, 10 November 1932, pp. 81–3.

36 WEBB, Sidney and Beatrice, *Soviet Communism: A New Civilisation?*, London, Longmans, 1935, 2 vols. p. (ix).

37 DALTON, *Diary*, vol. 53, 3 August 1932, p. 70.

38 WEBB, Beatrice, 'What I Think of Soviet Russia', *New Clarion*, 8 October 1932.

39 For details of these criticisms see my article 'La genèse d'un livre: les Webbs et la rédaction de la première edition de "Communisme sovietique: une nouvelle civilisation?"', *Relations Internationales*, No. 24, Winter 1980, pp. 443–463.

40 Notebook E, September 1934.

41 WEBB, Beatrice, *Diary*, 25 June 1934.

chapter fourteen

The Russian impact on the Labour Party's domestic economic policies, 1932–4

The debate about Soviet trade in 1932

The election victory of October 1931 put a strange coalition into power. Evidently dominated by the protectionist policies that it had inherited from the Joseph Chamberlain school of tariff reform, the National Government still had a Prime Minister (MacDonald), a Chancellor of the Exchequer (Snowden), and a Home Secretary (Herbert Samuel), who were believers in free trade. The main body of the House of Commons however was now made up of those who believed in protecting home industries from excessive competition. This had led in the long run, as Pollard points out, to 'a concentration of stagnant, rather than growth industries'.[1] In 1932 the great bulk of unemployment was in these stagnant industries – coal, iron and steel and shipbuilding especially – as had been the case in 1929. This unemployment was at its peak with 3,750,000 out of work in September 1932. The new government was thus pushed by its own grassroots and the objective situation into 'doing something' about the problems of free trade, especially dumping and goods produced by 'slave labour'.

The inevitable major target was the USSR, and there was not a parliamentary debate during 1932 about trade which did not have its attack on the USSR'S trade policies. However within the Cabinet the ex-Labour ministers and Walter Runciman at the Board of Trade did not wish to see a reduction of Anglo-Soviet trade which had maintained jobs in British manufacturing industries. The government was thus split as to what attitude should be taken against nations accused of trade misdemeanours.

One key external pressure came from the Empire. Canada had a new Premier, Richard Bedford Bennett, who wanted to force the British to exclude extra-imperial goods from imperial markets in order to safeguard Canadian employment. He therefore echoed some British voices that called for an 'Empire preference', including the Beaverbrook-run *Daily Express*. The Canadians put considerable pressure on Britain over imports of timber and wheat, of which the Russians also exported a great deal to Britain.

Given these various pressures it was decided in early 1932 to set up a Cabinet committee on trade with Russia 'in the light of its bearing on the adverse balance of trade'.[2] This adverse balance had been one of the major pieces of ammunition for those who were against the 1930 temporary commercial agreement with Russia signed by Henderson. Figures presented to the House of Commons seemed to bear out this criticism. Nineteen thirty-one had seen imports from Russia of £32,178,868 and exports (including re-exports) to Russia of £9,044,350. Other figures were rather different – the *British-Russian Gazette and Trade Outlook* in March 1932 came to an export figure of £15,018,106 for 1931, by including Empire goods shipped to Russia through British ports.[3] Defenders of the figures could also point out that nearly all the British exports were of machinery and equipment from industries with grave unemployment problems in the main. They could have added that the bulk of Russian imports were goods that the British had to import anyway, notably wheat and timber. The Labour Party of course took this line.

The internal debate over trade within the National Government was not an easy one. Even before the Ottawa Imperial Conference of July-August 1932 different and contradictory voices were heard in the Cabinet. Snowden said in the House of Lords that '80 per cent of the important machine-tool-making industry in this country should have to close their works' if Russian trade were to be broken off.[4] The Cabinet Committee on Russian Trade was also told by the Board of Trade that 'the effects upon our industry and trade of excluding Russian goods might clearly be considerable'. They also made the point about the necessity of Britain importing goods that it imported from Russia. The Board of Trade minimised the importance of the deficit in trade and concluded that the overall trade balance for Britain would actually be adversely affected by a break-off of trade with the Russians.[5] The Foreign Office view was that the trade agreement 'is perhaps more important from the political than from a commercial viewpoint; and that its existence has had some effect as a stabilising influence in Anglo-Russian relations and that its cancellation would undoubtedly be represented by the Soviet Government as a first step in some active anti-Soviet policy'.[6]

On balance the Cabinet Committee on Russian Trade decided to recommend the denunciation of the 1930 agreement in order for the British Government to 'regain full liberty of action' in its trading relations with the USSR. In spite of the Board of Trade's objections (and those of Snowden) they did not feel that trade would suffer nor, in spite of the Foreign Office's warning, would relations in the political sphere be adversely affected.[7] Snowden relinquished the Chancellorship to become Lord Privy Seal and was replaced by Neville Chamberlain in February 1932, like his famous forbear a believer in protectionism. The National Government subsequently engaged in a gigantic game of bluff with the Soviet Union. The hope was that the Russians would give in to the pressure and renegotiate the agreement of 1930 without too many unpleasant political side-effects. This renegotiation would have to be done by April 1933 and necessitated a reunciation of the agreement by the Government of either country six months in advance.

One immediate political side-effect was domestic, for although the committee's deliberations were highly secret, some small idea of what had been decided evidently reached the Labour Party.[8] Sir John Colville, Parliamentary Secretary to the Cabinet, released a few clues when he said to the House that the negotiations were 'to secure a better balance of trade between this country and Russia and to reduce the period of payment'.[9]

The *New Clarion*, in reply, carried an article pointing out that the Russians 'pay up', that is, were correct in their business dealings. The Labour press also continually sniped at the increasing protectionism of the government as a whole. When a 10 per cent ad valorem general tariff was imposed in February 1932, the *Daily Herald* warned that 'when you are in a lunatic asylum you behave like a lunatic'. The *Herald* also warned repeatedly about the dangers of increasing world tensions with the kind of economic nationalism of which all countries were becoming guilty.[10] But by and large there does not seem to have been a clear awareness that the National Government would go so far in any individual case as to denounce a commercial agreement.

Meanwhile, the quite successfully kept secret of exactly such a proposed denunciation figured large in the build-up to the Ottawa Conference. The Conservatives were themselves a little nervous about this course of action, and Sir John Colville came under some pressure from business interests to safeguard Russian trade. He also noted privately that 'prejudice in the House [from Conservatives] seems to be lessening . . . there is no doubt that the employment value of such orders is now being realised'. However, Bennett kept up his pressure for a denunciation of the agreement right until the conference, though tactically and temporarily reducing his demands slightly.[11]

The final document contained an anti-dumping clause (Article XXI) that was aimed at the Soviet Union. Litvinov certainly thought so and went to Leningrad to tell Strang as much immediately.[12] In the words of a British official who reported this development, Bennett put enormous pressure on the British, a position that must have been incredibly galling for the mother country to accept from its Dominion. The true position would now have to be explained by the British Government, or the danger that Bennett would do so might become overwhelming.[13]

In spite of their dislike of the 1930 agreement, the Cabinet was clearly embarrassed at the possible reaction to a denunciation in public, when they had hoped to renegotiate quietly. The October 1932 Leicester Conference of the Labour Party passed a resolution against the denunciation, concentrating on the unemployment effects and the good paying record of Russians. It emerged in the debate that a member of the TUC General Council, John Bromley, who had been invited to advise the Government at Ottawa, had been categorically told that no such denunciation would take place in spite of Canadian pressure.[14]

From denunciation to the Metro-Vickers Trial, October 1932–July 1933

In response the Labour Party unleashed a continual barrage of criticism in the Labour press and an increased pressure in Parliament. The slightest hint of a reduction in orders that might be imputable to the denunciation was reported. The government's own confusion was stressed as much as possible. Baldwin was quoted as saying that he did 'not know' what the effect of the Ottawa Agreement would be on trade. The Labour Party also adopted the line that the denunication of the trade agreement was solely directed as a political act against Russia – and this at a time when exports to the USSR were actually increasing. 'Viewed from every aspect, the Government's action is a damaging blow to British trade and utterly without justification'.[15]

Negotiations resumed in December between the British Government and the Russians to draw up a new agreement, after another note of 11 November 1932. The Russian Amabassador in London, Maisky, was to be in charge of these discussions, the Russians revealed on 10 December. This prompted the National Government to think that its bluff had worked and that the Russians would not take reprisals of an economic or political nature. Ovey told Simon in late 1932 that 'opinions [in

Moscow] are somewhat divided but the tendency is to accept facts and in due course to reply to Her Majesty's Government'.[16]

This sense of false security was to be rudely broken by the Russian arrest of several British engineers working for Metro-Vickers on 12 March 1933. There is no clear proof that the arrests were to put pressure on London to come up with a new agreement favourable to Moscow, or that the action was revenge for past slights, but there is no escaping the linked timing. The British Government evidently took the action as pressure on the trade talks and decided not to give in. Reprisal duly appeared in the form of an embargo on all Russian imports into Britain. Needless to say the National Government, advised by Ovey, who was hurriedly recalled from Moscow for consultations, felt the charges against the engineers were groundless.[17]

The immediate *Daily Herald* reaction to the arrests was to link them to what was presented as British provocation. The representative of the arrested mens' firm, Metro-Vickers, was reported as having told the paper that 'we are aware that the Russians have been upset by the attitude of the British Government ... it has been hampering our business for some time'. British reprisals in the form of the trade embargo were condemned as 'placating the wild-men who do not pause to think of the interests of the arrested men, or the interests of the country'.[18] As to the question of whether the men were guilty or not, the *Herald* decided that 'for one Government to pre-judge the courts of another before even hearing the evidence would be most improper'. The foreign editor of the paper, Ewer, was more definite. For him 'the whole fantastic story of sand and acids being used to damage the turbine blades of the great Dnieperstroi power stateion is a ... fabrication'. On the other hand nothing proved that the accused would be found guilty, he claimed. Another report had the men living a wonderful life, Monkhouse (one of the accused) reporting praise for his captors: 'Jails last word in efficiency ... prisoner fed on caviare'.[19]

The Labour Party's organ continued in like vein all though the trial, always pushing itself as the party of the 'calm survey', an expression used by Stafford Cripps in the Commons. The Conservatives were portrayed as a pack of baying hounds after the break off of relations with Russia. The Foreign Secretary, Simon, made speeches 'of an agitator fomenting international hatred'. The Labour Party was clearly beside itself with rage. Why? Some answer must lie in the international context of these early months of 1933. The Conservatives did not view Hitler's rise to power with too much worry; the Labour Party carried out an almost lone and mammoth opposition. Anything that might bring more of public opinion round in favour of Hitler, such as hatred of the USSR, had, therefore, to be quenched with the fire of reason. This was also an excellent opportunity for the Labour Party to get back at the government for the betrayal of Ottawa and countless other slights, real or imagined. And it is certain that a large sector of the party believed that the diehards were in truth behind the National Government's intransigence. A very revealing cartoon by Will Dyson in the *Herald* had 'Russian Die Hard' and 'British Die Hard' rowing in opposite directions as 'The Volga Boatmen (A Study in Progress)'.[20] The older Labour Party 1920s belief of 'moderates' and 'extremists' was seeing a new lease of life in the setting of early 1933.

The virulence of the attack on the National Government's handling of the crisis was due to fears of the impact on world peace. 'Have they no conception of the harm which an economic war, a rupture of friendly relations between two great powers, would do to the world in the present situation?'[21] asked the *Daily Herald*. Apart from the possibility of a new war there were the probable employment effects. As an MP for an industrial constituency on the Clyde David Kirkwood well realised the devastating possible consequences of the embargo on exports of machinery. Kirkwood was assured that Simon 'sincerely trust[ed] that this new complication [the arrests] may be swiftly removed and the prospects and interests you have in mind [trade] may not be prejudiced'. Simon later remembered this incident as being one of the Labour Party's major triumphs in the crisis: 'Kirkwood, the fiery Clydesider, spoke from the Labour benches in vindication of the men with immense effect'.[22]

Part of the government dispute with the Labour Party could possibly have been avoided had the government been slightly more frank about its own intensions. Strange in Leningrad, who had borne the brunt of the Russian end of the negotiation over the engineers, was told by a Foreign Office colleague that the *Daily Herald* was 'implying that the proclamation and embargo are directed to making Anglo-Soviet relations as bad as possible ... it is of course nothing but tendentious'.[23] The tactics of the government were a fairly widely recognised propaganda failure. By the end of April the criticisms that had previously only emanated from the *Herald* were also coming from elsewhere. The announcement of the embargo had in particular bought more of the British press into the critical camp. Even the *Times* correspondent was saying (again to Oliphant, Strang's contact) that 'he [was] hearing a good deal of this sort of stuff'.[24]

In truth the government was not at all sure about what to do, even if it would never have admitted this in public. The main problem was that of knowing with whom one was dealing. Litvinov of course disclaimed all responsibility for the Soviet judiciary. On 3 April Simon wrote to Thomas Wylie: 'We are dealing with a foreign Government whose outlook and reaction are beyond ordinary rational calculations'.[25] Hence Ovey had been sent for from Moscow. He merely complicated matters by saying that only financial pressure would have any effect on the Russians: 'they won't listen to pleas or threats'.[26] MacDonald was evidently not too impressed by this and doubted that the 'Russians would have any regard to our action'. He continued by saying that in Russia: 'Apparently there was no Government: he doubted if even Stalin was the Government'. Later on in the crisis Simon wrote that 'This Russian psychology is a thing none of the rest of us can claim to speak of with confidence'.[27]

The Labour Party had also shown a great lack of understanding of the Russians. They evidently could not believe that the Russians were so cynical as to use live hostages in their trade battle with the British Government. In trying to find excuses for Moscow's actions they showed themselves to have been as ignorant of Russian psychology as the Cabinent. The National Joint Council interpretation of 20 April 1933 and the NEC meeting that preceded it gave little clue that they realised that the Russians were possibly playing a rather dirty game. All blame was laid, as it had been throughout, on the Cabinet's handling of the crisis.[28]

It must be concluded that the Labour Party was on this occasion completely blinded to the reality of Russian power politics by its own obsession with unemployment and the international tensions of the period. This time the Russians had been able to use the opposition in the British Parliament and press as its best advocate, while not having to climb down an inch. The trials went ahead, the first of a new kind of show trial with Vyshinsky as public prosecutor, a role he was to carry out with great gusto for the rest of the 1930s. The Russians could even persuade the labour press that their trial was a fair one and then release the 'guilty' parties to another round of applause in the *Daily Herald* about how moderate they had been – decidedly an impressive performance. But the Russians ran the risk, later to be proved a grave one, of being found out. The Russians had exploited all their stock of credibility and goodwill with the trial. Should a repeat performance take place, it might mean a less sympathetic hearing from the Labour Party the next time round. This was especially so given that the party's two sacred cows, peace and jobs, had been used in the exercise as the main lever of support for the Russian actions. Although a short-term triumph for the Russians, the Metro-Vickers trial was to prove one source of a mounting distrust of the USSR in the Labour Party.

The post–1931 reassessment of Labour Party economic policy: 'What is to be done?'

Whatever the nuances of the different interest groups within the Labour Party at the end of 1931, all were agreed that the possible solutions to the overwhelming economic problems of Britian were as much political as anything else. Norman Angell, whose earlier writings, especially on Russia, had shown him to be a moderate on many issues shared the widespread belief that capitalism, or at least laissez-faire capitalism, had proved inadequate to the tasks facing it. The result was unemployment and financial crisis accepted, said Angell, 'by practically universal admission'. What was now needed was a better form of adjustment policy that would be more rapid and less vulnerable to outside influences. He proposed a first 'National Plan', one that 'will enable a Capitalist industry that does not believe in Socialism to work cordially with a Socialist Government that does not believe in capitalism'.[29]

That capitalism was doomed if drastic measures were not implemented was supported by the most impeccable of commentators. The Governor of the Bank of England himself was quoted by Angell and others as saying: 'Unless drastic measures are taken to save it, the Capitalist system throughout the civilised world will be wrecked within a year. I should like this prediction to be filed for future reference'.[30] Within the Labour Party itself, the date of the coming collapse was continually revised, even by the most confident of marxists, but one can take the Leicester Conference of the Labour Party in autumn 1932 as the culmination of a first, fairly wild, spate of doom-laden prophecy and searching for radical solutions. The vision of Soviet Russia played an important role in this early stage.

The aspect of Russia that increasingly fascinated was that of planning, as has been seen in the comments of the various visitors to Russia. This interest was a primary reason for an upsurge of planning literature, especially by Labour Party intellectuals. G. D. H. Cole was the most prolific of these. Of particular interest are his *Economic Tracts for the Times* (1932) and his *Principles of Economic Planning* (1935). These and other books such as *Plan or No Plan* by Barbara Wooton (1934) and Norman Angell and Harold Wright's of 1931 but were of course part of a longer standing intellectual current into which the model of Soviet

Russia came to be a new consideration. This intellectual environment must be examined before considering the purely Labour Party contribution and the role of Russia in this contribution.

The planning environment

The emergence of a widespread reflection about economic planning in Europe during the 1930s is now well documented. The essence of the argument is that the difficulties encountered in adapting to post-1914 conditions led to a progressive realisation that the old economic order was well and truly dead. Before 1914 'mutability in particulars seemed to be consistent with general stability', basking in a well-defined system of 'interdependence' and 'automatism' of economic adjustment. Keynes was one of the first to see that this cosy arrangement was gone for good or ill in 1918 and that the position of dominance held by Britain and sterling had especially faded. The increased importance of the economy of the United States, only gradually realised as the 1920s wore on, was forced into focus by the worldwide implications of the Wall Street crash of 1929.[31]

The new conservatives like Harold Macmillan were as convinced as G. D. H. Cole that the capitalist system was in deep trouble even if their solutions varied somewhat. If one takes foreign trade as a prerequisite of a liberal capitalism, the predominant autarky of the 1930s with attendant competitive devaluation and trade barriers gave an impression of capitalism failed.[32] Economics, it has often been pointed out, changed from a spectator activity to one of active intervention.

John Strachey, by the early 1930s in the Communist Party, via the New Party, popularised an extreme marxist view with his *The Coming Struggle for Power* (1933) and other works. Harold Laski was an important marxist influence within the Labour Party itself. However, his sympathetic biographer comments: 'His assertions [on economics] are often so vague as to be incapable of precise interpretations; when his statements are clear they are often inaccurate or unsupported by evidence'. Apart from that he held what were fairly current views that can be called 'semi-marxist' about the dire nature of the 1930s Depression and the unlikelihood of any solution.[33]

However, John Strachey, as all communists, continued as *persona non grata* at Transport House. He was undoubtedly, a Pimlott says, 'the most productive and widely read British Marxist theoretician of the decade',[34] but his main influence within the Labour Party was on the ILP's successor, the Socialist League, which was the main self-consciously 'marxist' wing of the Labour Party up to its disaffiliation in 1937.

So if Briggs is right to see planning's 'pedigree' as dating back to before the First World War, it is still with the crisis of 1929–32 that the idea really began to be developed. The failure of an orthodox (and widely respected) Chancellor of the Exchequer, Snowden, to avert catastrophe and a run on the pound during 1930 went in parallel with new thinking about economics. The classical laissez-faire had showed its limitations, which led to the exploration of different forms of a new rational distribution of scarce resources. This was the 1930s meaning of planning and clearly it englobed much. It could mean national or Empire, local or regional, micro or macro, or a host of other descriptive epithets.

Three essential types of planning were identified by the new organisation 'Political and Economic Planning' (PEP): 'a controlled planned economy', 'a free planned economy' and 'a mixed planned economy'. The first was the Soviet or fascist model, the second the 'contemporary model of laissez-faire' (i.e. Liberal) and the third 'in line either with progressive Conservatism or Socialism'.[35] The categorisation shows the links that developed in the aspirations of Conservatives like Blackett and Macmillan, who were in at least periodic contact with the group from early 1933 onwards and those of most of the Labour Party.

However, it can be shown that interests were similar. On the crucial point of interest in the Soviet model, the PEP were saying very early on that 'the USSR remains the sole extant example of a State with a national plan and an aim dominating it'.[36] A more detailed paper on the USSR's planning system was produced, by a Russian exile, in July 1932. The report was very factual with little polemic. It was noted in June 1932 that '[p]lanning in Russia is more all-pervading that it is in Italy'.[37]

Differences of emphasis were noted, and this led to the above-mentioned types being defined. The British economy was seen so far more dependent on world conditions, and thus any British model could not be so self-contained. But the major problem was identified as political. In a Western democracy the planning function had to be separated from the executive function. The state could not have total control. In Russia the PEP had noticed a growing tendency for this 'separation ... to disappear, and the consequences good or bad, remain to be seen'.[38]

Labour Party conception of planning 1931–2

The PEP's interest in Soviet planning, its lack of sufficient knowledge and therefore of understanding of where this planning would lead, and especially its worry about the impact on democratic traditions were all questions mirrored in the Labour Party about the subject.

The first problem, that of knowledge, was illustrated by the published NFRB and Webb accounts. In the aftermath of these visits there were several attempts to analyse what Soviet planning really implied in Russia itself. Upon his return, Dalton was still not too sure. Although the crisis in the West had convinced him that there was a need to 'plan or perish' he does not seem to have been absolutely sure that the Soviet Union was successful in its efforts to plan. 'In the Soviet Union ... at least they are *trying* to plan ... at least they are trying, and not impotently giving up the ghost'.[39] This energy was the main attraction, Dalton's 'exemplar'.

Other members of the Labour Party leadership saw and admired this energy as the result of either a personal visit to Russia or because of the account of a close colleague. Herbert Morrison railed against the 'opposition psychology' that was developing in the Labour Party: 'Defeatism is weakness – and weakness is next door to treachery'.[40] In a press release he prominently placed Russia as an example to everyone:

> I do not wish to be controversial, so by all means pass the point if you desire, but probably the country which has the least unemployment and preventable poverty is Russia, where the state is asserting its right of controlling the production and distribution of wealth ... I should be an unreasonable and prejudiced person if I did not draw attention to the great importance of what is happening in Russia where the government is endeavouring to operate an ordered economic plan.[41]

This quotation illustrates the same uncertainty as that expressed by Dalton. Morrison had, after all, long been the scourge of the Communist Party and its efforts to join the Labour Party, affirming in the same article: 'I am no Bolshevik'. Therefore in the early days after October 1931 planning was used as a rallying cry, not a policy. No policy existed. The Labour Party Manifesto of September 1931 had urged the idea, but with the only detail of note being that 'Socialism ... presses for the extension of publicly owned industries and services operating solely in the interests of the people'.[42] Attlee had extended this idea a little further in November 1931 with his thought about the nationalisations that were already *de facto*. The Post Office, the BBC, the General Electricity Board and the London Traffic Board were his models. But we can search in vain for any desire for total state control on the Russian model. What Attlee wanted was the right of information about the nationalised industry to be made widely available, not state control: 'I am quite clear that Treasury control as now exercised should be abolished'.[43]

The reason for this hesitancy was the realisation by leaders like Dalton and Morrison that the Russian model could not be applied to Britain. 'The Soviet Union is a raw young giant' with very different needs, a 'British Planned Economy should start from the available working population, and should aim to plan away unemployment and great inequality, and to raise average standards of life'.[44] Not very revolutionary, in fact. This was bound to annoy those in the Party who believed that only a real revolution would achieve what was necessary. The ILP held many such people and they were furious with the Labour leadership for what they considered a return to 'MacDonaldism', and the advocacy of 'corporatist' planning, more along fascist than socialist lines.

But even the ILP *New Leader* demonstrated that capitalism was in no real danger of imminent collapse. A quick opinion poll among intellectuals close to the Labour Party revealed that even by spring 1932 only Stafford Cripps now believed that a crash was imminent. The split in the ILP that came in August 1932 was the ultimate playing out of this disagreement: even Cripps, who stayed in the Labour Party, thereby showed he was not sure that capitalism was doomed.[45]

The remarks often made by the visitors to Russia of 1932 about the lack of democracy in the USSR also show a distinction between the Labour Party and ILP and are another clue to the chasm opening up between them. Dalton and Morrison clearly recognised the dangers of the Russian system for democratic procedures as understood in Britain. The ILP jettisoned the 'futility of gradualism', as Campbell Stephen put it, when it fell in love with the Russia of Lenin and his 'courage and independence'.[46] The unfortunate truth is that the ILP put itself out into the cold because it believed that the future would prove it was right about the coming revolution, a dangerous revolutionary illusionism that led it even further away from the mainstream of the Labour movement and from British politics as a whole.

It must be said that the Labour Party erred in the direction of caution in their espousal of the ideal of planning, but in so doing they were able to slowly introduce a new economic idea and practice by 1945. The British 'planning' of 1945 was far removed from the Russian model and owed as much to liberal economists such as the thinkers of the PEP and to Keynes. Nineteen thirty-one rather saw the beginning of the idea of state intervention on a large scale in Britian during time of peace (since it had already been tried in time of war) with the Labour Party as its main exponent.

Notes

1 POLLARD, p. 352.
2 Conclusion 7, 27 January 1932, CAB 27/480.
3 House of Commons *Debates*, vol. 269, 24 October 1932, col. 610 and *British-Russian Gazette and Trade Outlook*, March 1932.
4 Quoted in a Labour Party research document of early 1932.
5 Board of Trade memorandum of 13 May 1932, CAB 27/480, pp. 3 and 6. For more details see WILLIAMS, *The Attitude*, pp. 430–31.
6 Cabinet Committee on Trade with Russia, Third Report, 30 May 1932, CAB 27/480, p. 2.
7 Ibid., 'Conclusions and Recommendations', pp. 13–17.
8 For example, House of Commons *Debates*, vol. 261, end February 1932 and vol. 264, 19 April 1932, col. 1405.
9 House of Commons *Debates*, vol. 265, 9 May 1932, col. 1530.
10 *New Clarion*, 25 June 1932. *Daily Herald*, 5 February and 12 March 1932.
11 Colville to Runciman (Department of Overseas Trade), 5 July 1932, and F. Ashton-Gwatkin to Wellesley, 4 August 1932, FO 371/16320.
12 Strang to Simon, 28 August 1932, N.5006 FO 371/16320.
13 Ashton-Gwatkin to Wellesley, 18 August 1932, N.5011, FO 371/16320.
14 L. P. A. C. R., Leicester, pp. 317 and 181.
15 Cf. 'Notes for Speakers', 'Labour's Ottawa Challenge: How is British Trade Helped?', 26 October 1932, Labour Party. See also Anglo-Soviet Parliamentary Committee, *The Ottawa Conference and Anglo-Soviet Trade*, forward by John Bromley and W. P. Coates, December 1932.
16 Ovey to Simon, end October 1932, N.6163, FO 371/16320.
17 Cabinet Committee on Anglo-Soviet Relations, 3 April 1933, 16 pp., CAB 27/550.
18 *Daily Herald*, 13 March and 21 March 1932.
19 Ibid., 20 March and 15 March 1932.
20 Ibid., 6 April and 13 March 1932.
21 *Daily Herald*, 6 April 1933. Another example of this mood came in Lansbury's speech of 28 April. He had said: 'Britain . . . was at economic war with Russia . . . one of the most stupid and criminal acts any Government could take against a friendly power', *Daily Herald*, 29 April 1933.
22 Simon to Kirkwood, 29 March 1933, FO 800/288 and SIMON, Viscount John, *Retrospect*, London, Hutchinson, 1932, p. 194.
23 Launcelot Oliphant to Strang, 20 April 1933, Strang Papers, Churchill College, Cambridge, STRN 4/2.
24 Oliphant to Simon, 20 April 1933, FO 800/288.
25 Simon to Wylie, 3 April 1933, FO 800/288.
26 Oliphant to Simon 2 April 1933, reporting Ovey's views, FO 800/288.
27 Cabinet Committee on Anglo-Soviet Relations, 3 April 1933, p. 11, CAB 27/550 and Simon to Buckmaster, 10 April 1933, FO 800/288.
28 Labour Party NEC Minutes, and N. J. C. statement, 20 April 1933, Labour Party Archives, WG/RUS/37(i).
29 ANGELL, Norman and WRIGHT, Harold, *Can Governments Cure Unemployment?*, London, J. M. Dent and Sons, 1931, p. 1 (hereafter Angell and Wright).
30 Montagu in letter to M. Moret of the Bank of France in summer 1931, quoted by Angell and Wright, footnote on p. 16.
31 BRIGGS, Asa, 'The World Economy: Interdependence and Planning', *New Cambridge Modern History*, ed. C. L. Mowat, vol. XII, 'The Shifting Balance of World Forces, 1898–1945', Cambridge University Press, 1968 (hereafter 'Interdependence and

Planning'), p. 37 and GALBRAITH, John K., *The Great Crash, 1929*, Berkeley, California, University of California Press, 1973.

32 Cf. BRIGGS, 'Interdepedence and Planning', pp. 29–33.

33 STRACHEY, John, *The Coming Struggle for Power*, London, Gollancz, 1933, and *The Nature of the Capitalist Crisis*, London, Gollancz, 1935 and DEANE, p. 194.

34 PIMLOTT, *Labour and the Left*, p. 63.

35 NICHOLSON, Max, *Draft Study of Planning Field*, unpublished, 4 pp. PEP WGI 1/2.

36 PEP, *Third Interim Report*, 18 December 1931, circulated 2 February 1932, WGI 1/2, 1932.

37 PEP Report of 7 pp. dated 1 June 1932. WGI 1/2, 1932.

38 PEP, *Third Interim Report*, p. 17.

39 DALTON, Hugh, 'Plan or Perish', *New Clarion*, 12 November 1932.

40 MORRISON, Herbert, *The London News*, London Labour Party, June 1931.

41 MORRISON, Herbert, 'Capitalism. A Series of accidents', press release by the London Labour Party, 24 February 1932.

42 Labour Party, *Election Manifesto*, September 1931, printed in BEALEY, Frank (ed.), *The Social and Political Thought of the British Labour Party*, London, Weidenfeld and Nicolson, 1970, pp. 129–30.

43 ATTLEE, Clement, 'Post Office Reform', *New Statesman and Nation*, 7 November 1931. For more details on the policy discussions, see WILLIAMS, *The Attitude*, pp. 452–60.

44 DALTON, 'Plan or Perish', *New Clarion*, 12 November 1932.

45 'Will Capitalism Crash?', *New Leader*, 18 March 1932. Cole said: 'How do I know? How does anybody know?' Bertrand Russell expected capitalism to last 'fifty years at least'. J. A. Hobson felt it had plenty of life left yet. Even Cripps, who thought it would collapse, did not rule out a 'reprieve' if drastic steps were taken.

46 STEPHEN, Campbell, 'The Labour Party: The Case for Disaffiliation', *New Leader*, 15 July 1932.

chapter fifteen

Russia as an element in the Labour Party's foreign policy, October 1931—end 1932

The context of British foreign policy, 1931–5

The financial crisis of 1931 had thrown the limited nature of British foreign policy options into stark relief for all who wished to see them. The First World War had shown that 'splendid isolation' was no longer an option. Woodrow Wilson's departure from the White House and the re-emergence of US isolationism had ruled out the possibility of an Anglo-American axis. The only thing that was left was the League of Nations. Yet the sorry tale of British foreign policy under the National Government between 1931 and 1939 is a mixture of ostrich-like refusal to accept new truths of relative impotence and a lukewarm adherence to the League. This consisted in declarations of support in times of relative optimism and in declarations of blame for the idea of collective security in times of crisis. Later it meant the 'appeasement' of dictators.

Christopher Thorne has perhaps struck the best balance in his book on the Manchurian crisis of 1931–3. He points out that '[s]eldom has there been a period when men have been forced to re-examine so intensively their basic assumptions and approaches to international politics'. The questions he says were most important bear repetition: was there to be one final attempt to 'achieve a substantial measure of arms reduction and limitation, or to rearm for the purpose of deterrence?' and were Britain (and the other democratic powers) 'to rely on the League and collective security, or on the old diplomacy and "balance of power", or on what Simon [the new Foreign Secretary] described as a "judicious mixture" of the two?'[1]

The Labour Party's overall foreign policy, 1931–5

The best text on Labour's foreign policy in the early 1930s is Naylor's

Labour's International Policy.[2] Literature on the National Government is of course much larger.[3] On the major questions of the day before 1935, most current historiography of foreign policy has the Labour Party a small voice off stage left, not as a central actor. A new policy eventually emerged as one of a far more vigorous interpretation of collective security within the League, one that did not rule out military sanctions after 1935. The change was not often completely clear to the outsider since old-style pacifist, George Lansbury, was the leader of the party until the end of 1935. Occasional evidence of the fratricidal struggle going on in the National Executive Committee (NEC) did emerge, but it was not until the 'martyrdom' of Lansbury, to paraphrase Ernest Bevin's action at the Brighton Conference in October 1935, that the struggle was fully admitted in public.[4]

These debates, which will shortly be outlined in more detail, in themselves mirrored the problems faced by the National Government and Britain as a whole. Christopher Thorne says: 'Foreign policy goals remained ones of self-preservation, not of self-extension'. The period is one of 'retreat from power' as the title of one study indicates.[5] The Labour Party's discomfiture was therefore but the reflection of a wider one. The opposition had to face up to the same challenges as the government, and in the same developing knowledge that if domestic politics has been the main concern until 1930, the problem now lay in how to react to a volatile situation abroad. Maurice Cowling recognised this when he wrote of the 1920s as the 'age of Labour' and the 1930s as the 'Age of Hitler'.[6]

The main issues that faced the Labour Party in foreign policy between 1931 and 1935 – the rise of the dictators and the decline of the League of Nations – were discussed within a policy vacuum created by the departure of MacDonald and most of the old guard of the 1924–31 period. Of the four men who had formed an inner Cabinet, only Henderson remained – in self-imposed exile in Geneva at the disarmament conference – an old and rapidly weakening man. Snowden (who had negotiated the Young Plan), MacDonald (who had always seemed as much of a Foreign Secretary as a Prime Minister), and Thomas (who had held important foreign-related positions) were all gone. Who could replace such a cast?

As has been explained, the parliamentary defeat of the Labour Party led to a definite swing of power away from the Parliamentary Labour Party towards the General Council of the TUC and towards the Labour Party's administrative sector grouped in Transport House under the same roof as the TUC and the Transport and General Workers's Union.

Bevin, as the leader of this union and Citrine, the General Secretary of the TUC, thus assumed new and enormous power over the party's decision-making process. They were helped by a new generation of young Labour Party leaders, Dalton and Morrison in particular, who had their own legitimacy. The presence in Transport House of industrious if not particularly original party workers dedictated to a moderate re-think of the party's role also helped nudge the party towards new policy options. Collectively these men, with the tacit agreement of the remaining member of the old guard, Henderson, formed a foreign policy over the next few years that went in a far more realistic direction than that of the idealist pacifism of the old and new left. The struggle within the party was therefore between a new centre-right led by Bevin, Citrine, Dalton and Morrison (helped in Transport House by a few strategically placed officials), the old left made up of pacificists like Lansbury, and the new left led by Stafford Cripps.

This new left was the product of the Popular Front mentality which had started in the 1920s but which was a particular product of the 1930s and Hitler, and of the parallel fear of Germany that made up so much of the Soviet Union's foreign policy in the 1930s. Cripps and his Socialist League, which grouped most of the left that had not left the Labour Party with the ILP in 1932, staunchly supported a Popular Front with the ILP and the Communist Party after Hitler's arrival as Chancellor. This front was to devote much of its energy to ensuring that the National Government did not return to a diehard policy against the USSR or, as many on the left believed, make an actual alliance with Hitler against the USSR. That the National Government had no such intention is clear, even if there is evidence that many in the British establishment were 'Fellow Travellers of the Right'.[7] But the natural distaste of the Conservative Party for bolshevism lent some credence to the Socialist League's hysterical claims that any rearmament by Britian would be so that it could attack Moscow, and that the League of Nations was a club of those who wished to destroy socialism, with which they strongly identified the USSR.

The USSR's anti-Western diatribes of the 1920s had sown a deep distrust of Soviet motives in the now rising leadership of the Labour Party and in particular in Bevin, Citrine, Dalton and Morrison. All had been prepared to give the USSR many chances to redeem itself and they would continue to do so until the 1940s. But this warmth was now severely marred by the feeling that the USSR could only be trusted up to a certain point. The attempts by the Communist Party to infiltrate the Labour Party and the setting up of parallel trade unions, such as the

Minority Movement, had not been forgotten or forgiven by this new inner Cabinet than now ran the higher echelons of the Labour Party. There is thus the paradoxical but almost inevitable picture of a Labour Party wishing to learn from the USSR, as was explained in the last few chapters, and willing to cooperate with it in any internationally acceptable forum, especially in the League of Nations, while totally refusing to allow any domestic political alliance in a 'popular front' between the Labour Party and the Communist Party.

The question inevitably arises: 'Had the USSR changed its spots?' The answer in foreign policy is undoubtedly 'yes'. Literature on the USSR's foreign policy in the 1930s agrees that the Soviet Union was very worried about a two-pronged German and Japanese encirclement.[8] Much of the period from 1933 to 1939 was spent trying to gather potential allies, as with the Franco-Soviet Pact of 1935, the cordial greeting of Anthony Eden in Moscow in the same year, and membership of the formerly despised League of Nations in 1934. Stalin gave very clear indications of wishing to work with the League of Nations from late 1933 onwards.[9] These indications were taken at face value by a Labour Party looking for allies within the League of Nations and to further bolster this body faced with German, Italian and Japanese hostility. But nothing could persuade the National Government in London that the USSR was now a *status quo* country that must be supported against the dictators.[10]

The League, the Labour Party and the USSR, 1931-end 1932: the Manchurian crisis

The first three years of the 1930s demonstrated the myth of the League's capacity to ensure world peace.[11] It should perhaps be recalled that much of this myth was identical with the Labour Party's own policy and that many of the staunchest supporters of the League were in or close to the Labour Party. The most famous of these were of course Lord Robert Cecil, Arthur Henderson and his assistant at the Disarmament Conference, Philip Noel-Baker.

There is a certain acacemic consensus that the Labour Party's attitude to the events in Manchuria was more or less the same as that of the National Government. British interests in China and the 'open door' are thus supposed to have been the common ground of government and opposition. The difference is supposed to lie in the relative belief in Conservative and Labour circles in the possibility of a League settlement to the dispute between Japan and China. It should be considered whether this picture is entirely correct in so far as it concerns the Labour Party.[12]

It is clear that at the outset the Manchurian crisis was not taken too seriously in London or Geneva. The Far East had for long been a turbulent place and the Chinese were widely accepted as an anarchic race. The Japanese, on the other hand, had seemed to be coming well into the fold of western civilisation. Had they not been with the Allies in 1914–18 and had they not become an industrial nation quite as fast as any European power? Moreover they seemed, until 1931, to have become democratic. This rather condescending comparison between the 'yellow races' was held as true by Labour and Conservative alike. The Chinese 'provocation' invoked by the local Japanese commander in Manchuria in mid-September 1931 could therefore be taken as a relatively limited but acceptable excuse for a small punitive retaliation by the Japanese. Hence the slow reaction in London and Geneva. It must be stressed that it was not until much later that the Manchurian crisis was seen as the first battle of the Second World War, as Thorne emphasises throughout.

The Labour Party's attitude was different to the extent that it did have access to extremely detailed and well publicised accounts of Japanese actions in Manchuria, often by Edgar Snow. That these were published, frequently on the front page of the *Daily Herald* – which was now widely accepted as an official Labour Party newspaper – is very significant. The party was also different at least partly because it took very seriously the fear of the USSR being pulled into the conflict by the Japanese, who might try and seize the Pacific provinces of the USSR. The National Government would not have cared if they had, since to deny the Russians Vladivostok would have fulfilled an ancient Admiralty dream.[13]

If the Labour Party had no illusions about the impact of its protest on the National Government, it was severely worried about the probable impact of the Manchurian crisis on the League of Nations. As early as December 1931 the *Daily Herald* editorial was pronouncing that the League had 'failed' in Manchuria.[14] But such was the commitment of the party to the League at this period that some rather bizarre attitudes to the Manchurian affair became apparent. On one side the membership of the Party was regaled by the horrors being perpetrated by Japan and the lack of a National Government response of sufficient strength. On the other there was a gnashing of teeth in some of the higher echelons of the party that had more to do with the dangers of an upset in the delicate disarmament negotiations where the Japanese had to be present. As a result we see the (private) remarks from Noel-Baker to Cecil in early 1932 that 'only the damned Chinese question is spoiling the Conference'. Noel-Baker was nevertheless indignant about the Japanese and infuriated that Sir Eric Drummond of the League would not take any firm action.[15]

One problem that was recognised more clearly as a result of the Manchurian affair was that the League could never be an effective guarantor of peace, especially in the Far East, without the presence of the Soviet Union and the United States in its membership. The efforts of such as Noel-Baker and Cecil to get the Russians in had foundered throughout the 1920s on the hostile attitude of the Comintern to the League. This tradition of hostility was not dissipated so easily even when the USSR decided to change its approach during 1932–4. And what is more important, its changing policies were not so easily perceived at the time as they have been by subsequent historiography. Noel-Baker was one of those closest to the Labour Party and the League at this crucial juncture of 1932. He fully realised the importance of Soviet involvement with the League. And yet most of his speeches for 1932 stress the USSR's 'bitterly hostile' attitude to the League in the 1920s.[16] He actively worked for the inclusion of the USSR and the USA in a 'Committee of Twelve' to decide on ways to ensure peace through the League of Nations, but he distrusted the Russians profoundly. In a lengthy memorandum on the Manchurian crisis he wrote: '[an] objection to this plan [to include the USSR in the Committee] is that the policy of Russia in this whole dispute is ambiguous in the extreme. It is certain that she has been flirting with Japan. . . . If Russia thus desires to mix the cards her power for doing so will certainly be greater in such a secret conference as is here proposed'. This time it was Cecil, now back in London, having resigned as Britain's most important representative at the League, who urged confidence in the Russians on Noel-Baker. He wrote: 'it would be quite useless to go on without open consultation with Russia and America'.[17]

The source of this new debate about Russian trustworthiness arose from a new development in Manchuria. In mid-March 1932 there were reports of a Russo-Japanese clash on the Manchurian border.[18] The wildest reports now suggested that Sir John Simon, as Foreign Secretary, was quite willing to let the Japanese have Manchuria in return for wearing down bolshevism by force if necessary. An invasion of the USSR was considered in some quarters to be imminent. That this would be the line of the Communist Party is understandable, but it also reached the Labour and Socialist International. The LSI passed a long resolution in the presence of Compton, Gillies and Brockway of the Labour Party in late May which put forward at length the thesis of a likely invasion, with the implication of approval by the 'counter-revolution' and the 'duplicity' of the governments assembled at Geneva.[19] It is likely that Brockway, shortly to take the ILP out of the Labour Party, approved of the tone of this resolution more than Gillies. Gillies was to write later that 'the political realities were the fear that if Japan did not occupy Manchuria, Russia would'.[20]

This realistic, if not flattering, approach to Russian intentions was the general rule for Labour Party foreign policy experts. There was a general realisation that a Japanese attack on Russia was possible, especially during April 1932, but there was a fair dose of caution as to apportioning of ultimate blame. Good examples of this are the closely worded reports from the *Daily Herald*'s chief foreign correspondent, W. N. Ewer. He stressed that 'war clouds' were gathering in the Far East but that both Japanese and Russians were preparing for it, with the British Government taking on the really evil role of hoping to pick up the pieces of such a clash.[21] Commander Kenworthy warned that Japan would lose and that this would give rise to a heaven-sent chance for Russian propaganda. Russia would 'endeavour to arouse all Asia on its side in a Holy War against imperialism'.[22] It is clear from his other writings that Kenworthy wanted this even less than Sir John Simon. In evoking the 'yellow peril' as he had in his writings of the 1920s he shows how deep was the persisting suspicion of Russian motives in certain sections of the Labour Party.

There was, however, a current, strongly manifested in the LSI and the left of the Labour Party, of a more naive view of Soviet intentions. Gilies for one spent much of his career in combating this current, that was strongest in the ILP and in the Socialist League after 1932 and the ILP/Labour Party split. Manchuria here had another effect, in that it seems to have crystallised attitudes to the League of Nations among the non-communist left into two distinct schools. After Manchuria there were those who believed that the League of Nations could be saved and those who believed that it was entirely working in the interests of Western imperialism. Broadly speaking, these two groups became the left and the right of the Labour Party until the end of our period. Attitudes to the Soviet Union became a major touchstone of membership to these groups.

On the one hand there were those, such as Noel-Baker and the majority of the Labour Party NEC and the TUC General Council, who believed that it was necessary to implicate the USSR in the League as much as possible in order to minimise any danger of rash Soviet action on one side or rash western action on the other, against the USSR. On the other hand there were those who wished to work outside the League of Nations altogether and form 'popular fronts' with friendly socialist and communist parties ensuring world peace by refusing to fight in a capitalist war. It was in effect a plea for the return of the pre-1914 International. Most of the Labour Party thought that this was absurd and only the Socialist League, led by Sir Stafford Cripps, put any credence in it.

The disarmament conference of the League of Nations, 1932–3 and its effect on the Labour Party

This division was accentuated by the slowly developing disaster of the Disarmament Conference that opened in Geneva in February 1932. The remainder of the Labour Party old guard in the form of Arthur Henderson had made a complete commitment to seeing the success of these talks. The date of its birth could not have been worse, with Anglo-French contacts at an inter-war low and the spirit of revanchisme on the increase in Germany. Italy had already proved herself an untrustworthy ally for peace.[23] To pin too many hopes on it therefore seems to us today extremely naive. But to Henderson it was a last chance well worth trying. Lansbury, who replaced him as leader of the party in late 1931, totally agreed and the Labour press gave a good impression of agreeing, whatever private doubts may have existed. The problem, they said, lay not in the conference but in the statesmen sent to it. Perhaps Henderson could show the way.

But even before the conference was six months old the Labour press was disillusioned with its progress: 'The trouble with humanity is that it trusts too much to its generous feelings and to prayer', even if 'Providence ought to be given a fair chance'. By the time Hitler arrived to power in February 1933 on the anniversary of the conference it was all over and by January 1934 the *Economist* was not alone in calling it 'failed'.[24]

Among the schemes that were proposed to the conference during 1932 and the first half of 1933, only three were really of any impact on the discussions. These were the Hoover plan of June 1932, the MacDonald plan of March 1933 and the Russian plan of February 1932. The second of these came too late, since Hitler had already decided to rearm. The first foundered on Franco-German distrust. It was a wide-ranging plan for reductions of one-third in land forces, the abolition of tanks and heavy artillery as well as aerial bombing, and reductions in capital ships. In one swoop Hoover was able to alienate both the British and the French who were wounded in their amour propre and please the Germans. The plan seems clearly to have been an electoral ploy for a doomed President. It was rejected almost out of hand.[25] The first plan tabled to the conference, that of the French, was ruined from the outset, for it wanted a League of Nations dedicated to the defence of the Treaty of Versailles by force.

The Labour Party had no problems agreeing with the National Government in rejecting this.[26] They disagreed rather on the Russian proposals which were next put forward. Litvinov proposed nothing less than complete disarmament by all nations. The *Daily Herald* foreign editor, W. N. Ewer, was enthusiastic. Praise of the speech was 'pretty well universal' and 'he said what most people in the world are thinking' were two of his comments. 'There has been no speech yet that has so much set people thinking, wondering if, after all, this is not the right, at bottom, the simplest way'.[27]

It is perhaps symptomatic of a deeper distrust of Litvinov's motives in the Labour Party leadership that there was no *Daily Herald* editorial to go with this speech and Ewer's glowing comments. The explanation of this curiously lukewarm journalism is explained by this being during one of the worst periods of the Manchurian crisis. Even Ewer had to admit on 22 February that 'Japan has put Geneva in the shade'. The ILP, as has been stressed already, was coming round to the point of view that any effort in the League, even by Litvinov, was useless. The same week that Litvinov's speech was printed in the *New Leader*, its chief foreign journalist, H. N. Brailsford, announced: 'The League is dead'.[28] So this Russian initiative fell on deaf ears even in the Labour press as much because of its timing as anything else. If it had been intended as a propaganda ploy it failed even among its most sympathetic audience in Britain.

The Russian element in the ILP disaffiliation

The extent of the ILP's deception with the League now became total but they, unlike most of the Labour Party, now believed the Russian line that the League was actually an alliance against the USSR. Japan was now being portrayed in communist journals the world over as the head of a battering ram being wielded by all the capitalist nations, that is, by all of the League of Nations.[29] The Manchurian crisis was perceived by the ILP as an excuse to attack the achievements of the five-year plans, which were showing up the decline of the West. For the ILP the idea was being confirmed that an attack on the USSR was an attack on socialist principles and therefore on the ILP itself.

It was during this period, until mid-1932, that the basis of the rationale for 'popular fronts' was established. The first major discussions for a Popular Front between the ILP and the Communist Party took place at this time as did a whole series of policy debates within the ILP. Soviet Russia thus played the role of an important catalyst in driving the ILP from the Labour Party. The National Administrative Council of the ILP urged the TUC and the Labour Party to ensure '[b]y every means in their power [that] ... the workers of this country must cooperate with the workers throughout Europe in preventing the threatened attack on Socialist Russia'.[30] The clear implication was the drawing up of a new alliance that the ILP knew was deeply inimical to the Labour Party leadership.

The Russian state was to be the reference point for most major domestic and foreign policy attitudes in the ILP for the next two years at least, even if this was not supposed to be a slavish copy, as Brockway was always keen to point out. But it would be foolish to imagine that this fine print corrigendum had such an impact as the overall policy statement. E. F. Wise, who was to be the most respected voice for the ILP 'affiliationists' seems to have realised this inherent problem: 'The new ILP Manifesto was full of revolutionary phrases, but there was no difference between it and the new policies of the Labour Party ... all of which would be discussed'.[31] He urged a left-wing presence in the Labour Party to ensure that these policies were carried where it really mattered.

His advice was ignored and he resigned to be founder Chairman of the new Socialist League within the Labour Party until his death in 1933. As a long-time open friend of the Soviet Union he must have known that the best way to link its interests to the majority of the Labour Party was to stress it as an object lesson, 'an exemplar', and as a concrete contributor of wealth through trade, not as a political ally in the physical sense. He could see the dangerous simplicity of equating Russia with 'socialism' and the Labour Party with 'capitalism' or even 'fascism', as some wilder ILP members were in effect seemingly claiming.

To tie a party to such an untrustworthy and single float would be to ensure its sinking in line with the object of adoration. Whether there was a direct link or not between the decline of the ILP and the decline of love for the USSR as the 1930s wore on is difficult to prove, but there was a direct *prima facie* correlation. Brockway later admitted both the error of disaffiliation and that of excessive trust in the USSR.[32] The latter gradually dawned on the ILP ruling NAC. In 1933 ILP speakers were already being urged not to commit the party to a too Soviet line. Trade benefits should be stressed, as should the war danger, but 'ILP speakers should avoid dogmatic statements committing the Party in matters where neither Annual Conference nor NAC has given a decision'. What was more, speakers should carefully study both 'the present policy of the Russian Government and the Communist International (Stalin's policy) and the criticism of it by Trotsky and others'.[33]

This led to increasing ILP official contact with Trotsky himself in the wake of growing disappointment over contacts with 'official' Russia, and especially after continuing rebuffs from the Comintern. Trotsky was urged by one of his spies at the end of 1933 to exploit this by getting his works 'into the hands of ILP-ites. A fund should be raised immediately for this purpose'.[34] By January of 1934, Brockway was making his doubts public to his branch members: 'while my Council agrees that the USSR Government can render its best service by building up a strong Proletarian State and laying the foundations of the Socialist Commonwealth in Russia itself, it does not agree that the present tactics of the ECCI [Comintern] in this respect are invariably correct'.[35] By 1935 Brockway was inquiring after Trotsky's health and they were on the best of terms, Trotsky even publishing on occasion in *New Leader*.[36] The effect of this on Stalin's blood pressure does not need to be described. Brockway later said that he had had great doubts about stalinism from 1936.[37] 'Negotiating with Moscow' had, however, been the main eye-opener, and this dated from late 1933. Nineteen thirty-four had also had its share of disappointments for the ILP, the USSR joining the League of Nations and the purge trials being among them.[38] The ILP had indeed put itself out on such an unsteady political limb in 1932 with its USSR policies that the branch had snapped and with it a lot of the ILP's credibility. The Labour Party, precisely by not over-committing itself to a pro-Russian stance, was able to avoid this crash. How it did so, by accident or design, is the main theme of the next chapter. The ILP in the meantime was reduced to the status of an irritating 'flea'.[39]

The end of the left's influence on Labour?

The departure of the ILP left a free path for the more conservative elements of the Labour Party – Morrison, Dalton, Citrine and Bevin in particular – a heaven-sent opportunity to suggest a new policy that would incorporate what was useful in the Russian experience while disposing of what was undesirable or politically embarrassing. Although the ILP was replaced by the Socialist League as a ginger group of the left within the Labour Party, this never had the political and historical legitimacy of the ILP, a legitimacy that it had just voluntarily jettisoned. The Socialist League was also thus only an irritant, especially after the end of 1932. The Labour Party had never been marxist, its claim to socialism had always been relative and largely emotional. Now it was to return to its own version of working-class liberation, an alliance of the workers and middle-class intellectuals who had far less interest in any class war nonsense than in efficiency in parliamentary government.

The departure of the ILP, which was at least partly due to Russian considerations, can thus be seen as the beginning of a new era in Labour Party history, which culminated in the same leadership taking over from Churchill in 1945. Their pragmatic attitude to the USSR was formed in the next years. The initial stages of this process are clearest to discern in foreign policy decisions but it is obvious, once again, that the domestic debate cannot be divorced from these decisions.

Notes

1 THORNE, Christopher, *The Limits of Foreign Policy: The West, the League and the Far Eastern Crisis of 1931–1933*, London, Macmillan, 1973 (hereafter THORNE, *Limits of Foreign Policy*), p. 13.

2 NAYLOR, John F., *Labour's International Policy: The Labour Party in the 1930s*, London, Weidenfeld and Nicolson, 1969.

3 For example, NORTHEDGE, F. S., *The Troubled Giant: Britain Among the Great Powers, 1916–1939*, London, G. Bell, 1966.

4 Cf., for example, COLE, *A History of the Labour Party From 1914*, pp. 307–8.

5 THORNE, *Limits of Foreign Policy*, p. 47 and DILKS, David (ed.), *Retreat From Power: Studies in Britain's Foreign Policy of the Twentieth Century, Volume 1 1906–1939*, London, Macmillan, 1981.

6 COWLING, Maurice, *The Impact of Labour*, Cambridge University Press, 1971, and *The Impact of Hitler*, Cambridge University Press, 1975.

7 GRIFFITHS, Richard, *Fellow Travellers of the Right: British Enthusiasts For Nazi Germany, 1933–39*, Oxford University Press, 1983.

8 For example, KENNAN, p. 276.

9 Cf. what is still the best account of the Soviet entry into the League: DAVIS, Katherine W., *The Soviet Union and the League of Nations, 1919–1933*, Geneva Research Centre, 1934, 23 pp.

10 Cf. for a short appraisal of this global problem NORTHEDGE and WELLS, *Britain and Soviet Communism*, pp. 51–8.

11 A convenient summary can be found in EGERTON, George W., *Great Britain and the League of Nations; Collective Security as Myth and History*, paper presented at Geneva, September 1980, published IUHEI.

12 For example, HAGGIE, Paul, *Britannia at Bay: The Defence of the British Empire Against Japan, 1931–1941*, Oxford, Clarendon Press, 1981, p. 26 (hereafter *Britannia at Bay*).

13 For much greater detail on Labour Party reactions to the Manchuria crisis see WILLIAMS, *The Attitude*, pp. 470–71.

14 *Daily Herald* editorial, 10 December 1931.

15 Noel-Baker to Cecil, 12 February and 2 March 1932, Cecil Papers, Add.Mss.51107.

16 'Speeches on Disarmament – 1932', Noel-Baker Papers, 1/6 and Cecil to Noel-Baker, 25 November 1932.

17 'Notes on the Manchurian Dispute', 23 November 1932, Cecil Papers, Add.Mss.51107.

18 *Daily Herald*, 15 March 1932.

19 Labour Party International Department. Report of the LSI Executive Meeting of 19 and 20 May 1932.

20 GILLIES, William, 'The International Scene', *Labour Women* (official Labour Party magazine), April 1933, p. 57.

21 *Daily Herald*, 18 and 19 April 1932, reports by Ewer from Geneva.

22 KENWORTHY, Commander, 'The Shadow of War Over Asia', *Daily Herald*, 13 May 1932.

23 Good summaries of the Disarmament Conference can be found in CECIL, Viscount, *A Great Experiment*, London, Cape, 1941 and WALTERS, F. P., *A History of the League of Nations*, London RIIA, 1952. NORTHEDGE, F. S., *The Troubled Giant* also has a brief description on pp. 368–84. Good summaries of the problems involved in the conference from a paper very sympathetic to the Labour Party can be found in the 'Disarmament Supplement' of the *New Statesman and Nation*, 30 January 1932, pp. 132–46.

24 TOMLINSON, H. M., 'Torpedoes or Flower Pots?', *New Clarion*, 18 June 1932 and '1933, A Year of Drama', *The Economist*, 6 January 1934.

25 Cf. NORTHEDGE, *The Troubled Giant*, pp. 372–3.

26 See, for example, 'A Noble and Ingenious Plan', *New Statesman*, 13 February 1932.

27 'Mr Litvinov Puts Case for Complete Disarmament', *Daily Herald*, 12 February 1932.

28 *Daily Herald*, 22 February 1932 and *New Leader*, 19 February 1932.

29 Cartoon reproduced from *New Masses*, New York in *New Leader*, 11 March 1932.

30 'Hands Off Socialist Russia', NAC Declaration, *New Leader*, 22 April 1932, printed with an article by John Paton (General Secretary, ILP) entitled 'The ILP and the Attack on Russia'. For more details see WILLIAMS, *The Attitude*, pp. 478–480.

31 'The Critical Debate . . . E. F. Wise Pleads', *New Leader*, 5 August 1932.

32 BROCKWAY, Fenner, *Inside the Left*, p. 345.

33 Independent Labour Party NAC, 'Soviet Trade and Political Relationships', 1933, LSE Archives, NAC Print Item 70.

34 WEBER, J., 'Report of Talk Delivered by Fenner Brockway of ILP before Left Wing Socialist Forum – December 5th 1933', sent to Trotsky, 6 pp., Harvard Papers, no. 17344. In the same speech Brockway is reported as having said: 'I hope to God no representative of the Press or any spy has managed to sneak in here. I do not want this quoted in the English Press', p. 4.

35 Brockway to the ECCI, 8 January 1934, Harvard Papers, no. 13817.

36 Brockway to Trotsky, 2 December 1935, Harvard Papers, 378.

37 BROCKWAY, *Inside the Left*, 'Preface'.

38 Cf. Chs. 25 and 26 of *Inside the Left*, pp. 248–63.

39 The expression is Dalton's in a letter to Middleton (Labour Party Secretary) dated 8 February 1935, Labour Party Archives, JSM/ILP/15.

chapter sixteen

Russia as an element in the elaboration of the Labour Party's foreign policy, 1933–4

The defeat of Labour Party hopes of a world peace through the League of Nations was complicated in 1933–4 by the rise of new dictatorships in Germany and Austria. The rise of Hitler was to dominate the world's political scene for the next twelve years. The very concept of democracy seemed doomed to the dustbin of history. This the Labour Party could not allow, for it stood or fell after 1919 as the party that represented the democratic system through which it had gained legitimacy. The Labour Party had therefore to either submit to the tide of pessimisim or to fight back and postulate alternative possibilities for the system it had made its own.

This was particularly important in the light of the accusations of much greater 'efficiency' in dictatorships, a world that had always haunted European, and especially British, Labour politics since the late nineteenth century. Mosley's New Party and the British Union of Fascists, the latter proclaimed in late 1932, were a direct challenge to create a 'Greater Britain' of a kind that appealed to many ordinary Labour Party members.[1] It has been shown in a previous chapter how the Labour Party proposed to create its own greater Britain through planning. But how did it answer the fundamental question of its own supporters whether dictatorship was perhaps better than democracy in a political sense? It also had to convince an essentially conservative electorate that its methods were going to succeed where the National Government's would fail in creating a new Britain that would be authentically British, not a copy of some foreign model. Luckily for Labour, here the British propensity for distrust of 'abroad' helped the BUF to wither away. But Labour had to be careful not to be identified too closely with any foreign 'exemplar' itself.

The Labour Party leadership thus seems to have made a conscious appeal to what one writer has termed 'British tolerance and good sense'[2] but which could just as easily have been a dislike of foreign ideas. While the communists used the tactic of waging an illegal street war against the BUF, a tactic that had failed in Germany and Austria, the Labour Party and the TUC decided to retreat behind the walls of moral outrage and issue stern warnings against excess in politics. The resulting literature of 1933 shows once again how the Labour Party used a foreign example as a warning in its domestic politics while actually benefiting from examining that example *in situ* with great interest. Hence Sir Oswald Mosley's thugs could be roundly condemned as emissaries of nasty Italian fascism, while Hugh Dalton of the Labour Party NEC went to visit Mussolini and was, in private, impressed.[3] The same could be done with the USSR, the CPGB and the Comintern this time taking the role of scapegoat.

The period 1933–4 thus has its supreme importance in that the lines were clearly drawn between Italy and Russia and 'experiment', and the political systems of fascism or Soviet communism. There was a return to the policies of 1924–31, in that the old idea of 'moderates' and 'extremists' took clear form again. A slight window had been left open in late 1931 and 1932 for a rapprochement between the British communist left and the Labour Party. 'Class against class' and the ILP defection had very nearly shut this window. In 1933 the Hastings Conference of the Labour Party shut it for good. But this in no way meant discouraging the Soviet Union as a force for moderation in world politics. Whilst rebuffing the still 'extreme' Comintern and its agents, the Soviet Commissariat for Foreign Affairs and Ambassador Maisky in London could always be sure of a warm welcome at Transport House. When the same Maisky intimated that he wished to get the USSR into the League of Nations, the NEC did all in its power to help.

Finally, by the end of 1934, the clouds that were to lead to much worse disagreement were appearing in the form of the purges. But until the end of that year, the year of the Webbs' second visit, the distinction that was made between the 'exemplar' and the 'defender of world peace' on the one hand and the 'dictatorship' on the other was an almost universal categorization in the Labour Party.

The end of hopes in the disarmament conference and the revival of the idea of the 'united front'

The demise of Labour Party hopes in the disarmament conference took a certain time to take hold. Henderson, Noel-Baker and Zilliacus in

Geneva were particularly slow in admitting failure in spite of the evidence. In London, this failure seemed more obvious earlier, Dalton epitomising this on the Labour Party's NEC. When Dalton went to Geneva in early 1933 'with no great enthusiasm', he spent the time with this friends Zilliacus ('Zilly', as Dalton called him) and with Philip Noel-Baker. He commented: 'Phil still ridiculously hopeful about the prospects of the Conference ... But while I'm there, both the French and the German Governments fall in one day ... terrifying row of portents'.[4] By June of that year Henderson was just about ready to give up hope for his conference. Henderson had agreed to a three-month 'adjournment' and this was seen by Noel-Baker, rightly enough, as the equivalent of a death blow. Zilliacus agreed that it was all over, and was also 'upset'.[5]

This is in no way to imply that most of the NEC saw any alternative to the League of Nations, unlike the ILP and Socialist League left. The NEC held to its policy throughout that only by disarmament was world peace possible, but a League recourse to force was more and more implicitly accepted as 1933 wore on.[6] How was collective security to be enforced when disarmament seemed impossible to achieve and how were states to react when faced with such aggression as had been shown by Japan?

The Labour Party's ACIQ conceded defeat in the disarmament conference in March 1933. It also saw new clouds gathering, in Germany, in the Balkans and in the 'isolation of Russia'. A subsequent longer memorandum enlarged on these observations. It was now 'incumbent both upon individuals and on the Party very carefully to reconsider their attitude towards the League'. The alternative, 'a policy of alliances' was 'ruled out', and what was needed was a 'strong League of Nations ... a League system under which every State has to submit disputes to League settlement and cannot disregard a League decision'.[7] But what if they would not do so?

Cripps' argument concerning the League of Nations was that fascism was imminent and perhaps inevitable in Britain and that Russia was the target of the nations that made up the League, with Japan, Germany and Poland leading the way. The League of Nations could therefore not be trusted, as had been proved in the Manchurian crisis. Dalton could only agree with his analysis 'a little', and he clearly disagreed with Cripps's alternative policy, which was 'to declare a General Strike against sending munitions to Japan if she attacks Russia'.[8] The Socialist League went from this point on a diametrically opposed track to the majority of the Labour Party on the subject of the League of Nations.

The idea began to be floated by the Socialist League of a parallel of Nations, one made up of 'progressive states'.

This had very important repercussions on the way that the Socialist League and the rest of the Labour Party looked at Russia's place in the party's future foreign policy. The majority of the centre-right wanted to work with Russia within the League of Nations in order to reduce its dangerous 'isolation' and the left to work with it outside the League of Nations. What really crystallised this debate were differing attitudes that developed in the party in relation to the new threat of nazism in particular and totalitarian dictatorship in general.

'Democracy versus Dictatorship?': Labour Party reactions to totalitarian regimes, 1933–4

The Labour Party leadership had not forgotten the attempted infiltrations of the party by the communists in the 1920s. They were convinced that the Communist and ILP call for a 'united front' was but another such attempt.[9] The Labour Party NEC discussed the proposal at length in March 1933. To decide upon their reply they asked Compton, who with Gillies had long been the main Labour Party delegate to the Labour and Socialist International, for the LSI's view. He produced a lengthy decision of the Executive Committee of the LSI dated 19 March which pointed out that the Comintern had 'adopted the well-known method of laying down conditions and attacking the Socialist Parties before negotiations could begin'. This was 'an indication that the hope that Moscow would learn from the tragic developments in Germany that a frank and honest concentration of all the forces of the workers has become an absolute necessity which has not yet been fulfilled'. The LSI therefore suggested that member parties should refrain from cooperation with the communists. The Labour Party NEC agreed, in spite of the fact that a letter arrived from the Socialist League in the middle of the discussion urging consideration of a 'united front'. It was decided to issue a manifesto explaining the decision.[10]

The TUC General Council came to a similar decision and the National Joint Council of the TUC and the Labour Party decided to issue a series of replies to explain their lack of enthusiasm for a 'united front'. These replies were, of course, as much directed against their own left as at the CPGB or the ILP. The two most important of these replies are to be found in *The Communist Solar System* and in *Democracy Versus Dictatorship*. Both had important implications for Labour's Russian policy and both raised a storm of debate.

The expression 'Democracy versus Dictatorship'[11] first emerged in a National Joint Council tract of 24 March 1933 and dwelt mainly on the emergence of dictatorships all over Europe, with particular emphasis given to Germany. But some of the real virulence was reserved for the USSR. Some examples are as follows:

> The follies and furies of Tzarism led straight to Communist Dictatorship in Russia (line 9)
>
> Reaction on the 'Right' has bred reaction on the 'Left' (line 18)
>
> Before the War, British Labour denounced Russian tyranny (line 23)
>
> Today, in a world that is being driven by capitalist ruthlessness into Dictatorship, British Labour stands firm for the democratic rights of the people (lines 30–31)
>
> Workers everywhere should strengthen the Labour Party – the spearhead of political power against Dictators – Fascist or Communist (lines 53 and 54)

This tract was intended more as a rebuff to the communists than as an attack on the USSR but it swiftly became apparent that a least within the Labour Party fears existed that the linkage of Nazi Germany with Soviet Russia might work against the Labour Party. Even Gillies appears to have wanted the above-quoted lines 9, 18 and 23 removed. He also took exception to the 'spearhead' implications: 'This is not the function of British Labour. This is the function of International. When did London become a new Moscow?[12]

But it is clear that Gillies was overruled and the unamended tract was followed by a National Joint Council letter signed by Henderson for the Labour Party, Citrine for the TUC and the acting deputy head of the PLP, H. S. Lindsay. This detailed all the correspondence between the ILP, Communist and Labour Parties. Citrine further explained the impossibility of cooperation in the *Daily Herald*.[13] The ILP replied in most measured terms[14] as did, very surprisingly, the communists. 'We are honestly prepared to cooperate', said Harry Pollitt. However, not many days later this initial conciliation was countered by new attacks on the 'social fascists'. There must be a 'workers' dictatorship' and the only example for this was the Soviet Union.[15]

Mention of the Soviet Union itself was nevertheless markedly reduced in more humdrum Labour Party propaganda. 'Speakers' Notes' produced for Labour Party speakers the day that 'Democracy versus Dictatorship' was issued made no specific mention of Russia, even if 'all other forms of dictatorship' were condemned.[16] But in private memos Citrine kept to his initial condemnation of the Soviet Union. He did so mainly from the point of view of trade-union considerations. The Soviet Government had 'set out deliberately to obtain rigid control over the

Unions ... Now they are definitely organs of the Government'. After looking at German and Italian practice he thought it 'clear that industrial liberty is an non-existent as political liberty in Germany, Russia and Italy, this being an inevitable result of dictatorship whatever its political colour'. He then addressed himself to asking why it was necesary to point this out:

> Arising from the desire that fair play should be given to the Russian experiment, there has been a tendency to gloss over the results of Communist dictatorship and a disposition on the part of some people to see good features in the Russian method. It is shown that this reasoning is quite fallacious. Intentions cannot be taken as a criterion. The results themselves have to be considered and the results to trade unionism have been universally disastrous where dictatorships have been established.[17]

The cause and the effect were clear, said Citrine, and the main problem lay with 'confusion of thought in the Labour Movement'. Whenever such abuses of trade union rights had been made apparent in Italy or Germany, nearly all members of the Labour movement had condemned these abuses, but not when they had happened in Russia. 'Some indeed have usually sought to justify anything which the Soviet Government has done', and actions which would and had bought forth 'indignant protests' about Italy and Germany 'have passed almost without notice when done by Russia'.

Citrine analysed the reasons for this tolerance in terms that had been heard many times before. The Czar had been hated and his successors seen as liberators. The Labour movement had been convinced by the Allied intervention that capitalism wanted to squeeze the life out of the new revolution. In these circumstances he added that there was a natural desire to refrain from criticism which would be exploited by mutual enemies. But this 'has been responsible for the belief that the dictatorship of Russia is something desirable the merits of which the Labour Movement should be ready to defend'. The accounts of delegations of British workers had received '[w]idespread publicity in our Movement. An entirely one-sided picture is usually presented. Anyone who ventures to express doubts as to some of the achievements of the Soviet Government, runs the risk of being regarded as an enemy of Russia'.

More dangerous still for Citrine was his belief that 'this lack of discrimination had encouraged the belief that the form of Government in Russia is worthy of emulation'. This was 'confusion of thought' for it could lead to a confusion of the ideal and the real. The problem for Citrine was the ever-present danger of submitting to the communists' embrace. Moreover: 'It is not always easy to discriminate between the actions of the Communists as a political party and its actions as the Government of Russia'.[18] Both had proved their hostility to democracy which Citrine equated with trade unionism. What could be done to stave off the menace of this confusion? The answer, for Citrine, lay in a firm line against any united front, a constant reaffirmation of the benefits of parliamentary democratic institutions.

Citrine's action in releasing 'Democracy versus Dictatorship' was not a unanimous success among members of the Labour Party NEC or in Transport House. Gillies' objections have already been stated. Even much later Citrine's almost brutal approach made many of the Labour Party's leaders wince. Lansbury (the leader) wrote to Middleton (the secretary) in late 1934 that he 'hate[d] this controversy' because it distracted from the real work of the party, and gave propaganda to the communists at little cost to them. What he wished to be stressed was that the Labour Party was *already*, a 'United Front of Trade Unions, Cooperatives and Socialists'.[19] The Socialist League was, of course, against the Citrine declaration, as was Laski. This served to poison the atmosphere within the NEC and to add to the left-right split in the Labour Party. But Citrine's remarks were a crucial importance, since they constitute a distinct taking of position by the centre-right of the movement's leadership against the left, with Russia as a major touchstone.

This definition was further clarified by the publication of a pamphlet designed to expose Communist Party 'front' tactics, the *Communist Solar System* (referring to a 1927 expression coined by Kuusinen, then head of the Comintern), probably written by Gillies, with some help from Morrison and colleagues in Transport House, after an appeal for information from the National Joint Council.[20] The LSI was also prompt in sending material for Gillies to use.[21] The most important result of this pamphlet was that any body in which the directive force was seen as communist was now banned affiliation to the Labour Party.

Although directed primarily against the United Front, the pamphlet, as with Citrine's tract on dictatorship, could not be but partly construed as an attack on the USSR. Harry Pollitt, General Secretary of the CPGB, was quoted as saying: 'The Moscow road is the only road to working-class victory'.[22] Gillies might try and put the blame on the Comintern, rather than on Russia itself, but such was not the impression it gave to the left.

The 'United Front' quarrel came out into the open at the 1933 Conference of the Party at Hastings. The main criticism lay in what Ellis Smith called 'sidetracking the main issue' by refusing all cooperation with the communists. Ellen Wilkinson said that 'that pamphlet that Mr Morrison is so proud of, "The Communist Solar System", is a magnificent advertisement of the energy and drive of the Communist Party in this country'.[23] None the less, the left's attempts to refer the NEC's document back for further elaboration or even scrapping were roundly defeated. Undoubtedly one of the most telling statements in the debate about the 'The Communist Solar System' was when Morrison quoted none other than Stalin in his defence of the document: 'Let us go to the fountainhead, Mr Stalin', said Morrison, quoting Stalin's appreciation that United Front tactics were 'to make it easier for the millions of workers in capitalist countries who are infected by the prejudices of Social Democratic opportunism to come over to Communism'. There was, said Morrison, '[no] obscurity about that; perfectly honest, perfectly frank. The honesty of the Russians is like a breath of fresh air compared with the confusion among some of their friends in this country'.

The subsequent passing of the various Russian motions at this Conference in October 1933 must be seen as part of the growing desire of the majority of the Labour Party NEC to establish what Morrison referred to in the trade debate as 'business' relations with the USSR, not relations where the Labour Party ran the risk of being submerged by the Communist Party. An external cooperation with the Russians was more than possible, it was desirable: 'but a British Labour Government would have to have business heads on its shoulders and look after British interests as well as the Russians looked after theirs'.[24] The Labour Party would therefore not accept any relationship except on its own terms. Part of this relationship meant that the Communist Party of Great Britain and its Comintern masters were to have no role to play in the Labour Party or, if possible, in Britain as a whole. For all this, the problem and internal discussion within both the NEC and in the wider Party did not go away during the rest of the 1930s. Every annual conference had its supporters of a United Front, usually led by Cripps and the Socialist League. This was one of the main reasons that finally prompted Dalton to organise the disaffiliation of that body in 1937.

This resolute opposition to Communist Party alliances can be seen as part of the older policy of keeping the CPGB at arms length. It can also be seen in the continuing attempts to encourage the moderates in Moscow and to discourage the extremists. The Labour Party NEC had encouraged such a sympathetic line to the Soviet Union in the Metro-Vickers case to discomfort both the British and the Russian diehards of Will Dyson's cartoon. Having rejected the foreign wing of Soviet extremism in 1933 with the 'Demoracy versus Dictatorship' initiative, the Labour Party was to spend 1934 encouraging the Moscow moderates to take a more responsible attitude in the world arena, and particularly to get the USSR to join the League of Nations.

Labour Party efforts to bring the USSR into the League, 1933–4

The groundwork for this attempt was well prepared by a series of Labour Party policy documents and personal efforts, as well as a growing Russian and even National Government conviction of the usefulness of a Russian move into the League of Nations.

There had been no major policy statement on foreign policy since the 1931 debacle and yet events had moved to a point where one became imperative. The reason for this was that the disarmament conference and the League of Nations had remained the backbone of Labour Party endeavour. The secretary of the party, Henderson, had spent much of his time on this question, resigning his party post in May 1933. His partial departure from centre-stage left the scene even more dominated by Bevin, Citrine of the TUC, and Dalton and Morrison on the NEC. Lansbury was ill during most of this period, from December 1933 to the end of 1934. The only other figures of note were Attlee, who spent most of his time in the House of Commons and Greenwood, who did likewise. On the left of the party, Cripps continued as the left's main spokesman in both the NEC and Parliament – hated by Dalton and Morrison. He had failed to move the rest in his espousal of a United Front; he was now to fail in his broader foreign policy ideas.

Cripps and his Socialist League had already decided on an extra-League policy of support for Russia.[25] It was only a short step from here to rejecting the League of Nations altogether. The exact moment at which this happened is difficult to isolate but it was certainly by the end of 1933. In November 1933 Noel-Baker could still pretend there was no schism and write to Pierre Joxe to say that the Labour Party's policy 'is not a policy of pacifism. It is a policy of full-blooded support of the League' and that 'Sir Stafford Cripps (now our leading parliamentarian) was defending Article XVI [of the League Covenant] which must be "supported by armed force if necessary"'.[26] However at Hastings in October 1933 the only policy really backed by the left was that of a general strike against war, a motion forwarded by Trevelyan for the Socialist League. Henderson (in the chair) let it pass in an attempt to forestall a breach, but the fact remained that the general strike was an unworkable policy and one moreover that was open to ridicule, as

Zilliacus pointed out to Gillies in October, Just after the Hastings debates.[27] Noel-Baker in private realised this himself, whatever he might tell Joxe, and wrote hopefully to Zilliacus that 'as a force against us I think the Left have practically disintegrated'.[28]

The NEC therefore embarked on a series of discussions to try and give some concrete policy content to the 'Victory for Socialism' campaign declared at Hastings. The principal aim of this campaign was to be in the domestic sphere, to attack the record of the National Government, but it had foreign policy clauses. On 27 February 1934 Henderson issued what was to prove virtually his last impassioned and reasoned defence of the League of Nations and the disarmament talks. This was a reiteration of his ideas as expressed in his 1933 'Labour's Foreign Policy' broadly accepted at Hastings.[29]

The document was vague and excited a lot of disagreement in the NEC. All that could be decided was to set up a joint sub-committee of the TUC, PLP and the Labour Party to draft a statement which would then be rediscussed by the NEC.[30] The left were not strong enough to block Henderson's reliance on the League of Nations but they certainly were determined to make life uncomfortable. In these circumstances the members of the Advisory Committee on International Questions (ACIQ) started to get quite worried. The ACIQ had no real hard members of the left, Gillies, Noel-Baker and Leonard Woolf being its most faithful attenders. Woolf and Noel-Baker were very worried about the damage being done by the left, who were indulging in 'fatuous' argument and 'folly' said Noel-Baker, but in the midst of a 'great crisis ... the downright wickedness of such a position leaves me speechless'. Posing as 'friends of peace' they were doing unaccountable harm to the Labour Party and the cause they said they espoused: 'Cannot something be done to shut these devils up?' Even Harold Laski, he bemoaned, 'who admits that the League [of Nations] is the only hope ... spends his time sneering at it, belittling its achievements, using his immense influence and prestige to throw doubt, and indeed despair, into the minds of those who should be furnishing that driving power of public opinion without which the League cannot triumph'.[31] 'Those' were, of course, the members of the Labour Party. Woolf agreed with Noel-Baker's worries – 'the disorientation in the forces of the Left with regard to the League is appalling' – but he saw the problems of the left. He was sure that 'some restatement of the party's League policy is required'.[32]

As if like manna from heaven, Noel-Baker received a letter the next day from Zilliacus. He was sorry to bother Baker but said: 'I want you to take up what I think is the most important of all international questions today, namely, Russia's entry into the League'.[33] The obstacles were those of the National Government, and other national objections, but Zilliacus believed that other international opinion was moving in favour of a Russian entry. Maisky had also made it known that Russia might reconsider her refusal to cooperate with the Advisory Committee of the League in the Far East and even entry into the League itself with 'some encouragement from the Great powers'. Zilliacus also suggested getting a member of the left to act as go-between with Maisky. Noel-Baker could himself go or send Attlee (at this time sympathetic to the left view on the League, however temporarily), or Cripps or Laski. The idea was interesting for it would force the left back into support for the League if the Russians were also in it.

Noel-Baker was initially not so sure that this would work – he doubted the Russian desire to enter the League, but he did write that he would go and ask Laski to arrange a lunch with Maisky.[34] He also wrote to Attlee, asking him to come. Noel-Baker so phrased it to look as though it was the Chinese Minister, Quo-Tai-Chi, who had suggested talking to Maisky, and indeed Zilliacus had told Noel-Baker about the interest of the Chinese in a Russian entry. Noel-Baker now saw the lunch as a meeting between the Chinese, Henderson, Attlee and Lord Cecil to start a campaign for Russian entry. To get the Russians into the League would be a 'tremendous coup',[35] he wrote to Attlee.

On 24 April the National Joint Council issued a statement urging the government to bring the USSR and the USA into the League.[36] The NJC motion was forwarded to the government on 14 May. Cecil had seen Maisky with Quo-Tai-Chi on 28 March and wrote to tell the Foreign Secretary about his conversation. Maisky told him that the USSR would willingly join the League given a bit of encouragement from either France or Britain. Cecil expressed sympathy with Simon's dislike of bolshevism, one that he shared, but pointed out that the USSR was now a fact of life, had been recognised 'and however dangerous it may be it would be no less inside the League than out'.[37] He also had hopes that Russian entry would make the Germans and Japanese think again about withdrawal. Cecil had remained very close to Noel-Baker and Henderson due to their mutual belief in the League. He wrote to Noel-Baker to say that Attlee, also present, had 'made a very good impression on me. He is the best of your leaders that I have met'. Cecil also included his views on the left of the Labour Party and of the need 'to restrain the follies of Marley, Ponsonby and Trevelyan'[38] (all prominent in the anti-League of Nations campaign within the Labour Party).

The entry of the USSR into the League was consequently seen by the centre-right leadership of the Labour Party as a way of both reinforcing its League of Nations-based foreign policy and a method of outflanking the left. The most eloquent evidence of this two-birds-with-one-stone policy lies in a letter from Henderson to Middleton, now secretary of the party, date 18 July 1934. In it he started by admitting the 'great feeling in the country and throughout the entire working-class movement' due to the existence of fascism. But he noted that this ran the risk, as in France, of severely dividing the forces of opposition to this fascism. However, '[i]f Russia joins the League the position will be changed as the Communists cannot then continue their old form of opposition in the international field'. Henderson was not hopeful that this was bound to succeed, but it would be a positive policy to brandish at the Socialist League. The dangers of doing nothing and resting on a repressive policy such as that implicit in 'Democracy versus Dictatorship' and Gillies' and Morrison's purges of the communist front organisations were obviously feared by Henderson. As he continued: 'We must not play into the hands of the extremists in our own ranks by being too negative'.[39]

The International Committee decided to propose Russian entry into the League at its July session. Gillies, Woolf and Noel-Baker were all present. They took the Russian proposal of non-aggression pacts with various East European states as a very positive sign of Russian good faith.[40] The NEC added its agreement by proposing a resolution in the same direction shortly afterwards. They also supported a resolution to the forthcoming Labour Party Conference at Southport.[41] By the time this conference took place the USSR had already been accepted into the League and it could only congratulate the USSR on its entry.[42]

The question remains of the extent to which it was direct Labour Party pressure which persuaded the National Government to accept this entry. It is probable that it was a combination of factors, which included Labour Party pressure. According to a discussion made public in the NEC's report to the Southport Conference, when the NJC delegation had presented their statement of 14 May, the Prime Minister (MacDonald) had said that 'the British Government had no information from any quarter that the Soviet Government desired to enter the League',[43] – in the light of Cecil's letter of 29 March somewhat misleading.

Another factor is certainly that the element that had up till then most annoyed the National Government, and the Conservatives since 1917 – propaganda – was now perceived as having been considerably reduced in scope. Simon's deputy in the House of Lords, Lord Stanhope, had said in March that 'we have had little cause during recent times to complain of propaganda from the Soviet Government, either here or in other parts of the Empire'. Samuel Hoare, who was to replace Simon as Foreign Secretary in 1935, took great exception to this, since as Secretary of State for India, he believed that propaganda was still rife in at least his domain. Stanhope replied that he stood by his words since he had not claimed that there was *no* propaganda, but that he 'had in mind the amount of propaganda with which the Soviets at one time inundated this country and the Empire ... [he had] intended to speak only in a comparative sense'.[44] This all showed at least a Foreign Secretary who believed in the lessening of propaganda, and this must have had an influence on government attitudes. (There were even hints of a non-aggression pact, culminating in Eden's visit to Moscow in 1935, which came to nothing because of residual mutual suspicion).[45]

Cecil must have had an influence. The fact that he could write a personal letter to Simon, and on 'vulgar paper but I can find no other of decent size'[46] to boot, shows that they were on the most intimate terms. Moreover, Donald Birn's book on the League of Nations Unions (LONU) has demonstrated the power of that body as a force in public opinion. At this point the LONU had over a million members, even if a reviewer noted that only 400,000 were fully paid up.[47] The East Fulham by-election of 1935 was certainly won by Labour with support from the LONU and its 'Peace Ballot' on the issue of peace and a series of Labour victories in late 1933 also seem to have been so-linked. This almost obliged the government to make a popular gesture for collective security.[48]

Finally it must be reiterated that by the end of 1933 it seems that Russia (or rather Stalin) had decided that it must join the League of Nations. It was only a question of waiting for a grudging invitation from one or more of the League powers. It cost Baldwin very little and may have helped his reputation as a peace-maker to make moves in the direction of such an invitation.

Notes

1 MOSLEY, Oswald, *The Greater Britain*, London, 1932. A brief and convenient description of this can be found in MOSLEY, Nicholas, *Rules of the Game: Sir Oswald and Lady Cynthia Mosley, 1896–1933*, London, Fontana/Collins, 1982, ch 22 and SKIDELSKY, *Oswald Mosley*.

2 In BRANSON, Noreen and HEINEMANN, Margot, *Britain in the 1930s*, London, Panther, 1973, p. 321.

3 cf. DALTON, *Diary*, entries for December 1932 and early 1933, vol. 15A.

4 DALTON, *Diary*, 26 January 1933.

5 Ibid., 21 June 1933 and 14–16 July 1933.
6 GILLIES, William, 'The International Scene', *Labour Woman*, April 1933.
7 Labour Party ACIQ, 'The Labour Party's Policy With Regard to the League and Sanctions', March 1933, 2 p. and Labour Party ACIQ, 'The Labour Party's Policy Regarding The League of Nations', April 1933, 8 pp., pp. 5 and 7.
8 DALTON, *Diary*, 4 May 1933. Dalton thought he talked 'awful nonsense', that 'he ha[d] no judgement at all', in fact that 'this man [was] really becoming a dangerous lunatic. It may become a duty to prevent him from holding any influential position in the Party'.
9 For details cf. PIMLOTT, *Labour and the Left*, chs 8 and 9.
10 National Executive Committee, Labour Party, 22 March 1933.
11 National Joint Council, *Democracy versus Dictatorship*, 24 March 1933, Labour Party Archives.
12 Pencilled copy of above sent to Gillies, ID/CI/7/22 and Memo by Gillies to Middleton, 24 March 1933, ID/CI/21, Labour Party Archives.
13 N. J. C. circular letter, 31 March 1933 and *Daily Herald* (same date).
14 *New Leader*, 24 March 1933. That is, they replied to the earlier letters the day that 'Democracy versus Dictatorship' was released.
15 *Daily Worker*, 13 and 29 April 1933.
16 Labour Party, 'Speakers' Notes', 24 March 1933, 3 pp. typed.
17 CITRINE, W. M., *Dictatorships and the Trade Union Movement*, 23 May 1933, 18 pp., p. 2.
18 Ibid., pp. 13–14.
19 Lansbury to Middleton, 3 August 1934, Labour Party Archives, Middleton Papers, JSM/CP/92.
20 Labour Party, *The Communist Solar System: The Communist International*, London, Labour Party, September 1933, 23 pp. cf. Labour Party Archives file on Communist International and Proscribed Organisations, especially ID/CI/8/45, Gillies to Shepherd (National Agent), 23 October 1933, and ID/CI/8/31, Morrison to Gillies, 12 June 1933. The National Joint Council request is dated June 1933.
21 Cf. John Price (LSI staff member) to Gillies, 16 July 1933, ID/CI/8/38(i).
22 Labour Party, *The Communist Solar System*, p. 23.
23 Labour Party Annual Conference Reports, Hastings, 1933, pp. 218 (Ellis) and 221 (Wilkinson).
24 Ibid., p. 143 and p. 232.
25 Socialist League, *First Annual Conference, Derby: 3–5 June 1933*, private collection, Reginald Groves and Noel-Baker papers, NBKR, 2/14. For more details on this policy ref. WILLIAMS, *The Attitude*, pp. 498–500.
26 Noel-Baker to Joxe, 30 November 1933, NBKR 2/18.
27 Zilliacus to Gillies, 13 October 1933, copy to Noel-Baker, NBKR 2/18.
28 Noel-Baker to Zilliacus, 27 October 1933, NBKR 2/18.
29 Labour Party NEC, *War and Peace*, confidential memo circulated to NEC, 27 February 1934, by Arthur Henderson. Eight typed pages, p. 6.
30 NEC Minutes, 27 February 1934.
31 Noel-Baker to Leonard Woolf (Secretary, ACIQ), 8 March 1934, NBKR 2/18.
32 Woolf to Noel-Baker, 11 March 1934, NBKR 2/18.
33 Zilliacus to Noel-Baker, 12 March 1934, NBKR 2/18
34 Noel-Baker to Zilliacus, 16 March 1934, NBKR 2/18
35 Noel-Baker to Attlee, 19 March 1934, NBKR 2/23.
36 Annex to NEC Minutes, 24 April 1934, Labour Party Archives.
37 Cecil to Simon, 29 March 1934, FO 800/289.
38 Cecil to Baker, 8 April 1934, Cecil Papers, Add. Mss 51108.
39 Henderson to Middleton, 18 July 1934, Labour Party Archives, Middleton Papers, JSM/CP/69.

40 Labour Party International Committee Minutes, 11 July 1934, LP/IAC/1/527.
41 Labour Party NEC, 28–9 September 1934.
42 Labour Party Conference Report. Southport, 1–5 October 1934, p. 129.
43 LPACR, Southport, 1934, p. 15.
44 Hoare to Simon, 17 March 1934 and Stanhope to Hoare, 20 March 1934, FO 800/289.
45 See one description of this in BROWN, Anthony Cave and MACDONALD, Charles B., *On a Field of Red: The Communist International and the Coming of the Second World War*, G. P. Putnam and Sons, New York, 1981, pp. 451–4. This book must, however, be read with great caution since it is in places totally incorrect. The Metro-Vickers trial seems to have taken place, according to this book, after 1935!
46 Cecil to Simon, 29 March 1934, FO 800/289.
47 BIRN, Donald, S., *The League of Nations Union, 1918–1945*, Oxford University Press, 1981, reviewed by Ieuan G. John in *History*, vol. 69, no. 225, February 1984.
48 For details see STANNAGE, Tom, *Baldwin Thwarts The Opposition: The British General Election of 1935*, London, Croom Helm, 1980, Annex 2, pp. 274–81.

Conclusion

The story related here was by no means finished in 1934, but there is a certain logic in stopping this part of it in mid-1934 with the entry of the USSR into the League of Nations. At the end of 1934, on 1 December, the Leningrad Party boss Kirov was assassinated probably on Stalin's secret orders, an event which unleashed the purges of the 1930s. The wider implications of this have naturally been often explored.[1] The effect on the Labour Party was to produce a mounting distaste at the results of the 'experiment' which has never really abated. The 'business' relations described by Morrison were maintained and even saw a warming up between June 1941 and 1945 in line with the needs of defeating Hitler. But the enthusiasm that had existed even in 1934 perceptibly waned as the 1930s wore on. Among the leadership this was more noticeable than among the rank and file. Transport House knew the details of Soviet treatment of its own citizens, likewise it had good information about Comintern activities in Spain, which, incidentally, killed a good few Labour Party members.[2] From 1934 on all its official complaints were treated to insults, or as Roden Buxton put it, they 'frankly lined us up with Trotskyites'.[3] The Labour Party none the less never expressed regret about the Soviet Union joining the League; they continued to support the USSR's position, as before Munich over the need to defend Czechoslovakia.[4] Only in 1939 with the Nazi–Soviet Pact and the invasion of Finland did their patience give out.[5] The general Labour public was also still prepared to give the USSR the benefit of the doubt in its foreign relations. For them Spain was the fight of good, supported by the USSR, against evil, supported by Hitler and Mussolini.

But in the supposed quality of life in the USSR there was less and less belief. Not only the purges sounded warning bells but also the writings of trade unionists such as Walter Citrine, whose *I Search for Truth in Soviet Russia* was unremittingly negative about the life of the average Soviet worker.[6] It might be argued that this was none the less the era of the Left Book Club, which published many favourable accounts of life under the Soviets, but this publishing venture did not notably deflate Labour's electoral support in favour of the CPGB. Neither must it be forgotten that for many British workers the late and even middle 1930s saw a rise in employment levels and living standards. Some areas of the country, such as the Midlands, had an unprecedented boom.

The long-term effects of Labour's interest in the USSR are more complex, and would require a book in themselves. Bill Jones has given us one version which does a very competent job for the whole post-war period, if not a perfect one.[7] Kenneth Morgan's probably definitive study of the 1945–51 government and Lord Bullock's last volume of the life of Ernie Bevin provide food for thought about how far the Soviet experiment influenced later Labour policies, but of course they do not consider only this impact.[8] Certain points do emerge from these volumes however. One is that the membership of the 1945 government had much of its significant experience in the period dealt with by this book. Another is that the measures pushed through in the post-war period seem to have had their initial inspiration in the early 1930s. In foreign policy the new Permanent Under-Secretary of State to Bevin was Sir William Strang. Together they were the architects of a 'businesslike' but not friendly relationship with the USSR which toned down some of the more extreme American versions of cold war rhetoric but nevertheless went along with 'containment'. It would be wrong to draw too many conclusions as to the continuing importance of the USSR in such an atmosphere of distrust but equally it would be wrong to dismiss a lingering inspiration. Neither should we infer a hatred of the USSR in the post-war Labour leadership. Bevin once half-jokingly remarked that Stalin was 'just a fellow trying to make his way in the world like the rest of us'.[9] 'Realism' finally fully triumphed in 1947 but the 'idealists' did not wither for all that. Until 1956 there were always those in the mainstream Labour Party who could excuse even the USSR's excesses.

A conclusion is the opportunity for some well-deserved speculation and polemic. However I have taken great pains so far to eschew over-indulgence in such qualities. Clearly many other writers have not felt so constrained as is inevitable given the tumultuous nature of the subject under discussion. Neither were the actors of the time reticent about saying and writing what they thought, even if the leaders of the Labour

Party often had to give a cool-headed lead in the interests of political pragmatism.

As has on occasion been said here, I feel that many of the writers who have condemned 'fellow travelling' have both rightly attacked the positivist amorality of those who examined the 'experiment' and also over-stated their case. The tone of self-righteous indignation that pervades most of this literature does little but to pour scorn on a group of commentators in the 1930s who were faced with an entirely new phenomenon in the midst of the most trying period of domestic and international upheaval of this century, what is now becoming termed the 'Second Thirty-Years War'. Some intellectuals were undoubtedly wrong in seeing the USSR as a great model for mankind. But for every one that kept to this illusion there were hundreds who rejected the option in the light of subsequent experience. To say that they were duped is to restate the basic observation that mistakes can be made. The problem is that the temporary flirtation of the mainstream Labour Party with the five-year plans has been used to daub an entire generation of thinkers with essentially meaningless epithets. Mankind has always looked for models and always will. Not to do so would be to sink into a far worse intellectual parochialism.

A point that has been touched upon quite often in the text also bears repetition. Much of the criticism directed by the left-wing critics of the 'fellow travellers' is tinged with a 1970s horror of upper-class elitism and generalised racism. These are indeed regrettable features of both present day and 1930s British – indeed world – society. But they were universal in the pre-war period, not confined to any one party. Fenner Brockway was one of the very few that had any real feelings of sympathy for 'backward' peoples. Eugenic theories went very deep in the psyche of the British ruling class. Esmond Ovey's strictures about kulaks, Muslims and other beings were commonplace. The recent controversy about whether T. S. Eliot was an anti-semite is all the more farcical because his views were common currency. To blame Ovey, or the many millions who held his views, for collectivisation, is as ridiculous as blaming Eliot for the Holocaust. We were and are *all* responsible for these things and their inevitable imitators. To single out one group for blame is a classic case of projection and self-exculpation. We might also reasonably ask if attitudes have really changed? There *has* been a certain extension of those whom are accorded 'civilised' status, such as Romanian peasants being persecuted by Ceaucescu, for much the same reasons as Stalin persecuted his peasants, to 'modernise' them. But little real sympathy is evoked by the suffering of other, third world, peasants struggling for life against their own state or environment. There is still widespread hand-wringing at the 'inevitable' lot of 'backward' peoples.

The Labour Party of the 1930s demonstrated an intellectual and organisational vigour that resulted in the most radical social and political upheaval of Britain's twentieth century. That some of its achievements have proved to be misguided attempts at social engineering is undeniable. Even the party, or most of it, seems to have come to the same conclusion with its 'new realism', again, as in the 1930s, being elaborated by the twinning of a radical centrist leadership and a revamped trade-union movement. It would be foolish to predict such a happy landing for these attempts, and indeed there can be no real parallels except that the efforts are similar in totally different contexts. One major difference is also that there is now no 'exemplar'. Another is that the ideas now under review are at least to some extent those of a clearly defined 'enemy', whereas those of the 1930s were at least partly designed by erstwhile colleagues of the Second (Socialist) International.

The efforts of the 1930s were made in the face of a hostile environment that makes Thatcherism seem positively benign. It was also made by men and women of what seems, perhaps at romantic distance, of quite exceptional intellectual and physical courage. Can we really find parallels for Bevin, Dalton, Henderson, or even MacDonald and Snowden? Neither must it be forgotten that the realities of Europe, Hitler, Mussolini et al. required a much stronger stomach than anything in Europe since 1953. To attack the Webbs (even!) gives the inevitable impression of cats biting lions' ankles.

The cats, of course, have recently taken over the running. Until it was realised that some of the shibboleths of state security might also come crashing down it quite suited the Conservative Government of the 1980s to see the intelligentsia of the 1930s – mostly conveniently homosexual intellectuals – paraded in chains. 'They' were all tarred with the same brush by a sequence of Conservative writers intent on a wholescale demolition of left-wing ideas of social engineering and economic progress. The embarrassment over the *Spycatcher* rulings in Australia and in the House of Lords has contributed to a realisation that a return to a total ban on revelations about left-wing 'treachery' is better.[10] A revised Official Secrets Act has resulted.

The right's agenda for dealing with the USSR and other like-minded states can be equally criticised. There has never been much justification for the view that military intervention against revolutionary regimes can have anything but a converse effect to that wished for. There is now an extensive literature in international relations in this area.[11] The subsequent Conservative policy of either isolating or insulting the USSR has not worked either. The mishandling of the renegotiation of the Temporary Commercial Agreement of 1930 by the National Government at Ottawa merits scorn for its political ineptitude.[12] It also merits sorrow, for who knows what might have been if the narrow door opened up by a welcoming of the USSR as a (nearly) normal state might have achieved in the long run. One does not have to agree with the mendacious explanations put forward by the Russians to explain the Nazi–Soviet Pact of 1939 to feel that a more honest and open dealing with the USSR might have led to better international relations in the 1930s. It might also have served to defeat those like Stalin who believed that 'socialism in one country' was the only option.

Viewed in this light the Labour Party's attitude of involving the USSR as much as possible in the international intercourse of trade and diplomacy was the only viable policy to have. There is no ineluctable reason why the USSR had to go the way it did and if its course had been different so would all of ours.

Notes

1 The books of Robert CONQUEST inevitably spring to mind here, especially *The Great Terror*, London, Pelican, 1971. NORTHEDGE and WELLS, op. cit. can be referred to for the wider impact on British sensibilities.

2 A good history of the Labour Party and the Spanish Civil War has still to be written, *pace* Naylor. Jill EDWARDS, *The British Government and the Spanish Civil War*, London, Macmillan, 1979 can serve as an introduction. The relevant Labour Party files on the period are in WG/RUS/168–70. The Noel-Baker papers also have a deal of interesting material. See WILLIAMS, *The Attitude*, op. cit., pp. 513–16.

3 Correspondence between Middleton and Roden-Buxton, March 1938, LP/RU/21/14–15.

4 Cf. ROBBINS, Keith, *Munich 1938*, London, Cassell, 1968.

5 National Council Of Labour, 7 December 1939.

6 Walter CITRINE, *I Search for Truth in Soviet Russia*, London, Routledge, 1936.

7 Bill JONES, *The Russia Complex, op. cit.*

8 Kenneth MORGAN, *Labour in Power, 1945–1951*, Oxford, Clarendon Press, 1984 and Alan BULLOCK, *The Life and Times of Ernest Bevin*, London, Heinemann, vol. 3, 1984.

9 Quoted in Frances WILLIAMS, *Ernest Bevin*, London, Hutchinson, 1952, p. 11.

10 Peter WRIGHT, *Spycatcher*, New York, Viking, 1987, and Andrew BOYLE, *The Climate of Treason*, London, Coronet, 1979.

11 One useful introduction is Hedley BULL, *Intervention in World Politics*, Oxford, Clarendon Press, 1984.

12 Cf. my (as yet) unpublished manuscript 'Canada and Anglo-Soviet Relations: The Question of Russian Trade at the 1932 Ottawa Conference'.

Bibliography

Unpublished Labour movement sources

Labour Party, London

National Executive Committee (NEC) Minutes 1924–35, LP/NEC/.

National Joint Council, Minutes, memos, etc., LP/JEC/. (After 1934, National Council of Labour).

International Committee, Minutes.

Advisory Committee on International Questions (TUC and Labour party Joint International Department), LP/IAC/.

William Gillies Papers, Overseas Correspondence, especially 'Russia', WG/RUS/, 'India', WG/IND/.

International Department, subject files, especially 'Russia', LP/RU/.

Private papers: Aurthur Henderson LP/Hen/; James Smith Middleton LP/JSM/.

Communist International: Proscribed Organisations, LP/ID/CI/.

Labour and Socialist International (LSI), Minutes and Circulars.

Trades Union Congress, London

Minutes: General Council, International Committee, Economic Committee; Finance General Purposes Committee, 1927–35.

Various supplementary unpublished material (especially Russian visits, Box DK 266).

Cooperative Union, Manchester

Minutes of Executive Committee, Joint Parliamentary Committee, Cooperative Party.

British Library of Political and Economic Science/London School of Economics

Independent Labour Party (ILP) Papers:

1 National Administrative Council (NAC), Minutes and related records.
2 ILP Manuscripts.

Political and Economic Planning (PEP), PEP/.

Socialist League 1933–7: Papers in the possession of Reginald Groves and some in Noel-Baker papers, Churchill College, Cambridge.

Unpublished Official Sources

Individuals and Government Departments (All Public Record Office)

Cabinet papers:

1 Cabinet Conclusions CAB 23/.
2 Cabinet Memos CAB 24/.
3 Cabinet Committees CAB 27/.

Foreign Office:

- General correspondence: Political, FO 371/.
- Private collections, Ministers and Officials, FO 800/218–219 (1924), 280–284 (1929–31).

Arthur Henderson, private papers while Foreign Secretary 1929–31, FO 800/280–284.
James Ramsay MacDonald (as Foreign Secretary, 1924), FO 800/219.
Prime Minister's Papers, correspondence and papers, PREM 1/.

Private papers

Individuals

Alexander, First Earl of Hillsborough (and First Lord of the Admiralty, 1929–31), Churchill College, Cambridge, AVAR/.
Ernest Bevin, Churchill College, Cambridge (BEVN/...) and University of Warwick.
Lord Robert Cecil, British Library, London.
George Douglas Howard Cole, Nuffield College, Oxford. Includes: Society for Socialist Inquiry and Propaganda (SSIP), miscellaneous papers; New Fabian Research Bureau, miscellaneous papers; Cole manuscripts.
Hugh Dalton, BLPES/LSE, especially *Diary*.
E. M. H. Lloyd, BLPES/LSE, (especially material on Andrew Cairns).
James Ramsey MacDonald, PRO (PRO 30/69), 1919–1935 (c. 50 file numbers), includes Rose Rosenberg Papers.
Philip Noel-Baker, private papers, Churchill College, Cambridge, NBKR/.
Lord William Strang, private papers, Churchill College, Cambridge, STRN/.
Trotsky Papers (ILP, Reginald Groves correspondence), Harvard University Library.
Beatrice and Sidney Webb, Passfield papers, BLPES/LSE, especially manuscript *Diary*.

Published official sources

Official government publications:
Hansard, Parliamentary Debates, 5th Series.
Draft of proposed general treaty between Great Britian and Northern Ireland and the Union of Soviet Socialist Republics; 1924 (Cmd 2215) xxvi. 779.
Text of the draft Treaty as it stood when negotiations were suspended on 5 August, 1924; 1924 (Cmd 2253) xxvi. 793.
Draft of proposed treaty of commerce and navigation between Great Britain and Northern Ireland and the Union of Soviet Socialist Republics; 1924 (Cmd 2216) xxvi. 821.
Correspondence between His Majesty's Government and the Soviet Government respecting the relations between the two governments; 1923 (Cmd 1869), HMSO, xxv. 497.

Reply of Soviet Government respecting the relations between the two Governments; (Cmd 1874), HMSO, xxv. 511.

Note from his Majesty's Government to the Government of the Union of Soviet Socialist Republics respecting the relations between the two Governments, and note in reply, 23–6 February, 1927; 1927 (Cmd 2822), HMSO, xxvi 301.

Correspondence regarding the resumption of relations with the Government of the Union of Soviet Socialist Republics; 1929-30 (Cmd 3418), HMSO xxxi 769.

Decree of the All-Russian Central Executive Committee and the Council of People's commissars respecting religous associations, 8 April 1929; 1929-30 (Cmd 3511), HMSO, xxxi 785.

Certain legislation respecting religion in force in the Union of Soviet Socialist Republics; 1929–30 (Cmd 3641), HMSO, xxi. 799.

A selection of documents relative to the labour legislation in force in the Union of Soviet Socialist Republics; 1930–31 (Cmd 3775), HMSO, xxxiv. 369.

Report on the organisation of the foreign trade of the Union of Soviet Socialist Republics; 1930–31 (Cmd 3904), HMSO, xvii. 343.

Metropolitan-Vickers Employees: correspondence relating to the arrest of employees of the Metropolitan Vickers Company at Moscow; 1932–33 (Cmd 4286), xxvii. 589.

Further correspondence: 1932–33 (Cmd 4290), xxvii. 613.

Russian Goods (Import Prohibition): Bill [passed, cap. 10] to authorise the prohibition of the importation of Russian goods; 1932–3 (85), iii. 433.

Published documents on British and Soviet foreign policy

Series IA 1925–9, vol. IV (1927–8), ed. W. N. Medlicott, D. Dakin and M. E. Landers, London, HMSO, 1971, (xiv) 668 pp.

Second series, vol. VII (1929–34 – Anglo-Russian Relations), ed. E. L. Woodward and Rohan Butler, London, HMSO, 1958, (lxxxvi), 808 pp.

DEGRAS, Jane, Soviet Documents on Foreign Policy, vol. III, 1933–41, London, Royal Institute of International Affairs, 1953, (xxii) 500 pp.

Printed documentary sources

Labour Party, Reports of the Annual conferences (LPACR)

Labour Party, *The Communist Solar System: The Communist International*, London, September 1933, 23 pp.

Labour Party, *For Socialism and Peace: the Labour Party' Programme of Action*, London, 1934, 32 pp.

Trades Union Congress, Conference Reports.

Trades Union Congress, *British Labour Delegation to Russia 1920 – Report*, London, TUC and Labour party, 1920, 150 pp.

Trades Union Congress, *The Spanish Problem*, Report of Speeches at Plymouth, London, 1936, 39 pp.

Independent Labour party, *Revolution by Reason*, London, ILP, 1925.

Labour and Socialist International/Committee for Political Prisoners in Russia, *Bolshevik Terror Against Socialists*, New York, 1925, 60 pp.

Liberal Party, *Britain's Industiral Future: The Liberal Industrial Inquiry*, London, Ernest Benn, 1928, (xxiv) 503 pp.

Newspapers and Periodicals

(All for period 1924–35 unless otherwise stated)

Daily newspapers

Daily Herald, Labour Party/Trades Union Congress.
Forward, Glasgow ILP.
Manchester Guardian, independent.
The Times, independent.

Weekly

Birmingham Town Crier, Birmingham Labour Party.
Cooperative News, Cooperative Union, Manchester.
New Clarion, Labour party.
New Leader, ILP.
New Statesman, independent.
The Economist, independent.
Reynold's, Cooperative Union/Labour Party.
Weekly Bulletin, Anglo-Russian Parliamentary Committee (W. P. and Z. Coates).

Monthly

British-Russian Gazette and Trade Outlook.
Cooperative Review, Cooperative Union, Manchester.
Highway, Workers Educational Association.
ICA Bulletin, International Cooperative Alliance (until 1928).
Labour Magazine, Labour Party/TUC.
Labour Woman, Labour Party/TUC.
Listener, British Broadcasting Corporation.
The London News, London Labour Party.
Review of International Cooperation, International Cooperative Alliance (after 1928).
Russia Today, Friends of the Soviet Union.
The Socialist Leaguer, Socialist League (June 1934–September 1935). Became *The Socialist* after September 1935.
Socialist Review, ILP (ceased publication in 1933).
Soviet Union Monthly, Friends of the Soviet Union.
SSIP News, Socialist Society for Inquiry and Propaganda (1931–2). Latter copies called *ZIP News*.
Wheatsheaf, Cooperative Union, Manchester.

Quarterly

Political Quarterly, independent, commenced publication 1930.

Unpublished theses

ARCHER, J., 'Trotskyism in Britain, 1931–77', PhD thesis, CNAA, 1980.
HASLAM, Jonathan D., 'Anglo-Soviet Relations, 1924–27', PhD thesis, Cambridge, 1978.
JACQUES, M., 'The Emergence of "responsible" trade unionism: a study of the "new direction" in TUC policy 1926–35', PhD. thesis, Cambridge, 1977.
JONES, D. I. L., 'The "United Front" in the Communist International. The Debate on the

Affiliation of the British Communist Party to the Labour party, 1920–25', MPhil thesis, Ulster, 1977.

UPHAM, Martin, 'The History of British Trotskyism to 1949', PhD thesis, Hull, 1981.

Bibliographical sources

BELLAMY, Joyce M. and SAVILLE, John, *Dictionary of Labour Biography*, London, Macmillan, 1972–82, 6 vols.

COOK, Chris, *Sources in British Political History*, London, Macmillan, 1978, 5 vols.

Dictionary of National Biography, London, Oxford University Press, various volumes.

DOSSICK, Jesse J., *Doctorial Research on Russia and the Soviet Union 1960–73*, New York and London, Garland Publishing Inc., 1976, 248 pp.

GILBERT, Victor F. (comp.), *Labour and Social History Theses, 1900–1978*, London, Mansell Publishing, 1982, 194 pp.

HAMMOND, Thomas T., *Soviet Foreign Relations and World Communism, A Selected Bibliography*, Princeton, New Jersey, Princeton University Press, 1965 (with subsequent reprints), (xxiv) 1240 pp.

HARRISON, WOOLVEN and DUNCAN, *The Warwick Guide to British Labour Periodicals*, Brighton, Harvester Pess, 1977, (xxiii) 685 pp.

PHELPS-FETHERSTON, Iain, *Soviet International Front Organisations. A Concise Handbook*, New York, Praeger, 1965, (iv) 178 pp.

Society for the Study of Labour History, *Bulletin 1960–*, Manchester.

Published works

Contemporary

ADLER, Friedrich, *The Anglo-Russian Report: a Criticism of the Report of the British Trade Union Delegation to Russia from the Point of View of International Socialism*, London, P. S. King and Sons Ltd, 1925, 52 pp.

ANGELL, Norman and WRIGHT, Harold, *Can Governments Cure Unemployment?*, London, J. M. Dent and Sons, 1931, (xii) 147 pp.

ANGELL, Norman, *Must Britain Travel the Moscow Road?*, London, Noel-Douglas, 1926, 190 pp.

Anglo-Soviet Parliamentary Committee, *The Ottawa Conference and Anglo-Soviet Trade*, Foreword by John Bromley and W. P. Coates, ARPC, 1932.

BRAILSFORD, Henry Noel (and others in the ILP), *The Living Wage*, London, ILP, 1926, 54 pp.

BRAILSFORD, H. N., *Olives of Endless Age: Being a View of this Distracted World and the Possibility of International Unity*, New York and London, Harpers and Brothers, 1928, 431 pp.

BRAILSFORD, H. M., *How the Soviets Work*, New York, Vanguard Press, 1927, 169 pp.

CHAMBERLIN, William Henry, *Russia's Iron Age*, Boston, Little Brown and Co., 1934, (ix) 400 pp.

CITRINE, Walter, *I Search for Truth in Soviet Russia*, London, George Routledge and Sons, 1936, (x) 368 pp.

CITRINE, Walter, *A Trade Unionist Looks at Russia*, published by the General Council of the TUC, September 1936.

COATES, W. P. and Zelda, *The Second Five-Year Plan of Development of the USSR*, London, Methuen and Co., 1934, 144 pp.

COLE, G. D. H., *Principles of Economic Planning*, London, Macmillan, 1935, (xxiii), 435 pp.

COLE, G. .D. H. and M. I., *The Intelligent Man's Review of Europe Today*, London, Victor Gollancz, 1933, 864 pp.

Cooperative Movement, *Report on Visits to Russia by Members of Two Groups of Cooperators, July-August 1930*, Manchester, Cooperative Union Ltd, 1931, 71 pp.

Cooperative Movement, *Soviet Russia 1932* (Report of Two Groups of Cooperators on a Visit to the USSR in the Summer of 1932), Manchester, Cooperative Union Ltd, 1933, 60 pp.

DALTON, Hugh, *Practical Socialism for Britain*, London, George Routledge and Sons, 1935, (ix) 405 pp.

DALTON, Hugh, *Towards the Peace of Nations – A study in International Politics*, London, George Routledge and Sons, 1928, (xi) 316 pp.

DAVIS, Kathryn Wasserman, *The Soviet Union and the League of Nations 1919–1933*, Geneva Research Centre, 1934, 23 pp.

HAMILTON, Mary Agnes, *Arthur Henderson, A Biography*, London Heinemann, 1938.

HAMILTON, Mary Agnes, *James Ramsay MacDonald*, London, Jonathan Cape, 1929, 305 pp.

HENDERSON, Arthur, *Labour's Foreign Policy*, London, Labour Party, 1933, 34 pp.

HENDERSON, Arthur, *Labour's Way to Peace*, London, Methuen, 1935, 120 pp.

Meerut Prisoners' Committee, *The Meerut Trial: The Facts of the Case*, London, Meerut Prisoners, Committee, 1929, 16 pp.

MONKHOUSE, Alan, *Moscow 1911–1933*, London, Victor Gollancz, 1933.

MURRY, John Middleton, *The Necessity of Communism*, London, Jonathan Cape, 1932, 136 pp.

New Fabian Research Bureau, *Labour's Foreign Policy*, London, Victor Gollancz and NFRB, 1934, 27 pp.

New Fabian Research Bureau, *The Road to War*, London, Victory Gollancz, 1937, 207 pp.

New Fabian Research Bureau, *Twelve Studies in Soviet Russia*, London, Victor Gollancz, 1933.

New Fabrian Research Bureau, *Why the USSR Joined the League*, London, Victor Gollancz and NFRB, 1935, 36 pp.

NOEL-BAKER, Philip, *Disarmament*, London, Hogarth Press, second edition, 1927.

PONSONBY, Arthur, *The Anglo-Soviet Treaties*, London, Labour Party, 1924, 10 pp.

PURCELL, A. A., *Days in Leningrad*, Manchester, Manchester and Salford Trades Council, 1933, 4 pp.

SHAW, George Bernard, *The Intelligent Woman's Guide to Socialism and Capitalism*, London, Constable and Co., 1928, (xxxvi) 495 pp.

SHAW, G. B. (ed.), *Platform and Pulpit*, London, Hart Davies, 1962, (xvii) 302 pp.

SIEGFRIED, Andre, *England's Crisis*, London, Jonathan Cape, 1931, 256 pp.

SLOAN, Pat, *Soviet Democracy*, London, Victor Gollancz, 1937, 288 pp.

SODDY, Frederick, *The Impact of Science Upon an Old Civilisation*, London, ILP, 1928.

SPENDER, Stephen, *Forward From Liberalism*, London, Victor Gollancz, 1937, 295 pp.

STALIN, Josef, *Leninism*, London, George Allen and Unwin, 1928, 472 pp.

STRACHEY, John, *The Coming Struggle for Power*, London, Victor Gollancz, 1933, 399 pp.

STRACHEY, John, *The Nature of the Capitalist Crisis*, London, Victor Gollancz, 1935, (x) 384 pp.

TILLETT, BEN, *Some Russian Impressions*, London, Trades Union Congress, 1925.

Tilmanstone Miners' Report on Russia, Dover, St George's Press, 1929, 32 pp.

TOYNBEE, Arnold, *Survey of International Affairs*, London, Royal Institute of International Affairs, several volumes, 1925–36.

TROTSKY, Leon, *Leon Trotsky on Britain*, New York, Monad Press, 1973, 334 pp.

VIGILANTES (Konni Zilliacus), *The Dying Peace*, London, New Statesman and Nation, 1933, 55 pp.

VIGILANTES (Konni Zilliacus), *Inquest on Peace: An Analysis of the National Government's Foreign Policy*, London, Victor Gollancz, 1935, (vii) 360 pp.

WEBB, Beatrice, *Diaries 1924–32*, edited by Margaret Cole, London, Longmans, 1956.

WEBB, Sidney and Beatrice, *A Constitution for the Socialist Commonwealth of Great Britain*, London, Longmans, 1920, (xviii) 364 pp.

WEBB, Sidney and Beatrice, *The Decay of Capitalist Civilisation*, London, George Allen and Unwin, third edition, 1923, (vii) 182 pp.

WEBB, Sidney and Beatrice, *Industrial Democracy*, London, Longmans, ninth edition, 1926, (xxxix) 899 pp.

WEBB, Sidney and Beatrice, *Soviet Communism: A New Civilisation?*, London, Longmans, 2 vols, 1935, 1174 pp.

WELLS, H. G., *The Open Conspiracy*, London, Hogarth Press, 1928.

WELLS, H. G., *Stalin–Wells Talk*, London, New Statesman and Nation, 1934, 47 pp.

WERTHEIMER, Egon, *Portrait of the Labour Party*, London, G. P. Putnams and Sons, 1929, (1930 edition), (xxiix) 215 pp.

WICKSTEED, Alexander, *Life Under the Soviets*, London, John Lane, the Bodley Head, 1928, (xvii) 195 pp.

WISE, E. F., *Consumers Cooperation in Soviet Russia*, Manchester, Cooperative Union, 1929, 12 pp.

Other

ANGELL, Norman, *After All*, London, Hamish Hamilton, 1951, (xii) 370 pp.

ATTLEE, Clement, *As It Happened*, London, Heinemann, 1954, 227 pp.

BACKSTROM, Philip, *Christian Socialism and Co-operation in Victorian England*, London, Croom Helm, 1974, (vii) 238 pp.

BAILEY, Jack, *The British Cooperative Movement*, London, Hutchinson, 1955.

BALL, F. C., *One of the Damned: The Life and Times of Robert Tressell*, London, Lawrence and Wishart, 1973, (xiii) 266 pp.

BASSETT, R., *Nineteen Thirty-One, Political Crisis*, London, Macmillan, 1958.

BEALEY, Frank, (ed.), *The Social and Political Thought of the British Labour Party*, London, Weidenfeld and Nicolson, 1970, (xvi) 233 pp.

BEER, Max, *Fifty Years of International Socialism*, London, 1935, 239 pp.

BENTLEY, Michael, *The Liberal Mind, 1914–1929*, Cambridge University Press, 1977, (viii) 279 pp.

BERMAN, Marshall, *All That Is Solid Melts Into Air: The Experience of Modernity*, London, Verso Editions, 1982, 383 pp.

BIRN, Donald S., *The League of Nations Union, 1918–1945*, Oxford University Press, 1981, (vi) 269 pp.

BOYLE, Andrew, *The Climate of Treason*, London, Hutchinson, 1979, 574 pp.

BRANSON, Noreen and HEINEMANN, Margot, *Britain in the 1930s*, London, Panther, 1973, 384 pp.

BRAUNTHAL, Julius, *History of the International*, London, Nelson, 2 vols, 1967.

BRIGGS, Asa, 'The World Economy: Interdependence and Planning', *New Cambridge Modern History*, (ed. C. L. Mowat), vol. XII, 'The Shifting Balance of World Forces, 1898–1945', Cambridge University Press, 1968, (xxviii) 845 pp.

BRIGGS, Asa and SAVILLE, John (eds), *Essays in Labour History, 1866–1923*, London, Macmillan, 1971, 360 pp.

BRITTAIN, Vera, *Pethick-Lawrence*, London, George Allen and Unwin, 1963.

BROCKWAY, Fenner, *Socialism Over Sixty Years*, London, George Allen and Unwin, 1946, 415 pp.

BROCKWAY, Fenner, *Inside the Left*, London, New Leader Ltd., 1942, 360 pp.
BULLOCK, Alan, *The Life and Times of Ernest Bevin*, London, Heinemann, 3 vols, 1960–84.
CALHOUN, Daniel, *The United Front: The TUC and the Russians, 1923–1928*, Cambridge University Press, 1976, (xi) 450 pp.
CAMPBELL, John, *F. E. Smith, First Earl of Birkenhead*, London, Jonathan Cape, 1983, (xvi) 918 pp.
CARLTON, David, *Anthony Eden: A Biography*, London, Allen Lane, 1981, 528 pp.
CARLTON, David, *MacDonald Versus Henderson: The Foreign Policy of the Second Labour Government*, London, Macmillan, 1970, 239 pp.
CARR, E. H., *The Soviet Impact on the Western World*, London, Macmillan, 1946, (ix) 116 pp.
CAUTE, David, *The Fellow Travellers. A Postscript to the Enlightenment*, London, Weidenfeld and Nicholson, 1973, (vi) 433 pp.
CAVE BROWN, Anthony and MACDONALD, Charles B., *On a Field of Red; The Communist International and the Coming of the Second World War*, New York, G. P. Putnam and Sons, 1981, 718 pp.
CECIL, Viscount E. A. R., *A Great Experiment: An Autobiography*, London, Jonathan Cape, 1941, 390 pp.
CITRINE, Walter, *Two Careers*, London, Hutchinson, 1967, 384 pp.
CLARKE, Peter, *Liberals and Social Democrats*, Cambridge University Press, 1978, 344 pp.
CLINE, Catherine A., *E. D. Morel, 1873–1924. The Strategies of Protest*, Belfast, Blackstaff Press, 1980, 180 pp.
CLINE, Catherine A., *Recruits to Labour – The British Labour Party 1914–1931*, New York, Syracuse University Press, 1963, 198 pp.
CLYNES, J. R., *Memoirs*, vol. II, 1924–37, London, Hutchinson, 1937, 299 pp.
COATES, W. P. and Zelda, *A History of Anglo-Soviet Relations, Vol. I 1917–1942, Vol. II 1942–50*, London, Lawrence and Wishart, 1944, vol. I 816 pp. and vol. II 463 pp.
COLE, G. D. H., *A Century of Cooperation*, Manchester, Cooperative Union Ltd., 1944, (iv) 427 pp.
COLE, G. D. H., *The History of the Labour Party From 1914*, London, Routledge and Kegan Paul, 1948, (x) 516 pp.
COLE, Margaret, *The Life of G. D. H. Cole*, London, Macmillan, 1971, 304 pp.
COLE, Margaret, *The Story of Fabian Socialism*, London, Heinemann, 1961, (xv) 1366 pp.
COLE, Margaret (ed.), *The Webbs and Their Work*, London, Frederick Muller, 1949, (xvi) 304 pp.
COLVIN, Ian, *The Chamberlain Cabinet*, London, Victor Gollancz, 1971, 286 pp.
COLVIN, Ian, *Vansittart in Office*, London, Victor Gollancz, 1965, 360 pp.
CONQUEST, Robert, *The Great Terror*, London, Pelican, 1971, 830 pp.
COOK, Chris, *A Short History of the Liberal Party, 1900–1976*, London, Macmillan, second edition, 1984 (viii) 188 pp.
COOKE, C. A., *The Life of Richard Stafford Cripps*, London, Hodder and Stoughton, 1957, 414 pp.
COOPER, Duff, *Old Men Forget*, London, Rupert Hart-Davies, 1953, 399 pp.
COWLING, Maurice, *The Impact of Labour*, Great Britain 1920–24, Cambridge University Press, 1971.
COWLING, Maurice, *The Impact of Hitler*, British Politics and British Policy 1933–1940, Cambridge University Press, 1975 and Chicago University Press, 1977, (x) 445 pp.
CRICK, Bernard, *George Orwell: A Life*, London, Secker and Warburg, 1980, 473 pp.
DALLIN, David and NICOLAEVSKY, Boris, *Forced Labour in Soviet Russia*, New Haven, Yale University Press, 1947, (xvi) 331 pp.
DALTON, Hugh, *Call Back Yesterday. Memoirs 1887–1931*, London, Frederick Muller, 1953, (xii) 330 pp.

DALTON, Hugh, *Fateful Years: Memoirs 1931–1945*, London, Frederick Muller, 1957, (xvi) 493 pp.

DEANE, Herbert Andrew, *The Political Ideas of Harold J. Laski*, New York, Columbia University Press, 1955, (xii) 370 pp.

DEWAR, Hugo, *Communist Politics in Britain: The Communist Party of Great Britain From Its Origin to the Second World War*, London, Pluto Press, 1976, 159 pp.

DILKS, David, (ed.), *Retreat From Power: Studies in Britain's Foreign Policy of the Twentieth Century, vol. I 1906–1939*, London, Macmillan, 1981, 213 pp.

DISTON, Marshall, and FORGAN, Robert, *The New Party and the ILP*, London, New Party Broadcasts Pub., 1930.

DOWSE, Robert E., *Left in the Centre: The Independent Labour Party 1893–1940*, London, Longmans, 1966, (xi) 231 pp.

EDWARDS, Jill, *The British Government and the Spanish Civil War*, London, Macmillan, 1979, (xiii) 280 pp.

EGERTON, George W., *Great Britain and the League of Nations: Collective Security as Myth and History*, paper presented at Geneva, September 1980, 38 pp. not published.

ESTORICK, Eric, *Stafford Cripps: A Biography*, London, Heinemann, 1949, (viii) 378 pp.

FILENE, Peter G., *Americans and the Soviet Experiment, 1917–1933*, Cambridge, Harvard University Press, 1967, 398 pp.

FISCHER, Louis, *The Soviets in World Affairs*, London, Jonathan Cape, 2 vols, 1930.

FOOT, Michael, *Aneurin Bevan, Vol. I 1897–1945*, New York, Athenaeum, 1962, 536 pp.

GALBRAITH, J. K., *The Great Crash, 1929*, London, Hamish Hamilton, 1955, 186 pp.

GILBERT, Martin and GOTT, Richard, *The Appeasers*, London, Weidenfeld and Nicolson, 1963, 380 pp.

GORDON, Michael Robert, *Conflict and Consensus in Labour's Foreign Policy, 1914–1965*, Stanford, California University Press, 1969, (xiii) 333 pp.

GORODETSKY, Gabriel, *Cripps' Mission to Moscow*, Cambridge University Press, 1984.

GORODETSKY, Gabriel, *The Precarious Truce: Anglo-Soviet Relations, 1924–27*, Cambridge University Press, 1977, (xiii) 289 pp.

GRAUBARD, S. R., *British Labour and the Russian Revolution 1917–24*, Cambridge, Harvard University Press, 1956, 307 pp.

GRIFFITHS, Richard, *Fellow Travellers of the Right: British Enthusiasts for Nazi Germany, 1933–39*, Oxford University Press, 1983, 406 pp.

GUPTA, Partha S., *Imperialism and the British Labour Movement 1914–64*, London, Macmillan, Cambridge Commonwealth Series, 1975, (xviii) 454 pp.

HAGGIE, Paul, *Britannia at Bay: The Defence of the British Empire Against Japan, 1931–1941*, Oxford, Clarendon Press, 1981 (xii) 264 pp.

HARROD, Roy, *The Life of John Maynard Keynes*, London, Macmillan, 1951, (xvi) 674 pp.

HOARE, Samuel, *Nine Troubled Years*, London, Collins, 1954, 448 pp.

HOBSBAWM, Eric, *Labouring Men*, London, Weidenfeld and Nicolson, 1964.

HOLMES-LASKI Letters 1916–1935, Vol. II, 1926–1935, Cambridge, Harvard University Press, 1953, 1650 pp.

HOLTON, Bob, *British Syndicalism 1900–1914*, London, Pluto Press, 1976, 232 pp.

HOWSON, Susan and WINCH, David, *The Economic Advisory Council 1930–1939: A Study in Economic Advice During Depression and Recovery*, Cambridge University Press, 1977, (vii) 424 pp.

HYNES, Samuel, *The Auden Generation: Literature and Politics in England in the 1930s*, London, Faber and Faber, 1976, 428 pp.

JONES, William, *The Russia Complex. The British Labour Party and the Soviet Union*, Manchester University Press, 1971, 223 pp.

JUPP, James, *The Radical Left in Britain, 1931–41*, London, Frank Cass, 1982, 261 pp.

KENNAN, George, *Russia and the West Under Lenin and Stalin*, Boston, Mentor, 1960, (viii) 384 pp.
KENWORTHY, J. M., *Peace or War?*, New York, Boni and Liveright Inc., 1927, (xvi) 320 pp.
KENWORTHY, J. M. and YOUNG, George, *The Freedom of the Seas*, London, Hutchinson, 1928, 283 pp.
KEYNES, John Maynard, *The Economic Consequences of Mr Churchill*, London, L. and V. Woolf, 1925, 32 pp.
KEYNES, John Maynard, *The Economic Consequences of the Peace*, London, Macmillan, 1920, 1923, 298 pp.
KEYNES, John Maynard, *Essays in Biography*, London, Macmillian, 1933, (x) 318 pp.
KEYNES, John Maynard, *Social, Political and Literary Writing*, Vol.XXVIII of *Collected Writings*, London, Macmillan and Cambridge University Press, 1982, (xiii) 470 pp.
KUPFERMAN, *Le voyage francais en URSS*, Paris, Gallimard (Coll. Archives), 1979, 188 pp.
LEE, Ivy, *Present Day Russia*, New York, Macmillan, 1928, (viii) 206 pp.
LEE, Jenny, *My Life With Nye*, London, Penguin, 1981, 326 pp.
LEWIS, John, *The Left Book Club*, An Historical Record, London, Victor Gollancz, 1970, 163 pp.
LORWIN, Lewis, *Labor and Internationalism*, New York, Macmillan, 1929, (xviii), 682 pp.
MACFARLANE, L. J., *The British Communist Party to 1929*, London, Macgibbon and Kee, 1966, 338 pp.
MACINTYRE, Stuart, *Little Moscows: Communism and Working-Class Militancy in Inter-War Britain*, London, Croom Helm, 1980, 213 pp.
MACKENZIE, Norman and Jeanne, *The First Fabians*, London, Quartet, 1979, 446 pp.
MACKENZIE, Norman and Jeanne, *The Letters of Sidney and Beatrice Webb 1912–1947*, London, Cambridge University Press, 1978, 482 pp.
MARGULIES, Sylvia R., *The Pilgrimage to Russia: The Soviet Union and the Treatment of Foreigners, 1924–37*, Madison, University of Wisconsin Press, 1968, (ix) 290 pp.
MARKS, Sally, *The Illusion of Peace: International Relations in Europe, 1910–1933*, New York, St Martin's Press, 1976, 184 pp.
MARTIN, Kingsley, (ed.), *A Second Volume of Autobiography 1931–45*, London, Hutchinson, 1968.
MARTIN, Kingsley, *Tom Paine*, Fabian Biographical Tract, no. 10, printed in KATANKA, Michael (ed.), *Radicals, Reformers and Socialists*, London, Charles Knight and Co. Ltd, 1973, 24 pp.
MARTIN, R., *Communism and the British Trade Unions 1924–33*, Oxford, Clarendon Press, 1969, (xii) 209 pp.
MARQUAND, David, *Ramsay MacDonald*, London, Jonathan Cape, 1977, (xii) 903 pp.
McBRIAR, A. M., *Fabian Socialism and English Politics, 1884–1918*, Cambridge University Press, 1962.
McKIBBIN, Ross, *The Evolution of the Labour Party 1910–1924*, (Oxford Historical Monographs), Oxford, Clarendon Press, 1974, (xviii) 261 pp.
MIDDLEMAS, Keith and BARNES, John, *Baldwin: A Biography*, London, Weidenfeld and Nicolson, 1969, (xviii), 1149 pp.
MILIBAND, Ralph, *Parliamentary Socialism*, London, Merlin, 1973.
MINKIN, Lewis and SEYD, Patrick, 'The British Labour Party', in PATERSON, William E. and THOMAS, Alistair H., *Social Democratic Parties in Western Europe*, London, Croom Helm, 1977, 444 pp.
MORGAN, Kenneth O., *Labour in Power, 1945–1951*, Oxford, Clarendon Press, 1984, (xviii) 546 pp.
MORRIS, A. J. A., *C. P. Trevelyan 1870–1958, Portrait of a Radical*, Belfast, Blackstaff Press, 1977, (vii) 193 pp.

MORRISON, Herbert Stanley, *An Autobiography of Lord Morrison of Lambeth*, London, Odhams Press, 1960, 336 pp.

MOSLEY, Nicholas, *Rules of the Game: Sir Oswald and Lady Cynthia Mosley, 1896–1933*, London, Fontana/Collins, 1982, 274 pp.

MOWAT, C. L., *Britain Between the Wars*, London, Methuen, 1955, (ix) 694 pp.

MUGGERIDGE, Malcolm, *Tread Softly for You Tread on My Jokes*, London, Collins, 1967, 220 pp.

NAYLOR, John F., *Labour's International Policy. The Labour Party in the 1930s*, London, Weidenfeld and Nicolson, 1969, (viii) 380 pp.

NICOLSON, Harold, *Diaries and Letters 1930–1964*, London, Penguin, 1984, 436 pp.

NICOLSON, Harold, *King George V; His Life and Reign*, London, Constable, 1952, (xxiii) 570 pp.

NIEDHART, Gottfried, *Grossbritannien und die Sowjetunion, 1934–1939*, Studien zur britischen Politik der Friedensicherung swischen den beiden Weltkriegen, Munchen, Wilhelm Fink Verlag, 1972, 497 pp.

NORTHEDGE, F. S., *The Troubled Giant: Britain Among the Great Powers, 1916–1939*, London, G. Bell, 1966, (xii) 657 pp.

NORTHEDGE, F. S. and WELLS, Audrey, *Britain and Soviet Communism: The Impact of a Revolution*, London, Macmillan, 1982, (viii) 280 pp.

PELLING, Henry, *Origins of the Labour Party: 1880–1900*, Oxford University Press, second edition, 1965, (ix) 255 pp.

PELLING, Henry, *A Short History of the Labour Party*, London, Macmillan, fifth edition, 1976, (vii) 180 pp.

PERIGORD, Paul, *The International Labour Organization*, London, New York, D. Appleton and Co., 1926, 339 pp.

PETHYBRIDGE, Roger, *The Social Prelude to Stalinism*, London, Macmillan, 1974, 343 pp.

PIERSON, Stanley, *British Socialists: The Journey from Fantasy to Politics*, Cambridge, Harvard University Press, 1979, 403 pp.

PETHICK-LAWRENCE, F. W., *Fate Has Been Kind*, London, Hutchinson, 1943.

PIMLOTT, Ben, *Labour and the Left in the 1930s*, Cambridge University Press, 1977, (xi) 259 pp.

PIMLOTT, Ben, *Hugh Dalton*, Jonathan Cape, 1985, 752 pp.

PINCHER, Chapman, *Their Trade is Treachery*, London, Sidgewick, 1981.

POLLARD, Sidney, *The Development of the British Economy, 1914–1980*, London, Edward Arnold, third edition, 1983, (vii) 440 pp.

POPOV, Victor Ivanovitch, *Diplomaticheski Otnosheniia Mezdhu SSSR; Angliei* (1929–39gg), Moskva, Izd.-vo, Mezhduradnoye Otnosheniia, 1965, 515 pp.

POSTGATE, Raymond, *The Life of George Lansbury*, London, Longmans, Green and Co., 1951, (xiii) 331 pp.

ROBBINS, Keith, *Munich 1938*, London, Cassell, 1968, 398 pp.

ROSS, Graham (ed.), *The Foreign Office and the Kremlin: British Documents on Anglo-Soviet Relations, 1941–45*, Cambridge University Press, 1984, (xi) 303 pp.

SARTRE, J. P., *War Diaries: Notebooks From a Phoney War 1939–40*, London, Verso, 1984, (xix) 366 pp.

SETON-WATSON, Robert W., *Britain and the Dictators. A Survey of Post-War British Policy*, Cambridge University Press, 1938, (xviii) 640 pp.

SIMON, Viscount John, *Retrospect*, London, Hutchinson, 1952, 327 pp.

SKIDELSKY, Robert, *Politicians and the Slump: The Labour Government of 1929–31*, London, Macmillan, 1967, (xiv) 431 pp.

SKIDELSKY, Robert, *Oswald Mosley*, London, Macmillian, 1975, 577 pp.

SKIDELSKY, Robert, (ed.), *The End of the Keynesian Era*, London, Macmillan, 1977, (xiv) 114 pp.

SNOWDEN, Philip, *An Autobiography. Volume II: 1919–1934*, London, Ivor Nicholson and Watson, 1934, pp. 525–1094.

SPENDER, Stephen, *The Thirties and After: Poetry, Politics, People 1933–75*, London, Macmillan, 1978, 286 pp.

STANNAGE, Tom, *Baldwin Thwarts the Opposition: The British General Election of 1935*, London, Croom Helm, 1980, 320 pp.

STEVENSON, John and COOK, Christopher, *The Slump: Politics and Society During the Depression*, London, Jonathan Cape, 1977.

STEWART, Michael, *Keynes and After*, London, Penguin, 1967, 271, pp.

STRANG, Lord W., *Home and Abroad*, London, Andre Deutsch, 1956, 320 pp.

SWARTZ, Martin, *The Union of Democratic Control in British Politics During the First World War*, Oxford University Press, 1971, (xiv) 267 pp.

SYMONS, Julian, *The Thirties: A Dream Revolved*, London, Faber and Faber, 1975 (revised edition), 160 pp.

TAWNEY, R. H., *Equality*, London, George Allen and Unwin, 1964 (first published 1931), 303 pp.

TAYLOR, A. J. P., *English History 1914–1945*, Oxford, Clarendon Press, (xxvii) 709 pp.

TAYLOR, A. J. P., *The Origins of the Second War*, London, Penguin, 1965, 357 pp.

TAYLOR, A. J. P., *A Personal History*, London, Hamish Hamilton, 1983, (x) 357 pp.

THOMPSON, E. P., *William Morris: Romantic to Revolutionary*, London, Merlin, second edition, 1977, (xiii) 825 pp.

THORNE, Christopher, *The Limits of Foreign Policy: The West, the League and the Far Eastern Crisis of 1931–1933*, London, Macmillan, 1973, (xx) 442 pp.

TUCKER, Robert Charles, *Stalinism, Essays in Historical Interpretation*, New York, W. W. Norton, 1977, (xx) 332 pp.

ULDRICKS, Teddy J., *Diplomacy and Ideology, The Origins of Soviet Foreign Relations, 1917–1930*, London and Beverley Hills, Sage Publications, 1979, 239 pp.

ULLMAN, Richard Henry, *Anglo-Soviet Relations, 1917–21*, Princeton, New Jersey, Princeton University Press, 3 vols, 1961–72.

VOLKOV, Feder Dimitrievich, *Anglo-Sovietskie Otnosheniia, 1924–1929 gg*, Moskva, Gos.idz-iv polit. lit-org., 1958, 463 pp.

WALTERS, F. P., *A History of the League of Nations*, London, Oxford University Press, 2 vols, 1952, 833 pp.

WATT, D. C., *Personalities and Politics, Studies in the Formulation of British Foreign Policy in the Twentieth Century*, London, Longmans, 1965, (xii) 276 pp.

WEBB, Beatrice (ed.), *Our Partnership*, Cambridge, George Feaver, 1975.

WEINER, Martin, *English Culture and the Decline of the Industrial Spirit*, Cambridge University Press, 1981, 217 pp.

WHITE, Stephen, *Britain and the Bolshevik Revolution*, London, Macmillan, 1979, (xii) 317 pp.

WILLIAMS, Francis, *Ernest Bevin*, London, Hutchinson, 1952, (ii) 288 pp.

WILLIAMS, Francis, *Fifty Years March: The Rise of the Labour Party*, London, Odhams Press, 1949, 383 pp.

WINDRICH, Elaine, *British Labour's Foreign Policy*, Stanford, Stanford University Press, 1952, (ix) 268 pp.

WINTER, J. M., *Socialism and the Challenge of War. Ideas and Politics in Britain 1912–1918*, London, Routledge & Kegan Paul, 1974, (ix) 310 pp.

WRIGLEY, C. J., *David Lloyd George and the British Labour Movement*, Brighton, Harvester Press, 1976, 290 pp.

Articles

ANTCLIFFE, John, 'Politics of the Airwaves: Party Political Broadcasts in the 1920s and 1930s', *History Today*, vol. 34, March 1984, pp. 4–10.

CROWE, S., 'The Zinoviev Letter: a Reappraisal', *Journal of Contemporary History*, vol. 10, 1975, pp. 407–32.

GORODETSKY, Gabriel, 'The Soviet Union and Britain's General Strike of 1926', *Cahiers du monde russe et sovietique*, XVII, no. 2–3, 1976, pp. 287–310.

HOWKINS, Alan and SAVILLE, John, 'The 1930s: A Revisionist History', *The Socialist Register*, London, Merlin Press, 1979, 335 pp., pp. 89–100.

LAMMERS, Donald, 'Fascism, Communism and the Foreign Office 1932–39', *Journal of Contemporary History*, vol. 6, no. 3, 1971, pp. 66–86.

LAMMERS, Donald, 'The Second Labour Government and the Restoration of Relations with Soviet Russia (1929)', *Bulletin of the Institute of Historical Research*, vol. XXXVII, 1964, pp. 60–72.

LAQUEUR, Walter, 'Russia Through Western Eyes', *Survey*, no. 41, April 1962.

LIEBMAN, Marcel, 'Fabianisme et communisme: les Webb et l'Union sovietique', *International Review of Social History*, vol. V, 1960, pp. 400–423 and vol. VI, 1961, pp. 49–73.

LIEBMAN, Marcel, 'The Webbs and the New Civilisation', *Survey*, no. 41, April 1962, pp. 58–74.

MAEHL, William H. Jr, 'Jersualem Deferred. Recent Writings in the History of the British Labour Movement', *Journal of Modern History*, vol. 41, no. 3, September 1969, pp. 335–67.

OLDFIELD, Adrian, 'The Independent Labour party and Planning 1920–26', *International Review of Social History*, vol. 21, 1976, pp. 1–29.

PIMLOTT, Ben, 'The Socialist League – Intellectuals and the Labour Left in the 1930s', *Journal of Contemporary History*, vol. 6, no. 3, 1971, pp. 12–39.

SAMUELS, S., 'The Left Book Club', *Journal of Contemporary History*, vol. 1, no. 22, 1966, pp. 65–86.

SHERMAN, Alfred, 'The Days of the Left Book Club', *Survey*, no. 41, April 1962, pp. 75–85.

WILLIAMS, Andrew, 'Skin the Russian and Discover the Tartar: The Labour Party Looks at the Soviet Union, 1917–1939. Some Research Notes', *Cahiers d'histoire et relations internationales*, Geneva, no. 3, autumn 1984, pp. 98–121.

WILLIAMS, Andrew, 'La genese d'un texte: les Webb et la redaction de Communisme Sovietique: Une nouvelle civilisation?', *Relations Internationales*, 24, hiver 1980, pp. 443–63.

WILLIAMS, Andrew, 'The Labour Party's Attitude to the Soviet Union, 1927–35. An Overview with Specific Reference to Unemployment Policies and Peace', *Journal of Contemporary History*, vol. 22, 1987, pp. 71–90.

WILLIAMSON, Philip, '"Safety First": Baldwin, the Conservative Party and the 1929 General Election', *The Historical Journal*, vol. 25, no. 2, 1982, pp. 385–409.

WINKLER, Henry R., 'The Emergence of a Labour Foreign Policy in Great Britain, 1918–1929', pp. 247–58.

WINTER, J. M., 'Arthur Henderson, the Russian Revolution, and the Reconstruction of the Labour Party', *The Historical Journal*, XV, 4, 1972, pp. 753–73.

Index

Abramovitch (LSI) 16
Adler, Friedrich 48, 49, 75, 185, 186
All-Union Central Council for Trade Unions 27
Allied intervention (1919–21) 7
Angell, Norman 204
  Must Britain Follow the Moscow Road? 94–5
  War of Steel and Gold, The 54
Anglo-Persian Oil Company 111
Anglo-Russian Joint Advisory Committee (ARJAC) 31, 41, 42, 60, 69
  background to 22–3
  collapse of 44, 48, 71
  and the General Strike 27–8
  impact on future TUC attitudes 28–9
  period (1924–7) 23–5, 81
  splitting of IFTU by 36
  and struggle for power in the USSR 25–7
'Anglo-Russian Parliamentary Committee' 16
Anglo-Russian Parliamentary Committee Weekly Bulletin 105, 106, 115
Anglo-Russian Treaty (1924) 14, 30
Anglo-Soviet Conference (1924) 11, 13–15
Anglo-Soviet Trade Agreement (1921) 9, 12, 14
ARCOS affair 30, 33–8, 82, 141, 182
ASLEF 116
Astor, Lady 146
Attlee, Clement 151, 155, 167, 168, 194, 207, 232, 234

Baikaloff, A. V. 185, 186, 187
Balabanoff International Group and the I.L.P., 48, 49
Baldwin, Stanley 18, 31–3, 34, 36, 78–80, 95, 105, 200, 236
Ballard, Consul-General 169, 173
Baptists 106
Bauer, Otto 186
Beales, H. L. 169, 170, 171, 174, 177
Beaverbrook, Lord 198
'Benn' 138
Benn, Wedgewood 121
Bennett, Richard Bedford 197, 199, 200
Bevan, Aneurin 142, 143, 146
Beveridge, William 192
Bevin, Ernest 36, 115, 122, 140, 157, 194, 221, 240, 242
  at Brighton Conference (1935) 212
  as General Secretary of TGWU 151, 213
  role in TUC 153, 154–5, 159, 179, 232
'Birmingham Proposals' 69, 78
Birn, Donald 236
Birrell, Augustine 98
Blackett, Sir Basil 206
Blake, William 103
Bolsheviks and Bolshevism 7, 8, 10, 31, 32, 67, 74, 75, 84
Bondfield, Margaret 182
Bond-holders, Czarist 15
Boyle, Andrew 3
Brailsford, Henry Noel 32, 54, 61, 68, 69, 103, 108, 121, 158, 161, 219
  How the Soviets Work 72, 73
  Olives of Endless Age 57–8
  War of Steel and Gold, The 57
Bridgeman (League Against Imperialism) 123

Briggs, Asa 206
British Empire Union 82
British-Russian Gazette and Trade Outlook 198
British Union of Fascists (BUF) 224–5
Brockway, Fenner 48–50, 55, 73, 98, 123, 158–60, 217, 220–1
Bromley, John 116, 200
Bron (Russo-British Chamber of Commerce) 116, 188
Bukharin, Nikolai 12, 35, 37
Bullock, Lord Alan 157, 240
Buxton, Charles Roden 69–70, 239
Buxton, Dorothy F. 68, 69
  Challenge of Bolshevism, The 67
Buxton, Noel 61

Cairns, Andrew 165, 166, 167
Calhoun, Daniel 23, 24, 26, 27
'Campbell case' 17, 18, 25, 30
Carlton, David 91, 92, 120, 128
Caute, David 138, 142, 167
  Fellow Travellers, The 3, 137, 181
Ceaucescu, Nikolai 241
Cecil, Lord Robert 59, 125, 126–7, 129, 214, 216, 234, 236
Centrosoyuz 89, 188
Chamberlain, Joseph 197
Chamberlain, Neville 199
Chamberlain, Sir Austen 27, 29, 32–4, 58, 61, 119
Chamberlin, William 164–5, 166
  Russia's Iron Age 164
Chicherin, G. 13, 14, 22, 60
China 31, 53, 83
Christian Protest Society 105
Christian Science Monitor 164
Churchill, Sir Winston 70, 222
Citrine, Walter 29, 44–5, 74, 84, 153, 155, 167, 178, 179, 194, 221, 232
  attempt to influence the Webbs 193
  as General Secretary of TUC 116, 213, 228–30
  I Search for Truth in Soviet Russia 240
  visits to Soviet Union 146
Clynes, John Robert 46, 60, 97, 98
Coates, William and Zelda 16, 105, 106, 115–16, 135–6
Cole, G. D. H. 154, 155, 157, 168, 205
  Economic Tracts for the Times 204
  Principles of Economic Planning 204
Cole, Margaret 174
Colhos movement 137
collectivisation 1, 69, 77, 129, 135–6, 165–6, 171, 188, 192, 241
Colville, Sir John 199
Comintern (Communist International) 10, 14, 22, 34, 37, 49, 82, 90, 156, 160, 182, 185, 221, 225, 230–1
  activities in British Empire 81
  activities in India and China 31, 83, 120–3
  activities in Spain 238
  Congress (1928) 44
  control of 94
  'class against class' in 25, 45, 63
  distinction from Soviet Government 84
  ECCI 44, 221
  and 'Extremism' 33, 43
  hostility to League of Nations 216
  insults against British Labour Movement 55, 63
  1924 proposals 23
'comity of nations' 9, 72
Communist party of Great Britain (CPGB) 2, 9, 10, 12, 31, 37, 81, 82
  'class against class' policy 45, 225
  and the ILP 67, 68, 160
  Labour Party relationship with 42–5, 74, 84, 152, 156, 231, 240
  and the TUC 26
  'Unity Convention' 43
Communist Party of the Soviet Union (CPSU) 11, 12, 42, 49, 60, 63, 141
  Congress (1930) 140
Communist Solar System 227, 230, 231
Compton (TUC) 217
Congress Party (India) 121, 122
Comsomols 145, 180, 188
Conservative Governments 10, 26, 32
Conservative Party 78–80, 82, 115, 103, 122–3, 125, 201, 213
  Election Notes 1929 83
Cook, A. J. 27, 50, 144
Coolidge, President 61
Cooper, Duff 10, 17
Cooperative movement 30–1
Cooperative Party 67
Cooperative Reports on visits to Russia
  (1929) 144
  (1930) 144
  (1932) 176–7
Cooperative Society, Midland Division of 31

Cooperative Union 176
'Councils of Action' (1920) 7–8
Cowling, Maurice 212
Cramp, C. T. 48, 49
Crane, Mr (miner) 143
Cripps, Sir Stafford 151, 201, 208, 226, 232, 234
  and the Socialist League 161, 192, 213, 218, 231
Crowe, Eyre 119
Curzon, Lord 8–9, 10, 11, 18

Daily Express 99, 198
Daily Herald 9–10, 63, 67, 75, 80, 86, 90, 93, 94, 106, 137, 139–41, 144, 175, 176, 199, 215
  and China crisis 31, 33, 53
  financial dependence on TUC 29
  on Labour Party and religion 103, 104
  and Metro-Vickers trial 201–3
  and Russian disarmament proposals 60
  on Stalin 84, 140
Daily Mail 17, 135
Daily Worker 189
Dalton, Hugh 2, 57, 66, 70, 97, 99, 100, 124, 126, 146, 151, 153, 159, 191, 194, 207, 208, 213, 221, 232, 242
  attitude to fabianism 185
  and disaffiliation of Socialist League 231
  and Foreign Office 119, 131
  and New Fabian Research Bureau visit to Russia (1932) 155, 157, 167–70, 172–4, 177–9
  on religious persecution 105, 107, 108
  Towards the Peace of Nations 54–6
  on trade with Russia 110, 113, 114
  as Under-Secretary of State 88–9, 91–2, 95
  visit to Mussolini 225
  visit to Zilliacus 226
de Brouchère (LSI) 48
de Gruchy, C. R. 64, 70
Democracy versus dictatorship 227–30, 231, 235
Depression 1
'Detente' 22
Deterding, Sir Henry 111
Dillon, Dr E. J. 137
Dovgalevsky, Ambassador 89, 92, 94
Drummond, Sir Eric 216
Duranty, Walter 166
Dyson, Will 202, 231

Economist 166, 218
Eden, Anthony 214, 236
Eisenstein
  General Line, The 138
Eliot, T. S. 241
Empire Marketing Board 165
'Empire preference' 115
Ewer, W. N. 89, 140, 201, 217, 219

Fabian Society 155, 185
Farbman, Michael 104, 134, 136, 137, 138, 139, 187
February Revolution (1917) 7
  see also Russian Revolution
Federation of British Industry 50
'Fellow Travellers of the Right' 4, 213
Fischer, Louis 134, 137, 138, 140
Foot, Michael 142
Forbes, Rosita 175
Foreign Office
  and USSR during 1929–31 government 128–32
  view of Russia 119–23
Forward 134, 140
Franco-Soviet Pact (1935) 214
Friends of Soviet Russia 60, 123

Gandhi, Mahatma 121, 123
Gallen, Magda 108, 141, 142
General Elections
  (1924) 'Red Letter' 17–18, 25, 80
  (1929) 78, 119
  (1931) 82
  (1987) 46
General Strike 25, 27–8, 34, 46
Gillett, Sir George M. 110, 112, 114, 115
Gillies, William 48, 83–4, 123, 152–3, 155, 185–6, 217, 227–8, 230, 233, 235
Gorky, Maxim 138
Gorodetsky, Gabriel 11, 13, 18, 27, 31–2, 34, 36
Gosplan 188
Gough, Prebendary 105, 106
Graham, William 110–15, 120
Greenwood, Arthur 153, 182, 232
Gupta, Partha, S. 121, 122

Haldane, T. G. N. 168, 173
Halevy, Elie 184

'Hands Off China' 44
'Hands off Russia' movement 23
Hecker, Dr Julius F. 193
Henderson, Arthur 6, 7, 34, 66, 88–95 97, 99, 155, 198, 228, 242
and disarmament 124–6, 218, 225
foreign policy (1931–2) 212, 213, 214
as Foreign Secretary 119–20, 121, 128–9, 131
and Matteoti 71, 75
as President of LSI 62
and religion 103
as Secretary of Labour Party 9, 48, 152, 159, 232–3, 235
and trade with Russia 105–16
Hicks, George 23, 24, 29
Hilferding, Herr 70
Hill, J. 93
Hitler, Adolf 2, 3, 124, 194, 201, 202, 213, 218, 224, 239, 242
Hoare, Samuel 236
Hodgson, R. M. 11, 12, 17
Hoover, President 219
Hoover plan 218
Hughes, Emrys 144, 145, 146

Independent Labour Party (ILP) 2, 30, 32, 33, 46, 151, 161, 213, 226, 227
and analysis of USSR (1927–8) 67, 73–5
disaffiliation from the Labour Party 78, 158–60, 208, 217, 219–21, 222, 225
and 1929 election 78, 83, 85
and foreign policy (1927–8) 59, 61
(1929–31) 120–3
on five-year plans 140
in the Labour and Socialist International (LSI) 47–51
and Labour politics (1929) 91
(1930–1) 108, 114
National Administrative Council (NAC) 47, 220–1
Revolutionary Policy Committee 159
India 83, 120–3
International Federation of Free Trade Unions (IFTU) 23, 24, 25, 27, 29, 36
International News Service 166
International Wheat Conference (1931) 142
Isvestya 32

Jagger, John 176
Joad, C. E. M. 67
Jones, Bill 3, 240
Joynson-Hicks, Sir William ('Jix') 93
Joxe, Pierre 232

Kabul, propaganda in 10
Kalinin, Mikhail 129
Kamenev, Lev. B. 11, 35, 42, 60
Kellogg, Borah Proposals (LON) 61
Kenworthy, Commander J. M. 54, 56–7, 66, 217
Kerensky Government, British support for 7
Keynes, John Maynard 78, 85, 115, 140, 167, 205, 208
Khomeini, Ayatollah 3
King's speech (1929) 89–90
Kirkwood, David 34, 202
Kirov, Sergei M. 239
'kulaks' 69, 129, 131, 137, 143, 172, 189, 192, 241
Kuusinen, Otto 230

Labour and Socialist International (LSI) 16, 29, 62, 75, 84, 141, 216–17, 227
Congress (1928) 46, 50
ILP in 47–51
and 'united front' tactics 36
'Labour and the Nation' (1928) 47, 97
Labour Magazine 37, 44, 45, 73, 106
Labour Party
Advisory Committee on International Questions (ACIQ) 37, 59–61, 69, 124, 226, 233
birth of 8
Conferences
(1925) (Liverpool) 43
(1926) (Margate) 48
(1928) (Birmingham) 50
(1929) (Brighton) 123
(1932) (Leicester) 204
(1933) (Hastings) 225
(1934) (Southport) 235
(1935) (Brighton) 212
Constitution, Clause IV 2
International Department 124
see also Gillies, William
Manifesto
(1928) 'Labour and the Nation' 47, 85, 97
(1931) 207
National Executive Council (NEC) 2
condemnation of Meerut Prisoners'

Committee 123
and CPGB 44
and domestic economic policies (1932–4) 203
and 1929 election 80, 81
and foreign policy (1927–8) 60–2, 71
(1931–2) 212
(1933–4) 225–7, 230–3
and ILP disaffiliation 158–9
and Socialist League 161
National Joint Council (NJC) 9, 152, 153, 203, 228, 230
post-election rally (1924) 11
'Victory for Socialism' campaign 233
Labour Speakers Handbook for 1929 82
Lammers, Donald 90
Land Budgetary Limitation (Geneva Disarmament Talks) 127
Lang, William Gordon Cosmo 103, 105, 108
Lansbury, George 33, 34, 55, 68, 70, 97, 151, 158, 213, 232
'democratic methods and machinery' 41, 42
and disarmament proposals 60, 62
as head of PLP 153, 187, 212, 218
Laski, Harold 71, 95, 193, 205, 230, 233, 234
Law, Bonar 9
Lawrence, Susan 35, 71
'League Against Imperialism' 50, 84, 123
League of Nations 54–5, 124–6, 127, 152, 161, 224–7
Advisory Committee of the League in the Far East 234
and disarmament 59, 60, 61
disarmament conference (1932–3) 218–19
entry of USSR into 156, 225, 232–6, 239
and foreign policy (1931–2) 211–13, 221
and the Manchurian crisis 214–18
League of Nations Union (LONU) 236
Lee, Ivy 72
Lee, Jenny 141–2, 143, 146, 147
Leeds Convention (1917) 81, 82
Leeds Manifesto 7
Leeper, Reginald 13
Left Book Club 240
Lenin V. I. 1, 7, 11, 45, 67, 70, 94, 123, 140, 147, 188, 208
death 17
Lenin, Krupskaya 140
Liberal Industrial Inquiry 69
Liberal Party 1, 8, 33, 56, 73, 79
'industrial report' 78, 85
Liebman, Marcel 182
Lindsay, Sir Ronald 97
Litvinov, Maxim 22, 32, 60, 88, 107, 112–13, 126–7, 129, 200, 203, 219
Lloyd, C. M. 154
Lloyd George, David 8, 33, 78
Locarno Pacts (1925) 60
London Naval Conference (1930) 92, 127
Londonderry, Lord 81
Losovsky, A. 26, 27, 28, 45
Lunatcharsky (Soviet Diplomat) 126

MacDonald, James Ramsay 2, 6, 30, 31, 66, 139, 165, 167, 242
and ARJAC 23–4, 26
and 1931 crisis 150, 151, 153, 154, 155, 161
and domestic politics (1930–1) 103, 104, 106–7, 108, 111, 113, 114
and 1929 election 78, 79, 80–1, 82, 83, 84, 85, 86
and foreign policy (including USSR)
(1924) 15–17
(1927–9) 54, 55, 56, 57, 62
(1929–31) 119, 120, 121, 122, 125, 126, 128, 131
(1931–2) 212
(1933–4) 203, 235
and Labour domestic economic policies (1932–4) 197, 203
leadership (1927–9) 46–9
memorandum on Labour Party Policy (1928) 38–9
and Minority Movement 42–4
Plan (LON, 1932) 218
as Prime Minister (1924) 8, 10–15, 18
(1929) 88, 90, 91, 92, 93, 95, 99, 100
and trade with Soviet Union (1925–7) 30–2, 36–7
MacDonald, Malcolm 145, 146
Macmillan, Harold 205, 206
Maisky, Ambassador Ivan 187, 192–3, 200, 225, 234
Manchester Guardian 98, 105, 106, 116, 122, 134, 136, 192
Manchurian crisis (1932) 127, 211, 214–18
Margulies, Sylvia
Pilgrimage to Russia, The 3, 167
Marley, Lord 234
Marquand, David 11

Martin, Kingsley 109, 155, 166
Matteoti 71, 74, 75
Maxton, James 35–6, 47–8, 50, 55, 67, 72, 90, 122–3, 158–60
'Maxton-Cook Manifesto' 49, 61
May, Ernest 172
Meerut Prisoners' Committee 123
Mellor, William 155
Mencken, Louis 166
Mensheviks 16, 141
Metropolitan-Vickers Trial (1933) 112, 165, 200–4, 231
Meyendorff, Baron 187
Middleton, J. R. 152, 235
Miller, Margaret 187
Minority Movement 24, 25, 63, 74, 123, 214
  Labour Party attack on 42–5
Mirsky, Ivan 187
Mitchison, G. R. 168, 173–4
'Mond Moonshine' *see* Cook, A. J.
Morgan, John 168, 169, 171–2
Morgan, Kenneth 240
Morning Post 109
Morris, William 103
Morrison, Herbert 85, 151, 153, 159, 179, 194, 213, 221, 230–2, 235, 239
  and ARJAC 44–5, 63, 74
  as Minister of Transport 142
  on planning 207–8
Moscow Daily News 138, 186, 188, 189
Mosley, Oswald 49, 68, 78, 114, 147, 224, 225
Muggeridge, Malcolm 134, 164, 192
Munzenberg, Willi 50
Mussolini, Benito 3, 53, 67, 74, 146, 225, 239, 242

Narkomindel 22, 25, 60
National Union of Railwaymen Convention (1927) 28
Naylor, John
  Labour's International Policy 2, 211–12
Nazism 161, 170, 227
New Clarion 175, 176, 191, 199
New Economic Policy (1924) (NEP) 1, 136–7
New Fabian Research Bureau (NFRB) 153, 155–8, 185, 191, 207
  visit to Soviet Union (1932) 167–74, 177, 178
New Leader 44, 61, 67, 121, 139, 159, 160, 208, 221
New Party 78, 224
New Russia 159
New Statesman 93, 109, 166, 167
Newbold, John Turner Walton 30
Noel-Baker, Philip 2, 59–60, 104, 106, 110–12, 125–7, 155, 214, 216–17, 225–6, 232–5
Northedge, Frederick 1, 167

OGPU 164
Oliphant, Laurence 202
Optional Clause 93
Ottawa Imperial Conference (1932) 122, 198, 199
Oudegeest, J. 24
Ovey, Ambassador Sir Esmond 105–9, 112–13, 115, 119–21, 128–31, 164–5, 167, 169, 173, 184, 188, 200, 241

Parliamentary Labour Party (PLP) 33, 151, 152, 212, 233
Passfield, Lord *see* Webb, Sidney
Pethick-Lawrence, F. W. 157, 167–8, 169, 170, 172, 173, 175, 191
Pethybridge, Roger 135
Petrov (VOKS) 188
Piatakov, G. 85
Pimlott, Ben 153, 158, 160, 205
Pincher, Chapman 3
Pius XI 139
Politburo 31
Political and Economic Planning (PEP) 206, 207, 208
Political Quarterly 109
Pollard, Sidney 197
Pollitt, Harry 228, 230
Ponsonby, Arthur 10–13, 15, 16, 19, 61, 81, 119, 234
Popular Front 213, 220
Pravda 86
Preparatory Commission (LON) 124, 125, 129
Pritt, D. N. 169, 170, 171, 174, 177, 179
Propaganda 9–11, 14, 32, 83, 93, 99, 113, 131
Purcell, A. A. 23, 24, 27, 29, 44, 55, 176
purge trials 1, 203, 239

Quo-Tai-Chi 234

Radek, Karl 12, 188
Rakovsky, Kh. 13, 17
Red Army 95
Red International of Labour Unions (RILU) (or Profitern) 23, 25–6, 44, 45
'Red Letter' (1924) 82, 119
religious persecution crisis (1930) 102–10
'Revolution by Reason' *see* 'Birmingham Proposals'
Roberts, G. H. 7
Roome, Mr (miner) 143
Rosenberg, Rose 82
Rumbold, Sir Horace 105–6
Runciman, Walter 197
Russian Revolution 50, 66, 72, 136
Russian Social Democratic Party 73
'Russian trade card' 77–81
Rykov, A. 60

'Safety First' 78
Samuel, Herbert 197
Sankey, Lord 95
Schiller, Dr Otto 166
Selby, Sir Walford Harmood Montague 17
Sergius, Metropolitan 107
Shaw, George Bernard 67, 70, 74, 75, 98, 138, 145–6, 147, 164–5, 184, 193
Shaw, Tom 111
Shinwell, Emmanuel 50
'Shrine of the Iberian Virgin', demolition of 104
Simon, Sir John 34, 200–3, 211, 216, 217, 234–6
Simon Report (1930) 83, 122
Simpson, Celia 142
Sinclair, Sir Archibald 32
Skidelsky, Robert 77, 102, 110
'Smitchka' 69
Smith, Ellis 230
Snow, Edgar 215
Snowden, Philip 6, 15, 23, 24, 26, 33, 36, 47, 150, 178, 182, 184, 242
  and domestic economic policies (1932–4) 197–9, 206
  and domestic politics (1930–1) 102, 103, 108, 110–14
  and 1929 elections 81
  and foreign policy (1929–31) 120, 128 (1931–2) 212
Socialist League 155, 160–2, 192–3, 205, 213, 217, 222, 226–7, 231–2
Socialist Review 36, 65, 67, 68, 74, 98, 108–9
Socialist Revolutionary Party 16, 73
Society for Socialist Inquiry and Propaganda (SSIP) 153, 154–5, 160, 185
Sokolnikov, Gregori 104, 105, 113, 184, 187
Soukhoumlin Memorandum 16, 17
Spanish Civil War 2, 238
Spengler, Oswald 172
Stalin, Josef 11, 22, 25–6, 28, 31, 35, 37, 41, 43, 68–70, 72, 73, 92, 146, 155, 185, 188–9, 191, 203, 221, 231, 236, 239–41, 243
  and China 26
  and League of Nations 214
  presentation of, in Britain 139–41
  treatment of Trotsky group 84
Stalinism 131, 136, 177, 181
Stamfordham, Lord 107
Stanhope, Lord 235
Starr, Mark 69
  'Whither and Soviets' 69
Stephen, Campbell 208
Strachey, John 68–9, 73, 74, 78, 79, 98, 140, 142, 147, 205
  Coming Struggle for Power, The 205
Strang, Sir William 115, 128–9, 131–2, 135, 138, 164–5, 167, 200, 202, 240
Strauss, George 142, 143
Strong, Anna Louise 137–8, 139–40, 189

Tawney, R. H. 184, 185
  Equality 184
Third International *see* Comintern
Thomas, Albert 135
Thomas, James Henry 23, 24, 26, 28, 30, 31, 60
  and 1929–31 Government 182
  and National Government 128, 150, 212
Thomas, Will 34
Thorne, Christopher 211, 212, 215
Tilden-Smith, Mr (miner) 143
Tillet, Ben 122
Times, The 81, 104, 115, 202
Tolstoy, Leo 67
Tomsky, M. 23, 25, 27, 34, 140
Toole, J. 143, 144
Toynbee, Arnold 192
Trades Disputes Bill (1927) 28, 34
Trades Union Congress (TUC) 10, 41–3, 45, 53, 116, 225, 233
  Advisory Committee 115

and ARJAC 22–9
Congresses
(1924) (Hull) 25
(1927) (Edinburgh) 29
(1928) 46, 50
(1929) (Belfast) 93, 114–15
(1930) (Nottingham) 115
General Council of 2, 24, 27–8, 42, 44, 46, 114–15, 152, 168, 212, 217, 227
International Department 37
National Joint Council 37, 152
report on India (1928) 177
Transport and General Workers' Union (TGWU) 151, 212
Treaty of Versailles 219
Tressell, Robert
Ragged Trousered Philanthropists 103
Trevelyan, Charles 161, 232, 234
Trotsky, Leon 11, 16, 17, 22, 32, 33, 35, 37, 69, 72, 84, 105, 160, 221
and ARJAC period 25–8
Autobiography (My Life) 95, 140
as critic of British Labour Party 42, 95
'debate' 94–9, 100
expulsion from Communist Party 45, 60, 68, 74
meeting with the Webbs 95–6, 182
Tung, Mao-Tse 3
Turin, Victor
Turksib 138

Uldricks, Teddy 22
unemployment 110, 197
in Britain 9–10
Union of Democratic Control (UDC) 6, 125
United Front 63, 230

Vandervelde, Emil 16, 48
Vansittart, Sir Robert 88, 107, 108, 114, 132
Versailles Treaty 55, 57
Voikov assassination and reprisals (1927) 58, 72, 73
VOKS 188
Vyshinsky, Andrei 203

Wake, Egerton 47
Wall Street crash (1929) 71, 110, 205
Wallhead, R. C. 90
Webb, Beatrice 2, 3, 68, 70, 95–6, 124, 128, 130, 145, 146, 147, 155, 242
Industrial Democracy 41
My Apprenticeship 96
Soviet Russia: A New Civilisation? 191
visits to USSR 167, 175–6, 179, 181–94, 225
Webb, Sidney 2, 15, 68, 70, 95, 96, 104, 106, 121, 122, 128, 145, 155, 242
Industrial Democracy 41
Soviet Russia: A New Civilisation? 191
visits to USSR 167, 175–6, 179, 181–94, 225
Weekly Bulletin 135
Weekly Record and Textile World 33
Wellock, Wilfred 66, 67, 79
Wells, Audrey 1
Wells, H. G. 70, 74, 98, 167
Wertheimer, Egon 46, 47, 53
White, Stephen 8, 10
Whitehead, E. T. 73
Wicksteed, Alexander 134, 138, 140–1
Wilkinson, Ellen 44, 231
Wilson, Woodrow 211
Wise, E. F. 30, 79–80, 89, 91, 92, 114, 121, 141, 155, 158, 161, 220
Woolf, Leonard 155, 233, 235
Wooton, Barbara
Plan or No Plan 204
World Economic Conference (1927) 59
Wright, Harold 204
Wylie, Thomas 203

XYZ Club 153

Young Plan 93

Zilliacus, Konni 126, 226, 233, 234
Zinoviev, Grigorii 11, 12, 22, 26, 32, 33, 35, 37, 42, 45, 60, 74, 84, 94, 95
'letter' 17, 18, 25, 30, 43, 46, 72, 81